WITHDRAWN

FAREWELL *to the* HORSE

FAREWELL
to the
HORSE

A CULTURAL HISTORY

ULRICH RAULFF

Translated by Ruth Ahmedzai Kemp

LIVERIGHT PUBLISHING CORPORATION
A Division of W. W. Norton & Company
Independent Publishers Since 1923
New York · London

For information about permission to reproduce selections from this book,
write to Permissions, Liveright Publishing Corporation,
a division of W. W. Norton & Company, Inc.,
500 Fifth Avenue, New York, NY 10110

For information about special discounts for bulk purchases, please contact
W. W. Norton Special Sales at specialsales@wwnorton.com or 800-233-4830

Manufacturing by Quad Graphics, Fairfield

ISBN 978-1-63149-432-1

Liveright Publishing Corporation
500 Fifth Avenue, New York, N.Y. 10110
www.wwnorton.com

W. W. Norton & Company Ltd.
15 Carlisle Street, London W1D 3BS

1 2 3 4 5 6 7 8 9 0

Contents

CONTENTS

PART IV
The Forgotten Player
Histories

List of Illustrations

PLATES

The Long Farewell

To be born in the countryside in the mid-twentieth century meant growing up in an old world. Little had changed from the way of life that existed a hundred years before. Sluggish by nature, the agricultural realm ticks over at a sleepy pace. Not so for the children of the city; their environment was one of engines and decay, the result of mechanized destruction. The countryside lagged behind, dragging its feet for nearly a century before the sudden leap into technological modernity. Farm machinery was on the increase in rural settings, certainly, whereas back in the mid-nineteenth century such machines were still rare, experimental exceptions. Over the course of the twentieth century, these machines became smaller and more practical, gradually shaking off the resemblance to medieval siege engines or huge, robotic dinosaurs. With increasing regularity they would be seen in the fields, tugged along now by small tractors; if such vehicles were known at all a century ago, they tended to be colossal steam engines. By the mid-twentieth century, tractors could muster 15 or 20 horsepower; they had short, catchy names such as Fendt, Deutz, Lanz or Faun, and with few exceptions, such as the grey Lanz, they were painted green. Looking back, they seem like fragile grasshoppers compared to the mammoths of today with their 200 h.p. engines and soundproof cabs.

Aside from these noisy pioneers of rural mechanization, whose jerky movements and clamour were at odds with the pastoral idyll of the nineteenth century, little had changed. Horses – heavy Belgian coldbloods, strong Trakehners and stocky Haflingers – were still the most commonly used and most widespread forms of transport and draught power on narrow, winding byways, on sloping fields and in wooded ravines. My winter memories are of the water vapour rising from their breath and their warm flanks; my image of summer is filled with the scent of their brown hair and glossy manes. I still shudder when I recall the horror I felt when I first saw the square-headed iron nails being hammered into what I thought of as the soles of their feet. It was only in church, in the Passion of Christ, that I had seen such grim scenes. Later, whenever I heard someone say they had 'nailed it', in the sense of successfully achieving something, I couldn't help but picture those square-headed horseshoe nails.

For farmers who still lived off the land and had not yet exchanged their modest economy for factory work, the stables were one of the smaller but nobler parts of the enterprise. Cattle, pigs and chickens were more omnipresent, more pungent and made a far greater racket; in a word, they were the plebs of the farmyard. The horses, in contrast, were rare, precious and sweet-smelling. They were more refined in their eating habits and more spectacular in their suffering: their bouts of colic were especially fearsome. Standing in their stables like living sculptures, they would nod their shapely heads, signalling distrust or suspicion with a twitch of their ears. The horses had their own pasture, to which never a cow would stray, to say nothing of the pigs or geese. No farmer would consider surrounding his horses' meadow with the barbed wire which was often used to enclose sheep and cattle. For the horses, a bit of wood or a simple electric fence was sufficient to stop them escaping. One does not incarcerate aristocrats. It is enough to remind them of their word of honour.

I picture myself and my grandfather, one day in the mid-1950s, standing on a hill from where we could see our farm and the surrounding land. In the distance was a patch of deciduous woods, through which a narrow track wound its way up the hill. For a while, the silence that usually hung over the rural solitude had been ripped apart by something that resembled a hunchbacked ant slowly and noisily heaving itself up the hill. As it approached, this gigantic ant revealed itself to be one of my uncle's ancient Mercedes diesel cars. The weighty vehicle drew nearer with Olympian gravitas. My grandfather made a disparaging remark about it, which included the words 'threshing box', and watched with growing scepticism as my cousin, the man at the helm of this beast, turned off the hard track

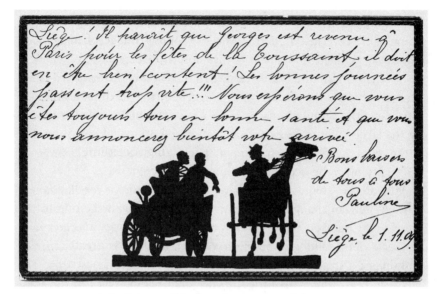

A fond farewell before the parting of the ways.

Horsepower contest: the diesel engine has 12 h.p.; the oat-powered engine has only 2 h.p., but it smells a darn sight better.

and headed across the horses' paddock straight towards us. After just a few metres on the damp grass, he lost control and the vehicle jolted sideways, skidded and made a dive for the electric fence where it became entangled and finally came to a halt by a tree stump in a cloud of dark blue smoke. As the smoke receded, the Olympian emerged into view, the thunderbolts he hurled now trapped within: ensnared by the electric fence, the car was transformed into a kind of inverse Faraday cage, its numerous metal parts conducting each surge of electricity onto the occupant within.

After all the attempts by the driver to extricate the vehicle had failed, a heavy Belgian draught horse came to the rescue. Hitched up to the diesel's rear bumper, this good-natured giant heaved the wrecked vehicle back onto solid ground. Everyone knows the J. M. W. Turner painting of a steam tug puffing away as it tows a proud warship, *The Fighting Temeraire*, sails furled, to her final resting place in the ship-breaking yard. In our case, though, fate intervened – with accustomed irony – to turn the tide of history: here it was the horse, history's retired war veteran, who was called on to tow the diesel engine. The old world was back in the harness, slogging away in the service of the new.

In fact, by this point the matter had already been decided once and for all: man and horse had set off on their separate paths. Since man preferred in future to travel his path in a motor vehicle, he then had it levelled and topped with asphalt. Our equine friends were literally outrun, overtaken, left behind. Horses were consigned to that part of reality which Condoleezza Rice, former US Secretary of State, once described as '*the roadkill of history*'. For centuries, mankind had always pictured the fate of the vanquished as those who had been trampled under the hooves of the triumphant. Now, in the transition from the nineteenth to the twentieth century, it was the horse that was trampled under the hooves, or rather the wheels, of history. For most of recorded history, horses had helped man defeat his most dangerous enemy: other men. Now they were relegated to the edge of the road and to seeing their conqueror trundle off into the distance. Six hundred years of gunpowder had done nothing to move horses from their rightful place as man's most important weapon of war. But one hundred years of mechanized warfare sufficed to render them obsolete, vanquished by recent history.

As simple and straightforward as the parting of the ways between man and horse seems – the segregation of mechanical and animal strength – it was in reality nothing like as clear-cut. Mankind was not made up of riders and coachmen one day and motorists the next. It took several phases over the course of one and a half centuries for man and beast to go their separate ways, from the early nineteenth century which saw engineers experimenting with steam-powered vehicles and motors, through to the mid-twentieth century, when motorized automobiles overtook the horse numerically as the prime mode of transport. The most surprising thing at first glance is that for most of this period, the use of horses continued to increase, rather than to fall as one might expect. It was only towards the very end of the period, the years following the Second World War, that the use of horses receded, and rapidly at that point. To that extent, the last century of the era of the horse witnessed not only the exodus of the horse from human history, but also its historical climax: never before had humanity been as heavily dependent on horses as when Benz and Daimler's first internal combustion engines began rattling away in Mannheim and Stuttgart.

Having said that it took one and a half centuries, when I occasionally speak of the *last century of the horse*, it is not out of intellectual laziness or because it has a better ring to it. The end of the horse age fits almost exactly with what has tended to be called 'the long nineteenth century': the period starting with Napoleon and ending with the First World War. Since then, virtually every kind of technology for which horses traditionally provided the necessary traction power – from the transport sector to the military – has switched over to combustion engines or electric motors. In practice, this changeover was a considerably drawn-out process:[1] the two world wars prompted a mercilessly heavy reliance on horses and it was only after the middle of the century that traction power was cheap enough to lead to a dramatic decline in horse numbers in Europe. Now, though, the separation of man and horse is not only a done deal, it is also a finished process.

Seen through the eyes of a historian, the parting of man and beast forms the central chapter in the story of the demise of the predominantly agricultural world. Until the mid-twentieth century, the landscape of the mechanized and technically advanced civilizations of the Western world was still strongly influenced by rural constructs, by farming villages, markets, livestock herds and crop fields. Going another fifty years back in time to the beginning of the last century, the dramatic departure from the apparently pastoral, natural environment is even more conspicuous: 'In 1900,' writes the philosopher Michel Serres, 'most people on our planet were working in agriculture and the food industry; nowadays in France, just as in comparable countries, farmers make up barely 1 per cent of the population. This is without a doubt one of the most profound historical breaks with tradition since the Neolithic era.'[2]

It is also through the prism of this radical transformation to life and working conditions in the rapidly industrializing countries that we need to view the departure of the horses: this farewell represents a phase in the withdrawal of mankind from the analogue world. Nietzsche referred to the death of God to describe one of the most unsettling experiences faced by nineteenth-century man: the loss of a transcendent sphere formerly deemed to be secure. People felt that the metaphysical realm was slipping out of their grasp. The citizens of the twenty-first century know a similar discomfort, finding themselves in the process of losing their grip on the physical realm.

In a traditionally agrarian country like France, where the ancient Roman sense of 'culture' has never been forgotten[3] – namely agriculture and viticulture – the disruption to farming was naturally perceived as particularly dramatic. The gods of wine and fruit withdrew from sight and with them disappeared the old way of life for mankind. The farewell to the horse has become a historical marker for the loss of the rural world. 'I belong to a vanished people,' laments art historian and writer Jean Clair. 'When I was born, we still made up 60 per cent of the French population. Today, it is no more than 2 per cent. One day it will be appreciated that the most important event of the twentieth century was not the rise of the proletariat, but the disappearance of farming.'[4] Farmers and producers have vanished, and with the farmers, and sometimes before them, went the animals. 'The horses were the first to go, in the late fifties. They became redundant and they disappeared forever.'[5]

Viewed through the lens of the philosophy of history, the separation between man and horse seems like the dissolution of an idiosyncratic workers' union. In a communal effort, albeit one imposed unilaterally, the two species together accomplished what Hegel called 'the work of history'. By strange coincidence, which may invite speculation, this age-old workers' union came to a bitter end during almost exactly the same time period as that which divided Hegel's *Lectures on the Philosophy of World History*[6] from the mid-twentieth-century theories that declared the 'end of history'.[7] Exactly fifteen decades span the end of the age of the horse from the first hints in the early nineteenth century up to the final nail in the coffin in the middle of the twentieth. Those decades stretch from Hegel, who in 1806 described the French emperor as a 'world-soul' on horseback, to Arnold Gehlen, who in the 1950s and 1960s developed his theory of the *'post-histoire'*.

The philosopher and anthropologist Gehlen distinguished between three distinct world eras: a very long period of pre-history was followed by a phase of intrinsically agrarian history, which was in turn superseded by industrialization and the entry into the phase of 'post-history'.[8] As though clinging to this schema, the historian Reinhart Koselleck, speaking for the first time in 2003 of the 'age of the horse', also outlined three great world epochs: he splits the entirety of history into the pre-horse age, the horse age and the post-horse age.[9] The historian resorted to the simplicity of this chronological three-field system because he saw in it a new perspective on world history: 'Knowing full well that any attempt to divide history into periods . . . relies on questions which alter our perspective, I'm searching for a criterion that avoids all boundaries between old, middle and recent history . . .'[10]

With my exploration of the *end* of the era of the horse, I share Koselleck's aspirations. Unlike him, however, I am focusing attention on the relatively narrow transition zone in which this particular departure from history takes place. The process of *dehorsification*, as Isaac Babel described it (*obyezloshadenie*),[11] has its own duration and its historical power. It occurs as a result of the dissolution and transformation processes that dragged on for over a century; in certain respects they are still unfinished to this day. It is not only in Koselleck's narrative of 2003 that we see the long shadow of the era of the horse. It is also felt in our stories, in our images of everyday life and in our figures of speech. In fact, the end of the era of the horse spans not only a relatively long time period, but also a wealth of realities and observations from the most diverse spheres of life. No other historical and natural being, except man, presents such a compelling case for an *histoire totale*.

There are countless histories waiting to be told in which horses play a major role: the story of technology, of transport, agriculture, energy, war and urbanization. But alongside these 'physical' histories of the material world, other less tangible histories jostle for attention: stories of knowledge, ideas and concepts, stories of art and symbolism. Even recent approaches in historiography, such as 'sound history' – the acoustic texture of worlds long gone – find a privileged subject in the horse. All these narratives are plausible, and all the horses they describe did indeed exist: whether they were the products of breeding, the outcome of research or artistic creations, none of these beings is more real or more valid than another. Graffiti on a wall, a metaphor, the shadow of a dream – none of these is less real than a being of flesh and blood. History is made up of one as much as the other, and not only the history of the horse. Jules Michelet once said that history seemed to him at the same time to be insufficiently material and insufficiently spiritual. This is perhaps a risk worth taking when we embark on the history of the horse, seeking to capture both the material and the spiritual – or intellectual, as we might call it today.

*

At the beginning of the era of the horse there is a paradox – as it were, the paradox of the entire history. An intelligent mammal – man – asserts its power over another mammal – the horse. We domesticate and breed horses, befriend them and use them for our own ends. The astonishing thing is that the whole process still functions even if mankind's end goals run contrary to the nature of his four-legged colleague. Unlike man, the horse is by nature a prey animal which flees at the slightest hint of danger. When it is not competing with peers for sexual purposes (the famous sparring stallions), it has no need of confrontation or quarrels; the instinct to seek out prey is quite unknown to the great vegetarian. It is the horse's speed when it needs to flee that allows it to escape the threat of hunters and carnivores. This is precisely the characteristic that attracted the attention of another mammal: the human. It was not as a source of protein, not even as a beast of burden or of tensile strength, that the horse first came into the spotlight in human history. Had it been restricted to the role of pack animal, it would have languished with the ox and the ass in the backyard of history, lurking by the tradesmen's entrance. It was only as a swift animal of flight that the horse took its place at the forefront of the symbiosis of history and nature, the top spot to which, for all the historical success of the camel and the elephant, the horse could assert its right unchallenged for 6,000 years.

Above all, the merit that earns horses their place in history is their *speed*, something which was clearly recognized by German historian and philosopher of history Oswald Spengler. For almost 6,000 years, rapid acceleration and high velocity were characteristics associated with the horse, although also with the camel in Arabia. To be fast meant being mounted – a unique historical discovery which, five generations after the invention of motorized vehicles, is now largely forgotten. The horse was the *speed machine* par excellence; as such it allowed the domination of territory to a degree that would have been unthinkable without this capacity for speed. Thanks to the horse, distant territories could be conquered and vast dominions could be established; indeed, they could also be secured and maintained. Following on from Nietzsche, Spengler called it *great politics* (*die große Politik*): the horse paved the way, historically speaking, for a new kind of power politics, the politics of conquest, to be engaged in on a major scale. As a machine of speed, the horse was a first-rate weapon of war; its ability to make light work of great distances led to an exponential increase in the scope of communication networks. The horse's capacity to be tamed and bred turned the swift horse into a domestic animal that could be steered by man. In a word, as a *vector in animal form*, the horse became a *political animal* and the most important companion of *Homo sapiens*.

Thus, we return to the initial paradox. As a vector, it is far from rare for the civilian saddle horse or draught horse to be transformed into a military warhorse. Time and again, the peaceful grazer is denied its natural instinct and forced by man to accompany him into battle, to trample his enemies into the soil. Against its nature, the terrified prey animal is turned into an incarnation of terror which drives the predator, man, to flee in droves: who would risk being trampled under a horse's hooves? The prey animal, put to use as a physically superior weapon in the battles between the predator, man and his own kind – this is the primary dialectic of the age of the horse, the source of tension which spans the 'Centaurian Pact'.

Compared with this historic alliance, every other covenant into which mankind has entered within his history has been fragile and ephemeral; not even man's relationship with his gods has shown a comparable degree of stability. All the more remarkable, then, is its sudden break-up: at the very moment when the alliance had reached its strongest and most intense bond, it began to fall into inexorable ruin. Almost silently and quite unnoticed by most contemporaries, this alliance disintegrated into its component parts. The great edifice crumbled, bringing about the unsung demolition of 6,000 years of centaurian companionship. What happened next is the stuff of a satyr play: while one party to the treaty, the human side of the old alliance, entered into all manner of short-lived dalliances with various kinds of machinery – automobiles, aircraft and computers – the other party, the horse, went into semi-retirement with a part-time job as a recreational item, a mode of therapy, a status symbol, and a source of pastoral support for female puberty. Henceforth, horses would be granted only fleeting appearances in their archaic role as inspirer of terror, when required to intimidate picketing workers or drive rallies of protesters out of shopping precincts.

Alongside its ultimate rise and fall, throughout the nineteenth century the horse enjoyed a colossal literary and iconographic career. The great novels of the last century of the horse – the ones set on terra firma rather than on the high seas, at any rate – have horses in their very fabric, equine motifs running through them like tendons and veins. This is true even for the most cosmopolitan writers of the time: one thinks of Stendhal, Balzac, Flaubert, Tolstoy and Robert Louis Stevenson. Every single great idea that fuelled the driving force of the nineteenth century – freedom, human greatness, compassion, but also the sub-currents of history uncovered by contemporaries such as the libido, the unconscious and the uncanny – can be traced one way or another back to the horse. Of course, the horse is no sphinx. But the animal was certainly the bearer of many of the great ideas and imagery of the nineteenth century; it was its intellectual assistant, its speech therapist. Whenever nineteenth-century man reached a mental brick wall, an emotional barrier, he would call upon his horse to help him advance: his horse was his flight animal that gave flight to ideas, his beast of burden who shared the burden of his suffering.

In the background to the story of a separation that I will narrate in the following pages runs a process of *sublimation*. Just as the old, solid world of horses, carriages and cavalrymen begins to crumble under the pressure of an increasingly mechanized civilization, horses take on a more imaginary and chimeric form: they are reduced to an existence as the ghosts of modernity, and the more they forfeit their worldly presence, the more they haunt the minds of a humanity that has turned away from them. Perhaps this is the price we pay for the 'enormous loss of naïve, historical tradition', as Hermann Heimpel lamented at the 1956 annual German historians' convention in Ulm. 'With every horse we lose, we also lose something of a way of life that connects our era with that of Charlemagne.'[12]

When an era ends, as far as Karl Marx is concerned (and he himself quotes Hegel), what was historical drama makes a comeback as farce. Thus, at the dawn of its demise, the era of the horse flares up in one final comic glow. It was the glow of a reddish *ponytail*, bobbing up and down enticingly, as the door of history slammed shut in the background. It was 1957, the year Max Frisch's novel *Homo Faber* was published. The age of the centaurs was over: this was the first blush of the youthful era of schoolgirl Amazonian warriors wearing cowboy jeans, and Frisch worked hard to capture the contours: 'Her reddish ponytail dangling down over her back, her two shoulder blades under her black sweater, the notch in her firm and slender back, then her hips, her youthful thighs in her black trousers, rolled up at the calves, and her ankles . . .' And yet all of these secondary details – her back, hips, thighs, calves and ankles – are tertiary when seen against this combination of innocence and animality, this hurricane of social change about to sweep in. It would be another seven years before the Ford Mustang became the appropriate mode of transport to ride out west. But the messenger of history was already fluttering enticingly, the ponytail that waved in the new era.

*

The grandiose achievements made by horses during the era of the centaurian pact were now, in the post-horse era, heading rapidly towards oblivion. However, the horse is not *la part maudite* of history, a page ripped out and crumpled up; it is simply a forgotten element. Though it might have been overlooked, its reach is extensive and complex: it is very tempting to narrate every aspect of equine history in one breath. The temptation is great to plunge in and get carried away, drifting between primary sources and theories, novels and reconstructions, bridles and destinies. As appealing as it might be, aesthetically speaking, it isn't a very practical approach. For the sake of dealing with stories systematically, I will introduce in succession the versions of history which strictly speaking should be told paratactically – that is, side by side. This will be done in the four sections of this book.

In the first part, I will narrate real histories: the stories of cities, of roads and of accidents, of rural doctors and cavalrymen, of spaces, paths and energies. In Part II, I'll focus on an intellectual, scientific and academic history. This will be a narrative of the leading lights in the history of the equine knowledge developed by centuries of horse fanciers, breeders, painters and scholars, now partially if not totally forgotten. In Part III, I will discuss the horse as metaphor and the history of its representation. We will consider images and perceptions of horses through which the nineteenth century's ideas of power, freedom, might, compassion and terror played out. In these three sections of the book I reflect on three economies where the horse has played its ancient, pivotal role as a converter or conveyor of energy, of knowledge and of pathos. In the fourth and final section, I gather together the narratives of horses and people I have heard, read and experienced. I have ordered my material into categories as best I can, by tracing the contours of the three economies, by showing how the horse and its history have been presented by other historians, and finally by proposing my own suggestions for tales that should be told.

So, as we embark on a re-enactment of the dramatic story of the horse, how should it be staged? Should it be framed as tragedy or farce? As an ascent or a decline? As cultural critique or detached structural analysis? The theme of separation, of leave-taking, suggests it would make sense to adopt the aesthetic form of the *eulogy*. After all, are we not bidding farewell to a living environment, a

The old world comes to the rescue; horses drag a car out of danger
on the beach at the Baltic Sea. Photo: Max Schirner, 1935.

History in the rear-view mirror: *Les Embarras des Petits
Champs*, Robert Doisneau, Paris, 1968.

natural civilization, a sophisticated culture, an analogue world? But this farewell is already done and dusted; it's a story that ended a good half a century ago. Is everything we might say about it not therefore more suited to being presented as an *epilogue*? Both approaches have something attractive about them and I'm sure both would be effective on the stage. They might well give us an emotional picture, but how much would they offer in terms of knowledge? If we want to know how the story plays out and what it has to say to us, we might do better to adopt a more open, more porous approach: more comparisons, fewer conclusions.

Besides, the history of the horse is not one suited to final words. The subject matter calls for an *histoire totale*, as I mentioned above, recounting how my early reflections came about. How little I knew then of the spirits I was summoning! For the sake of the horse, rivers of ink have flowed, creating an ocean of printed literature. But a synthesis such as I hope to achieve with this book will never escape the labyrinth of print; an all-encompassing archive remains a distant dream. The horse was born not in Troy, but in Alexandria: it is a phantom of the library, and whoever has experienced the representations in text and pictorial form with which this phantom has filled the minds of artists, writers and scholars – indeed, colonized their thinking to the point of obsession – will struggle to recover that harsh world of the stable, the manège and the pasture.

That is not all. The epistemic problems run deeper and bring into question the possibility of representation itself. Whoever writes about two or three hundred years of equine history begins to see himself hemmed in by dense heaps of literature on the role of the horse in various very distinct cultural contexts. With every step he takes, he moves across chasms of scholarly controversies of which he can scarcely take stock, let alone render in his own words. A hundred years of research into North American Indian anthropology cannot be neatly summarized in a handful of pages. Trying to be a scholar like Franz Boas, one risks ending up a genre novelist like Karl May. The sense of digging in a bottomless pit is one that will be familiar to all authors of synthetic history, especially global historians. With the plethora of references I litter throughout my text, I will, as far as possible, be laying my cards on the table. But the question of evaluation is perhaps one I manage to skirt around without truly answering it; more than something to have and hold, such a question is more of a desideratum: something to hope for or aim at. And the more garrulous the discourse and the more scholars and specialists babble away, the more unmistakable is the silence of the real protagonist: the horse holds its tongue.

Le cheval n'a pas de patrie: the horse has no fatherland, as Marshal Ney put it, but is it not high time to grant it leave to remain in our tales of the past? It is nearly two decades now since I first had the idea of writing the story of the long nineteenth century, focusing not on the usual suspects, from Napoleon and Metternich to Bismarck, but on the unsung hero and protagonist of this century: the horse. Back then, I still dreamed of giving a voice to this historic kingpin. If this dream has faltered, it is not for want of material or because of the obscurity of the subject; on the contrary, the archives are full and overflowing. One never writes from the stable, but always from the ivory tower of the library. When a writer grants the horse the lead role or even the first-person narrative voice, as we see with certain sensitive authors of equine and world literature from Théodore Sidari (*Mémoires d'un cheval d'escadron*, 1864), John Mills (*Life of a Racehorse*, 1865), Anna Sewell (*Black Beauty*, 1877), Leo Tolstoy ('Kholstomer', 1886), Mark Twain (*A Horse's Tale*, 1905) and D. H. Lawrence (*St Mawr*, 1925), to Michael Morpurgo (*War Horse*, 1982), their words do still stem from the ivory tower. I do not mean to suggest that we cannot truly get close to the special intelligence and emotional life of the horse; and indeed I attempt with a few brief references at the end of this book to propose that it is possible. But nevertheless I found that in what I initially hoped to achieve, I have failed. My first genuine horse book will have to wait until my rebirth as a horse. This tome in the hands of the reader is not the horse's book, but rather the work of a historian about the end of an era in which mankind and horses made history together. And I stress *made* it together, as clearly they didn't write it together: only one party to the alliance did the *writing*, and one human life is not sufficient to read everything that mankind has had to say about the other side of the partnership.

For a long time I thought I would write this book for historians, as if the point was to reveal to my colleagues the historical protagonist they had overlooked all these years and the opportunities for understanding they had missed. I would still be happy if one single historian read my book and found a loose end tied up or a new beginning opened up. But in the end I wrote it, to quote a charming, if immodest dedication, for all and for none. That, too, is of course only partly true. I have written it for my mother, who loved horses and understood them. Whether she would have liked it I will never know. Ten years have passed since I could have asked her.

PART I

The Centaurian Pact
ENERGY

Six stallions, say, I can afford,
Is not their strength my property?
I tear along, a sporting lord,
As if their legs belonged to me.

Johann Wolfgang von Goethe, *Faust, Part One*,
translated by P. Wayne, 1949

The centaur dominates the nineteenth century like a landmark. No other creature from the Greek fables and legends embodies quite so well the direction of movement of an age that was bewitched by the promise of increased energy. This is the era of the horse-man, the creature who is more than man. The centaur is the very epitome of energy, the troublemaker in the mythological menagerie, a young ruffian who loves to carouse and get into fisticuffs; invite him to dinner and you risk more than a few broken dishes. No other mythological wild child carries within him such an ever-present possibility of violence. He's an explosive machine of strength and vitality where man's wisdom and cunning combine with the horse's power and speed; he is wild belligerence coupled with methodical compulsion. What manifests itself as a centaur's aggression is a pure eruption of energy. In the world of this hoofed reveller, the female exists merely as a prey to be snapped up, as a Sabine to be whisked away. He might act the gallant gentleman and offer a beauty his hand to help her up onto his equine back,[1] but the next moment he's galloping off with her, sparks flying and the air trembling with erotic energy. When it comes to romance, he hasn't moved on much since the time of Ovid.

On catching his first glance of a human male, the young centaur can only be disappointed. He sees a defective creature, a mere half a being. 'One day, as I walked in a valley where centaurs rarely roam, I chanced upon a human,' writes Maurice de Guérin. 'It was the first upon which my eyes had fallen, and I despised him. This thing is but one half of what I am, said I to myself . . . This must surely be a centaur overthrown by the gods, which they have reduced to having to crawl along in such a manner.'[2] Man is well aware of his inferiority and weakness. And thus he seeks to domesticate and breed horses, to nurture and train them, the animal aspect of his mobile existence. The closer and stronger the bond between the two, the more 'centaurian' their partnership becomes, the greater the energy, power and speed that is channelled to the rider holding the reins. It was inevitable that as the sun set on the era of the horse, a new centaurian culture would arise: with their horseback battles for dominance, the "Cowboys and Indians" of the American West – in the vein of the Mongols, Mamelukes and Cossacks before them – brought to life the age-old fantasy of the fusion of man and beast for one last time, colonizing as they did so the minds of generations of children.

The discourse about the impending demise of riding and horse-drawn transport started early, a human life before the first automobile tentatively rolled out onto the road. Prompted by a natural disaster, this discourse was the trigger for invention. In 1815, the eruption of Mount Tambora, a volcano on the Indonesian island of Sumbawa, to the east of Bali, darkened the sky of the southern hemisphere, and of the northern hemisphere the following year, to such an extent that the global drop in temperature caused a series of failed harvests. The consequences were widespread famines and rising oat prices: 'Horses competed for scarce grain and hay stocks and either starved or had to be slaughtered and eaten out of severe food shortages.'[3] As hauntingly illustrated by Hans-Erhard Lessing, an expert in the history of technology, this was the hour of the inventor: in 1817, Karl Drais revealed the first model of his 'dandy horse' or '*Laufmaschine*' ('running machine'), which he described as 'a horse-less transportation device'. The underlying intention from the start was to unilaterally terminate the old Centaurian Pact, a contract that was unilaterally entered into in the first place. Once it was brought into the world, the conversation about the impending end of the horse era would never run dry; the fantastical spirit of innovation and experimentation kept the discourse alive until the late nineteenth century when the process of phasing out and replacement started in earnest, powered by both electrical and internal combustion engines, and quickly gained momentum.

A farewell ode to the old equine world, now sunk into oblivion, was published in 1935 under the title *Das Reiterbuch*. This 'Rider Book' was the debut work of the as yet unknown psychologist Alexander

Mitscherlich. This young writer captured the 'look' of the horseman and traced his changing appearance throughout the millennia. The splendour of the historical sunset glowed on every mountaintop, filled with the sweet sound of the elegy: 'The spotlight no longer falls on the horse and its rider ... Their trotting tempo has faded away. Their hoof tracks are covered over. The domain of the horse has dwindled ... The tracks man follows are of another timbre, since he fell in step with the turbine's beat.' [4]

Mitscherlich's historical 'review' led to criticism of the mechanized and motorized civilization. In contrast to mankind's 'eternal tools' such as the sword and the steed, which served as a natural expansion and augmentation of man's strength, 'inspired by his *original* thinking',[5] the machine robbed men of their vital expression: 'Mankind yields his physical expression and vitality to the neutrality (of these machines), hiding himself *inside* the apparatus.' [6] In these 'total prostheses' cowered a being who was depleted of strength and alienated from himself: ' ... the more of these prostheses are put into service, the weaker becomes the man whom they serve'.[7] Judging by the vocabulary Mitscherlich uses and the intellectual landscape he depicts – prosthetics, the neutrality of machine-generated energy, the disempowerment of the subject – his eulogy to the horseback rider who climbed down from the saddle and disappeared into the cab of his motorized vehicle belongs firmly in the context of a conservative perspective on culture and technology in the 1930s. In the form of a footnote to Ernst Jünger's book *The Worker (Der Arbeiter)*, Mitscherlich counters Jünger's aggressive techno-vision with sentimental, idyllic scene-setting.

When in the following pages I describe how the horse, that animalistic supplier of energy, was replaced in various aspects of life (agriculture, the transportation of goods, public transport, the military ...), I won't adopt a mournful, elegiac tone, bemoaning the cultural changes. The dissolution of the Centaurian Pact was not accompanied, after all, by the complete disappearance of our hoofed friend.[8] On the contrary, since the all-time low of 250,000 horses in Germany in 1970, their number has again been on the increase and is now estimated at over a million. There are also thought to be over a million men and women regularly involved in equestrian activities in Germany – with a significant bias in favour of women and girls. The riding industry employs some 300,000 people in Germany, whether it's in breeding, veterinary services, training or day-to-day care. People earn a living from riding equipment, riding lessons, staging competitive events, riding holidays, writing for equestrian magazines. The average German station bookshop stocks some two dozen periodicals for the riding community. And then there's the specialist academic subject of equine studies, which students can study at several colleges in the Federal Republic, with undergraduate degree courses available in Berlin, Osnabrück and Nürtingen, and a postgraduate Master's course at Göttingen.

Besides those who make a living in the equine industry, this revival of the horse age, filled with sporting achievements and tender love and care, has all but lost its former historic solemnity. The connections forged between humans and horses nowadays are relationships based on love, communities of interest and sporting camaraderie. The Centaurian Pact by contrast was made of much sterner stuff. It was a covenant of the old style, still governed by the law of necessity. People and horses were comrades in fate – that is, until the day when they went their separate ways. In this section we'll look at how that came about and what happened next.

Hell for Horses

Since we've got the railroad, horses have been running worse
than ever.

Theodor Fontane, *The Stechlin* (1898),
translated by W. Zwiebel, 1995

A TRINITY WITH DANTE

When playwright and poet Friedrich Schiller passed away in May
1805 after a long terminal illness, he left behind him a considerable
number of unfinished plays. One of the drafts, entitled *Die Polizey*
('The Police'), was a tragedy set in pre-revolutionary Paris, a colossal
amphitheatre where citizens and information are subjected to sinister
monitoring by the authorities. At the heart of the drama is the bureau
of the omnipotent police chief. His real nemesis is not the shadowy
criminal world, but the intrigues of the nocturnal city. Paris becomes
a superhuman protagonist in its own right. As in most of the draft
manuscripts cut short by Schiller's early death, the playwright had not
yet made a start on the rhyming verse of the police drama. The play is
instead sketched out in prose dialogue, swarming with excerpted quotations and draped with the fruits of his reading and turns of phrase
he had picked up here and there. One of the most striking is the phrase
'Paris is paradise for women, purgatory for men, hell for horses'.[9]

Schiller did not invent this memorable tripartite dictum, he merely
tweaked the rhythm. Louis-Sébastien Mercier, whom he quotes,
speaks of 'le paradis des femmes, le purgatoire des hommes & l'enfer
des chevaux'.[10] For his Paris drama, the poet Schiller finds in

Mercier's *Tableau de Paris* an inexhaustible source of quotations and observations. Schiller adopts from him the seemingly contemporary depiction of the police force as a great machine, along with the city as a kind of Moloch who comes into his own in the night. It is clear from the following sentence in Schiller's notes that he had not over-looked the demographic context of Mercier's aperçu: 'Mortality rate in P. – 20,000 per year.'[11] This statistic is also derived from Mercier, who under the heading *'Population de la capitale'* furnishes evidence that the men of Paris died at a more tender age than women. This, Mercier argues, is why people speak of Paris as the paradise of women and purgatory of men. Only the horses and flies dropped faster.

But this elegant axiom was not coined by Mercier either. The trope about women, men and horses was doing the rounds a whole two centuries earlier. It seems that it was the French author Bonaventure des Périers who first composed the expression in 1558. In the thirty-first short story included in his posthumously published collection *Nouvelles récréations et joyeux devis*, Paris is described as 'paradise for women, hell for mules and purgatory for petitioners'.[12] Towards the end of the sixteenth century, John Florio in his *Second Fruits* was the first to express the idea in the classic formation: paradise for women, purgatory for men, hell for horses.[13] And again, thirty years later, in 1621, Robert Burton brought the concept of a paradise for women and hell for horses back to England in order to contrast his homeland with Italy, where everything is reversed and it is the horses that are in paradise.[14] But it was Mercier who brought the memorable phrase into such wide currency. This tricolon reminds us of Dante, who is never far away when it comes to talking about hell. But everyone made use of it to suit their needs. The canon of Hamburg cathedral, F. J. L. Meyer, followed up his 1802 trip to France by pub-lishing his *Letters from the Capital and the Interior of France (Briefe aus der Hauptstadt und dem Innern Frankreichs)*,[15] in which he praises the quality of the police and bemoans the lot of the horses in Paris. You can get there very cheaply, he writes, but the horses and their harnesses are in a dreadful state. Women, men, mortality rates – the whole demo-graphic context is left out of the picture and all that remains is the misery of the horses, which henceforth survives as a topos that spreads throughout the Parisian literature of the nineteenth century.

Savage energy: *The Centauresse*, pen and ink drawing by Eugène Fromentin.

'Tolstoy often went riding in winter and summer. In the morning, he worked, drank coffee, then left the house. With a practised hand, he would take hold of the reins and the horse's mane at the withers, pull himself up on the stirrup, throw one leg over the horse's back and sit up, light and elastic. . . . Kramskoy said Tolstoy when riding was the most handsome man he had ever seen.' (from *Lev Tolstoy* by V. Shklovsky, Moscow, 1974). Tolstoy on his horse Demir, 1908.

It comes up again in the work of Eduard Kollof, the Paris corre-spondent for the *Morning Journal for Educated Readers* (*Morgenblatt für gebildete Leser*), published by Cotta. Kollof reported in 1838 on 'The Paris transport industry' and employed the following description of the hellish traffic in the capital: 'When one sees the great quantity of carriages that trundle back and forth ceaselessly through the streets of Paris from morning 'til night, one wonders how it is possible that there are still pedestrians to be encountered on the sidewalks. Cabrio-lets, fiacres, deltas, lutétiennes, tilburys, barouches, calèches, coupés, landaus, gigs, curricles, four-horse post-chaises, six-horse diligences – all of these ride up and down, day in day out, weaving and winding, breaking axles, tipping over, causing untold accidents in the French capital, which has long been known as a *paradise for women*, but has more right to be known by its other nickname, a *hell for horses* and equally fitting would be *hell for pedestrians*.' (see Plate 2)[16]

Even among Arab diplomats and writers, *a hell for horses* is a famil-iar watchword. Among them is the vizier Ibn Idriss Muhammad al-'Amraoui, who in 1860 visited the court of Napoleon III as an emis-sary of Sultan Muhammad IV of Morocco (1859–73). Al-'Amraoui adopts the formula from his experienced predecessor, the Egyptian Sheikh Rifa'a Rafi'a al-Tahtawi, who had travelled to France a few years earlier.[17] The vizier shows little interest in the demographics of Paris or in the traffic conditions in the capital. In his eyes, the reference takes on a slightly different significance: he refers to the dominance exerted by women within their domiciles and sometimes even beyond their walls.[18] The Oriental visitor senses a cultural danger in the power wielded by women, which makes it advisable, as far as he is concerned, to keep one's distance from the West. The sight of the Frenchmen's horses prompts condescension from the Arab connoisseur: 'Excellent horses such as we have are not to be found over there.'[19]

THE GENTLEST TOUCH

The *Tableau de Paris*, Mercier's panorama of the Paris of the 1780s, on the eve of the revolution, consists of numerous prose sketches or essays which read like the captions to paintings. The entire composition breaks down into kaleidoscopic shards, a series of frames, many filled with mayhem, shouting, shoving, the hustle and bustle, clamour and odours of the city. Like the illustrations of a children's book, swarming and teeming with activity, in Mercier's detailed descriptions we recognize characters, familiar faces, well-known scenes. There is also one particular ever-present protagonist, whom we see lurking in every shadowy corner of his intricate cityscape, utterly indifferent to the topic under discussion, be it the spirit, the economy, wealth, the state of the city or the morals and health of its residents. Whatever the headlines, the gossip, the talk of the day, the horse always turns up where you least expect it.

In such moments, Mercier's great cityscape almost becomes a novel about the two species sharing a common space. In the *Tableau*, the tale of the *grandeurs et misères* reveals an exceedingly close cohabitation. We speak of *biocoenosis*, an ecological community where several species live together in one space, one biotope. In this narrative, there are only two species sharing the biotope, their common habitat, while all their other fellow residents – the city's dogs, cats, rats, pigeons – are pushed out of the picture, historically speaking. In the urban realm, the coexistence of people and horses is perceived as a *ménage à deux*. Of course, humans and animals cohabit very closely in the countryside, too, and have done since time immemorial, even sharing one roof, cosying up in one household or *synoecism*. But in a rural farmstead, the horse is not a farmer's only housemate: the domain is also shared with cows, oxen, sheep, goats, pigs, geese and hens, not to mention the mice, lice and other parasites. The lives of humans and animals are often divided by only a very thin wall; one hears the other eating and chattering, one is aware of the other's smells and both chase away the same flies. The city with its reduced biodiversity gives the impression of allowing men and horses greater distance from one another. In truth, they are welded more closely together than ever, with the common habitat that is imposed on them, merging the two tribes into a common destiny.

All this is not without friction or tension. Reports of late eighteenth- and nineteenth-century Paris echo complaints about cramped conditions and the stench of the city, the dangers for pedestrians, the cacophony of the horse-drawn carriages. There are still places in

Europe where we get a sense of how a horse-filled city must have looked and smelled; in Vienna and Rome, there are squares where fiacres and dozing horses wait for tourists. But can we imagine how a nineteenth-century city would have sounded? Everyone knows the rumble of a scooter on its nocturnal newspaper delivery rounds, the screech of a tram, the honking of taxis and the death knell of a braking bus. But who can conjure up the cracking whips, the wagon wheels and horseshoes on the cobbles, in the early morning hours when sleep is fragile and ephemeral? The roar of the city becomes unbearable when the two species, horses and humans, come into too close quarters, when a rough carriage driver thrashes his weary beasts of burden. Arthur Schopenhauer denounced the cracking of whips as 'the most irresponsible and shameful din', which breaks the concentration of one who labours with his mind. 'This sudden, sharp thwack which slices through one's brain and shatters one's thoughts must strike agony into every man who carries anything so much as resembling a thought in his head . . . The emotional effect on the horse, which is surely intended to be the same . . . is dulled and indeed annulled by the habitual use and incessant abuse of the thing: the horses do not accelerate their pace in response; even when driving an empty fiacre on the prowl for custom, trotting at the slowest tempo, they swat away constantly. The gentlest touch of the whip would be much more effective.'[20]

The clamour of horses, carriages and coaches sets the pulse of the trembling city. Mercier describes how, at every hour of the day, the noise of the city subtly changes. From early morning until dusk, the soundscape shifts with each hour that passes. The worst is the racket at about five o'clock in the afternoon, when everyone is driving towards each other, pushing to get past, clogging up the roads. At seven o'clock in the evening, the noise fades out, the city becomes still. The workers go home on foot, but by nine the clamour rises anew, as the bourgeoisie head out to the theatre. Around midnight, silence reigns again, broken only by the occasional rumble of the cabs bringing city dwellers home. At one o'clock in the morning, 6,000 farmers descend upon the city, laden with vegetables, fruit and flowers. By two o'clock, the gigs and coaches of those returning late to their beds tear Parisians from their sleep . . .[21] In Mercier's prose, we hear not only the stagecoaches rattling and the horseshoes clattering on the cobbles, but we also sense the growing awareness among city dwellers of the din created by the sheer numbers of their equine companions.[22] The rhythm which pulsed through the city would not change for some time. When Emile Zola wrote of the 'belly of Paris' a hundred years later, the noise that echoes around day and night is this same infernal din, and those who are to blame for it are also still the same people.

EVERY THIRTEENTH FRENCHMAN

On 18 January 1766, a dispute arose at the edge of the Place des Victoires between a cab driver and an elegant aristocrat, the consequences of which were investigated by the police and registered in the archives.[23] A driver stopped to let out his customer; on seeing that he and his own carriage were thus prevented from moving forward, the aristocratic gentleman flared up in anger and, stepping down from his carriage, beat the horse with his sword and stabbed it in the abdomen. He was eventually made to pay the cab driver for the care of the injured horse. The signature on the ensuing legal document was that of an irascible character whose name went down in history as a byword for cruelty: the Marquis de Sade.

As early as the mid-eighteenth century, Paris was the horse capital. The political, economic and cultural revival that Paris underwent, briefly interrupted by the Revolution but then strongly reinvigorated, was unthinkable without a great number of horses in the capital city. The horse at once represented the economic means and the energy required for everything that Paris had on show, everything that made the world marvel, from the new forms of symbolic politics and real warfare, the exercise of cultural hegemony, the rapid circulation of money, goods and news, the spread of the arts and fashion, to the ostentatious display of wealth and a certain *savoir vivre*. Nearly 80,000 horses populated the city at the height of the horse era in 1880.[24] In the capital, we see the reflection of a nation rich in horses: in 1789, on the eve of the Revolution, almost 2 million horses grazed the pastures of France; by 1850 their number had increased to nearly 3 million, a level which remained consistent, with only slight fluctuations, until the First World War.[25] Had it not been for the loss of

Alsace-Lorraine, France would have owned an estimated 3.8 million horses on the eve of the First World War. Of course, the human population also rose, from 36.5 million in 1852 to 41 million in 1906.[26] But the ratio of one species to the other, of horses to men, changed by only one percentage point. Even then, every thirteenth Frenchman was a horse.

Yet France was by no means in first place in terms of national horse populations. In the UK in the nineteenth century, there was one horse for every ten residents, while in the USA the ratio was 1:4 and in Australia it was 1:2. In the late nineteenth century, there were 300,000 horses living in London.[27] Although the nineteenth-century city developed a higher requirement for horses than at any previous point in history, the number of horses per human inhabitant in the densely populated agglomerations was still likely to be lower than in the rest of the nation. Even between cities within one country there were differences, as we see in the United States, for instance: the more spacious and provincial-feeling cities of the Midwest had a far higher ratio of horses to men than the highly compressed metropolises of the East Coast.[28] Even where the ratio was 'only' 26.4 inhabitants per horse, as in New York in 1900, the absolute numbers are still staggering. Imagine what life must have been like in Manhattan when there were some 130,000 horses working within the city at any one time.[29] What must it have felt like to walk along Broadway and have to dodge horse carcasses and carriages wedged into gridlock?[30] How must a city like New York in 1900 have reeked, when its horses produced 1,100 tonnes of manure and 270,000 litres of urine daily, and when twenty dead horses were transported away every day?[31] The figures are even higher for the considerably larger city of London: at the knacker's yard, 26,000 horses per year were turned into cat food and fertilizer.[32] Photographs from those times convey only a pale reflection of the cramped coexistence humans and horses had to endure in the city at the *fin de siècle*.

The life of one species means the death of the other. For the horses living in and consumed by the nineteenth-century city, seized by the storm of mechanization, it was no healthy environment. Their muscles, tendons, hooves and joints could only endure the harsh work of providing draught power for the urban modes of transport for a few years, before they were sold on for commercial use to pull lighter loads, or allowed to return for their final years to the country-side. City horses went into retirement at the age of five and had an average lifespan of ten years. This was true of omnibus horses, while tram horses tended to be exhausted after four years.[33] For many the end came even sooner by way of permanent lameness, a sad fate con-cluded with the veterinarian's bullet. Between 1887 and 1897, the employees of the New York ASPCA (American Society for the Pre-vention of Cruelty to Animals) put down between 1,800 and 7,000 horses annually. Contrary to the popular notion, the dead animal was not left to rot in the gutter; the disposal of carcasses was a mech-anized process: a winch powered by horsepower hauled it onto a cart, a tarpaulin was thrown over it and it was transported out of the city.[34] In the cities of European countries where horse meat was eaten, you would often see groups of horses, many limping on three legs, making their weary way to the slaughterhouse. In France, owners had their horses shaved before slaughter to make use of the horsehair. Mid-century Paris saw growing indignation among the populace at the desperate sight of shorn horses on their last legs.[35]

The increasing reliance on horses for the expansion and mechan-ization of urban transport changed the relationship of the city to the surrounding countryside. No longer were farms responsible only for supplying vegetables, meat and milk for consumption by the human population of the city; throughout the course of the nineteenth cen-tury they increasingly took on the role of breeding and supplying the dietary needs of the city horses. The requirements of the horse indus-try opened up new, lucrative business opportunities. 'A horse-based economy,' say the American historians Clay McShane and Joel A. Tarr, 'demanded enormous inputs of land, labor, and capital . . . The horse-powered economy required massive amounts of land, both for grazing in rural areas before migration and for food supplies after.'[36] The 3 million horses that inhabited the cities of the United States in 1900 consumed 8 million tonnes of hay and almost 9 mil-lion tonnes of oats per year. Twelve million acres of land were needed to produce that quantity of fodder – about four acres per horse.[37]

It was not only for inner-city traffic that the demand for horses rose; from the late eighteenth century horses also finally took over from the ox and the ass as the main supplier of draught power in farming (Plate 5). The main reasons for this shift, besides the expansion and improvement of the road network and road paving,[38] were improvements made to vehicles and agricultural tools, namely the plough and harrow, later also the mower. Speed became the most important factor in the economy: saving time reaped profits. Thanks to its speed, the horse more than made up for what the ox offered in terms of power and modest nutritional requirements. The constantly growing demand for horses from this point on led to a similar increase in the number of stud farms. By the mid-century, horse breeding was at the heart of the agricultural system of most European and North American countries. No other agricultural product, be it meat, crops or wool, held anything like as high a systemic value. The horse provided something that would become more important and more fundamental for the modern economy than protein, carbohydrates and textiles: the provision of energy, in a pure, immediately available form, with no further requirement for transformation or transference. If, as Michel Foucault put it, the *régime scolaire* produced the 'scholars', that is the pupils and students, and the *régime pénitentiaire* governed the inmates of the modern penal system, so the modern agricultural regime produced the familiar repertoire of proteins, fats and carbohydrates, but above all animal-powered kinetic energy, which by the nineteenth century was supplied mainly by horses. The great powerhouse of the horse provided the prerequisite for the modern logistics and transportation systems in the expanding cities. Of course, the domestication and breeding of a second *habile* animal, besides the *homo habilis*, came at a price, and was not without social and technical preconditions.

BREAKDOWN IN THE SYSTEM

Paris, the nineteenth-century world capital, was also the capital of traffic: it was little wonder there were so many accidents. Wherever there is mention of the traffic, sooner or later we hear of an accident. Regardless of who or what supplies the motive power, be it horse, ox, locomotive or combustion engine, there always seems to be an injury or fatality in the margin of the texts dealing primarily with the technical means, costs and risks of the act of transportation. It begins with Icarus, and Concorde was not the end of it: each and every mode of transport brings with it inherent risks and its own distinctive kind of accident. In the history of technology, each epoch has its own 'True Stories' chapter cataloguing the associated disasters, as though it were in the mishaps, the collisions, the pile-ups and the systemic break-downs that we see the true essence of a technology.

Again Mercier presents himself as an early and fruitful informant. 'Cabs and cabbies cause untold accidents,' he writes in *'Gare! Gare!'*,[39] 'which do not interest the police in the slightest.'[40] To lend legitimacy to his critique of the traffic system, Mercier draws on his own experiences. He was present at one of the earliest urban pile-ups (at least of those that were recorded): 'I witnessed the disaster on 28th May 1770. Its cause was a mass of vehicles blocking the road, across which poured the most enormous stream of people, a huge crowd in the dim light of the boulevards. By a hair's breadth I avoided losing my life. Twelve to fifteen people were killed, either on the spot or later as a consequence of their injuries, having been crushed so terribly. Three times I was hurled to the ground, each time by a different coach, and I was almost crushed alive under the wheels of one.'[41]

It was not the criminality of certain residents that made the city of the late eighteenth and nineteenth century a dangerous place, but the forced *centaurism*, the horse-powered street traffic, the obligatory close coexistence of men and horses. Throughout the nineteenth century, the number of accidents in the cities and on the highways rose steadily, caused by bolting horses, overturning carriages, collisions and driving at excessive speeds. In 1867, horse-powered transportation on the streets of New York caused an average of four fatalities per week, with another forty pedestrians injured; in other capitals the incidence of accidents was also well above what is typical of today's motorized traffic.[42] Even at the beginning of the twentieth century, when automobiles were beginning to be found on the streets, the cause of traffic accidents was still overwhelmingly the use and abuse of horses. Fifty-three per cent of accidents registered in France in 1903 involved horse-drawn carriages: one-third in the cities, two-thirds on the country roads.[43] Figures for the United States around the turn of the century come out at an annual average of 750,000 accidents and serious injuries.[44] The literature of the nineteenth century, whether descriptions of cities or travel, is full of lamentation about reckless drivers, drunken coachmen, toppling carriages, injured passers-by and terror-stricken travellers. It's not the dreaded highwayman who is the traveller's worst enemy, but his best friend: the horse.

But the beast is not the true cause of the accident. The problem is the *system* of horse-drawn transport, with all the associated cab drivers, riders, travellers, hauliers and policemen, and all the vehicles, harnesses and other equipment. A not inconsiderable role is played by the lamentable condition of the paths and roads, and the poor monitoring of the speed of the moving elements within the system. If we want to dig down to the root cause of so many accidents, we need to look at the *centaurian system* as a whole, considering all the individual parts that make up the entire horse-powered ensemble, evaluating how the players interact and how each element is articulated. It all starts with the intrinsic nature of the lead player. Horses are flight animals, easily startled and quick to resort to their instinctive flight reflex. A sudden movement in their peripheral vision, the bark of a dog, a sheet of newspaper caught by the wind, and that's it – before you know it, the horse loses its head and bolts. A bolting horse can have fatal consequences, especially in the crush of the city, and if other horses are also alarmed. The largest horse-related catastrophe in recorded history was in New York in 1823, involving a chain reaction of panicking horses.[45]

Urban workhorses need to become accustomed to the traffic and the sights and sounds of the city, just as in a military context warhorses need to become attuned to gunfire and cannons. But not only did the industry need horses to be bred and trained in a certain way, the men working in this new environment also had to adjust to the increasingly complex and fast-moving traffic conditions: the human animal also needed training to cope with the challenges of modern traffic. The drunken cabby given to spouting profanities and reckless driving was no longer merely a nuisance for sensitive souls, a moral irritant, he had become a *risk factor*. He needed to be put in his place, rules needed to be imposed and their compliance monitored by the police and, where necessary, enforced by the courts. Efforts to regulate the speed of horse traffic go back as far as the Renaissance: in a

Broadway in the rain, 1860. Photo: E. Anthony.

Paradise for women, purgatory for men, hell for horses: Paris in 1880.

decree of 1539, Francis I of France spoke for the first time of the dangers of speeding, overtaking and turning abruptly in the streets of the cities and on the highways of the kingdom.[46] Yet it was not until the end of the seventeenth century that the first steps were taken by police forces to confront excessive speeding and careless driving. It was around 1780 that a new invention started to appear on the streets in England and France – one of those developments explored so eloquently by Bruno Latour[47] – which in a seamless solution to both social and technical challenges was able to protect urban pedestrians and implement a physical division of the road by creating different levels. What we are talking about is of course the *trottoir* or pavement: a clearly delineated, elevated walkway whose kerbstone forms a physical border between the carriageway of moving vehicles and the dedicated space for pedestrians.[48]

The kerb – this partition of a mere hand's breadth – which just decades later snaked for hundreds of kilometres throughout the entire city, is not merely a response in urban architectural form to the creeping centaurization of the metropolis and its inhabitants. If the growth of the city in the nineteenth century profoundly changed the ecology of the countryside and the economy of agriculture by placing the horse at the centre of the agricultural system, then it also in turn led to changes in the horse's ecology and the architecture of the city. The tens of thousands of horses living and working in the cities needed not only to be fed and watered, they also required accommodation. On a scale that is barely imaginable now, the nineteenth-century city consisted of rows upon rows of urban stables, whose often haphazard construction out of wood and brick made them a liability in terms of both sanitary conditions and fire safety.[49] Boston in 1867 boasted some 367 stables, each housing on average 7.8 horses. These stable blocks were dotted across the entire city, with work and transport horses deployed at the port and the railway stations, while the riding and carriage horses of the well-to-do needed to be housed within easy reach of their owners.[50] Just like the outbuildings with coach houses below and coachmen's living quarters above that are still to be found today in the courtyards of European townhouses, or the mews lanes of London, the stables were mostly located behind the houses or accommodated in the central courtyard of a block of dwellings. Most had one or possibly two storeys, though in some cases three- or four-storey stables were built. In the largest bus depot in south-west London, 700 horses were accommodated on two floors around a huge square courtyard.[51] Just as the cramped cohabitation of people and horses had altered the structure, and the infrastructure, of aristocratic life – including the installation of palace staircases for horses – so too had the obligatory centaurization of the nineteenth-century city altered its architectural features.

This was also a boom time for street furniture: from the middle of the nineteenth century onwards, European and American cities were enhanced by the installation of troughs and drinking fountains for horses.[52] The ASPCA counted over a hundred in 1890. One of the grandest drinking spots for horses was set up on West 155th Street in New York in 1894, thanks to a legacy left by the entrepreneur John Hooper. Besides a large drinking trough for the horses, the fountain, designed by George Martin Huss, included a number of smaller drinking points at ground level for dogs and a tap for the people of the city.[53]

THE GOLDEN AGE

There was another significant factor in the tension between city and country. A certain crop had a very important place at the intersection of technology and society, particularly the upper class elites, and that crop was oats. In addition to hay and water, oats represent the main fuel in a horse-drawn economy. Oats are rich in protein and good for horses' sensitive digestive system; oat straw is also nutritious. With the increased use of horses, there was a clear spike in the cultivation of oats to fill their bellies; and as the use of horses declined, so too did the oat fields.[54] The increasing use of maize as a plant-based biofuel supply in the current energy market recalls the upsurge in oat production in the eighteenth century. Oats boost a horse's vitality and bring a shine to its coat, which explains why the cereal was so intensively consumed in the stables of the upper classes. 'Thanks to a wealthy population of 4,000 aristocratic families in the 1780s,' writes the historian Daniel Roche, 'Paris becomes the showcase of beautiful horses.

It is also the place where we see the most sophisticated care being lavished on horses.'[55]

With the horse, the city of the nineteenth century is filled with new dangers, but also new beauty. The city positively swells with unremarkable and wretched creatures, but it is also increasingly filled with swift, elegant animals and luxurious vehicles. Horses and carriages alike become objects of *conspicuous consumption*. 'The fast horse', writes Thorstein Veblen, 'is in general expensive, wasteful and unusable as a work horse. The use to which such a horse can be put . . . at best takes the form of an ostentatious display of power and agility, which may at least satisfy the aesthetic sensibility. Perhaps we may concede that therein lies some benefit.' [56] It is this aesthetic sensibility that stimulates the ingenuity of craftsmen and entrepreneurs, prompted, not least, by a desire for variety. Even Mercier in the late eighteenth century found himself admiring the sheer abundance of various types of carriages, a range which grew from year to year. In 1838, Eduard Kollof wrote that, if he wished to describe all the carts and carriages that trundled through the streets of the French capital, he could easily fill an entire book.[57] Between the cabriolet and the fiacre was a huge spectrum of light, mostly open-topped 'mongrel carriages' including the '*Françaises, Parisiennes, Eoliennes, Zéphyrines, Atalantes* and *Cabriolets compteurs*'; nevertheless it was the classic fiacre that 'despite its numerous competitors and rivals . . . remained the firm favourite among fathers, grandmothers and lovers'.[58]

Towards the end of the era of the horse, in 1941, the Italian author Mario Praz voiced a great paean to the time of the carriages, their noble elegance and their 'steady and solemn rhythm', which 'no automobile will ever achieve'. As long as there were magnificent equipages, Praz argued that 'amidst the drumroll of scraping and pounding', the aristocrats could claim 'to have preserved an outward symbol of the chosen class – one last stamp of the old cavalry at the threshold of the modern age. A train of opulent carriages once resembled a frieze like the gallant young riders of the Panathenaic procession, where men and horses marched on as if in a ceaseless, wonderful, graceful and joyful dance of the earth . . . Vienna was once a city "on four wheels", where beautiful Viennese ladies sat in their open carriages showing off their elegant dresses.'[59]

Fashion is the art of making fine alterations to a product for which strictly speaking there is no genuine need. Differentiation on exclusively stylistic and aesthetic grounds was a feature of carriage design for the entire century. Back in 1910, Studebaker, the USA's biggest manufacturer of horse-drawn carriages, was producing 115 different types of light, two-wheeled gigs and as many types of coaches. The end of the horse era stole up in the shadow of such numbers. Twenty years later Studebaker, who had been experimenting with horseless carriages since 1895, had completely moved over to automobile production.[60]

Besides agriculture and the armed services, the city was the heaviest consumer of horses in the nineteenth century. Officers, whether they were leading the French army or the armies of other nations, proved to be willing disciples of Napoleon; while they were continuously beefing up their armies, they focused particularly on a massive expansion of the cavalry and the horse-drawn artillery. In 1900, the peacetime reserves of the French Army comprised 145,000 horses, a number which in the event of mobilization would rise to 350,000.[61] Despite early experimentation with steam engines, reliance on horses was continually on the rise in the agriculture of the industrialized countries too. Machinery such as the mowing machine, patented in 1834, did not reduce the requirement for horses, but on the contrary encouraged it to climb; the first combine harvesters that appeared fifty years later in California were drawn by twenty to forty animals, 'about as many horses ... as were needed to transport an obelisk', writes Sigfried Giedion, reminding us in passing of the wonders of antiquity.[62] Agricultural machinery could only save manpower by increasing the use of animal labour instead. Since one main purpose of agriculture in the nineteenth century was breeding horses and providing for their nutritional requirements (as urban, military and coal and steel industry workhorses), we see at this point a kind of feedback loop within the horse-powered economy of the nineteenth century.

In the city, the use of horses essentially served two main purposes: the conveyance of goods and of passengers. The rapid growth of cities in Western Europe and North America prompted the need for public transportation, that is, inexpensive transport connections along fixed routes at scheduled intervals. Horse-drawn omnibuses, in circulation in Paris since the mid-1820s and in London since the 1830s, also made inroads into America at this time; in 1833, New York was dubbed the 'City of Omnibuses'.[63] That same decade the new mode of transport conquered virtually the entire urban road network of the United States. The omnibus carried that sector of the public who, as McShane and Tarr put it, 'could afford the fare but couldn't afford carriages'.[64] As fares dropped and the middle and lower classes swelled, there was a corresponding expansion in bus traffic in the cities. There was mounting competition in the second half of the century from horse-drawn trams: that is, buses which ran on rails. They combined increased comfort for passengers with reduced effort for the draught animals: a tram carriage could carry about three times as many passengers as a bus and this efficiency brought the fare down. This is how rail transportation, so inconspicuous in its nature and yet so successful, would come to change the face of the city, just as a few decades later high-rises would transform the skyline. By 1880, New York's 'horse cars' were being drawn by nearly 12,000 horses and mules, and were carrying an average of over 160 million passengers per year.[65] The disproportionately high numbers of passengers, draught animals, wagons and miles of track laid, given the size of the population,[66] can be seen as evidence of the suburbanization of cities: the expansion of the public transport network made it possible to commute into the city to work, while living and sleeping in the suburbs.

The same processes could be seen, a little later, in continental Europe and Japan. Berlin, a metropolis that was rather late to the party, lagged somewhat behind international developments, before it too was suddenly hit by the storm of technological modernity. The first Berlin omnibuses appeared in 1846, connecting central Berlin with its suburbs such as Charlottenburg. Running rather infrequently initially, the city's omnibus service saw an upswing in the 1860s, which was then curbed again by competition from horse-drawn trams (from 1865); the faster, more comfortable and cheaper trams pushed the buses, which were no faster than a pedestrian's walking speed (an average of 3.5 mph), out of the suburbs and back into the city centre. On 25 August 1923, a mere three-quarters of a century after their introduction, the very last Berlin omnibus set off for Halensee station from Potsdamer Platz.

The short summer of urban horse-drawn mass transport was already over.[67]

The expanding horse economy of the nineteenth century not only changed the way of life and modes of transport of the city dweller, it also allowed new occupations and ways of working to flourish, distributing them according to new criteria rather than the traditional determiners of status and rank, and thereby modifying the class structure. 'The ubiquity of horses,' writes French historian Jean-Pierre Digard, 'turned figures like teamsters, coachmen, cuirassiers, knackers, breakers, hussars, farm workers, horse traders, farriers, grooms, stable masters, stage drivers and veterinarians into trusted members of nineteenth-century society . . . Horses had penetrated every area of society; they had spread through the entire culture.'[68] Breeding, husbandry and the horse's many uses were all highly skilled subjects which required training and expertise. A knowledge of horses was no longer the preserve or the natural privilege of the nobility. The *homme de cheval*, who makes an appearance in the course of the nineteenth century, is a new kind of character of indeterminate provenance.[69] Undetected, an agent of democratization had entered the scene.

Nevertheless, the nineteenth century was not the golden age of the horse. The sacrifices made by the animal as a universal pulling machine on the streets and in the fields, and as combatant and comrade on the battlefield, were too great, too cruel and too painful to be able to call it that. The nineteenth century ratcheted up the use and consumption of horses to a historically unprecedented level, and for a time the twentieth century carried on the same trajectory.[70] And yet the nineteenth century saw horses not only exploited, tortured and slaughtered, but also studied, bred, cared for and admired; they were loved, in their own way and for their own potential. As the period's main supplier of universally usable energy – besides human workers – the horse was placed at the heart of the economy, and around this bipolar centre were aligned society's spectrum of requirements, as well as the expression of its desires and passions, its sensitivity and its appreciation of beauty. If we consider this unprecedentedly tight network of economy and ecology, technology, society and aesthetics as a *centaurian system*, then we find that for this system the nineteenth century was indeed a golden age. To be more precise, it is perhaps only the second half of the nineteenth century about which this can be said. The huge boom in the exploitation of horses did not really kick off until the late 1840s. From the turn of the century onwards, both the number and the efficiency of mechanical competitors started to multiply, most notably the automobile and the electric tram, leading to the inevitable decline of horsepower. The golden age lasted barely half a century. In 1903, Paris could already boast some seventy factories manufacturing motor cars.[71]

THE PRICE OF ENERGY

When we speak of the Industrial Revolution of the eighteenth and nineteenth centuries, we tend to think of the great technical inventions like the steam engine and the spinning jenny, and the changes to the mode of production, the division of labour and the way of life which these innovations triggered. In this regard, we in the twenty-first century are still the children of Karl Marx. Here Sigfried Giedion, the historian of technology in modernity, has vastly broadened the perspective of his readers, highlighting the impact that mechanization has had on every one of our elemental human processes, be it walking, sitting, living, eating or killing.[72] Nevertheless, his attention to detail and to anonymous history notwithstanding, Giedion did not appreciate the contribution made by the horse as a forced labourer for hire, working in order to give birth to modernity, itself a historical effort of enormous proportions which yet today is hardly recognized at all. The horse's role is like a lost continent that, even after all the historical research carried out in France and in the United States in recent years, is still waiting to be discovered: a worthy task for a new realism informed by ecology, anthropology, visual cultural studies and the history of ideas.

The industrialization of production and the mechanization of the living environment led above all to a massive hike in the demand for energy, the response to which came in the form of steam power, improvements in harnessing water and wind power, and the production and use of electricity, which itself required a greater and more efficient consumption of fossil fuels. A large proportion of the demand for energy, namely kinetic energy, needed, of course, to be met by draught animals, because with the newly available products, raw materials and markets, and with the rapidly increasing need for transport capacity for people, goods and, not least, news and communications, there came a corresponding surge in demand for traction and transport. With the exception of heavy steam ploughs and tractors, the steam engine could be exploited only in conjunction with rails; it was only with the emergence of the relatively small, lightweight Otto and Diesel internal combustion engines that this technology could make the great leap onto the streets. Horses had to bridge both the spatial distance (from the station to the back of beyond) and also the temporal gulf of just over a century. At the end of the eighteenth century, when traffic speeds had reached a critical point and the more sluggish ox – the horse's age-old, mighty competitor when it came to traction power – was left behind, the horse rose to the status of king of the road. For a century, the *oat-powered engine* was the universal and irreplaceable power unit in the forced mechanization of the world.

Over three centuries have passed since mankind first attempted to measure the working capacity of a horse. If we want to measure a force, we need a scale against which to measure it; to this end, a comparison was made with another source of power. On the evening of 10 July 1688, the members of the Academy of Sciences in Paris discussed the strength of the horse, comparing it with that of men.[73] A horse, the scholars determined by means of a special pulley, could lift a weight of 75 kg one metre high in one second – a task that it took seven men to perform. A horse was therefore the equivalent of seven men, they reasoned. The capacity of one half of the centaur was reflected in the strength of the other. But is man not already reflected in this equation, reduced to his mass alone? Is 75 kg not the weight of an average adult male? Although the ratio remained fixed at this suggestion of 75 kg per metre per second, it was the Scottish engineer James Watt (1736–1819) who is considered the inventor of *horsepower*, a term that is used to this day as a measure of the performance of vehicle engines, although in most countries it has long been replaced by kilowatts. The unit of measurement has been kept alive by its familiarity, its clarity, but also the magic number at the heart of the relationship between the two species: a horse is equal to seven men.

The visible and measurable impact of the energy exerted by a horse can not only be measured by a scale, it also commands a price. As long as there was no viable alternative to the use of horses in agriculture, goods and passenger transport, in the postal sector and in mining, the horse reigned as the undisputed, universal tractor. It was not until the rise of the electric tram from the 1880s, and two decades later the advance of the automobile (followed by the motorized bus, truck, tractor and all manner of vehicles with caterpillar tracks), that the oat-powered workhorse's sovereignty came under fire. It took just two generations to realize that the railway was far superior to the horse in terms of power, speed and stamina. The last generation of the nineteenth century realized that as motors, horses were costly, sensitive and unreliable. Horse-powered energy was *more expensive* than that generated by electricity or internal combustion engines. 'Not satisfied with displacing the horse from the rails,' ran an article in a German transport journal of 1899, 'the engine is now beginning to push the horse off the streets, too. The mechanical horse is lighter, stronger, faster, more enduring, cleaner, easier to steer and, under certain conditions, already cheaper than the other kind. Once the conditions are fulfilled, which form the prerequisites for the greater affordability of the self-driven vehicle, the horse will disappear as a draught animal on our streets.'[74]

In the countryside, where the horse was able to dine and lodge at less expense, the balance fell in its favour for a considerable time, in comparison with the use of motorized tractors. In the city and in cross-country transportation, on the other hand, the horse was soon superseded by its mechanized rival. These motor engines were superior to our equine friend in three respects. First, they had the economic advantage: the motor vehicle offered better performance at a lower price. Fodder, stabling and water all came at a high price, especially in the city. The second advantage was technical: horses are sensitive animals, they can withstand the stresses of urban transport work for only a few years, and one cannot exchange their used or defective parts.[75] The third is an ecological or sanitary advantage: workhorses placed a not insignificant burden on the city with their faeces and

Traffic chaos in Chicago, *c.*1905.

Three-storey stables at a bus company depot, Berlin *c.*1900.

urine, as well as the flies these attracted. While in our time, the motor car has a poor reputation for polluting our cities, at that time the horse was the one condemned for contaminating the city and endangering the health of its residents. Around the turn of the century, the opinion that horses had, in today's parlance, too great an ecological and economic footprint started to become entrenched. The German Emperor Wilhelm II could talk all he liked about the motor car being 'a temporary phenomenon', insisting defiantly that he believed in the future of the horse, but in reality it was merely a question of time before the biggest revolution in energy since Neolithic times.

It was a case of déjà vu when, during the 2013 New York City mayoral election campaign, Bill de Blasio declared that, if elected, he would finally banish from the city the last remaining working horses. While such a policy was boosted by the familiar arsenal of animal welfare – the polluted air, the hard road surface – anyone with a knowledge of the local property market saw other motives behind this campaign: the stable blocks near the Hudson, of the classic two-storey design, constituted highly desirable real estate, in which the patrons of the anti-workhorse campaign may have had a speculative interest. Whatever the reason, the struggle for the rights of horses in the city went viral; animal rights organizations and the media raised the rallying cry. As the correspondent for the *Süddeutsche Zeitung* put it, clearly 'the latest fashion on the streets of New York is the nineteenth century'.[76]

A Pastoral Incident

THE GOD OF SPARROWS

A small town in Westphalia was dominated from the late 1950s by two rival gangs. One was called the Forest gang, the other the Village gang. Both recruited boys who had recently turned ten. The good boys went to high school, the bad ones joined the gangs, and then there were a few who did both. The gangs were basic social structures with a vague hierarchy, that is to say, there was a chief, but the others did more or less what they wanted. In contrast to this weak organizational structure stood the strong tradition of the initiation ritual. I cannot comment precisely on the initiation ritual for the Forest gang, but I can vouch for the Village gang's rites of passage. The underlings were subjected to a test of courage by the gods on high before being admitted to the illustrious club, and it clearly drew upon the old way of life. In front of their assembled peers, new boys were made to eat a local 'delicacy', a prominent agricultural product found in great abundance in the country: a ball of horse dung.

This was common practice until 1960, at any rate. Ten years later, another item would be needed to test the mettle of would-be recruits. The supply of horse dung had dried up, the producers had vanished. The era of the horse was already over, so it was no coincidence that the consumption of their by-product, the 'horse apple', came to an abrupt end. Hadn't the doors to paradise slammed shut in similar circumstances for the tasting of forbidden fruit? In 1960, the horse population in the Federal Republic of Germany was in free fall. While more than 1.5 million horses grazed the pastures of Germany in 1950, by 1970 the total figure was a mere 250,000, a sixth of what it had been two decades before. The decline seems greater yet when we bear in mind that before the First World War there were 4 million horses in Germany, although of course then they were spread out over the larger territory of the German Reich, of which little remained after the Second World War.

Of course, there were still horses in Germany after 1960. Since 1970 their number has even been on the increase again, as the horse began its new career as the plaything and soulmate of the pubescent girl.[1] But the pony club is an enclave on the margins of the real world. The year 1960 was also the one in which the television set conquered the German living room, a pony club for the armchair rider, bringing magical horses into the homes of viewers, from *Fury* and *Bonanza* to *Mister Ed*, the talking horse. It was the dawn of a new world of equestrianism and a new experience of nature, beyond the village and the forest. Of the previous partnership of man and horse, only the human half remained. The other half – the horse – was subsumed into the secondary reality of the media; it had become a *cultural icon*. With the exception of certain provincial backwaters, like the villages of Westphalia, by 1960 the age of the horse was over. The horse had become the Native American of the Western world: a species that survived only in isolated conservation areas.

By 1960 television sets were arriving in the homes of farmers as well as city dwellers, while at the same time the stables, where until recently horses had pawed the ground and slept on the straw, were starting to empty. In areas where the land had long ago been given over to farming on an industrial scale, with endless fields, intensive use of fertilizers and widespread use of machinery, the farewell to the horse was a relatively unceremonious affair. One morning, all that remained was one lonely animal left in the barn, which the farmer occasionally took out hacking or let his children ride, while a new, more powerful tractor had moved into the converted garage next door. In areas where villages eked out a more traditional way of life, and farming was more fragmented and old-fashioned – with a dung heap in the yard and apple orchards behind the house – the farewell was a rather slower, protracted and more solemn affair. In some villages of the southern German and Austrian region of Allgäu, where the young men's traditional Easter ride marked the climax of the village year, this ritual still continued years after the horses were gone, the only difference being that now it was an Easter outing for young tractor drivers.

The tangible lack of horse dung since 1960 caused difficulties not only for the traditionally minded section of the village youth; it was also tough on some much smaller creatures: the sparrows. For as long as there were horses, there were also sparrows, whether it was in the countryside or in the city, living in the lap of luxury. Horse droppings still contained a considerable quantity of leftovers of the horses' favourite food – oats. At any rate, what remained was more than adequate for a sparrow's appetite. This is due to the nature of the oat grain, which is more robustly packaged by the surrounding husk than the grains of other cereals. Just as small birds roam with herds of large animals in the African savannah, living in symbiosis with the rhino and buffalo, so the European sparrow lived for centuries in symbiosis with horses, albeit at a slightly greater distance and with horse dung as an intermediary. In the eyes of sparrows, blessed God took the form of a horse. The end was all the more tragic then for them: the twilight of the equine gods also meant the disappearance of one of the main food supplies for European sparrowdom.

As the horses disappeared, so was oat cultivation scaled back. Until the twentieth century, oats and rye were the most important and most widely cultivated cereal in Germany; today, oat production plays a very minor role. Its rise to become one of the most important fodder crops began when, in the eighteenth century and decades before the advent of the railways, the first revolution in transport occurred. When the faster horses took over the harness from the strong but slow oxen, and when passenger and freight transport on a growing network of paved roads increased in speed, rural producers had to react in terms of both livestock breeding and crop cultivation. 'Paved roads were laid and farmers acquired draught horses. These had to be fed in the stable for a time, and for that they needed to grow more oats.'[2] The cavalry brigades of European armies were also major buyers of this crop; besides its ration of hay, a nineteenth-century German cavalry horse was given an average 5 kg of oats per day.

Even the pastures of the farming community were organized differently. There were changes to the way that land was being used and administered, including the pastures of the farming community, the

forests and the so-called 'common land'. The old common land, or
'*Allmende*' as it was called in German, was gradually carved up, bringing to an end its historic shared use; the ecologist Garrett Hardin
referred to this change in 1968 as the 'tragedy of the commons'. Farming methods developed, becoming more intensive, new breeds of farm
animals were introduced, and the agricultural economy was increasingly aligned with the major markets (meat and grain). In short, in
parallel with the transport revolution, there was a total transformation of the system of land use, the *régime agraire*, as the French call it.
At its centre now stood our fleet-footed friend, the horse.

The basis of the economy had shifted and with it certain fundamental
aspects of life had changed. The shift in the use of the land had a vivid
impact on its morphology or, rather, its perceived form as a landscape.
After all, just as the terms *countryside* and *land* imply a number of economic and ecological facts, *landscape* denotes an aesthetic category.

STUCK IN THE MUD

Swiss cultural historian Jacob Burckhardt saw the discovery of the
landscape as a characteristic of the new relationship with the world
that man entered into during the Renaissance. Starting with Dante
and Petrarch, nature is opened up to the aesthetically critical beholder.
Describing the contrast between a practical and an aesthetic relationship to nature, German philosopher Joachim Ritter noted that for a
man of the land, 'nature is divided into that which is used and that
which is unused . . . It is only in the eyes of one who is capable of free,
aesthetic contemplation that nature exists as a landscape . . .'[3] Even
more radically, German sociologist and philosopher Georg Simmel
described 'landscape' as an *artefact*, a work of art: 'When we see a
landscape and no longer see a sum of individual natural objects, we
have before us a work of art *in statu nascendi.*'[4] In fact it was artists,
poets and painters, as we see in Ritter's historical sketch, who discovered the landscape first of all, sculpted it into a certain form and
moulded it into a genre of painting. Since the eighteenth century, the
concept of landscape has also existed as a category of geography, as
a description of the 'typical structures of the earth's surface'.[5]

This sense of a subjectively perceived excerpt of nature is also how German economist and sociologist Werner Sombart describes the landscape in his history of the German economy of the nineteenth century.[6] However, nature considered in economic terms bears the footprints of history and trade; it is shaped by the work of men and women and the imprint of industry. In the morphology of the landscape, we read the history of agriculture and the progress of mechanization. Sombart's economic history of Germany begins with an opening sequence that's reminiscent of an early film, a kind of road movie. As if filmed with a jerky hand-held camera, in the first twenty pages the author follows a carriage ride through Germany a hundred years ago. The ride is jarring and uncomfortable, the picture jumps and wobbles; there is constant cause to grumble.

It begins with a lack of paved highways and the miserable state of the byways: 'Endless reports of carts getting bogged down, including postal workers asphyxiating in the mire.'[7] The state of the roads corresponds to that of the vehicles: 'At that time, the post-chaise was one of the most popular and most plentiful laughing stocks.'[8] Sombart cites Ludwig Börne's classic piece of satire, *The Natural History of Molluscs and Testacea*, a 'monograph on the German post-snail' that opens with the author's jest that, although his journeys had provided him with an endless supply of comical anecdotes, he had failed to note any of them down, for it had been quite impossible to capture a single word on paper: 'I struggled to write down a single observation, for every jolt caused my thoughts to bolt.'[9]

The rattled traveller in Börne's send-up goes on to voice his mockery of every single participant in the postal service: the coachmen, the horses, the packers, the postmasters and the passengers. They all play their part in the great snail project of slowing everything down. According to his 'Statistics of the Post-chaise' (where Börne interprets 'Statistics' as 'remaining static'), the route from Frankfurt to Stuttgart is reckoned to be a drive of forty hours, but with fourteen rest-stops adding up to a total of fifteen hours of idling, so that over certain stretches the carriage has trouble keeping up with a sturdy pedestrian. In this case, it wasn't even the quality of the highway that was under fire: Börne suffered less from impassable terrain and inclement weather than from the inertia of the personnel. Goethe, on the other hand, in his notes on a journey, recorded the deterioration of the roads as he crossed from one state into another or from one religious denomination to another. This was his third trip to Switzerland. No sooner was Tübingen behind him and he had entered into the Catholic region of the Hohenzollern, than the dreaded bone-shaking commenced. 'The moment one leaves the Wirtenburg region, the treacherous roads begin . . . The reason the bridge needs the good St John of Nepomock is surely because of the terrible road surface.'[10]

If a carriage is sent skidding, it is not always the dreadful quality of the track that is to blame. A harmless dead creature in the road is enough to stop the wheels. In Laurence Sterne's *A Sentimental Journey*, it is a dead donkey that causes the *bidet*, a small French post-horse, to lose its wits. The horse flinches and, refusing to pass the corpse of its deceased colleague, it throws La Fleur, the postilion, from its back. Cursing, the rider mounts his stead again, 'beating him up to it as he would have beat his drum. The bidet flew from one side of the road to the other, then back again—then this way— then that way, and in short every way but by the dead ass.—La Fleur insisted upon the thing—and the bidet threw him. What's the matter, La Fleur, said I, with this bidet of thine?— *Monsieur*, said he, *c'est un cheval le plus opiniâtre du monde*— Nay, if he is a conceited beast, he must go his own way, replied I.'[11] And as Yorick, the narrator, suggests, this is what happens.

Land, considered in economic terms, is either arable land or forest, used for pasture or for industry. From this perspective, it is termed a 'terrain', or *Gegend* in German, depending on its condition or status. The terrain is the epitome of what stands in the way of or opposes man's desire to proceed and progress. When seen as a terrain, the land is quantified in terms of distance and breadth, peaks and chasms; it is rock and mountain, water and marsh; it may be passable: ford, ravine and clearing; or impassable: thicket, wilderness and swamp. Until the late eighteenth century and the early days of modern road construction, with its fixed carriageways supported by bridges and arches, the road is a tortuous labyrinth winding its way around a thousand obstacles, man's meandering compromise with the obstinacy of the unsystematic opponent that is nature. In other words, the path is the complicated, not exactly mathematical function of human will to overcome a distance multiplied by the indomitable resistance of natural objects. It is not until the railway's iron will breaks the landscape's resistance[12] that the road can then hesitantly meander alongside it. Even today, the curve of the highway preserves the memory of the twisting old road as it once snaked between river and mountain, forest and valley.[13]

If we consider the concept of the terrain more closely, wrote Prussian staff officer Carl von Clausewitz, and don't lose sight of the lie of the land, we become aware of three means by which a terrain can distinguish itself from the base line of pure, level ground, as it were: 'firstly, the contours of the earth, that is the elevations and depressions; secondly, the natural phenomena covering it, whether it's forests, marshes or lakes; and finally, the product of its cultivation'.[14] It is this same unholy trinity that the horse-drawn carriage had to contend with as it traversed the rural terrain. As in the case of the General Staff, the coachman on his box wrestled not only with the inertia of his draught animals and his own beastly exhaustion; in a literal sense, he experienced the obstacles the terrain had to offer and the friction (as Clausewitz puts it) of the track as his first natural enemy. 'In all three cases,' wrote Clausewitz, perceiving the relief of the terrain, the vegetation and its cultivated products, 'war is made more intricate and more elaborate.'[15] Things were no different in war, when every post-chaise was commandeered as a lonely *détachement*: beyond every bend in the track lurked trouble, or 'friction', as Clausewitz puts it. An unexpected rockfall, storm damage after the autumn gales, a mule carcass at the edge of the path, and this battle also became more intricate and more elaborate.

'One cannot seek out one's preferred theatre of war, as one might choose a product from a range of samples,'[16] Clausewitz reminds us. Might the same not be said of the terrain to be traversed? One does not always have a selection of routes to choose from. What if there is only one? And what if the gloom of dusk and inclement weather come into play? To illustrate what we might understand as 'friction' in war, Clausewitz offers the civilian example of a traveller under the dark of night: 'Let's picture a traveller who imagines he will easily cover the remaining two stations of his day's journey by evening. A mere four to five hours with post-horses on the road; a doddle. But when he reaches the penultimate station, there is no horse or only a very poor one. Then he encounters a mountainous terrain, damaged roads, and meanwhile the twilight gives way to pitch black. He is relieved when, after many hardships, he reaches the next station and finds himself some austere accommodation for the night.'[17] It's not unlike wartime life: no sooner have you got around one hindrance than you are halted again by another spanner in the works.

Particularly ominous are circumstances in which the soil and weather form a vicious alliance. Mud is the worst enemy of the horse-drawn vehicle. Woe to the coachman who fails to see it coming! As Pierre de Marivaux wrote in 1714, 'The conversation about love was very heated, while as a result of carelessness, the coachmen, having downed a stoneware bottle behind our backs, proceeded to drive our wayward horses headlong into thick mire, into which the poor animals sank deeply along with the wheels of our heavy carriage, which became thoroughly stuck. Noticing the horses had ground to a halt, the drivers went at them with many a "Gee up" and a crack of the whip, while the horses strained and pulled, sinking yet deeper the more they struggled. The coachmen shouted their thirsty throats hoarse, lashing at the beasts like savages: in vain, for the horses were already short of breath. Cursing the phaeton, which hadn't budged a fraction, we got out, while the coachmen redoubled their blows and curses, but not even the Bastille stands as firmly on its foundations as our wheels in this accursed mud.'[18] In *The Life and Opinions of Tristram Shandy*, this same substance brings a sticky end to an unexpected encounter between two mounted men, the 'man-midwife' Dr Slop and the servant Obadiah, on the muddiest stretch of a treacherous track not far from Shandy Hall, which leaves Dr Slop stranded 'with the broadest part of him sunk about twelve inches deep into the mire'.[19]

What was it Werner Sombart wrote in his economic history of Germany in the nineteenth century? 'Endless reports of carts getting bogged down, including postal workers asphyxiating in the mire.'[20] Sombart did not live to hear the accounts of the Wehrmacht facing their first tribulations in Russia in September 1941, pitted against the enemy alliance of soil and weather; he died in May of that year. But he would not have been surprised. No conqueror can retain a firm grip in the face of the resistance of the elements, Sombart would have

A pastoral incident. Photo: André Kertész.

Sisyphus on the treadmill: a horse providing the motor for an early
threshing machine, Saint-Pierre-en-Port, *c.*1900.

said. Indeed, he might have added, that law and order itself – the 'Nomos of the Earth' – would one day sink into the mire, parodying his friend Carl Schmitt, the author of such a work.

A COUNTRY DOCTOR

Beside the historic world figures like Bonaparte and his many imitators, as well as the revolutionaries, poets and scholars so revered by the nineteenth century, not to mention the balloonists, it is easy to overlook the everyday heroes. With time, individuals are given the credit they're due: we do justice to the engineers, the architects of steel bridges and glass palaces, when we say that they were the true heroes of the nineteenth century. At a certain point we also rediscovered the great doctors, the explorers and innovators – the heroes and heroines of humanity. Then there are the philosophers, the inventors of the -*isms* of the twentieth century and those who prophesied their coming. But there is still one figure who sits in his modest practice, listening out for the sound of the night bell, awaiting recognition by posterity. And indeed it was the literature of nineteenth and twentieth centuries, the stories and novels of the likes of Honoré de Balzac, Gustave Flaubert and Franz Kafka, that immortalized this unsung hero.

The country doctor's was a thoroughly equestrian, as it were *centaurian* existence. Nobody, besides the cavalry, depended on his horse as much as he. If he drove instead of riding, he used the lightest and most manoeuvrable vehicle the market had to offer. He waived prestige in favour of speed and agility; instead of a team of two or even four horses, which his modest fees would not allow, he opted for a one-horse set-up. The rural doctor was not only a contemporary *Hippocrates* (whose Greek name, 'horse tamer', says it all), he was also a roaming missionary of enlightenment in the provinces. Balzac presented him as counter-figure to a cavalry officer who has taken part in every single battle against Napoleon – in Italy, Egypt and Russia through to the last campaign in France – while the country doctor waged his long, patient campaign against the ignorance and lethargy of the rural population.

Kafka depicts the rural physician as a wretched soul vexed by anxiety, plagued by images of unbridled power: the lecherous and aggressive groom, the fleshy horses, the 'mighty creatures with powerful flanks',[21] the maiden Rosa, who is initially 'willing', but who then flees in fright. Reaching his destination, the doctor is himself stripped and laid down in the patient's bed to become the remedy, lying alongside the sick man's terrible, festering wound, while up above sway shadowy horses' heads. When the doctor finally escapes, making as fast a getaway as he can, the straps 'trail loose, one horse barely attached to the other, the carriage wandering about behind'. With aspects of Heinrich von Kleist's novella *Michael Kohlhaas* peeking through the cracks in the text, the doctor is every bit the lost soul – 'Naked, exposed to the frost of this unhappiest of ages, with an earthly carriage, unearthly horses ...' – an embodiment of all fatal misfortunes that can befall a country doctor and a keeper of horses on this dark earth.[22]

Perhaps literature's most famous country doctor is Charles Bovary. Around the middle of the nineteenth century, he practises his humble art in the small villages near Rouen, Normandy. Like all men of his standing, he is constantly on the go: 'Charles, in rain and snow, rode along the country lanes.'[23] His wife dreams of a groom, but as he cannot afford one, he saddles up the horse and looks after it himself. Occasionally, he also makes use of a lightweight carriage which he bought for his young wife, a 'second-hand gig which, with new lamps and splash-boards in mottled leather, looked almost like a tilbury'.[24] With Charles at the reins, this gig makes just as unfortunate an impression as anything the hapless soul touches: 'Charles, perched on the very edge of the seat, was driving with his arms held wide, and the little horse was ambling along between the shafts, which were rather too big for him. The loose reins were slapping on his rump, sopping in a frothy sweat, and the box tied on behind kept banging about.'[25]

The doctor's name says it all. Does Bovary not echo *bovis*, the ox?[26] He is the epitome of inelegance. To emphasize his clumsy awkwardness, Flaubert contrasts him with the sophisticated men who dance as outrageously as they ride, 'laughing, with cigars in their mouths'.[27] It is one of these dashing rascals who tempts Emma into her first fling, during a horseback ride for two, which offers the lady a sensual thrill from the outset: 'Her head slightly bowed . . . she yielded to the rocking motion of the saddle.'[28] Just before the two riders, Emma and Rodolphe, pass beyond the edge of the forest – an invisible line which seems to divide good morals from sin like light from dark – we read: 'The horses were blowing. The saddle-leather was creaking.'[29] The interplay of light and sounds, evoking an atmosphere full of colours, noises, movement and smells, is the signal for something inevitable that can be delayed, but can no longer be held back entirely. Again, as the scene draws to an end towards the evening, the horses play a pivotal role: 'Entering Yonville, she pranced her horse on the cobbled street. Eyes examined her from the windows.'[30]

Besides the slights to his honour as a husband, to which Bovary is oblivious, the novel also charts the slights to his social and professional standing. The worst defeat suffered by the doctor, little more than a nursing attendant whose meagre training has taught him only the rudiments of the medical arts, is an incident which occurs when he attempts to cure Hippolyte, the ostler at the local inn, of his club foot.[31] While the groom was hitherto quite cheerful about his '*equinus*, actually as large as a horse's hoof, with rough skin, stiff tendons, huge toes, and black nails just like the rivets on a horseshoe',[32] and 'galloped about like a stag', nevertheless now that Science had descended on the village, represented by the pharmacist Homais, it had been declared that he was suffering and needed to be cured. The surgery – cutting the Achilles tendon followed by treatment in a home-made stretching apparatus – ends disastrously. In the allegorical web woven by Flaubert at this point, almost exactly halfway through the novel and shortly after the climax of Emma's affair with Rodolphe, the fatal snip made by the doctor is like a spark in the tinder.

It was a British country doctor, specifically a vet with a practice in Ireland, who in the 1880s invented the pneumatic tyre for the second time, and this time successfully. John Boyd Dunlop was a Scottish veterinary surgeon who was a friend of Queen Victoria. Tired of the discomfort of driving on unmade roads, he experimented with air-filled pneumatic tyres and developed a usable bicycle tyre, which was launched to the public in 1887. Two years later, Willie Hume, the captain of the Belfast Cruisers Cycling Club, won a series of bicycle races in Ireland and England on a bike equipped with Dunlop's tyres. This was the start of the bicycle's rapid triumphal march as the racehorse of the poor. But thanks to Dunlop's invention, country doctors were also able to reach their patients more quickly and more safely than before. A few years later, the country doctor would also become one of the first intensive users of the fledgling automobile. In this profession, speed is not a luxury but a vital necessity: it is speed that saves lives.

FROM ONE INCIDENT TO ANOTHER

Doctors travelling by horseback or by carriage would often be called out to accidents involving other riders or coachmen. Horses are jumpy animals, easily spooked and quick to yield to their natural flight reflex; once one bolts, it is no easy matter to catch it and calm it down again. Of course, Hippolytus, the son of Theseus and Hippolyta the Amazon, knows a thing or two about horses, as his name suggests. He is blessed in this regard from his mother's side: as Queen of the Amazons, she would hardly have qualified for the job without some skill in the saddle. Yet, for all his flair as a charioteer, he falls victim to a classic traffic accident, behind which lurk the usual Olympian intrigues. Love, hate and revenge all conspire and the story ends with Poseidon sending an enormous sea monster to scare the horses pulling Hippolytus' carriage, causing them to bolt. The chariot crashes into an olive tree; its passenger is killed.

The *bolting horse* is the terror of all horsemen, a nightmare for anyone who travels in a carriage. But it is not the horse in isolation that made travel so risky before the age of mechanized transport. Other factors played a part: bad roads, bad weather, darkness, the laziness and drunkenness of the personnel, including the driver. Finally the carriage itself: if the brakes are not applied properly, the carriage wobbles and overturns, and once it's landed in the mud, it's as good as stuck. The accident caused by bolting horses and an overturned, shattered carriage has been a topos of travel literature since its beginnings in the Renaissance. A famous engraving in Ulrich von Richental's fifteenth-century *Chronicle of the Council of Constance* shows an upturned carriage at Arlberg in 1414: it is that of anti-pope John XXIII, fleeing from the Council of Constance where he had been deposed. The widespread fascination with the accident captured in this historical snapshot (although it possibly had no real basis in fact) reflects a morbid curiosity that continues to this day: no anthology of travel writing, no cultural history exhibition on the age of horse-drawn carriages in Germany, is complete without a passing mention of Georg Christoph Lichtenberg's satire on the dangers of travelling or Karl Immermann's 1821 satirical account of an accident.[33] Thomas De Quincey's account of an imaginary collision between two horse-drawn vehicles – a heavy stagecoach and a light-weight gig – on the highway at night is, for all its rhetorical bombast, a masterpiece of literary suspense.[34]

Especially popular were the accounts of grisly accidents and miraculous escapes which filled eighteenth-century almanacs and collections of anecdotes. One example is the breathtaking description in the 1799 edition of the 'Handbook for Horse Lovers, Riders, Breeders, Veterinary Surgeons and Supervisors of Large Stables' (*Taschenbuch für Pferdeliebhaber, Reuter, Pferdezüchter, Pferdeärzte und Vorgesezte großer Marställe*), an annual publication issued by the German publisher Cotta: 'An Englishman by the name of Luthbret Lambert of Newcastel, was riding over Sandfort's stone bridge ... when upon this bridge he wished to make an about turn, causing his horse to come to a halt so abruptly that the swift and sensitive horse suddenly reared up into the air and the very next moment leaped over the railing of the bridge into the river below. A low-lying branch of an ash tree, hanging with good fortune so close to the bridge, saved this rider from death: he clung firmly to this same branch and remained hanging there until some passers-by delivered him from this uncomfortable and indeed fearsome position. The horse, which plummeted with all its might onto the riverbed some 20 foot below, lay in the place where it had died.'[35]

In addition to the literary archives, we also have a long history of chronicling horse-riders coming a cropper in illustrated form, with the most recent and most spectacular additions to the genre available on YouTube (Plate 9). The historical forerunner to these pictures and videos was a sort of European image gallery of every conceivable kind of accident involving a horse, a carriage or a wagon which was the tradition of ex-voto paintings (see p. 76). The catalogue of horrors and miracles spans the same time frame as this book: the long swansong of the age of the horse, from the end of the eighteenth to the mid-twentieth century. Browsing through its images, we might take a pilgrimage to a famous Catholic site such as Altötting or consult an ethnographic collection such as that at Hellbrunn Palace, Salzburg.[36] In the small votive illustrations expressing prayers and giving thanks, people's beliefs give form and colour to every imaginable incident involving horses and intercessions by Mary and the competent saints: an overturned carriage, the coachman trampled, the horses fled. A frantic horse bolting with a carriage still attached, the coachman under the wheel, his cap flung to the ground in the corner of the picture. Two draught horses that have jumped over a wall, smashing the wagon and injuring the driver. Three horses in a stable, a stable boy lying by the hindlegs of one, two men rushing over in horror. A horse and coachman lying on their backs, their carriage overturned and in pieces. A carriage with its driver fallen into a ravine, the horse standing at the edge of the cliff. A collision between a wagon and a carriage, the driver hurled to the ground, the injured horse trying to break free. A collision between a horse-drawn cart and a motorcycle; the driver is on the ground, the injured horse is on its knees.

Since 1970, when the annual death toll on the roads in the Federal Republic of Germany reached almost 20,000, there have been intensive efforts to improve traffic safety and reduce the harm caused by collisions, resulting in considerable improvements to accident statistics. Similar efforts were made with regard to horse-drawn traffic some 200 years earlier. As in our time, it was not merely a matter of the regulation and control of the traffic; it also involved technical improvements to the two main components of the locomotor system: in our case, the car and its engine; in those days, the carriage and the horse. First, the carriage: in 1756, a French handbook for stable masters presented the allegedly 'untippable' *Berline* model.[37] Johann Poppe's *History of Inventions* focuses on efforts to improve vehicle safety (higher wheels, broader axles, greater agility and solidity of the parts) carried out a quarter of a century earlier.[38]

Any industrious cartwright can improve a carriage. But how does one improve the nature of a draught animal? How does one help a horse to keep its nerve, or if it loses it and bolts, how does one bring it to a halt? In 1802, J. G. Herklotz launched his 'Description of a machine that prevents riding and carriage horses from bolting';[39] three years later, J. Riem recommends 'two failsafe, tried and tested means of protecting against danger in the event of runaway horses'.[40] Poppe's *History of Inventions* is systematic in its approach and distinguishes between three procedures that might prevent horses from bolting, or mitigate the consequences when they do. These are: 1) a full braking system; 2) the separation of the horses from the carriage; 3) 'rapidly covering the eyes of the frenzied beasts'.[41] A residual risk remains, of course, in every event. After all, you can't simply switch off an 'oat-powered engine' like you can a petrol engine.

The comic theatre of the nineteenth century had audiences in stitches laughing at all the overturned coaches and carriages that were constantly toppling over on the boardwalks and boulevards.[42] Who knew who the next victim would be – found head over heels in the most embarrassing and laughable confusion of limbs and clothing? The horror of public indignity found a beloved home in the anarchy of the stage. The upturned carriage unleashed social chaos and satirical laughter that brought the stage to life; the spotlight shone on what, behind the curtains, was sending the city and country reeling.[43] In the early 1850s, when Flaubert was working on *Madame Bovary*, hardly a year passed without a new play about 'Jean the postman' or 'Jean the coachman' hitting the stages of Paris and the provinces – whether it was vaudeville, a one-act operetta or a five-act play.

Just as in the following century, the movies indulged in a never-ending romance with the motor car, so in the nineteenth century the theatre flirted endlessly with the horse-drawn carriage, especially in popular musical theatre such as operetta, vaudeville and variety shows. The twentieth-century arts critic Siegfried Kracauer once commented that the music of Philippe Musard reminded him of an old Napoleon film where the emperor was riding in a carriage to a remote battlefield, surrounded by a swarm of rushing mounted orderlies and messengers, all giving the impression that the Emperor was racing through the world at tremendous speed: 'Musard's balls must have been dynamic events with no less power.'[44] Returning to Flaubert, it is the theatre – albeit a more 'serious' kind of performance, the opera *Lucia di Lammermoor* – that occasions a fatal reunion of Emma Bovary and the apprentice Léon, triggering similarly 'dynamic' events which reach their climax two days after the evening at the theatre during an aimless, six-hour carriage ride through Rouen and the surrounding countryside. 'It's what people do in Paris,' Léon comments as he calls for a cab;[45] in rural France, on the other hand, the unusual spectacle attracted the suspicious attention of the locals: ' . . . down by the harbour, in among the wagons and the great barrels, and in the streets, on every corner, the bourgeois gaped in amazement at this extraordinary thing appearing in a provincial town, a carriage with its blinds shut, coming into view like this over and over again, as secret as the grave and shuddering along like a ship at sea.'[46]

Unlike the vaudeville librettist, the author of *Madame Bovary* could not allow the coach, in which Emma surrenders to her lover, to overturn and burst open to reveal the events unfolding within the hidden, moving space. The readers of the novel write the continuation of the story for themselves, filling in the vacuum of what is left unsaid within the coach, which orbits like a sombre moon through the space between the town and the country. As secret as a grave, writes Flaubert, and shuddering like a ship: the coach is a cell, it is a cavern and a vessel that bobs about getting bumped and bruised and yet is oblivious to its surroundings; an absolute interior that exudes an atmosphere both claustrophobic and erotically intimate. 'A closed carriage', writes Mario Praz, 'was like the cosy corner of a drawing room, only the chests and luxurious divans had been shifted outside.'[47] Flaubert leaves his parlour firmly closed off, describing only the orbit of the black monad and reminding the reader of the two sweaty horses and the weary coachman, half insane from thirst, who are facilitating the endless circulation of this strange space capsule.

THE SOUND OF THE COUNTRY

A familiar topos of cultural criticism is the image of the city as a raucous monster, a sleepless Moloch, surrounded day and night by noise. The countryside, on the other hand, is characterized as a blissful kingdom of silence. The city is as loud and shrill as a saw; the country is either silent or murmurs softly like a gentle rain. The only thing that's true about such stereotypes is the differentiation of the contrasting soundscapes. The world of the city is indeed typified by an orchestra of mechanical noises, but the clatter of horses' hooves and cart wheels is also at home here: the screech of metal against metal or clanging on cobblestones. But the sound space of the country is most certainly not limited to the rustle of the wind, birdsong and the grunts and snorts of farm animals; the countryside has its own mechanical sound corpus. The cacophony of hammering, pounding, mowing, sawing and milling; workers all busy eliciting specific sounds from the plants and metals of the earth, from their houses, tools and everyday objects. 'When a body makes a sound,' writes Hegel, it is, so to speak 'mechanical light'; it touches us, because tone is itself 'inwardness and subjectivity, it speaks to the inner soul'.[48]

In an insightful study of the folk songs associated with working on the land,[49] economist Karl Bücher manages to trace the source of rhythms and melodies back to the sounds of physical labour: 'When a maid scrubs the floor, the forwards and backwards motion of the scrubbing brush emits tones of varying strength. Similarly, when mowing the grass, the backswing and swish of the scythe resounds with tones of varying strength and length . . . Hammering the hoop of a barrel into place with blows of varying intensity, the cooper also creates a kind of melody, while the butcher's boy, with the chop of his cleaver, summons up an entire drum march.'[50] What Bücher doesn't mention is the lovely resonance of the whetstone grinding and knocking on metal that rings out when one sharpens a scythe or sickle, a sound that would have been heard in all rural areas across central Europe until the mid-twentieth century.

Against the constant murmur of the rural backing track, we hear the sometimes quiet, sometimes relatively loud contribution of a combination of various, all clearly audible instruments. For the agricultural symphony orchestra, there was no need to wait until the first ploughs were pulled across the fields by steam engines, followed a few decades later by tractors, or until the first combine harvesters were dragged clattering by some thirty horses across the endless wheat fields of the Midwest. Even the time of carriages brought a particular song of sighs and groans to the country. The language used by Flaubert as he captures the motion of the lovers' fiacre in the famous scene simultaneously evokes the rhythm and sounds of heavy machinery: 'And the big engine began to move . . . The vehicle set off again . . . gathering speed on the hill, she drove at full gallop . . . trotted gently along . . . She rolled along very peacefully, with the unpolished straps cracking in the heat.'[51]

Like the windmill, the ship and the railway, the horse-drawn coach, with its large, wooden resonating body and its many moving parts, is a musical instrument of a particular size and quality. Its wooden structures are constantly chafing against iron, leather and other wooden parts; the box is constantly rising and falling, taking air in and out with a sigh and a hiss. Ludwig Börne recorded the many sounds associated with a carriage filling with air: 'groaning, sighing, moaning, clattering, grunting, purring, rattling, hissing, mewing, barking, growling, chattering, squawking, growling, jangling, whistling, murmuring, sobbing, singing, grumbling and sulking'.[52] Even if the satirist exaggerates, the sound history of past centuries forms a musical corpus dedicated to a very different set of composers from those of classical music: the anonymous builders of carriages, carts, windmills and cranes, the stone beaters hammering down the cobblestones of squares and bridges. And we certainly mustn't forget the bell-makers.

In one of the most beautiful books on French cultural history, Alain Corbin reconstructs the sound space of the bell, describing the fullness of its chime, a resonance which rippled through every corner of pre-revolutionary France. 'It is not easy', writes Corbin, 'to picture the emotional power wielded by bells at the end of the Old Regime.'[53] Despite the cultural associations of city belfries, such as London's 'Oranges and lemons say the bells of St Clement's', the staggering power of the chiming bells was by no means a purely urban phenomenon. On the contrary, 'abbeys covered the verdant wildernesses with networks of rings, although it is hard for us to gauge how far their sound carried . . . The abbeys of Normandy were capable of achieving a particularly high volume of sound. Indeed the most significant changes to the auditory landscape and the most acute sense of loss and deprivation probably occurred in the Normandy countryside

Early mechanization in the country: the machine cuts the crop and bundles the stalks into sheaves. They are collected by hand to be threshed. Österlen, Sweden, 1947.

Making progress: a harvester drawn by thirty horses, California, *c.*1904.

between the eighteenth and the nineteenth centuries . . . On the eve of the Revolution, thirteen bells used to ring out on days of religious festivals in the small town of Saint-Pierre-sur-Dives. Some episcopal towns could likewise produce a sound disproportionate to the size of their populations.'[54]

Wilhelm Heinrich Riehl, a writer and cultural historian who originally intended to become a parish priest, recalls in his *Cultural Studies from Three Centuries* that another form of music that rang out from the church towers was that of the tower watchmen or trumpeters. 'In many Protestant towns and villages,' writes Riehl, 'until recent times, it was customary for a horn player to play a chorale every morning and evening, and even at midday. The workers in the field would halt their ploughs for a moment when the solemn tones rang out through the quiet of the morning landscape; in the workshops, all was still for a few minutes . . . It was through such music, that everyone was granted spiritual and artistic consecration for at least a few moments each day.'[55]

In addition to the bells and choral song of the churches, and in addition to the woodwind instrumentation of the carriages, boats and mills, the soundscape of the rural world had a third component. This was the percussion of the blacksmith, the drummer of the countryside, the rhythm section of the village big band. The forge has long been considered the birthplace of the Western perception of the mathematics of music. Pythagoras, it is said, passed by the smithy one day and was astonished to notice that the sound of the hammers rang out at pure intervals of fourths, fifths and octaves. 'He ascertained that the only difference among the hammers was their weight, and found that their weights were related in the ratios 4:3, 3:2 and 2:1 . . . The story goes on that Pythagoras hung weights corresponding to these hammers from equally long strings, and found, on plucking them, that the same intervals were produced.'[56] Despite the physical impossibilities of this legend, there is something in it, argues the classical scholar Walter Burkert, something that refers back to the Idaean Dactyls, the mythical blacksmiths associated with Orpheus, who were regarded as the inventors of music. The story brings to light the 'the secret of magical music which was discovered by the mythical blacksmiths'.[57]

The soft fabric of bell ringing, as Corbin put it, may have been thinner and more threadbare since the Revolution. But who else has described the vast change to the rural world since the rhythmic hammering of the blacksmith fell silent? The village forge gave the day its beat, its melody; it may have been a less festive and emotional form of music than that of the bells, less closely associated with the villagers' celebrations and their grief, but it was nevertheless an integral part of daily life. The ever-present clang of hammers on the anvil was an acoustic sign of industriousness, the surest sign of life of the organism that is the village. The forge was the heart of the local community of producers and suppliers: this was where its tools were made, where its horses were shod.[58]

In 1888, just as the first automobiles were coming into the world, Arnold Böcklin painted *Centaur at the Village Blacksmith's Shop* (Plate 4). A bearded centaur, light brown with flecks of white, has trotted into the village smithy and presents his right front hoof to the blacksmith, as if to say, 'Here, Master, your help is needed.' It is not out of the question that Böcklin, who had a passion for flying machines, was also observing the increasing mechanization of land transport as he transformed the old era of horseshoes and smithies into the realm of myth. Whatever his intention, with his humorously cryptic image of the centaur stopping by the village forge, he succeeded in creating one of the most charming icons of a rural world – a world which, like the century, was coming to an end.

It was not the first time that Böcklin had attempted to convey this creature – half man, half horse. In 1873, he painted *Battle of the Centaurs*, followed five years later by a peaceful portrait of a centaur sitting quietly beside a lake, not troubling the water. In *Battle of the Centaurs* (Plate 1), he presents his unmistakable response to the much-debated question, among classicists, of the nature of centaurian sexuality.[59] Incidentally, with this picture he remains true to a very classical mythology which presents the centaur as a belligerent and quarrelsome creature. Again, he respected tradition when in 1898 he painted *Nessus and Deianeira* as a scene of sexual violence with fatal consequences for all three protagonists.

How different, then, is the portrayal in *Centaur at the Village Blacksmith's Shop*. Here we have a perfectly civilized customer who has politely trotted in to give instructions to the blacksmith. The notorious rascal of mythology appears here as peaceful visitor to the village, a customer in need of the services of the capable craftsman. The village women at the edge of the scene look on inquisitively, while 'the blacksmith seems to be assessing the scale of the damage,' wrote Petra Kipphoff, like a 'car mechanic *avant la lettre*'.[60] As we consider this scene, at every moment we expect to hear the first blow of the hammer as the whole village rouses from its slumber. Now, creaking and rumbling, a carriage might roll up, the bells begin to ring, and the rural orchestra stirs into life. Finally, all that remains is for the sparrows to swoop in, eagerly awaiting the centaur's offerings. Incidentally, with his robust figure, Böcklin's centaur also fits perfectly into this rustic environment: in his lower half, he's a sturdy farm horse. The countryside is a world apart from the aristocracy of the slender racehorse.

Riding West

I don't get on a horse unless they pay me.

John Wayne

COWBOYS AND INDIANS

The riderless and bridleless horse that staggered through the main street of Fort Lincoln was clearly drunk. The bay stallion was single-mindedly rummaging through garbage cans before casually kicking them over. If he found the contents to his taste, he would gleefully wallow in the pickings before carrying on, covered in coffee grounds and potato skins. In the evening, he would pop in to see the soldiers, and they would share a beer or two with him. Then he'd amble on over to the officers' mess to have a drink with them too, perhaps even a drop of the harder stuff. There was no doubt about it, the old boy was a boozer. But no one thought of prescribing cold turkey or hitching him up to a cart. It was forbidden to ride the old chap; he was a war hero and since 1878 had borne the title of Second Commanding Officer. The name of this stallion with a taste for liquor was Comanche. He was the only non-Native American survivor of the Battle of the Little Bighorn,[1] later known as Custer's Last Stand.

The former owner of the veteran stallion was an Irishman by birth, Myles Keogh. As courageous and as fond of a tipple as his horse, he left home early and emigrated to America, where he climbed the ranks to cavalry officer. As a regimental commander under Lieutenant Colonel Custer, he rode his stallion into the battle of 25 June 1876, where he was killed along with his leader and his entire regiment. When the

70

battle was over, the field at Little Bighorn was littered with human and animal corpses. In the words of one historian,[2] the 'horse cavalry, was reduced to a 'horse calvary', and Comanche, with several bleeding wounds, was the only creature still standing. Miraculously, the gravely injured animal was rescued and, as a precious living testimony, was transported back to Fort Lincoln, the garrison from which Custer's regiment had set off some weeks before. The only obligation incumbent on this animal henceforth was to participate in the annual commemorative parade on the anniversary of the battle, which passed imperceptibly from the narrative of history into the realm of myth.

The American Indian wars, which came to a bloody climax at Little Bighorn and a cruel end at the Massacre of Wounded Knee (1890), began in the seventeenth century and increased in violence and intensity throughout the nineteenth as the result of the brutal government policies towards native inhabitants and the gradual shift of the frontier of settled population westwards beyond the Mississippi. It was no coincidence that its last and bloodiest phase was in the period following the Civil War. Wars do not end on the date of the ceasefire or at the moment of surrender; they move underground, shoved along to other theatres of war until the lethal energy is finally spent. When, after the Homestead Act of 1862 and reinforced by the end of the Civil War in 1865, ever greater masses of settlers poured into the Great Plains and pushed the frontier of conquest westwards, this led to an escalation of conflict with the tribes already living there, including the Sioux, Cheyenne, Kiowa, Blackfoot, Crow, Arapaho and others.[3]

To protect the settlers, the federal government deployed a cavalry regiment made up of former members of the armies of both sides in the Civil War. The internecine conflict among the white settlers spawned a bitter war with the Native Americans, lasting over two decades. The radicalism that characterized the Civil War in its final phase was also felt in the subsequent racial war. But unlike the fighting in the previous conflict, this one was fought almost exclusively on horseback. The American cavalry found a well-matched foe in the tribal horseback warriors of the Great Plains.

Or to be more precise, the warring Native American horsemen found an evenly matched foe in the cavalry of the reunified country. For a long time, the uniformed riders had been hopelessly inferior to their native counterparts, both in agility on the field and in battle tactics and shooting technique. During the Civil War, both sides – Union and Confederate – had vastly refined their cavalry tactics and improved their weaponry. The militaries had swapped their heavy horses for more agile and tougher Mustangs; now they rode faster, fought more flexibly, and with their new handguns they shot more quickly and hit their targets better. The cavalry had successfully modernized, and was now taking part in an archaic war, led by their opponents in the style of the Mongols and Saracens centuries before.

The American Civil War (1861–5) occupies a special position in the history of the waning era of the horse, being at once an integral part of it, but looking beyond it. On the one hand, the infantry's improved firepower and accuracy since the middle of the century robbed the cavalry of their status as the most powerful and decisive offensive weapon, a reputation they had still been able to claim for four or five decades after the Napoleonic wars.[4] Large, soft targets like horses and men are as good as useless against automatic, rapid-fire weapons. The flamboyance of cavalry shock tactics lost their value on the modern battlefield. One-and-a-half million dead horses and mules compared to 600,000 human casualties in a five-year conflict says a lot about the nature of this war. Its prelude was also significant in this respect. The bombardment of Fort Sumter on 12 April 1861, which opened the floodgates to spiralling military engagement, claimed just one victim after thirty-three hours: a horse.

As in most armies of the world, in the American Civil War the cavalry had three core tasks to fulfil. The first was in reconnaissance and securing communications lines, the second was actual combat use as a high-speed shock weapon, and the third was surprise attacks behind enemy lines and sabotage. For all the success that the cavalry could claim on the battlefield in the Civil War, it was this second task – the offensive role in combat – that became problematic: thanks to improved infantry weapons, namely the breech-loader with its increased rate of fire, and thanks to the supporting field artillery, firing with all barrels blazing, the use of cavalry became more difficult and more expensive. In the days when it was cavalry fighting cavalry, their skirmishes were balanced, but if they were up against well-equipped infantry, it was quite a different matter. The unmounted infantry – for long historical periods, the classic prey of the cavalry, so easily trampled and hacked down if they could not flee in time – had suddenly become a dangerous predator: their firepower had increased and therefore so had their security and their self-confidence.[5] This required a change in tactics to be adopted by the warring sides of the American Civil War. First, it meant an increase in the already considerable speed and agility of their cavalry, giving more flexibility to switch positions between rider and foot soldier, allowing them, secondly, to continue fighting, dismounted, with their carbines.[6] Thirdly – and this made the difference – they were much more restrained in their deployment of the cavalry in its classic function as a shock attack weapon.[7]

In the 1860s, after the Civil War and when the American Indian wars were in their final stages, many of the native tribes were decimated and robbed of their horses.[8] The mass slaughter of horses was an integral part of the war against the native horseman tribes of the Great Plains. These massacres were aimed at robbing the Native Americans of the very foundations of their existence and thus their ability to resist. From the Civil War, the army learnt the lesson that the most effective form of war was total warfare, targeting the enemy's entire society and seeking to destroy its economy.[9] On the night of Thanksgiving, 27 November 1868, George Armstrong Custer executed a shock attack on the small Cheyenne community which had survived the Sand Creek Massacre in Colorado four years earlier and had resettled by the Washita River in Oklahoma.[10] The almost complete annihilation of the tribe was followed by that of its ponies. With the help of two captive Cheyenne women on horseback, they rounded up the tribe's entire herd, some 900 animals. Initially they tried to lasso the horses and cut their throats, but in the face of fierce opposition from the captive animals, Custer's soldiers gave up and shot the rest.

When Comanche died in 1891 at the grand age of twenty-nine, the University of Kansas had his body stuffed by a taxidermist. Two years later he was one of the main attractions at the World's Fair in Chicago, appearing alongside survivors of Little Bighorn, including Chief Rain-in-the-Face.[11] After the World's Fair, it was intended that his body would be returned to Fort Riley, where Comanche had spent the two last years of his life. But because the taxidermist's bill had not yet been paid, the University kept him and put him in their

Natural History Museum, where he remains to this day, partially renovated over the decades, not unlike Lenin in his mausoleum on Red Square.

TEACHER AND STUDENT

In the white imagination, the Native Americans are horse riders. Often depicted as "noble savages,"[12] it's hard to picture them without their horses. Like the aristocrats of Europe, the prairie noblemen are at home on horseback. Like their legendary counterparts, the cowboys, the popular perception of the Native Americans is of them fused with their horses in a thoroughly equestrian existence. The Western – that epic genre that sings of the glorious deeds of Cowboys and Indians – is a cloak-and-dagger fiction of the movie era, where the Colt is the weapon instead of the dagger. The ubiquity of this image in the white imagination makes it all the more astonishing when we learn that the horse-riding Native Americans were in fact latecomers in the history of the native Indian tribes, even in the horse-rearing era, and that the use and breeding of horses was far from typical of all the tribes of North America.[13] On the contrary, the Eastern Woodland Indians, and also the tribes of the Midwest and the South, did not have horses and neither did they adopt them later on as other tribes did; they hunted on foot and trod the warpath as infantrymen. Even the tribes who did at some point discover horses and learn to use them, did not by themselves become wild horseback warriors. Only a small part of the total tribal population learned to fight on horseback. Even the famous Apache, the glorious Winnetou tribe, only rode up to the point of engaging the enemy; they dismounted to fight the battle itself.[14] The same phenomenon can be found at different times and in different cultures: not every population that learns to ride necessarily goes on to become a nation of cavalrymen. This historic role is reserved for those who from the outset were tutored in the school of the great outdoors, the hunters and nomads of the steppe, the desert and the prairie.

For about 10,000 years, from the end of the Pleistocene epoch,

America was a continent without horses. The loss of many species of megafauna, including mammoths, camels and lions, as well as horses, from the American mainland is today thought to have been caused primarily by changes to the climate and the vegetation, and not least by overhunting, or 'overkill', by the Paleo-Americans, the Clovis culture.[15] Another tenacious theory is that of a meteorite strike unleashing a 'mini ice age' which caused the mass extinction. Whatever the reason, America was a continent without horses when the Spanish Conquistadores introduced them at the end of fifteenth century as domestic animals, thus setting in motion some of the most amazing dynamics of modern history, in both zoological and anthropological terms.

The Spaniards were experienced and skilful importers. It was not just a first-class product they were introducing in the form of the Ibero-Arabian horse; they also possessed a considerable amount of associated cultural knowledge. From their former masters, the Moors, they had adopted not only horses themselves but also the related culture and the *gineta* riding style (known as *à la gineta* or *à la jineta*).[16] They came from the most highly developed equestrian civilization of the Western world, where the cultivation and breeding of horses, and all the knowledge that goes with it, were no longer the exclusive privilege of the nobility. The Spanish horse, the best in Europe at that time, emerged from crossing the fast and resilient Iberian horse with the Arabian breeds which came with the Moors from North Africa.[17] Their horses lent the Spanish military superiority over their indigenous foes and allowed them to rapidly whisk away their booty, particularly precious metals, as well as paving the way for the large-scale cattle ranches that became typical of colonial America.[18]

The horses had a hard time of it with their new mission. First of all, very few even survived the passage by sea – the windless zones between the trade winds and westerly winds were called the *horse latitudes*, because of the countless horses that perished in the heat and were thrown overboard. If they did survive the journey, many died shortly after reaching the hot and humid climate on the islands off the coast of Mexico. Their situation improved when the Spaniards on the Mexican mainland continued to penetrate towards the north and the animals were able to acclimatize. Between 1530 and 1550,

A Roman chariot-racing accident, 1st century CE.

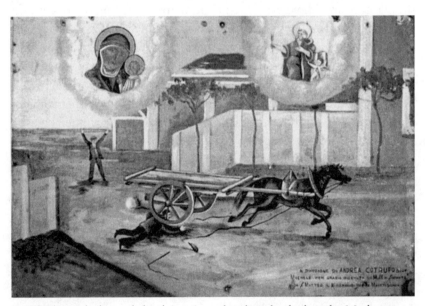

The horse bolts and the driver is under the wheels, but the Madonna
prevents the worst. Italian ex-voto.

there was the first explosive increase in the population of horses in North America.[19] The first large herd of horses reached New Mexico with Juan de Oñate in 1598. The Spaniards had little trouble initially with the Pueblo Indians, who learned to look after the Spaniards' horses without showing any particular interest in them. This was not the case with the Apaches, who lived in the same region. They stole the Spanish horses and learned to ride by imitating the incomers, including adopting the Spanish custom of mounting the horse from the right.[20] From the middle of the seventeenth century, according to Spanish sources,[21] the new Apache riders had made life difficult for their former teachers: they attacked their settlements in New Mexico, not even sparing the Pueblo Indian communities, stole their horses and disappeared from whence they had come, in the vastness of the prairies and deserts. Unlike the later Comanche, the Apaches never learned how to breed horses or to fight on horseback. But they were the first Native Americans to undergo a major technological revolution and enrich their arsenal with a weapon that, at that point, no other indigenous tribe had mastered: *speed.*

The revolt of the Pueblos against the Spaniards in 1680 and their temporary expulsion from New Mexico brought a turning point for the horse culture of North America. When the Pueblo Indians returned to their agriculture and pottery, they abandoned the horses they had travelled with and a mighty river of horses spilled into the prairies of the Midwest. The animals found similar living conditions to those their Spanish ancestors had known on the high plains of Andalusia, and within a comparatively short time their population had soared, producing large herds of wild Mustangs, which were seized upon by about thirty Indian tribes of the Great Plains, following the example of the Apaches.[22] The so-called Great Horse Dispersal from 1680 resulted in a permanent change to the power structures of North America's geographical centre.[23]

The process was rapid. While in 1630 no Native American had ever sat on a horse, by around 1700 all the tribes on the plains of Texas were riding horses, and by 1750 even certain tribes of the Canadian plains were hunting bison on horseback.[24] It was not a huge step then from hunting technique to military tactic. A number of tribes – including the Sioux, Cheyenne, Kiowa, Arapaho, Blackfoot, Cree and

Crow – took horses into battle at some point, with the Comanche the most thorough and successful. They were the undisputed champions in the new war of speed and over the eighteenth century they rose to supremacy among the indigenous tribes of the south-west, a plague to the Spaniards. Their ownership of horses towards the late eighteenth century was legendary. The only tribe to truly master the art of breeding and raising horses, the Comanche linked their fate and their economy closely with the life of an animal that until a few decades ago had been unknown to them. Neither was their language unaffected: their otherwise rather modest vocabulary contained an amazing wealth of adjectives describing every conceivable shade of brown, black, red, beige and grey, and all shapes and sizes of patches and blazes.[25]

For the indigenous tribes of the Great Plains, the period from 1540 to 1880 was the 'epoch of horse cultivation', as Clark Wissler, a student of Franz Boas and pioneer of research into Native Americans, puts it. For many tribes, the era began later and for some it ended earlier. It was an era that began with the acquisition and first use of horses, while its end was marked by the extinction of the bison from the territory of one tribe.[26] The latest research dates the beginning of the age of Amerindian horse culture one hundred years later, in the mid-seventeenth century.[27] Since the beginning of the twentieth century, American anthropologists – first the students of Franz Boas and later researchers associated with Alfred L. Kroeber – have examined in detail the astonishing process by which the tribes of the Great Plains expanded, and eventually completely altered, their ecological system through the adoption of two items, namely horses and firearms.[28]

The Apaches were the first Native superpower of the south and south-west, until they were overtaken by other tribes militarily and technologically, sending them headlong into insignificance. The development of horses and firearms did not occur simultaneously or in the same place: the horses advanced northwards from the south, from Mexico, while the firearms made their way from east to west. Firearms reached the tribes via the fur trade, and while the Spanish strictly forbade any arms trading with the native inhabitants, the British and French gave free rein to hunters and dealers. So it was that two separate cultural patterns existed in isolation for several decades before they finally crossed over and combined. The first phase seen in the south and south-west was the post-horse and pre-gun phase, while the north and east of the Great Plains initially experienced the post-gun and pre-horse phase.[29] In other words, the Plains formed a kind of *horse frontier* that, from the mid-seventeenth century, edged gradually from south to north, and a *gun frontier*, which over the same period gradually shifted from east to west. By 1800, the two migrating frontiers intersected over an area covering the entire eastern half of the Great Plains.[30] Within this ever-expanding territory, the remaining tribes learned how to manage firearms and horses, and how to trade them as items of economic value.[31]

The ascent of the Apaches in the south began around 1650. It was through their direct contact with the Spanish that they learned how to ride, adopting not only the Spanish riding style, but also the Spanish saddles and tack, leather shields and armour for horses and riders. The Apaches, their newly formed cavalry being militarily far superior to their neighbours' infantry, expanded the area of the prairies under their control further and further to the north and successfully broadened the sphere of the post-horse, pre-firearm model.[32] However, since they remained only semi-nomadic, like many other tribes, and did not give up their agriculture and partially settled way of life, when their nomadic rivals, especially the Sioux and Comanche, began to outstrip them in terms of riding technique and belligerent tactics, they became the victims of a violent roll-back.[33]

The step from settled to nomadic life was indeed decisive for the military power of a tribe. The next step – from superior hunting technique to superior military technique – happened as if by itself. Prerequisites for both were the possession of horses and the ability to put them to optimal use.[34] Moreover, in order to make that decisive step from settled village life to nomadic life on the Plains, the tribes needed 'a critical mass' of about six horses per head – men, women and children counted individually – and twice as many to lead a secure life, in the sense of being economically secure.[35] The fateful conversion from settled to nomadic life was not a sudden, one-off shift; for the Cheyenne it began around 1750, but even after 1790 a few villages of that tribe still continued farming. On the whole, for most native tribes of the Great Plains, the years 1780–1800 appear to have been a *saddle period*, quite literally.[36]

It was in the south, closer to the old Spanish source of this wealth of horses, that certain tribes learned more quickly and more thoroughly. As early as the mid-eighteenth century, the Comanche tribe had 'laid the foundation for their legendary status as the most skilled and fearsome horse-back warriors of the Plains . . . The new masters of the region were the linchpin in the communication between the plains and the peripheries . . . At the beginning of the nineteenth century, they had consolidated their dominion over a vast area from the upper Arkansas valley to the mountains of the Edwards Plateau in mid-Texas.'[37] In the 1820s and 1830s, their hegemony over the south-west, thanks to their military superiority, posed a considerable threat to the stream of American colonialists flowing into Texas without the Mexican army being able to do anything to stop them.

Even the *Texas Rangers*, a militia launched by Stephen F. Austin in 1823 to protect the settlers, needed over twenty years before it was ready to take on the wild hegemon of the prairie. Their old-breed cavalry horses were cumbersome, clumsy and too quickly exhausted to keep up with the Native Americans' swift, tough Mustangs or ponies. Their weapons consisted of single-shot pistols and long-barrelled rifles, ideal as duelling or hunting weapons, but of little use in combat with an enemy who could shoot up to twenty arrows per minute while riding at full pelt. Out in the open, with no palisade to take cover behind, the Texas Rangers were hopelessly inferior to the Comanche. The average life expectancy of a Ranger was two years.

The turning point came in 1840, when John Coffee Hays, known as Jack Hays, a firebrand of twenty-three years, assumed command of the Rangers' garrison in San Antonio. Hays provided his unit with new, lighter horses, crossbreeds of Mustangs and thoroughbreds. He taught his men to live like the Native Americans, always alert and ready to fight; and to ride in their style, which he had observed from the Comanche. Hays' men shot and loaded their weapons faster than any other *and* in the saddle, which at this time no other white militia or cavalry could manage, even in battle.[38] In riding style and battle tactics, Hays' Rangers got closer and closer to the Comanche; it was only in firing speed and firepower that they lagged behind their teachers.

'The Indian, the horse and the gun formed a perfect unit. They were

well matched and as a whole added up to an excellent fighting unit,'
Walter Prescott Webb wrote in his epic depiction of life on the Great
Plains.[39] The most advanced opponent of the Native Americans on
Texan soil, the Texas Rangers, would achieve a similar status as a unit
only when they had in their hands the invention of a young, technically gifted Yankee. Armed with Samuel Colt's five-shot, later
six-shot, revolver, from 1843 Jack Hays' Texan militia finally had a
weapon which balanced out the hitherto existing asymmetry. Walker
and Colt's new improved revolver, in production since 1847, was the
perfect weapon for firing on the move in quick succession. In an environment in which, as Webb wrote elsewhere, 'men survived solely
thanks to weapons and speed',[40] this technical leap was crucial. While
the six-shot reduced the risky time it took to load the weapon, it also
shifted active warfare into the saddle once and for all, and thus to the
centre of the mobile system of man and beast.

For a long time, the American cavalry remained practically the
only cavalry of a large nation that included the revolver – alongside
the sabre and carbine – as the main weapon in its arsenal. The cavalries of European countries were all still armed with swords and
bayonets, which were supplemented with various types of rifles and
later also carbines. The reason for the American cavalry's preference
for the Colt revolver lay in the experience garnered in the fight against
the Native American horsemen. But the revolver found its way back
into the white men's war: in the Civil War, the cavalrymen of both
the Union and the Confederacy were armed with weapons that had
debuted barely twenty years earlier in the hands of the Texas Rangers, and with them they caught up with their opponents' technical
superiority in terms of weaponry.[41]

In the relative balance of mobile *man–horse–weapon* systems achieved
at that time, two very long historical lines divided the nineteenth century roughly down the middle. There stood on either side of the middle
of the century what Webb would have called 'an excellent fighting unit':
on the earlier side, the system comprised of *human, horse, bow-and-
arrow*, and on the later side, the system was made up of *human, horse
and revolver*.[42] Here were two systems in which animal elements
(humans, animals) were functionally connected with specific technical instruments (light firearms with high firing frequency) and the

requisite skills (riding, shooting). Both systems, the settlers' and the natives', differed in technique when it came to firing their weapons and yet resembled one another when it came to moving around: for both, the essential element was the producer of speed, the horse. Tracing either system back to its origins half a millennium earlier, we encounter a major equestrian culture: that of the Arabs.

JEWISH COWBOYS

The Moors, who dominated the Iberian peninsula from the early eighth century CE, transformed their adopted home into a second riding school. They crossed the fast, tough Spanish horses with the purebreds they brought with them, thereby improving the Iberian breeds which had long been considered the best in Europe, and were highly coveted across the continent. From the Moors, the Spaniards also inherited the nomadic style of riding, the famous *gineta* style, where the rider has short stirrup straps and appears to float above the horse, while keeping his thighs and lower legs in close contact with the animal. The contrasting *brida* style, where the rider sits deep in the saddle with outstretched legs, took the backseat,[43] with the *gineta* style becoming the dominant riding style in the New World, including among the native horse tribes.[44] But the cavalries of the northern and western Europeans who spread across the continent from the east from the sixteenth century also learnt from the Arab school. In the Middle Ages and the early modern era, the Arabs' knowledge of horses reached Western Europe via a great number of paths, not least the cultural transfer unleashed by the Crusades.[45]

Even more important was the influx of equine noble blood, for which the West had the Arabs to thank: all thoroughbred breeding since the second half of the seventeenth century, started by the English, was based on a certain proportion of Spanish or Arabian blood.[46] In the mounted battle for the heartland of North America, the Great Plains, around the mid-nineteenth century, the horses of both protagonists – the Native Americans and the Rangers – brought together two hitherto isolated bloodlines which both originated in the Arab cultural sphere. One might even speak of a *translatio arabica*, seen in such a pithy way only in the history of horses. In this, the Arabs were the masters of the world: the native language of equine history is Arabic.[47]

When cultures function like languages and follow a grammar, as certain structuralist schools used to think, then cultural transfers act as a translation from one language to another. In this respect, the Jews who lived scattered among various cultures, in the *intermundia* of the Old World, as Karl Marx put it, brought particular skills into play. The transfer of the Arabian or Moorish culture to the Christian inhabitants of the Iberian peninsula was in large part the work of skilled and learned Jews.[48] What is less well known is that Jews also played a decisive role in the translation of Spanish equine knowledge into the technological culture of indigenous North America: not just the first ranchers of the New World, they were also the first cowboys in America.[49]

The Jewish conquistadores, who came to Mexico in 1519 with Hernán Cortés, led by Hernando Alonso, were emigrants fleeing the Inquisition, which was nevertheless still hot on their heels on the other side of the ocean: Alonso was burnt alive on 17 October 1528.[50] They understood cattle and horse breeding, and in order to survive in the New World unseen by the Inquisition, they became ranchers and moved northwards in the wake of the gradual Spanish expansion towards Nueva España, present-day New Mexico.[51] They were, as one explorer of their history writes, 'the ghostly ancestors of the founders of our Western history' and their cultural transfer included proven techniques and objects: 'These Jews were the first to bring the *gineta* riding style, the high-horned Persian, now Western saddle, the tossed lasso and the Andalusian ancestors of the quarter horse to the deserts of the Southwest. They did it in their particular and peculiar way – as Jewish ranchers.'[52]

The Spanish Jews, who brought both cattle and horses with them – the two emblematic beasts of the American West – were not the only Jewish cowboys in the history of the United States. With the wave of German emigrants after the failed Revolution of 1848, many Jews settled in the United States, of whom, in turn, a considerable number headed west and became ranchers.[53] If we picture American Jews exclusively as the descendants of Eastern European Jews and the residents of the *shtetl* transported en masse to the East Coast, we overlook the diversity of their origins and fail to see the appeal of the Wild West to young Jews, eager to leave behind the cramped conditions of European living. At the end of the century, in 1898, when Theodore Roosevelt rallied together his infamous 'Rough Riders'[54] – a volunteer cavalry regiment as colourful as it was unruly, made up of businessmen, scouts, Native Americans, policemen, miners and cowboys – to fight against the Spaniards in Cuba, his motley crew also included many Jews. The first casualty to fall from the ranks of the Rough Riders was a sixteen-year-old Jewish cowboy from Texas, Jacob Wilbusky, who had signed up as Jacob Berlin from New York. One of the first of Roosevelt's cavalrymen to storm San Juan Hill on 1 July 1898, in the most spectacular and bloody action of the campaign, was a Jewish corporal named Irving Peixotto.[55]

The storming of San Juan Hill has been represented in several paintings, perhaps most impressively by the Russian war painter Vasily Vereshchagin.[56] The most famous American representation of the event, however, is by the illustrator, painter and sculptor Frederic Remington, whose dramatic portrayals of the old Wild West are deeply imprinted on America's collective visual memory (Plate 7).[57] Horses and paintings of them had brought Remington and Roosevelt together some twenty years previously, making them business partners initially and later friends. Roosevelt went to Dakota in 1884 where he set up a cattle ranch, while Remington attempted the same with sheep in Kansas. A year later, his sights already firmly fixed on a political career, Roosevelt began writing his book about ranch life in the West,[58] published initially in serial form in two periodicals. Looking for a suitable illustrator for his series, he was thrilled to discover Remington's early work. For the hitherto unsuccessful artist, this was a turning point in his career.[59] The opportunity for Remington to return the favour came when he was sent to Cuba as special correspondent for *Collier's Weekly* in February 1898. The picture he painted, drawing on eyewitness accounts of the battle for San Juan Hill, showed the Rough Riders boldly charging up the hill on foot, the first men being mowed down by Spanish guns, led into the charge by the only mounted soldier – their leader, Colonel Roosevelt, brandishing a

Comanche, the US cavalry's sole survivor of the Battle of
Little Bighorn. Photo: John C. H. Grabill.

On the trail of history: *Skirting the Sky-line*. Photo: Rodman
Wanamaker, 1913.

pistol in his right hand. This image, Roosevelt later acknowledged, won him the presidency in 1901.[60]

Remington's paintings and the numerous photographs of Roosevelt surrounded by his 'Rough Riders' in victorious pose sealed his reputation as cavalryman and war veteran and shaped the image of the future cowboy president. For his part, Roosevelt never missed an opportunity to consolidate the popular image. In his version of the Rough Riders' Cuban campaign, published just a year after the event,[61] he described the colourful uniform of his volunteer regiment which looked exactly 'as a body of *cowboy cavalry* should look'.[62] From this point on, the image of the cowboy was anchored not only in the popular imagination, but also in the political iconography of the time. There was a certain permeability, a transparency, between these images and the iconography of politics, so that the newly and roughly simultaneously emerging Western art forms – the book[63] and the movie[64] – could also always be read as political allegory. Though it may not seem it on the surface, the Western is no trivial genre like the costume dramas or adventure movies of the era. It is the American epic par excellence, a reliable reflection of the political fate of the nation, especially in times when it was often afflicted by doubt.[65]

While the cowboys rode at 'Teddy' Roosevelt's side into the American realm of myth and metaphor, the real military world lost its interest in the cavalryman as a soldier. A mere few years after the official closing of the Frontier in 1890, the United States had other horizons in its sights and was set to ascend to the status of a globally operational naval power. No one was more keenly aware of the new scope of American foreign policy than Theodore Roosevelt; no one took advantage of its potential as unscrupulously as he. And no one was more consistent than 'Cowboy' Roosevelt at putting into political action his friend Admiral Mahan's theories about the historic global dominance of sea power.[66] The intervention in Cuba brought the phase of the land-based land grab to an end and, with it, the end of the era of the horse as its most visible protagonist. The world, it is said, is conquered by saddle and sail. It was under Roosevelt, the cowboy president, that America rose from its saddle and unfurled the sails, transforming from a land power to a naval nation. In fact, Roosevelt was himself the only cavalryman who ever fought in Cuba while in the saddle. The rest of the regiment had to leave their horses in Florida and fight on foot in Cuba: so much was true in Remington's dramatic and iconic depiction.[67] From this perspective, the storming of San Juan Hill was not only one of the last cavalry battles in history, but also the birth of the Marine Corps Infantry.

WHITE HORSES, BLACK BOXES

Theodore Roosevelt, we read from time to time, was the first media-hyped president of the United States. But could we not also say that of every president before him? Without exception, they all ran their election campaigns with the help of the entire media apparatus at their disposal at the time: printed books, the press, posters, and later increasingly printed images – sketches, woodcut prints and photographs. By 1900, however, there was a kind of revolution in the media, not unlike the moment when Johann Gensfleisch Gutenberg invented the printing press with movable letters, only this time it was inventors like Thomas Edison, who created the mechanics of moving images and revolutionized the way film could capture events and influence audiences' perception of them. And Theodore Roosevelt had a particular flair for the media of the time – pictures – which could win his contemporaries' hearts, win presidential election campaigns and ultimately even win wars.

Even when, in 1884, at the age of twenty-five, politically defeated and widowed young, he turned his back on Washington and went to set himself up as a rancher in Dakota, he did not for a moment stop working on his public image and reputation. Every line that he wrote, no matter how intimate, was addressed to an imaginary reader or audience. At the heart of it was always the image that he, Teddy Roosevelt, intended to project to the wide-eyed world; the spotlight was always on the accessories and the details. When he described himself as a rancher and cowboy, he always drew attention to his tanned complexion, the golden glint of his sun-bleached hair, but above all to the trappings of his legendary cowboy get-up: 'I now look like a regular cowboy dandy, with all my equipments finished in the most expensive style,' he wrote to his sister, while to his friend Henry

Cabot Lodge he described his 'broad sombrero hat, fringed and beaded buckskin shirt, horse hide chaparajos or riding trousers, and cowhide boots, with braided bridle and silver spurs'.[68]

The paraphernalia worn by the Rough Riders – a curious mix of Wild West costume and military uniform – was of Roosevelt's own design. He had specific ideas about how a real 'cowboy cavalry' should look, as much as he did about the provenance of its Riders and their talents. Even if his men had never stuck their noses outside Brooklyn and had barely ridden more than a rocking horse, he testified to his troopers' Wild West gun-slinging skills and unrivalled riding technique. Even the name 'Rough Riders' almost kicked up a trademark dispute with Bill Cody ('Buffalo Bill'), whose Wild West show had, since 1893, also been billed as a 'Congress of Rough Riders' – a cavalry parliament bringing together a whole host of horsemen from Berbers, Cossacks, Prussian Uhlans and British Lancers to Mexican gauchos, which Cody led as a kind of President of the World Cavalry.[69] The unstoppable rise of Roosevelt as war hero and his political comeback made it advisable for Cody to drop the charges and instead include 'The Battle of San Juan' as a brilliant finale in the programme of his 1899 show.

While the mounted showman took the classic route and turned war into a circus act, turning reality into entertainment, the media-savvy statesman, Roosevelt, pursued a more complex route. He brought elements of a historical costume drama (because this was precisely what the story of the Wild West had become)[70] into the bloody reality of the battlefield, only to reimport heroic posturing into the cynical gameplay of political stakeholders: it was a circular logic rather than an 'invasion' of reality into the world of fiction. Wild Bill Hickok, a gunslinger, gambler and sheriff, played himself in his 1899 show: he was Wild Bill Hickok on stage, until he left the boards and was shot in a saloon in Deadwood.[71] Try to break the circuit connecting stage show and real life, and you wind up a dead man.

From the early 1890s, the new, unheard-of power of film began to creep into this cycle, undetected at first. Unaware that they had entered the cave of a lion that would later devour them, Bill Cody and a few Native American members of his troupe played in the first short filmstrip that Edison recorded in September 1894 in West Orange, New Jersey. Film history began with these 'circus versions of Western subjects, demonstrated by authentic figures of the West'.[72] Just a few years later, the circular logic had shifted in favour of the movies: in 1908, Cody introduced one piece into the arena, a train robbery in the West, which did not have a foundation in a historical or mythical subject, but was instead based on the plot of a film that was the first Western in film history, Edwin S. Porter's *The Great Train Robbery* of 1903.[73] But by now, Cody's historical fate was already sealed. In 1912, he even became the subject of his own film biography (*The Life of Buffalo Bill*) which, while it feted his historic screen persona, ruined the real Bill Cody in terms of his business.

The arrival of the movies was more than a second conquest of America. The Wild West had been conquered with horses, and it was with the Western that the United States of America now conquered the world. The first Westerns were, incidentally, branded as 'horse operas'. A few years after Theodore Roosevelt, the cowboy president, was sworn in at the White House in September 1901, one of his former comrades from Cuba rose to stardom as one of the first heroes of the Western. Thomas Edwin Mix, better known as Tom Mix, became one of the 'idols of the American public', as the French historian of the Western, Jean-Louis Rieupeyrout, put it. An early American film critic described Tom Mix as the dandy of the Westerns and the beau of the big screen prairie: 'He is an average actor, but an exceptional rider.'[74] In fact, Tom Mix owed much of his fame to his white horse, an animal that appeared to have leapt straight out of the realm of mythology. It was said of Herman Melville that he had wavered for a while, and 'toyed with the idea of narrating the hunt for a sacred white buffalo, or a sacred white stallion', before settling for a whale.[75] Also in *Moby-Dick*, he recalls 'the White Steed of the Prairies; a magnificent milk-white charger, large-eyed, small-headed, bluff-chested, and with the dignity of a thousand monarchs in his lofty, overscorning carriage'.[76]

Faced by the choice of land or sea, Behemoth or Leviathan, Melville opted for the mythical beast of the sea, the white whale. He left the kudos of becoming the mythologizer of the prairies not to another writer, but to an up-and-coming artist. Frederic Remington, who like

The Oklahoma Land Rush: from the film *Cimarron* by Wesley Ruggles
and Howard Estabrook, 1931.

Even the Western speaks of the end of the horse era:
'*Lonely are the Brave*', 1962.

Roosevelt had left the East coast in 1883 to go to Kansas, and had become a rancher and horse-handler there. He studied the life of the cowboys, trappers and natives, and in his imagery he delved deeply into the life of the Wild West. While 'Buffalo' Bill Cody was refashioning the old West as a circus act, where one-time protagonists were starring in cameo roles as themselves, Remington's paintings – much sought after by museums and reproduced in the press – gave the Wild West its own iconographic stamp. Anyone who described or depicted the West after him, including the great directors of Westerns like John Ford and Sam Peckinpah, was standing on Remington's shoulders, seeing the West through his eyes. Even Owen Wister, author of the first Western novel, *The Virginian*, looked to Remington with reverence: everything that permeated the image of the West was his doing, from the characterization of American soldiers, to the life and the tragedy of the Native Americans, to the prototypes of depravity and squalor, the prospectors, gamblers and bandits.[77] There was only one figure that Wister forgot to mention, perhaps the greatest of all Remington's icons: the horse. This was the painter's main subject – the country's mythical beast. It had, after all, made possible both the conquest of the West and the invention of the Western.

The Shock

THE END OF A RIDING NATION

It's mid-September 1939; in his billet, just west of Warsaw, a German officer is going over the events of the past few days. He is still young; until two weeks ago, he knew war only as a game and a manoeuvre. Now he's experienced it as a cacophony of rapidly changing high-risk situations and logistical challenges, with fleeting moments of rest in the drawing rooms of hastily abandoned stately homes. The pictures still hang on the walls, the Empire furniture remains; the only thing that is nowhere to be found is wine. The chronicler belongs to a motorized unit, but his writing betrays the perspective of a former cavalryman.[1] Besides the human casualties, he witnesses the other victims of war. Claus von Stauffenberg writes to his wife Nina on 17 September 1939: 'Today, on the main road west out of Warsaw, I saw the remains of an entire column, all shot. Over 100 horses lay by the roadside. Civilians are still burying the carcasses. It was a sight I'll never forget.'[2]

Meanwhile, a Polish child experiencing the war is taken aback by the sight of the masses of dead horses. For him, too, the image of the stiff, fallen animals will be burned forever in his memory. In his childhood memoirs, Ryszard Kapuściński writes: 'The air was thick with the smell of gunpowder, fire, rotting flesh. Again and again, we stumble across the carcasses of horses. This large, defenceless animal, the horse; it cannot hide, it stands there frozen when the bombs fall, stands there and waits for death. At every step, we see dead horses, here in the middle of the road, there at the roadside in a ditch, again a little further away in a field. There they lie, with stiff legs stretched up to heaven, shaking their hooves at the world. I don't see dead people anywhere, because they are buried straight away; just everywhere I look I see the carcasses of horses – blacks, bays, piebalds, pintos, chestnuts – as if this weren't a war of the people, but of horses, as though it were these animals who were fighting a battle of life and death, as though they were the only victims of the war.'[3]

Just as in the last days of the Second World War, when Cossacks dismounted and brought their horses down to drink at the Elbe, so too were the first days of the war characterized by the horse. Poland, the old cavalry nation – according to the myth that lingers to this day – perished in mounted battles.[4] From the mid-nineteenth century, every great battlefield campaign involving cavalry is somehow or other described as the last of its kind in history. But in the desperate, defensive battles of the Polish cavalrymen against the advancing troops of the Wehrmacht, we see yet again traces of the twilight of a human epoch: this is the final farewell to a long era of horses in Polish history and it could scarcely have been more dramatic. Never mind that this farewell did not actually ever take place – the same old pictures hang in the parlours of our collective memory as those in her abandoned Polish stately homes.

Like love and the stock exchange, our historical memory is a motherland of wishful thinking, sacrificed to our faith and blind to known facts. History is written in the indicative mood, but lived and remembered in the optative – the grammatical mood of wishful thinking. This is why historical myths are so tenacious. It's as though the truth, even when it's there for everyone to see, is powerless – it can't lay a finger on the all-powerful myth. But there is a trade-off: for a myth to survive, it needs not only to become widespread, but also to have some dramatic or sensational core that captures and excites the popular imagination more than pure historical critique ever can. One of the most resilient myths of the last century is the story of the attack by Polish lancers against German tanks on the first day of the Second World War. The confirmed factual context of what was in reality a historical accident or a fatal fluke, rather than the blood-soaked and quixotic act of insane courage it is billed as, is now freely accessible online.[5] But all the same, the sensational image of the death-defying Polish riders proves far stronger than all historical reason and logic. *Morituri te salutant*: the more hopeless the battle, the better the story.

On the evening of the first day of the German invasion of Poland, 1 September 1939, legend has it that a detachment of the Polish cavalry attacked a German Panzer division, with courage stirred up by despair at the foreseeable deadly consequences.[6] This spectacular image of galloping cavalrymen brandishing outstretched sabres was even embellished to feature lance-wielding Uhlans, a detail that heightens the atavistic sense of it being lifted from a temporal context: it is as if the first evening of the Second World War brought about the unlikely clash of primordial and contemporary warriors. It's as if the archetype of the Mounted Warrior has risen from the strata of historical time: defiantly, the terror of the steppe emerges to confront the steely paradigm of modernity. The Polish Rider in a hopeless duel with the German tank: how apt an image of the end of the era of the horse.

The actual sequence of events in this unequal encounter was somewhat different. It was a random collision of a Polish cavalry unit with German tank troops; instead of performing a manoeuvre to turn away from the machine-gun fire, which few were likely to have survived, the riders seized the bull by the horns and charged straight at the tanks in the hope of squeezing through (and about half of them actually succeeded). The legend sprang originally from the report of an Italian journalist. From there, the German propaganda department picked up the thread and wove it further. Two films, *Campaign in Poland* (1940) and *Battle Squadron Lützow* (1941), anchored the fictitious, or embellished, events in the contemporary consciousness and successfully lodged the story in the memory of posterity. Even in 1959, when Polish director Andrzej Wajda attempted to conjure up a counter-myth with the film *Lotna*, he didn't think he could completely dispense with the scene of the cavalry armed with lances coming up against tanks.[7] It simply fitted the self-image of the Polish nation too perfectly to shake off.

It was a trope shaped by the perception of the Polish nobility, who saw themselves as a riding elite more emphatically than any other strand of the European upper classes. And the Polish nation, so many times partitioned, humiliated and left historically unstable, drew confidence and pride from the concept of being an equestrian nation. More than any other European military, Poland had since the sixteenth century made the cavalry the central branch of its armed forces, replacing the traditional sword with the light, swift sabre. The horse was an integral component of Polish self-representation, in literature as well as in the visual arts. Paintings of horses, so highly esteemed in the nineteenth century by the nobility and the newly established bourgeoisie throughout Europe, inherited a thoroughly political undertone in Poland, especially as part of the genre of historical painting.[8] Always looming in the background was the august portrait of the greatest Polish rider, Jan III Sobieski, King of Poland and Grand Duke of Lithuania, who defeated the Turks at the Battle of Vienna in September 1683 and was henceforth regarded by Poles as the saviour of the Christian West.

Shortly before the late afternoon of 1 September 1939 and the fatal encounter with a German tank column, the Polish cavalry also rode against some German infantry positions. As heavy in casualties as the attack was, it still had the impact of the old shock tactics against the infantry, who beat a hasty retreat. Even German general Heinz Guderian speaks in his memoirs of the 'panic of the first day of war'. [9] Again, on subsequent days of this short war, the Polish cavalry launched occasional surprise attacks on German troops and broke through the enemy lines. But the Polish cavalry was ultimately powerless against the superior German, and later Russian, motorized and armoured units. Added to that were the attacks by fighter-bombers, which brought casualties among the cavalry in particular. Some units managed to escape to Hungary in the last days of the German annexation campaign; the last cavalry soldiers still fighting under General Kleeberg, a total of 5,000 men, capitulated on 5 October. Only in the woods in the foothills of the Polish Central Mountains did a few hundred Polish riders fight on under Major Dobrzański, also known as 'Hubal', as a 'separated unit of the Polish Army'. On 30 April 1940, the guerrilla group was encircled and defeated by German troops, their leader meeting a savage and ignoble death.[10]

THUNDERBOLT ANNO DOMINI

The outbreak of the Crimean War in 1853 brought an end to almost forty years of peace in Europe. Once again the continent was launched into a phase characterized by military conflicts, where the rapid advancement of technology was plain to see. The swift changes in power relations on the battlefield were especially felt by the cavalry. For a very long time, ever since mankind had been fighting wars and involving animals in the process, horses and riders had been the masters of the battlefield. The centaur was the lord of battle and the terror of its enemies. Under Napoleon, the cavalry had again risen to become the most visible and in many cases decisive weapon of battle; it was often the cavalry charge that decided the outcome of the battle. The idea of a 'decisive battle', as Clausewitz had termed it, demanded an appropriately decisive weapon, and this is what the cavalry promised.[11] The cavalry was the section capable of the fastest motion, the wedge which at the height of the struggle broke the resistance of the hostile masses, the blade that at the decisive moment was thrust into the heart of the enemy army. The cavalry was the shimmering weapon, a large, colourful, many-limbed being, and at the same time it was a monument to its own brilliance and ebullience. But the new wars from the mid-nineteenth century on saw the start of its long, slow fall from grace. Initially, there was only a slight crack in the monument, a chink that escaped the attention of most onlookers.

After the end of the American Civil War, it took Europe three-quarters of a century to understand the lessons that America had learned in four bloody years. Nations and armies do not draw lessons from observing far-off disasters; they learn, if at all, from their own crushing defeats. But what lessons could the European staff officers and cavalrymen have drawn from the battles of the Civil War?

What was apparent first of all was the rapid slump in value of the cavalry as an offensive weapon in comparison with the infantry's breech-loaders and repeating firearms, which enabled them to fire faster and more accurately. The cavalry, once a source of terror for foot soldiers who feared being trampled down, now faded in contrast with the increased firepower of the infantry, which allowed it to keep the cavalry at bay. Secondly, less obvious but no less important, was the operational capacity of the cavalry beyond the 'classical' battlefield role, for example commando operations aimed at interrupting enemy supply and communications lines, or raids on ammunition depots. On both sides, the Union and the Confederates, riders made extensive tactical use of these swift, flexible operations targeting enemy logistics, where the moving elements of bandit or nomadic warfare were combined with the objectives of a modern, hi-tech conflict.[12]

Furthermore, observers of the Civil War and the subsequent American Indian wars would have been able to study the benefits of modifications to the cavalry's armoury. While the cavalry commanders and strategists of the old world without exception swore by traditional bladed weapons for thrusting and slicing, the North American cavalry was consistently equipped with revolvers and repeating rifles, in line with the new style of cavalry warfare. Sending a squadron with sabres drawn at full gallop up against enemy lines was tantamount, in terms of physics, to hurling a gigantic, multi-part projectile of high penetrating power to break through a kind of hot wall. What it meant, in psychological terms, however, firstly for the riders – largely robbed of control over their half-deranged animals, in constant danger of being thrown off and being tramped under hoof – to charge towards the defensive enemy line, and secondly for the defending side to see an infernal gigantic, snorting, roaring, thundering and flashing monster come hurtling towards them, is hard to imagine from today's perspective.[13] But if the main purpose of the cavalry was no longer to thrust a tremendous thunderbolt into the ranks of the infantry, but rather to sabotage the railways behind the enemy line or to stand up to mounted guerrilla fighters, then the tactics, arms and equipment all had to change. This was precisely what happened in America, while European armies still clung to the dated notion of the offensive campaign using conventional weaponry such as sabres and spears.[14]

In the key battle of the Austro-Prussian war of 1866, the Battle of Königgrätz, the same phenomena could be observed as in the American theatre of war: the increased risks facing the cavalry, now that they were encountering not their own kind but a modern-style infantry, and the consequently decreased likelihood of their taking a decisive role in the battle, as the cavalries under Napoleon or Frederick the Great, Joachim Murat or Friedrich von Seydlitz had been able to.[15] Even more spectacular were the debacles suffered by the French cavalry, the elite units of what was seen as the continent's best army, in the late summer and autumn of 1870 during the Franco-Prussian War (Plate 27).

The worst disaster unfolded on 1 September 1870 outside Sedan, when under the watchful eyes of the Prussian King Wilhelm and his staff, the French cavalry suffered heavy losses as they made three consecutive and ultimately unsuccessful attempts to break through the German infantry lines. After the final attack failed, so legend has it, the French commander General de Gallifet paused a moment, exhausted, in front of the foremost post of German infantry regiment; the Germans ceased fire, saluted and let the last vestiges of the French cavalry drag themselves slowly away.[16] The less chivalrous reality of the battlefield, in the very literal sense of the word, was reflected in the numbers of casualties of this murderous war. On both sides – French and German – the number of slaughtered horses outweighed that of fallen riders. The horses, as the larger targets, were not only easier to hit, but they also brought their riders down with them as they fell, making them easier to kill or capture. But the history books are so often silent about this less glamorous aspect of warfare between infantry and cavalry, Man vs. Centaur.[17]

Here we enter the era of the final battles. Since the days of the Franco-Prussian War, historians have never tired of constantly declaring a new 'final' cavalry battle in military history. Prussian cavalry commander Adalbert von Bredow's 'Death Ride' of 16 August 1870, at the battle of Mars-La-Tour, was, as historian Michael Howard puts it, 'perhaps the last successful cavalry charge in Western European warfare'.[18] The huge melee at Rezonville that same afternoon, comprising some 5,000 riders, is considered the last great battle of cavalry against cavalry.[19] Like no other branch of historiography, military history has preserved its romantic spirit and sense of historical empathy. Where else would we see these impassioned reports of such an exit from the stage of world history? At the end of the day, this stage needed to be cleared for the cruel spectacle of the First World War: if you were going to ride into the line of fire now, you had to be insane, a general, suicidal, or all three at once.

The only European nation that showed signs of revising its cavalry tactics before the First World War was Britain. The British had learned not from the American Civil War, but from the unrest in the colonies and from the guerrilla war that the Boers had forced upon them.[20] For all the grandeur of the Victorian age, it was anything but a peaceful time. During the sixty-three-year reign of the eponymous queen, Britain fought in eighty military confrontations, large and small, and 'in every one of them,' argues a recent historical study, 'horses proved to be as essential as men'.[21] One of the more political and cavalier engagements was the campaign in Sudan against the Islamic Caliphate established by force following the siege of Khartoum in 1885 by the self-proclaimed Mahdi, Muhammad Ahmad. With his conquest of Khartoum and the death of the entrenched British governor, General Gordon, the Mahdi had stuck two fingers up at the British Empire. But it wasn't until several years later, in 1898, that the Empire struck back. With hindsight, the campaign, in which the British turned north-eastern Africa into a laboratory for modern weaponry, looks a lot like a harbinger of the Great War. Seen from the opposite historical perspective, it resembles a last gasp of the nineteenth century: a campaign with a decisive battle, where the cavalry played a highly visible role that ultimately tipped the balance. It's no wonder that the Battle of Omdurman is yet another of those cavalry battles often credited as being the *last* of its kind in history.

A young officer of the British cavalry, who led a squadron at Omdurman, a year later devoted a book, *The River War* (1899), to the campaign, thereby laying the first foundations of his later (also literary) fame. In fact, in Winston Churchill's portrayal of the campaign against the Mahdi, we can sense the lion's paw. His elliptical images of a fierce clash between the 21st Lancers and the militant dervishes are among the most impressive descriptions that war literature has to offer, because they do justice to the speed and elegance of the appalling ballet, without taking away from the horror of the carnage and the confusion of the protagonists. 'The collision', wrote Churchill, 'was prodigious. Nearly thirty Lancers, men and horses, and at least two hundred Arabs were overthrown. The shock was stunning to both sides, and for perhaps ten wonderful seconds no man heeded his enemy. Terrified horses wedged in the crowd, bruised and shaken men, sprawling in heaps, struggled, dazed and stupid, to their feet, panted, and looked about them. Several fallen Lancers had even time to re-mount. Meanwhile the impetus of the cavalry carried them on . . . On this occasion two living walls had actually crashed together. The Dervishes fought manfully. They tried to hamstring the horses. They fired their rifles, pressing the muzzles into the very bodies of

Clash of the ages: Andrzej Wajda's 1959 film *Lotna* made a Polish
epic out of the Nazi legend of a Polish cavalry attack on German
tanks on 1 September 1939.

The Royal Scots Greys regiment, at the roadside in
northern France, May 1918.

their opponents. They cut reins and stirrup-leathers. They flung their throwing-spears with great dexterity. They tried every device of cool, determined men practised in war and familiar with cavalry; and, besides, they swung sharp, heavy swords which bit deep . . . Riderless horses galloped across the plain. Men, clinging to their saddles, lurched helplessly about, covered with blood from perhaps a dozen wounds. Horses, streaming from tremendous gashes, limped and staggered with their riders.'[22]

The war against the Boers, which broke out shortly thereafter, in October 1899, quickly spiralled from a conventional confrontation of two similar opponents into a guerrilla war where horses played a pivotal role. After the Boers realized they were inferior to the British Expeditionary Force in pitched battles, they focused instead on surprise attacks by smaller commando troops on tough African ponies. Lord Kitchener, British commander-in-chief and the victor at Omdurman, responded with a series of measures, all aimed at limiting the free movement of the combatant Boers while at the same time increasing that of the British troops. The campaign's most important element was the increased deployment of mounted troops which, at the height of the war in 1901, constituted almost a third of the entire expeditionary force of 250,000 men. Sending some 80,000 horses into the field threw up some not inconsiderable logistical problems. Since the British authorities restricted the purchase of remounts (military horses) to the domestic market – the horses needed for the Boer War had to first complete a tour on the London buses before they could serve in South Africa – only the London transport companies were importing from the US and Canadian markets.[23]

A GHOST AT NOON

The catastrophe did not happen overnight; some had seen it coming. In 1913, in his book *Der Kaiser*, Paul Liman quoted a warning by Baron von Gühlen: 'The German nation will have to pay for the Kaiser's impressive cavalry manoeuvres with the gushing blood of its sons.'[24] After the experiences of the American Civil War and the Franco-Prussian War of 1870, there was no lack of voices in the European countries stressing the dangers the cavalry faced with the infantry's increased firepower. If the cavalry was to have a future, it would not lie in the classical offensive campaign with sabres drawn. They would need to adopt the military approach of nomadic warriors and irregular troops, breaking up into small commando forces that would attack at lightning speed and just as quickly disappear again, coming at the enemy from behind their lines and sabotaging communications and supply lines. For this purpose, they would need to develop new tactics and update their training and equipment; such skills don't just come out of nowhere. However, the rules of the game were still being written by men who were former or active cavalrymen and threw all caution to the wind: they continued to teach the value of the offensive attack and in the face of rapid-fire weapons they recommended at most a dispersal of the formation. Indeed, the last German cavalry protocol before the First World War, from 1909, described the offensive campaign as a decisive instrument in cavalry warfare.[25]

The political and strategic discourse was not determined by the few individual tactical instructors at army and cavalry academies, who saw things more realistically and advised more deployment of offensive tactics, but rather by authors such as the experienced cavalry commander Friedrich von Bernhardi, who in 1908 was still urging the cavalry, 'to put the enemy firearms out of action, as far as is possible' in order to then attack the enemy cavalry with cold steel: 'Because an energetic and dashing opponent must have the same desire, it seems to me, that even future warfare will bring forth battles that can be characterized as real mounted fighting. Likewise, in terms of the cavalry's battle function, the offensive attack will remain of paramount importance in combating the use of firearms.'[26]

What sounds so cheerfully militaristic was nothing more than whistling in the dark. No one knew this better than Bernhardi himself, which is why he was usually much more prudent in his utterances, tending to caution against the 'gung-ho spirit'[27] of most of his fellow officers. The nature of the battlefield had, within a few decades, undergone a complete transformation from the ground up, he argued. More and more, the losses outweighed the gains, and the 'firearms coverage' had become so thorough that it was now 'impossible to ride directly through the covered areas'.[28] In this situation, Bernhardi recommended that the cavalry focus on attacking strategic mobility[29] and, like the once despised infantry, 'protecting and defending the territory'.[30] His cautionary proclamations, however, were acted upon less often than his more aggressive pronouncements.

Both the American Indian wars and the Boer War showed that the contemporary military value of the cavalry lay in the 'combination of firepower and mobility'.[31] But this evidence was paid little heed in the strategic and tactical thinking of military leaders entering the First World War. Even the British Army, who were forced by the Boers to adapt their fighting style, just as two or three decades earlier the American cavalry had been forced by the Native Americans, remained deaf to the voice of experience. Certain young officers might have learned from the experience in Africa, but the old guard had not. Douglas Haig, Commander-in-Chief of the British Expeditionary Force on the Western Front from December 1915 to the end of the war, had indeed taken part in both the Sudan campaign and the Boer War, but as an avowed cavalryman who had served in India as Inspector General of the Cavalry, he wore his spurs even in his headquarters, rejected the impact of modern weaponry and insisted on the superiority of will power, determination and surprise – that is, the psychological elements of warfare. Just as at the time of the Napoleonic campaigns, which Haig studied intensively and taught at the military academy in the 1890s,[32] he saw the task of both the infantry and the artillery as being preparation for the decisive final attack, to be led by the cavalry. This remarkable defiance and refusal to learn from experience among many senior commanders at the time came at great cost and the price was paid by the cavalry in the great battles between 1916 and 1918.[33]

In his novel of the Great War, *Heeresbericht* (Army Report), Edlef Köppen describes an offensive against the German trenches by a British cavalry troop, which ends with the gruesome demise of the attacking troopers in the face of infantry fire: 'The first row, the second row, no longer separated but colliding together, running aground, crushed together as one mass, too densely packed to be able to move. And it snorts and stamps and throttles and scrabbles and gobbles. Machine guns between the thrashing legs of horses, hacked stumps shuffling across the ground, shrapnel into their chests, grenades under their bellies . . . Arm-thick fountains of blood and gore, limbs and torsos of humans and animals hurled into the air . . . It is bedlam let loose: fear upon fear, horror upon horror. Not a horse turns back. The dead still press forward . . . The dead march on forever, mangled and mauled forever. Hands rise from the thick parapet of blood; faces rise, unrecognizable; arms flutter. Standing, empty-handed, the German infantry despatch the finishing blow. Until everything falls motionless, drowned in the bath of blood.'[34]

Even John French, Commander-in-Chief of the British Expeditionary Force (until December 1915), had been, like his competitor and successor Douglas Haig, a cavalry commander in the Boer War. Against all empirical evidence, both held firmly to the traditional understanding of 'their' branch of the army. French dreamed of dashing cavalry charges and loved nothing more than to inspect the troops from his white steed.[35] Douglas Haig, or 'Butcher Haig' as he was known after the battles of the Somme in July 1916, even maintained as late as 1927, an entire decade after the end of the Great War, that aeroplanes and tanks were mere accessories to a man on horseback.[36] At a time when aerial warfare was already all too familiar, when man dreamed of sending a rocket to the moon, this stubborn adherence to the cavalry as an offensive weapon seems like a cynical kind of atavism – evidence of the headstrong refusal to adapt of an entire stratum of military leaders concerned only with winning the wars of times gone by. It's with good reason that this duality – the obsolescence of the cavalry and the stubbornness of the generals – characterizes the historical images of the First World War to this day.

In addition to this, or rather in spite of it, over the last three decades a revisionist school of English historical scholarship has emerged, inspired by John Terraine (d. 2003), a biographer and defender of Haig, which endeavours to prove that the cavalry did indeed have an important role on the battlefields of the Great War, including in the trenches of the Western Front.[37] The idea that the breakthrough in the West was the result of modified battle techniques and new weapons, especially tanks, is labelled by this school as 'technological determinism'.[38] Notwithstanding this revisionist heroism, it is hard to dispute that the battlefields of the First World War were an environment dominated by new technology, where the chances of mounted troops carrying out their operations successfully were radically decreased. This was not just because of the increased firepower

of the machine gun. Since the late nineteenth century, another technical enemy had emerged to threaten the cavalry. It was as dangerous
as it was unimpressive: a simple stretch of iron wire. It did not even
need to be the infamous barbed wire of the First World War; the
straightforward iron fence found around fields on a farm served to
hold the animals back. 'Nearly all scholarly attention focuses on the
development of firearms, nearly none on the development of the terrain,' notes mathematician and historian Reviel Netz, adding 'there is
something extremely exciting about violent instruments such as the
rifle and the machine gun. A piece of wire that a cow farmer has laid
on his land does not produce the same kind of excitement.'[39]

As Netz argues convincingly, changes in the ecology of Europe and
North America, and more specifically the changes in land use in
the second half of the nineteenth century, meant that ever greater
areas of open country, which the cavalry needed for confrontations,
were cut off by enclosures and fences. Even if a few of America and
Europe's farmers pulled down their fences, there was still little space
for the cavalry to pick up speed; the minute-long run before they
reached another fence was not enough for a classic attack.[40] Years
before the trench warfare and infantry weapons of the First World
War, modern land management had literally taken the ground from
under the hooves of the traditional cavalry with its fluttering banners
and outstretched sabres. But it was not until 1916 that the tank
offered a weapon which could replace heavy cavalry as a classic
'shock weapon' in combat and which was not to be stopped by barbed
wire, ditches or infantry fire.

By contrast, the horse as a traction engine experienced a sinister
boom. While its application as a *vector* would henceforth be limited,
as a *tractor* it was still in as much need as ever, and in rising numbers.
The logistical complexity of the massive armies and the physical
battles, but also the expansion and improvement of the medical service,
led to an upsurge in the number of horses in use and with it the challenge
of replenishing stocks.[41] As the war became more and more protracted,
the replacement of horses became a growing problem. The more
horses were requisitioned from farmers in the hinterland, the more
precarious things became for agriculture, as yields depended not only
on human effort but also on the animals. As during the Boer War, the

British Army drew its horse stocks largely from Canada and the United States. But submarine warfare threatened these supply lines too. On the whole, the First World War resulted in what one American historian describes as 'a massive . . . forced migration of millions of animals'.[42]

The reason for the high demand for draught horses was not least the increase in the number and weight of heavy weapons. The enhanced importance of artillery in the First World War was expressed in a far greater demand for traction. Apart from the heaviest siege guns, which needed to be transported by railway, horses were used for the transportation of all light and medium-sized pieces of artillery. It was not an infrequent sight to see teams of twelve or more horses dragging their heavy load along rain-sodden roads, churned up by wheels and grenades, towards the artillery positions: an arduous and treacherous procession. Neither did chemical warfare, launched in 1915, spare the lives of horses. They were also helpless in the face of attack by enemy aircraft; horses could not duck for cover. That's why it was seen by pilots as more effective to bomb horse-drawn convoys than marching columns: the animals were easier to target and harder to replace than men.[43] By the final climax of the fighting on the Western Front in August 1918, the life expectancy of an artillery horse on the front was ten days.

The number of horses deployed by all parties in the First World War is currently estimated at 16 million, of which half the total, 8 million, met their death before the end of the war.[44] This figure stands alongside an estimated 9 million people killed by the war. The survival rate for animals in the Boer War was even lower: between 1899 and 1902, of the 494,000 horses employed by the British, some 326,000 died, i.e. nearly two-thirds. In the First World War, the loss of horses on the German side is estimated at a million, or 68 per cent.[45]

It's only very recently that literature, most notably Michael Morpurgo's 1982 children's book *War Horse*, adapted for the screen by Steven Spielberg in 2011, and research leading up to the commemoration of the First World War began to recall the achievements and suffering of animals in the war, and especially the horses.[46] Much earlier war literature and the memoirs that were so popular in the

Hellfire Corner: horse-drawn artillery and logistics on a service
road under enemy fire.

187. Guerre de 1914 — Enfouissement de chevaux sur le champ de bataille de HAELEN

A mass grave for horses after the Battle of Haelen, 12 August 1914.

period soon after the war were not aware of horses. The American naturalist Ernest Harold Baynes dedicated an early memorial to the fallen animals with his monograph *Animal Heroes of the Great War*,[47] and in 1931 Major General Sir John Moore, head of the British Army's Veterinary Corps, paid homage in his pamphlet, *Our Servant the Horse*.[48] In Franz Schauwecker's 1928 collection of photographs from the front, he presented pictures of war animals complemented by a touching narrative.[49] Ernst Johannsen ought perhaps to be seen as Morpurgo's direct predecessor, having told the story of the war from the perspective of Liese, a Great War veteran mare. His book is dedicated to 'the 9,586,000 horses . . . casualties of the Great War'.[50] And one of the most shocking scenes in Erich Maria Remarque's novel *All Quiet on the Western Front* is the description in chapter 4 of the suffering of the wounded horses.[51]

Erased from the battlefields of the West, the cavalry lived on in the memories, myths and political cartoons of the Great War.[52] It made only the occasional, fleeting reappearance, like a ghost at noon, in the everyday theatre of war. At the end of August 1918, lieutenant and company commander Ernst Jünger was wounded in a battle with British troops, as we read in his war diaries. After an emergency tourniquet is applied, Jünger is picked up by a comrade by the name of Hengstmann (literally 'stallion man' in German)[53]and carried away on his back, until he is himself hit by a bullet. Jünger was an infantryman, but he had to learn to ride to become an officer, and when he recalls this strange moment in his diary, we hear an echo of the language of the cavalry: 'I heard a faint metallic buzz and felt Hengstmann collapse beneath me. He had been hit by a shot through the head . . . It's a curious feeling when a person who is physically so close to you is knocked out from under you.'[54] Jünger appeared never to have shaken off this surreal scene with its echoes of the legend of St Christopher carrying Christ (and Jünger seemed in his writing to obsessively seek out the symbolic): the editor of his posthumously published war diary recalled that even in old age, Jünger dwelled on the fatal moment and remembered the centaurian name of the man who had saved him.[55] Throughout his life, Jünger had a photograph of Corporal Hengstmann hanging over his desk.

THE NOBILITY MATRIX

The fate that awaited horses during the Second World War was hardly any gentler. Progress in mechanization and motorization was still not so advanced that horses were no longer required as draught animals. This was due to the low level of mechanization in many units, the logistical problems, difficulties in the supply of fuel and spare parts, and also the lamentable state of most roads and paths. Where the terrain was impassable for motorized vehicles, where mechanized columns would be engulfed in mud, it was only horse-drawn vehicles that could get through. The historian Reinhart Koselleck experienced the Eastern Front of the Second World War as a member of the horse-drawn artillery. This war, too, 'though bomber planes, fliers and tanks certainly played the decisive role, was still mostly fought – at least on the German side – by troops reliant on horsepower. While, in the First World War, the Germans used some 1.8 million horses, in the Second World War it was almost a million more, namely 2.7 million. And of these, 1.8 million perished. In terms of percentages,' Koselleck concludes, 'that is a far higher death toll than that paid by the soldiers.' He chalks up the figures as 'evidence of a murderous end to the era of the horse'.[56]

Compared to the First World War, the demand for horses saw another sharp hike. 'At the beginning of the Second World War,' writes historian Heinz Meyer, 'an infantry division possessed more than twice as many horses as an equivalent division in the First World War. The greater number of heavy weapons and the more widespread use of such equipment necessitated this increase in the supply of horses. In the non-motorized troops in the First World War, there was one horse for every seven men; in the Second World War, it was more like one horse for every four soldiers.'[57] The enormous rise in demand for horses brought its own problems. It did not just take significant capacity away from agriculture and civilian transport. It also meant an escalation of the units' demand for fodder and required additional military personnel for the care and veterinary treatment of the animals. On top of this, as was becoming increasingly clear in the course of the war in the east, even the fully motorized troops could no longer get by entirely without horses – the state of the roads was simply too dire. 'Even the smallest vehicles,' we read in the April 1942 war diary of a middle-ranking soldier, 'were often only loosened from the spot by a team of four.'[58]

The war on the Western Front was conducted largely without horses; the familiar images of helmeted, mounted German officers leading their troops through defeated Paris were just propaganda. Things were different in the east: here, besides providing draught power, the horse had a genuine cavalry role, even if it was not on the front line. New uses were emerging for the cavalry in the rear guard. With greater distances between the troops, terrain becoming less accessible and guerrilla attacks on the increasingly stretched supply lines on the rise, the military unit once declared dead made a comeback: in 1942, a German cavalry unit was deployed under Baron von Boeselager. Their regiments fought alongside both Kalmyk and Cossack cavalry corps, as well as the cavalry units of the SS. But these are stories which can be read elsewhere.[59] In technical terms, the war in the east was another, as it were, 'older' war than the one raging in Western Europe, where mechanized armies were grappling with one another and horses played a minimal role. 'The Russian campaign,' writes Reinhart Koselleck, summarizing what he had seen and experienced in the east, 'with its structural conditions, belongs back in the horse age. It could not be won with horses, and certainly not without them.'[60]

Again, the same questions arise as had done in the First World War: why was the cavalry so persistent and why did so many die? Why did the armies of the West not simply abolish their cavalry regiments after the experience of 1914–18, leaving just the horses for the horse-drawn artillery units, which could not yet give up their old traction engines and grant the remaining horses leave to return to civilian life? The suggestion that this was the result of the impact of the traditional and conservative spirit of the general staff does not explain everything. Time and again, history gives examples of successful operations by the cavalry – coups, raids and covert actions – that seem to contradict all the naysayers' prophesies of the end of the military cavalry. They include the operations of guerrilla combatants as well as of the cavalry troops who were deployed to combat them.

In the First World War, it was the dazzling actions of British commander and cavalryman Sir Edmund Allenby that had his contemporaries spellbound. In 1917–18 his Egyptian Expeditionary Force drove the troops of the Ottoman Empire out of Palestine; he rode up to the gates of Jerusalem on 9 December 1917, and nine months later took Amman and Damascus. His success gave a polish to the old shield of the cavalry, letting it shimmer in the desert sun. Not far from the battlefields where once Alexander the Great had shown his enemies what a well-trained, quick and agile rider was capable of, Allenby's light cavalry triumphed in battle – in a war of combined arms that pre-empted the blitzkrieg strategy of the next world war. Few observers of the campaigns of Megiddo and Palestine seem to have recognized that the real secret of Allenby's success lay in the tactical integration of cavalry, infantry and air force. Most onlookers were intoxicated by the image of the old aristocratic cavalrymen gracing the same ground in the theatre of war that had once been ridden by the splendid cavalries of Alexander the Great and Napoleon.

Immediately after the Great War, the cavalry enjoyed another late renaissance in Eastern Europe. Just as in the earlier Russian civil war between the Whites and the Reds, the Polish-Russian War of 1919–20 also had substantial cavalry units fighting on both sides. On the Russian side, there was the famous *Konarmia* ('cavalry'), also known as the Red Cavalry or Budyonny's Cavalry – successful initially, until it was thwarted at Lvov and pushed back in the late summer of 1920. On 31 August 1920, ten days after the Russian debacle at Warsaw, Komarów, not far from the headquarters of the Red Cavalry, was host to a cavalry engagement which – yet again – has been described as 'perhaps the last pure cavalry battle in European history'.[61] Although this battle did not decide the outcome of the war, the Polish Lancers also dealt a further painful blow to the ailing Red Cavalry. The fast, energetic and brutal forays by Budyonny's riders in the early days and, later, the success of the Polish cavalry, provided the desired arguments to advocates of cavalry warfare. As at Warsaw, the siege war, they argued, could have been decided by the tanks, but the horse was far superior to the tank in long and fast offensives. In both Russia and Poland, therefore, prominent cavalry commanders were able to maintain their prestige and their status,[62] and even in Britain,

France and America, argues historian Norman Davies, 'cavalrymen took heart from what they believed to be the lesson of the Polish campaigns'.[63]

Military leaders, particularly in the higher echelons, are certainly prone to conservative thinking and traditional attitudes, and a desire to repeat the battles of yesteryear. The First World War is full of examples of this, and Haig and French are merely prominent cases of this professional obstinacy and blinkered thinking. But one of the reasons why the cavalry, in particular, was prone to succumb to this malady of conservatism was the deep-rooted connection it had with the aristocracy, a phenomenon we might call the *nobility matrix*. The close connection of man mounted on his steed has an aura of inherent nobility to it. It is imbued with an air of mystical faith, a kind of fetish for the dyad of man and beast. But it is also a striking embodiment of an age-old, aristocratic bearing, an attitude or pose that suggests distance and superiority. Thanks to the speed and height the mounted position gives man (the 'cavalier perspective'), the horse acts as an excellent medium of distance. A horse grants his rider power at any moment to create a spatial distance, horizontal or vertical, between the rider and the lowly men on foot, his pedestrian entourage. In the collective memory of Europeans, the image of a rider atop his horse – an image which cavalrymen such as Haig consciously evoked – embodies an eternal paradigm of chivalry: every armed horseman reminds us of St George.[64]

The classic close-range combat weapons such as the sword and lance, also known as melee weapons, fitted with this sense of distance, even if at first glance that seems paradoxical. Despite all their experience of the continuously growing firepower of the infantry, the cavalrymen of Europe, with very few exceptions, held firmly to the 'chivalrous' ideal of hand-to-hand combat. 'The heroic conception of combat between a cavalry formation armed with short-range weapons charging against the enemy is fundamentally distinct from the artifice of the infantryman who ambushes his opponent or shoots them down from afar like fleeing prey.'[65]

The cavalry was not only lost in tradition, it was captive to its noble ethos, or what was perceived as such; captive to images of long-gone wars which were still revered for their beauty. Until very recently, the cavalry still claimed to be more than a mere branch of the armed services like the infantry or artillery; it wore the badge of military aristocracy long into the modern era. Even after it had long since become obsolete as a military unit, it still paraded itself as a monument to another, unforgotten world. The cavalry had its own metaphysics, beside which the physics of the battlefield fell short; the *idea* of the cavalryman survived his real demise in a hail of bullets. Wherever a uniformed man showed up on a horse, whether or not it was in the carnage of mechanized warfare, the age-old drama still played out on the stage, a dramatized conflict like a duel of warring peoples, battles over the scraps of cavalry banners, an echo of pomp and circumstance.

What we might take from all this is that since the tail end of the nineteenth century, the cavalry has seen a great number of final battles and died a great number of deaths. Even its death on 17 May 1940 was not its last. On this day, a small troop of French cavalrymen – the scattered remains of a regiment, decimated by the Luftwaffe – was making its way between Solre-le-Château and Avesnes in northern France, near the border with Belgium. Their end came at the hands of a machine-gunner hidden behind a hedge. With the exception of two riders who escaped, every man was killed. One of the two survivors was the future Nobel Prize-winner Claude Simon, an author of the *nouveau roman* movement. Simon returned many times to this moment: the colonel riding on ahead, apparently raving mad and desperate for a soldierly death, the shots out of the blue, the flashing sabres held aloft one last time as if ready to attack, the dazzling light, the slow-motion collapse, like a slowly tumbling statue. More than once he deconstructed the scene into kaleidoscopic fragments,[66] where along with the figure of Colonel de Reixach the entire world of the aristocracy also perishes as it crashes to the ground, together with its ethos and its pathos, its pride and its folly: 'he saw him raise the sparkling sabre in his outstretched arm, everything, rider, horse and sabre slowly collapsing to one side, exactly like one of those lead soldiers whose base, the legs, would begin to melt, still seeing him collapse, sink down endlessly, the sabre raised in the sun . . .'[67]

This famous scene, whose repetition has often given rise to interpretations revolving around the concept of trauma, can also be viewed as

Behind the scenes: in the First World War, horses stopped falling on the battlefield; now they died on the supply lines.

Russia 1944. The war in the East could not be won with horses, and certainly not without them, as Reinhart Koselleck put it.

an ironic epilogue to the traditions of historical painting and the cavalry portrait. Like Simon, who makes use of this slow-motion narrative device, the nineteenth-century painters solved 'the problem of the supreme, highest point, the acme of motion' by leaving 'an emphatic sign of the unstable' – that 'which one might call the *numen*, the solemn petrification of a pose which it is impossible to maintain over time,' as Roland Barthes put it.[68] But the image of the cavalryman's anachronistic, final gesture followed by the long, slow descent of man and rider, responds not only to artistic traditions, but also, ironically, causes the narrative to disintegrate. The flashing sabre is a twinkling hint of the transcendence so long enjoyed by the celestial duality of a man astride a horse. In the next moment, Simon's narrative comes crashing down to the terrestrial, the legendary moment fracturing into a panicked flight, hooves kicking up mud and dust.

The last great cavalry units of the world – the Red Army's – survived an entire decade after the end of the Second World War; it was not until the mid-1950s that their regiments were finally disbanded.[69] Hiroshima was a whole ten years in the past.

The Jewish Horsewoman

THE PALE RIDER

In the years 1984 to 1985, the London-based painter R. B. Kitaj was working on an allegorical portrait of a man in a railway carriage. He gave the final work the title *The Jewish Rider* (Plate 10). The process involved numerous sittings with his model, the art historian Michael Podro. The academic and the artist were long acquainted; in their own ways, both were associated with the Warburg school, which lived on in exile in London and became a powerful influence in British art history. In the late 1950s, Kitaj had studied as a young man in Oxford with Edgar Wind, one of the brightest thinkers of the Warburg movement. In his early pictures Kitaj makes several references to art historian and cultural theorist Aby Warburg; in the 1960s, he portrays him as a dancing maenad. Other giants of the Jewish intelligentsia such as Walter Benjamin wander through the world of his paintings; Kitaj is a scholarly painter, rather like the *poeta doctus,* or scholarly writer, in the manner of T. S. Eliot or Ezra Pound, two more of his guiding stars. Podro, for his part, combines strong theoretical interests with a clear inclination towards contemporary art (neither of which is common among art historians); he was also friends with other artists of the London School of painting such as Frank Auerbach, for whom he occasionally sat for portraits.

Like Kitaj, Michael Podro was from an Eastern European Jewish family and in their work both reflected the experience of exile and the obliteration of European Jewry. This also created the context for Kitaj's portrait of the travelling Jewish scholar: the smoking chimney whose smoke wafts over to the cross on a mountain, and the peripheral figure

of the guard, whose whip gives him the ominous look of a camp over-
seer or a commanding officer.

Among the principles of the Warburg school is the idea that pictorial representations and elemental innovations in form, especially
when combined with strong expressive energy, have the potential to
travel, or roam, long distances in time and space. Kitaj's painting of
the travelling Jewish art historian seems like a commentary on this
very idea: the traveller is a Wandering Jew, who in turn references the
idea of the picture's ability to roam. But Kitaj's work is no simple
illustration of a theoretical idea; it reads like an erratic translation
into a foreign language. Everything begins very simply. The conceptual inspiration behind it, hinted at in both the painting's title and in
the posture of its protagonist, is clear to see. Its forerunner is entitled
The Polish Rider and is the work of Rembrandt (Plate 6). Since 1910,
it has been part of the New York collection of American steel and
railway tycoon Henry Clay Frick.

It was disputed for a while whether this famous painting could
truly be attributed to Rembrandt, although now it is generally confirmed that it can be.[1] Its title, however, is pure fabrication based on
the painting's provenance in the collections of Polish aristocracy. It
first came to light in 1793 in a list of art treasures owned by the Polish king Stanisław II. Its history before this date is unknown. The
title has over the last century given rise to many interpretations of the
enigmatic young rider it depicts. Most of them link him to Eastern
European subjects, including Poles, Hungarians, Cossacks, aristocrats, poets and theologians; the Mongol hero Tamerlane, the young
King David and the Prodigal Son have all been touted for consideration. In 1944 the art historian Julius Held dismissed most of these
attempts to identify the subject as mere myth-making and proposed
that the subject be seen as an idealized, youthful Christian soldier, a
miles Christianus.[2]

The anonymity of Rembrandt's horseman fits neatly with Kitaj's
intentions in his painting. His 'Rider', as Kitaj calls him, 'is on his
way to visit the sites of the death camps in Poland, many years after
the war. I was inspired by a report someone wrote, who travelled on
a train from Budapest to Auschwitz to see what the doomed souls
might have seen. He said the countryside was beautiful.'[3] By alluding

to the Wandering Jew, Kitaj makes a 'Jewish Rider' of Rembrandt's anonymous subject, replacing the confident youth, looking out into the distance, with an older scholarly type with his gaze lowered, immersed in his book. The conspicuously bright, almost white coat worn by Rembrandt's rider is echoed in the loose, casual jacket worn by Kitaj's subject, which together with his bright shoes and red shirt gives the rail traveller a certain conspicuous elegance, not unlike that of Rembrandt's youthful rider. The numerous weapons Rembrandt's horseback warrior carries – two swords, a bow, a quiver full of arrows and an axe in his right hand, which is twisted so that the palm faces out – are transformed into the train passenger's three books.[4] But Kitaj's 'Jewish Rider' maintains the same pose with the right arm bent and the – now empty – right hand twisted outwards and resting against the right thigh: an awkward, tense position which seems not to suit the otherwise rather melancholy portrayal of a figure immersed in thought, and yet is unmistakably reminiscent of the pose of Rembrandt's subject.

There is another, stronger reference which we perhaps only notice at a second glance: the horse which appears like a spectre of Rembrandt's mare squeezed in between the reading passenger and the train seat. There is no mistaking the likeness of the horse to that of *The Polish Rider*: the head stretching forwards with an open mouth, the pale colouring, the truncated tail – all the details correspond perfectly with Rembrandt's animal, which in turn defies all conventions of contemporary cavalry portraits. Countless art historians have racked their brains trying to make sense of Rembrandt's strangely ghostly-looking old nag; where one reckons it is a thoroughbred, another sees only a plough horse. It was Held in 1944 who was first to come up with a conclusive theory. 'The horse', he writes, 'certainly has something unusual about it. Compared with the rider, it is small and strangely fleshless ... The general lack of flesh is particularly noticeable on the head where the exaggerated "dryness" lends the horse a cadaverous expression.'[5]

Held finds an answer in a sketch by Rembrandt, which is believed to be based on an anatomical specimen which could be seen at the time in Leiden's anatomical theatre. The drawing is of the skeleton of a horse being ridden by the skeleton of a man, who is holding a bone aloft in his right hand as though it were a weapon, while the left hand holds the reins.[6] Rembrandt's horse in *The Polish Rider*, Held argues, is literally just skin and bones: a skeleton over which the painter has stretched a skin. Might Kitaj, the *pictor doctus*, scholarly painter, have recognized this possible background to Rembrandt's picture? Given his iconographic training and the fact that with Michael Podro as his model he is putting an art historian into his picture, we can't be sure either way. The idea that beneath both Rembrandt's young warrior and his steed lurk two barely veiled skeletons fits well with the eerie voyage of a man travelling to see the murdered Jews.

If Kitaj was, on the other hand, not aware of this 'role model' behind Rembrandt's cavalry portrait, he must surely have recognized the deathly pale colour that unfailingly evokes the fourth horseman of the apocalypse, and the curious shape of the head – described by Held as 'exaggerated "dryness"'. Of course, this 'dryness' might not necessarily suggest a horse's cadaver or skeleton, but could be seen as a reference to a possible Arab origin of the horse, which presupposes, of course, that the painter of *The Polish Rider* was aware of this genetic characteristic, and therefore was familiar with Arabian horses or at least with pictures of them – which for a seventeenth-century Dutch painter cannot be taken for granted. 'Insofar as we really engage with a past work we must re-make it for ourselves,' wrote Michael Podro, referring to the 'fundamental indeterminacy which marks all our knowledge', which we encounter as soon as we try to determine the exact dividing line between what we – as interpreters – see in a picture, and what is actually present in it.[7]

THE HEN

By shifting from *miles Christianus* (Christian soldier) to *migrator hebraicus* (Jewish traveller), Kitaj's paraphrase gives rise to a number of other shifts: from young man to old, from warrior to scholar, from activity to reverie, from weapon to book. It is as though the painter – of whom his critics often complained that he was too literary, too intellectual, and who used to reply that some books have pictures and some pictures have books[8] – wanted to reveal the Jewish rider's hidden 'weapon'. Another detail stands out when we consider this change of key from Rembrandt to Kitaj. Again, it is a gesture: the raised and bent left leg, which brings the Jewish rider's extended foot to the epicentre of the painting. The stretched foot now forms a contrast to the curled hand, and if we draw a line through these poles, the diagonal line would extend out to the smoking chimney in the landscape outside. While the shape of the hand links back precisely to the inspiration in Rembrandt, the position of the leg is in direct contrast: while the Polish rider sits atop his horse in a manly riding position, Kitaj's train traveller is 'riding' side-saddle.

The reason may be purely practical: how else could the painter convey a riding posture in a train carriage? But with Kitaj, we can bet there is also a literary allusion at play here. 'The way a Jew mounts his horse,' Friedrich Nietzsche once commented, 'is quite incredible and gives the impression that the Jews have never been a chivalrous race.'[9] In contrast to this historical cultural condescension, Theodor Herzl in his 1902 novel *Altneuland* developed the idea of a virile young Jewish man, who rides like a Cossack or the American Indians, singing Hebrew songs all the while.[10] In fact, this debate about how virile or 'chivalrous' the Jews are or were, continually came back to the question of how well 'they' could ride. The historian John Hoberman has traced this discussion, equating the exclusion of Jews from the riding experience with their exclusion from the experience of nature more generally.[11] But even Hoberman cannot avoid noting the deep ambivalence within Judaism itself and its literature with regard to the phenomenon of the rider (and the representation of power in the figure of a rider).[12] Kitaj's *Jewish Rider*, who rides in his train carriage sitting side-saddle on the cushion, still seems to have the shadow of this ancient discourse looming over him.

The Jew who does not ride: an anathematized image that emerges even in the lightweight novels penned by Pyotr Nikolayevich Krasnov, the ataman of the Don Cossacks and a White general in the civil war, when he wasn't out clashing with the Reds or leading his Cossacks into senseless, bitter combat. The most prominent representative of this trope is Leon Trotsky, the founder and commander of the Red Army. Placing the Cossack general at the centre of a historical search for clues, Italian scholar Claudio Magris considers his depiction of

Trotsky. 'To judge by the bilious portrait which Krasnov sketches in his novel, Trotsky's worst fault would seem to be that he didn't know how to ride a horse properly, like all Jews, like all new men – those spiders, as Krasnov thought, spinning the web of mediations which in our world binds the individual.'[13]

The anthropology of the Cossacks followed simple laws. Man is by nature a horseman; atop his steed, he is in the image of God. The Cossack is born into the world a horseman, and everything he may lack before reaching complete manhood he learns from his horse. The Jew, however, never learns to ride, and therefore never fully becomes a man. He finds an uncertain status somewhere halfway between humans and animals. As a Cossack and ataman, Krasnov shared this way of thinking; as an author he drew inspiration from the literary sources of anti-Semitism. From Gogol and Dostoevsky to more westward-looking, 'enlightened' writers such as Turgenev and Chekhov (and others after them), there stretched a tradition that placed Jews somewhere in the animal kingdom: the Jew is defined according to 'an animalistic correlation' as writer Felix Philipp Ingold put it, 'and thereby denies him any metaphysical dimension, assigning him a monstrous . . . existence and sphere of experience.[14]

Between Gogol and Dostoevsky a type developed by which one could allegedly recognize a Jew. The cliché of the plucked chicken, pale, scrawny and fidgety, with fuzzy hair and beard: this was the hackneyed depiction of the Jewish anti-hero.[15] This pale, nervous little bird, the epitome of a lack of strength and courage, was introduced in the nineteenth century to replace the age-old stereotype of the 'Jewish swine'. Little had changed: Jews were depicted as animals, just with different features.

Until the end of the nineteenth century, the non-assimilated Jews in Russia occupied a 'position midway between a monkey and a dog' writes Ingold, and many testimonies show they were treated not merely *like* animals, but as though they actually *were* animals. It is to Gogol's animal comparisons and their influence on Russian literature that we can attribute the fact that 'in Russia, there was barely a single . . . positive image of the Jewish people until the time of the great pogroms and the anti-Jewish laws, regulations and court cases of 1880'.[16] Turgenev finally rounds off the animal comparison when, in *Sketches from a Hunter's Album,* he contrasts a thoroughbred, noble and intelligent horse called Malek Adel – 'a marvel, no ordinary horse' – with the wretchedness of the gaunt, miserable and hysterical Jew Moshel Leiba: the humiliation and bestialization of the Jewish man is compared to the elevation and humanization of the horse.[17]

Malek Adel, whose name historically was Saphadin, the brother of Saladin, is an unusually noble animal, a kind of *über-beast* whose beauty and perfection requires admiration, even worship. Ordinary animals, on the other hand, are as neglected and abused as the Jews – and vice versa. As Jewish philosopher Michael Landmann explains, for Jews this engenders the feeling of a kind of common destiny: 'Just as people see animals as outsiders and mistreat and kill them without any qualms, when and where they please, they do the same with the Jews: with contempt . . . Animal and Jew are comrades in misfortune. This is why the Jew is doubly sensitive to the suffering of animals. He feels their suffering like his own . . . What looks like ethics is only the tip of an iceberg of mystery: the mystification of what is felt inside.'[18]

RED HORSEMAN

Mea Shearim is the name of a district west of Old Jerusalem, inhabited exclusively by ultra-Orthodox Jews. It is reminiscent of the Eastern European *shtetl* and sounds like it, too, with its residents often speaking Yiddish. The first time I wandered around it in the evening, I felt as if I had drifted into a bygone world, which seemed all the more alien and forbidden to me, belonging as I do to the nation that like no other bears the blame for the disappearance of this world. It was only at the end of the main street, from which the district inherits its name, that I was brought back to the present with a bump, or rather it was something that seemed more modern to me anyway. I was standing in front of a living statue. Before me loomed the largest equestrian monument I had ever seen. But this statue moved; from time to time, the horse nodded his head, the metal on his bridle clinking.

In the previous weeks, there had been some unrest in Mea

Shearim, linked to the refusal by members of the Orthodox community to fulfil their civic duties. No longer stopping at passive resistance as in the past, they had begun to forcibly restrain young men from their community who had defiantly signed up to join the army. Since then, this mounted policeman had been standing guard at the end of the road, on the lawn in front of the Ministry of Education: a large, heavily armed man on an enormous horse, watching out for the smallest sign of restlessness. As this centaur stood there in the half-light of dusk, he seemed to represent more than an ordinary security measure. He was a philosophical statement, a metaphysical proposition.There must have been a historically minded philosopher somewhere in the Jerusalem police department who thought up this antagonism of absolute tropes: the pure type of religious wrath, ready to surge at any time, and in opposition, the pure type of secular power, ready to strike at any time.

The question of why the police officer should be mounted continued to puzzle me, however, and it was a while before I found a solution that seemed plausible. Jakob Hessing, a Jerusalem-based academic, showed me the historical constellation behind it. 'The man on the horse', he replied without hesitation, 'represents the Cossack. The Jews in Mea Shearim see a man on horseback watching them or perhaps threatening them, and without realizing it they react like their ancestors in the *shtetl* when they saw the Cossacks at the gates. Even if their children and grandchildren cannot say what it is they fear – there is something in them, you might call it the collective memory, which feels a sense of alarm at the sight of the Cossack guard.'

As speculative as it was, Hessing's response was backed up by history. If we consider the history of Eastern European Jewry, we see a steady stream of pogroms. Starting in the mid-seventeenth century, it swelled up towards the end of the nineteenth century (with major pogroms in 1881–4 and 1903–6), before finally coming to a climax with the catastrophes of the Russian Civil War, the Polish-Russian War, and the Nazi extermination camps and the *Sonderkommando* units. The Cossacks played only a peripheral role in the latter crimes against the Jews by Germany, insofar as some of them fought alongside the Wehrmacht against Russian partisans. But in almost all previous acts of mass violence against the Jewish population of

Berlin in late summer 1946: the trees of the Tiergarten were cut down and replaced with fields of cabbages. Russian tanks are parked in front of the ruins of the Reichstag. *Amazon on Horseback*, Louis Tuaillon, 1895.

The Jewish Rider: art historian Michael Podro sits for a portrait by R. B. Kitaj, London, 1984.

Galicia (a historical region, parts of which are now in Poland and Ukraine), the Cossack troops played a leading role. Even historians minded to be sympathetic towards them do not downplay the scale of the Cossacks' part in anti-Semitic violence, which recurred constantly from the time in 1648 that Bogdan Khmelnitsky went murdering and pillaging through the Jewish villages and neighbourhoods of Ukraine.[19]

As noted in one recent study of anti-Semitism at the time of the Russian Revolution, their conduct meant the Cossacks were 'firmly integrated within the dominant anti-Semitic ideology of tsarism'.[20] Their conduct did not change in the slightest during the Revolution and the subsequent civil war. It was not only under White commanders such as Anton Denikin that the Cossacks regularly spearheaded the increasingly brutal, systemic violence against the Jewish people.[21] Even when they entered the service of the Bolsheviks, they carried on – the moment they were left to their own devices – hunting out Jews, murdering and looting. 'Like no other unit of the Red Army, Budyonny's Cavalry, made up largely of Cossacks who had defected to the Red Army, was known for its anti-Semitism and propensity for carrying out anti-Jewish pogroms.'[22]

The young Jew who set off in midsummer 1920, at the peak of the Russo-Polish war, riding with the Cossacks in Budyonny's Red Cavalry, had to be on his guard. Besides coming from the deep South, the Crimean city of Odessa in his case, he had nothing in common with his new comrades. A bespectacled writer and intellectual who did not ride well and was interested in neither looting nor killing: the contrast to the rough riders of the *Konarmia* could hardly be greater. As a war correspondent, Isaac Babel enjoyed a certain amount of freedom and was able to watch the commanders, Budyonny and Voroshilov, from close quarters, but he had to take constant care not to fall between the lines that opened up behind the actual front lines – the zones of hatred where there was the constant threat of looting and pogroms. No one could wax more lyrically than Babel about the virtues of Soviet power, no one could rekindle extinguished hopes for better times like him, but was he himself truly convinced by his own words?

Babel sees what he sees, and in his diary – the basis for his elaborately detailed stories, published as *Red Cavalry* – he holds firmly to what he believes: 'We are the vanguard, but of what? The population await their saviours, the Jews look for liberation – and in ride the Kuban Cossacks.'[23] Previously they rode with the Whites, now they had sworn allegiance to the Soviets, but in reality they were waging their own war on their own terms. The atamans, their leaders, writes Babel, acquired machine guns and joined up with the Red Army. That's as far as the heroic epic goes. The reality is much more profane: 'This isn't a Marxist revolution, it's a Cossack rebellion, out to win all and lose nothing.'[24] This is to be understood in material or materialistic terms: 'our army is out to line its pockets, this isn't a revolution, it's a rebellion of Cossack wild men.'[25]

What was it that motivated Babel to sign up to go to the front? The hope of fame? It certainly came – practically overnight – in the wake of the publication of *Red Cavalry* in 1924. Was it an adventurous streak? A desperate attempt to prove his virility? The senselessness of the violence he witnessed left no room for heroic posturing. Did he want to see the war up close, to understand it warts and all? He certainly had an eyeful. Isaac Babel, propagandist for the Red Army, became the Thucydides of the last European cavalry war. His writings form the bulk of the very few accounts we have of these most obscure campaigns of the twentieth century. Often his observations are no longer than two lines: 'The village, deserted, a light at HQ, Jewish detainees. Budyonny's men bring communism, a woman weeps.'[26]

Day after day, Babel, the Jew riding with the cavalry, has to watch as other Jews are humiliated, raped, robbed and murdered. And what of it? Perhaps a soldier gets the whip for stealing from a comrade; perhaps a brigade will be punished for disobeying orders and shooting prisoners. But who is going to trouble themselves about a little pogrom here and there? Who cares about a handful of dead Jews, two dozen women raped, a crowd of howling and bleeding children? Burning synagogues, looted houses – all that is the daily stuff of war. Only a madman like Babel takes any notice. Yet even he tarries with those trampled and crushed by history no longer than necessary. The war goes on, and somehow everything returns to how it was before: '. . . night, Cossacks, all just as it was when the Temple was destroyed. I go out to sleep in the yard, stinking and damp.'[27]

Babel rides, though badly. As far as the Cossacks are concerned he's a coward: he has to kill a goose in front of them before they're

even halfway convinced of his manliness. The fact that he is still able
to sympathize with them is not a feeling based on identification with
the aggressor of his people. Babel does not hide how raw, greedy and
violent the Cossacks are. But he also sees what they are not: they are
not bureaucrats, ideologists or strategists. They are wild riders, primitive and unrestrained, a 'hot' and unpredictable culture; the
revolution ought not to be left in their hands.[28] And they ought not to
be left in the hands of the revolution: the terror of Galicia now, but
tomorrow they will be devoured by the war and the next day they
will be swallowed up by the post-war reality, the plan, the state, the
party; then they too will be the victims, downtrodden like those they
massacre now. People like the Cossacks are not made to be leaders on
the world stage, they lack the cold, calculating instinct for power:
'Splendid comradeship, solidarity, love of horses, a Cossack's horse
occupies a quarter of his day, endless bartering, arguments. The role
and life of the horse.'[29]

'I understand now,' Babel wrote in August 1920, just before the
tide turned in the Russian civil war, 'what a horse means to a Cossack or cavalryman.' He saw horsemen who had lost their horses
wandering in a daze as bereft infantrymen along the dusty roads in
the blazing heat: 'Unhorsed riders on hot, dusty roads, carrying their
saddles, sleeping like the dead men on other people's wagons, rotting
horses everywhere, the talk is all about horses . . . horses are martyrs,
horses are long-suffering.' And later, 'The horse is everything. Their
names – Stepan, Misha, Little Brother, Old Girl. The horse is his
saviour – the Cossack is aware of that every minute of the day, but
can nonetheless thrash it like mad.'[30]

Far from wanting to discover the noble savage in the Cossack,
Babel finds a level on which Cossacks, Jews and horses all come
together. It is the realm of the animal, the realm inhabited by those
who are destined to die, sooner or later, probably very soon. But perhaps everyone and every horse he encounters in this hot Galician
summer are not merely *morituri* – doomed to die – but are in fact
already long dead, or shot, slain; deceased on leave. 'Must not forget
Brody and those pitiful figures – neither the barbers nor the Jews, like
visitors from the other world, nor the Cossacks on the streets.'[31] History repeats itself, and the historian, well versed in deciphering the

signature of the future in the past, sees figures of the past emerging from the future. 'The Jewish cemetery outside Malin,' Babel writes in July 1920, 'hundreds of years old, gravestones have toppled over, almost the same shape, oval at the top, the cemetery is overgrown with grass, it has seen Khmelnitsky, now Budyonny, unfortunate Jewish population, everything repeats itself, now that whole story – Poles, Cossacks, Jews – is repeating itself with stunning exactitude, the only new element is communism.'[32]

Eleven decades after Paris had feted the victorious Cossacks in 1814, when in reality the French were frightened to death of them, the same city received many Cossacks after their anarchic cavalry adventure of the Civil War came to a bitter end. While Budyonny would rise swiftly through the Soviet nomenclature and survive all the purges, for those who were late to change sides in 1919–20, Russia and the old motherland on the rivers Don and Dnieper were cut off forever. Impoverished Cossack noblemen had to scrape a living working as doormen in Paris nightclubs or as taxi drivers, if they did not join a circus troupe and continue to live the nomadic life.[33]

R. B. Kitaj, the painter who in 1984 began painting *The Jewish Rider*, his paraphrase of Rembrandt's *The Polish Rider*, had twenty-two years earlier produced a painting that alluded to the image of the riders, horses and Jews of Galicia. It is considered one of the key works of the then emerging London School and is now owned by the Tate Gallery. Its title is *Isaac Babel Riding with Budyonny*.

In the late 1930s, Isaac Babel was targeted by the Soviet secret police, the NKVD. The fact that he could just about ride a horse saved his life a couple of times in 1920; it couldn't help him now. On 27 January 1940, Babel was shot at Butyrka prison in Moscow. This is also a date to remember when we recount the many points in time that marked the end of the age of the horse.

The first decade of the twentieth century did, however, bring one Jewish rider to prominence. She, a young Russian Communist, came to Palestine for the first time in 1904. From 1907, she was involved with Bar-Giora, a Jewish self-defence group led by Israel Shochat, her future husband. The historian Tom Segev describes this militant woman as 'the mother of the kibbutz movement'. 'A fanatical young woman who rode through the hills of Galilee in Arabian robes. Her

Jews don't ride: *Benjamin Disraeli as a child*, George Henry Harlow, 1808.

Jews *do* ride: Hashomer, Jewish militia in Galilee, *c.*1909.

name was Manya Wilbuschewitz . . . In Palestine she was one of the co-founders of a rural community, an early form of the kibbutz, and one of the first members of the Hashomer ("Watchman") militia, the forerunner of the Israel Defence Forces.'[34] Even the male members of the new security force, founded in April 1909, did not think of abandoning their Arab-style robes. Once they had managed to raise enough money to arm themselves and to acquire horses, the young Jews formed a colourful cavalry inspired by Bedouin, Druze, Circassian and even Cossack influences. For a moment it looked as though Theodor Herzl's dream of strong, riding and singing Jews had come true: the terrifying spectre of the Cossacks was momentarily chased away.

Ten years later, in 1920, Hashomer was superseded by the better organized and better armed Haganah, the next intermediate step towards the army of the state of Israel, founded in 1948. The strong man behind this new paramilitary organization was Vladimir (Ze'ev) Jabotinsky, who, together with Joseph Trumpeldor, founded the Jewish Legion during the Second World War. Like Babel, fourteen years his junior, Jabotinsky also came from Odessa, where his widowed mother ran a stationery shop. It may well have been in this store that the young Isaac Babel bought his first pencils when he started to write.

PART II

A Phantom of the Library
KNOWLEDGE

It would have been the summit of good
fortune, if the lad had got the horses ready
for his master in Heßstraße – the bay that
Bob had taken a shine to and the chestnut.
They would have been standing there, with
their long necks and their snaffle bits, flicking
their tails, clattering gently as they lowered
their hindquarters. It would be like a Munich
child seeing the world like a painting that was
brought to life, a vision from an otherworldly
world, like the horses Albrecht Adam from
Nördlingen painted: *An Evening's Rest After
the Battle, Russia, 1812*

Hermann Heimpel, 'The Half Violin'

At some point in every historian's professional life, he feels that Rousseauian temptation. He finds a new source, poses an original question and starts to dream that he might be the first to have reached some unchartered territory, a new South Pole of historical inquiry. Might he have stumbled upon an *as yet unexplored subject*? It was a thought that crossed my mind too, in the early days of my research into the horse as the focus of a possible history. For a moment, I too dreamed I held something like an *objet brut* in my hand, a crude mineral, not yet laboured with interpretations. Over time, I could not help realizing that the opposite was the case: horses had more meanings than bones. Since the time of Xenophon,[1] horse experts of every kind – whether they be connoisseurs, handlers, breeders, farriers or cavalrymen – have never tired of sharing their equine knowledge in lengthy tracts with a readership which appears at any time in history to have been broad and extensive. The result is we see not only long diachronic investigations into the traditions of horse-related knowledge, but also the migration of this practical and theoretical knowledge amongst the most diverse cultures and environments.

This book cannot contain every thread of research into hippological knowledge throughout history from Plato to NATO, or every trail it has followed from the ancient Orient to the stables of modern-day Asil breeders. To capture it all would far exceed the scope of this book and the chronological period of interest. My focus is to try to understand and describe how the end of the equestrian age played out: how it was that humans and horses went their separate ways and yet, at the same time, remained so interconnected in the literary, metaphorical and imaginary realms. But to understand how the fringes originated, we have to look into the fabric of the rug. To make sense of the process of man and horse's separation, we need to go back and examine their coexistence. This includes looking at the extent and quality of knowledge resulting from man's work with horses. We need to pinpoint the locations where this knowledge was traded, identify the agents and reconstruct the negotiations carried out between them. In other words, we need to delve deeper into the history of equine knowledge, picking up the thread an entire century earlier.

This knowledge of horses, which has grown continuously since the beginning of the modern era, saw a particular boom from the second half of the eighteenth century. As the study of horses flourished, it found new markets and new media: magazines, almanacs, engravings, paintings and a deluge of literature which flooded the continent. England became the laboratory for racing and breeding, while France witnessed the birth of the veterinary clinic. The other horse cultures of Europe also picked up speed and, following these two guiding stars, they began to establish schools and clinics, to open racecourses and to restructure stud farms and cavalries. If it was already seen as a science, or a scholarly subject, the study of horses in the eighteenth century did not in any way correspond to today's academic standards. Structured according to the practical needs of the *connoisseur*, this 'science' offered advice and instruction, training and warnings. But it remained a science of passionate *amateurs*. The know-how of the aficionado gradually morphed into the beau monde of the breeders and buyers, racehorse owners and the bourgeois parvenus who adopted a cavalier perspective and managed to leap over class barriers. A knowledge of horses was a tangible skill possessed by farriers and riding instructors, dealers and owners, including practical guidance about feeding, stabling and doctoring, including what to do when the mare is in heat but the stallion is inexperienced, plus any other complications of these *liaisons dangereuses*. It could also take the form of artistic proficiency, training the hand and eye of the artist seeking success as a painter of sport and animal portraits. Not unlike the link that developed between the visual arts and human medicine, there was also a lively give and take between the veterinary and the art worlds: the dissecting table and the drawing board were never far apart. And the windows had a shared view onto the racetrack.

The nineteenth century built on the practical traditions of animal husbandry and breeding, horsemanship and dressage, and saw the publication of classic texts such as Count Georg von Lehndorff's *Handbook for Horse Breeders*.[2] As veterinary surgeons gradually split away from the smithy, the traditional setting for horse-doctoring, finding a new home in veterinary colleges and clinics,[3] the nineteenth century's zeal for knowledge opened up new conundrums, giving rise to new research styles and techniques that were no longer limited to the human sciences. The horse – in the early days of mechanization still man's most important companion economically, militarily and socially – became the prominent subject of a new kind of positivist research.[4] In studies and laboratories, the horse became the focus of research into linguistics, economics, iconography, geography and intelligence. The results of these empirical and experimental studies were of varying quality. Some had political implications, while others appear curiously idiosyncratic, and not just from a modern perspective. But besides the political and cultural relevance, all were also of significance militarily.

Knowledge is not a static entity – on the contrary. Indeed, it is a pleonasm when we speak of *migrating knowledge*. The question is not *whether*, but *how* knowledge travels. What material form does it take, which social groups control its dissemination, and which institutions prevent its disappearance? The following chapters will delve deeper into what we explored in the previous chapters: besides looking at the *media* of the age (books, sculpture, painting, graphics, photographs, technical objects, lists and pedigree records), we will explore the *places and institutions* (the stud farm, racecourse, clinic, artist's studio and publishing house), the *social communities* (farmers, handlers, anatomists, blacksmiths, military men, researchers, authors and conmen), and finally the *knowledge-related practices* (selection, breeding, medical care, training, collecting, anatomy, drawing and taxidermy).

Every artefact of horse history, seen in this light, contains a narrative of migrating knowledge. Each carriage tells of the landscape it was originally associated with, of the craftsmen who for generations had harnessed knowledge of different woods and metals, of the quality of the draught animals and the challenges of the roads, of traders who took into account their customers' ever-changing tastes. Every saddle speaks of riding positions and postures, of social hierarchies and codes of power, of hunting techniques and the tactics of war. Like Tolstoy's *Kholstomer: The Story of a Horse*, every animal tells the tale of its birth and happy youth, the distinction of its stables and the social classes it has passed through, of the misfortunes it has survived and the plight of old age. Every whip tells the story of pain endured, every sword the vicissitudes of a military campaign, every stirrup the epic rise and fall of the feudal world.

On these migratory trails of knowledge, occasionally it is historical accident that seizes the reins, prompting the formation of allegorical constellations: after the death of the painter Peter Paul Rubens in 1640, for example, an exiled English general rented his residence in Antwerp.[5] It was here that William Cavendish, Earl and later Duke of Newcastle, a supporter of the defeated Royalists in the Civil War, pursued his passion for breeding and training horses. In the grounds where until recently Rubens had created his masterpieces, Cavendish now set up a riding academy where he developed his new English school of dressage, which quickly made him famous throughout Europe and helped sales of his work on horsemanship, *La Méthode et Invention nouvelle de Dresser les Chevaux* (first published in French in 1657). It would run to ten editions in English, French and German over the next hundred years, a success which owed some debt to the dynamic illustrations by Abraham van Diepenbeeck, a former pupil of Rubens. At first glance, the transformation of Rubens's former home and studio into Cavendish's riding school may seem like a profanity, whereas in fact it was simply one Baroque art form being replaced by another: a ballet danced by beautiful horses.[6]

Blood and Speed

FALL FROM THE CAROUSEL

In the late nineteenth century, between 1896 and 1898, Edgar Degas was working on a painting which represented an unusual departure from his previous work (Plate 11). Its subject is a riding accident. A fallen rider lies on his back on the grass, while a horse – possibly his? – gallops past or jumps over him. Four-fifths of the canvas is filled with green grass, one fifth is sky. Beyond that there is nothing to see: no excited audience, no panicked running about, no furious gestures. The picture is strangely still and quiet in comparison with the dramatic events it portrays. The title is *Jockey blessé* (*The Injured Jockey*), but there is nothing to see that indicates an injury. The rider's right leg seems to have slipped out of his boot, the left leg is bent and could suggest a fracture, but it is not obvious. It is the flat, immobile position of the man which does not bode well: the injured jockey could be dying or indeed already dead. The horse – a bay thoroughbred whose head shape betrays its Arabian extraction – thunders past, empty saddle on its back, front and hind legs outstretched like a wooden horse on a fairground carousel, tail flowing behind and mane braids standing on end. All these movements seem frozen in time, captured quickly with a high shutter speed; the painter makes no attempt to make the scene dynamic. The viewer is not given any explanation of the causality nor any narrative complement that might hint at the before and after.

If we want to find out what is concealed within the taciturn image, there are three different archives we might consult: the painter's records, those of the events of the time, and the iconographic context.

In the first of the three, we find an early horse-racing tableau by the painter, a *Scène de steeple-chase*, whose subtitle is *The Fallen Jockey*. Degas submitted the painting to the Salon of 1866.[7] It shows a racing accident, a fallen jockey who is lying on the ground, with a riderless horse passing by, while two other jockeys ride by, unmoved. Thirty years later, the mature Degas takes up the scene again, reducing the formula to the fallen man and the riderless horse (Plate 11). Accidents on the racetrack are not uncommon and if, like Degas, you spend days and weeks at the track, you've got a good chance of witnessing such an event. With the help of the newspapers of the time (the archive of the events), it would be possible, with some meticulous research, to track down the details of the accident the painter observed – whether the horse bolted, who the injured jockey was, and what became of him.

It becomes more complicated in the third dimension: the archive of iconography. The title seems to allude to a picture by Géricault from 1814 – a good seventy years earlier – which at the time was assumed to refer to the defeat of the French armies in the Campagne de France. But the *Cuirassier blessé, quittant le feu*, who also has no visible external injury, has very little in common with Degas's injured jockey, except for his diagonal orientation across the composition of the picture – unless we wished to see in the boots of the jockey, his bright trousers and his bulky cuirass-like jersey an allusion to the uniform of the cavalry. Despite his invisible injury, Géricault's cavalryman remains a son of Mars, summoning his remaining strength to rein in his horse's impetuosity, while Degas's jockey resembles a carelessly knocked-over chess piece or an abandoned toy lying wearily on the ground. And while Géricault's hero still grips his weapon in his hand, Degas's jockey is stripped of all accessories – there's not even a lost whip to be seen.

However, there is one more card we can draw from the archives, and that's the image of possibly the most prominent victim of a horse-related accident: Saul on the road to Damascus, who is resurrected as Paul the Apostle as a result of his fall. Let us consider the perspective that Parmigianino put on the event in *The Conversion of Saul*. Again we see the fallen rider (albeit uninjured) in front of or beneath the horse, which rises up over him, still wearing the bridle. But the tone of the horse, the majestic white, the colour of the light that breaks through the clouds behind him, the ermine blanket and beneath it the noble animal form with the full-bodied rump, suggesting an official rather than sporting function, but especially his stance, rearing up in the levade – all this locates the horse within the occidental iconography of sovereignty. Like Saul – the fallen nobleman, the Roman knight, whose sword lies beneath his leg – the horse at this moment undergoes a resurrection as the docile mount of a *miles Christianus*, a Christian soldier. It is not a fall that Parmigianino depicts, but rather a new, spiritual elevation. Degas's injured jockey is no fallen Saul on the road to Damascus. The jockey lies between the legs of his horse as though within the brackets of a mathematical equation. Degas painted a green chalkboard on which he wrote the equation of modern racing. In front of the brackets is *speed* and within the brackets are *beauty and death*.

Everyone imagines that they know where Degas most loved to spend his time, where he drew his inspiration and where he encountered the personalities that emerged as ideas and colours in his paintings and pastels: in the ballet studio. Nobody thinks of the racecourse, and yet Degas admired the flanks of the racehorses and the jockeys' colourful jerseys almost as much as the slender legs of the dancers and their rosy tutus. He was as thrilled by thoroughbred racing in Boulogne as by the *contretemps* and *glissades* of the slender ballerinas; the dance hall and the racecourse both provided his muse. Had he lived two centuries earlier, a subject of the 'Sun King' and not a citizen of the Third Republic, he would have been able to indulge both pleasures at the same location: in the seventeenth and well into the eighteenth century, the dance hall and indoor riding arena were largely identical.[8] The famous riding teachers from Antoine de Pluvinel (1623) to François de la Guérinière (1733) taught riding, or rather the exemplary movement of rider and horse, as an advanced form of court dance, where the aim was to replicate the elegance and grace of the dancers. The most important dance step of the unequal pair was the levade, where the horse rests its weight on its hind legs while the rider sits 'perpendicular to the ground, forming a softly and gently closing cross' with the horse's body.[9] Together, rider and horse adopted the classic pose of sovereignty, an age-old obsession of painters and sculptors and an integral part of the Western repertoire of the

Jewish riders: Meir Dizengoff, the mayor of Tel Aviv (on the right), and Avraham Shapira riding in the Purim Parade in Tel Aviv, 1934.

THE REPOSITORY·
OR TATTERD-SALE·

A catwalk for horses: *The Repository, or, Tatter'd-sale*, Mary Darly, 1777.

iconography of secular rule. During the eighteenth century, the schools of dance and riding would go their separate ways. The riding school came into the hands of the military before it became the domain of racing trainers. It was only on the ballet stage that the *Ancien Régime* lived on with its strict forms – the ritual of pirouettes, leaps and airs above the ground and the poised geometry of bodies hovering beyond gravity.[10]

As at the ballet, from which it had been separated for more than a century, the racecourse of the *fin de siècle* also conveyed the notion of a possible and sometimes tangible victory over gravity. The speed of the animals and the low weight of their riders produced the impression of levitation without the levade; the appearance was no longer of a bird in flight, but of an arrow zipping from the bowstring. At the moment of a fall, the two bodies, combined as one vector during flight, are broken up into their constituent parts, and gravity, momentarily overcome, now reels these parts back in. This is the moment that Degas captures in his painting. Perhaps this is his real subject: the jockey does not lie on the ground, but appears to levitate, frozen in the falling motion, an endless free fall propelled by his returning weight, while the horse galloping on without its rider continues to convey the sense of weightlessness.

BORN UNDER A SOLAR ECLIPSE

The history of English horse racing is, like the rise of the Suffolk market town of Newmarket, closely linked to the rule of the Stuarts. As in other European countries – we might think of the *Palio* of Siena – there had been horse racing in England before the seventeenth century, run at a local level or organized by individual members of the landed gentry. But with Newmarket and the Stuarts, a new dynamic came into play.[11] The first race in this still relatively insignificant location took place in 1622. James I of England, son of Mary, Queen of Scots, had discovered the small village in 1605, identifying its broad heath as the perfect ground for racing. Over the next few years he developed it into his personal estate for hunting and sport.[12] Under his son, Charles I, the sleepy hamlet was promoted to 'a kind of second capital of the kingdom',[13] where from 1627 regular spring and autumn races took place. However, the crucial phase of racing as a sport funded and promoted by kings only really began in 1660, when after years of the Puritan republic, which took a hostile attitude to sport, the monarchy was restored and Charles II returned from French exile. In 1671 King Charles II, a great lover of speed,[14] himself won the race for the Town Plate, which he had established five years previously. In the same year, the world's first training stable was established at Palace House. The years after his death (1685) saw the rise of English racehorse breeding, where the three famous Arabian foundation stallions played their role in founding a dynasty: Byerley Turk (imported in 1687), Darley Arabian (1704) and Godolphin Arabian (1729) became the founders of the three main lines of Arab blood in English breeding.[15] *Thoroughbreds* or *blood horses* were the offspring of the deliberate combination of the oriental and English lines – the 'hot-blooded' horses whose proven quality on the racetrack was much sought after.

The close association of the English monarchy with breeding and racing did not end with the Stuarts. As historical accident would have it, the news of the death of Queen Anne in August 1714 spread just as the country's nobility were congregated at York racecourse. It was at this very location that the decision was taken for the crown to be passed to the Hanoverians. The monarchs who came to the throne as a result of this decision, from George I onwards to Queen Victoria, carried on the country's hippophile and racetrack traditions with vigour, making England the world power of thoroughbred racing. When Daniel Defoe travelled through the British Isles in 1720, he saw in Newmarket an established racing industry and 'a great concourse of the nobility and gentry, as well from London as from all parts of England'.[16]

According to official statements, when oriental horses were imported – initially individual stallions, but later also groups of mares (such as the *royal mares* in the first decades of the seventeenth century) – to be crossed with examples of indigenous breeds, it was with the intention of improving the genetic characteristics of native horse breeds in general. In fact, it was primarily about speed. The aim of breeding was a fast horse, one that won races. It was not only a certain landowning and animal-breeding section of the English nobility that identified with this goal; it was a project that had the backing of the English Crown. From the seventeenth century, the English monarchy was a kingdom of speed.

The appeal of horse racing, writes a historian of our day, lay 'not only in the fact that nowhere else were such high speeds achieved, but also in its symbolic value as the "sport of kings" '.[17] English monarchs raced (occasionally winning) and in the records of the racing calendars, which appeared regularly from 1727, they were listed as racehorse stable proprietors, horse owners, breeders and employers of jockeys. They also belonged to the Jockey Club, founded in 1750, in London initially but based since 1752 at Newmarket. The club, founded to organize races and regulate betting debts among its members, also gained in authority as it undertook to establish rules for competitions and to implement them nationwide.[18] Started by the royal family, its membership included broad swathes of the nobility and went through a process of secularization and bourgeoisification, though this was not recognized by its members. The Jockey Club, writes historian Otto Brunner, 'was not only an organizer of events, it was also the "social" hub of the nobility. Its members did not appear to be aware of the extent to which they were functioning in a typically "bourgeois" social structure.'[19]

Procuring Arabian horses, or rather oriental breeds, which also included Turks and Berbers, was no easy matter in the seventeenth and well into the eighteenth century; on the contrary, it was a costly and time-consuming, not to mention dangerous, enterprise. The prestige that the possession of such horses brought with it, and which could be further increased by success in racing and breeding, also came at a social price. The nobility saw itself as reliant on a class of indispensable professionals – buyers, trainers, jockeys, handlers and grooms – mostly recruited from the rural population and who advised them and supported them in many ways. Besides the civil service, diplomatic service, the military and the law, a new, modern type of professional expert now emerged on the stud farm and racetrack. At the same time, an unexpected rival to the nobility arose in the competition for social glitz, fame and survival in the memory of posterity: this rival took the form of the celebrity racehorse, whose name as a race-winner or sire (or mare) was recorded in the annals of the racing calendar and studbooks. In fact, eighteenth-century England experienced a second birth of the celebrity cult: alongside the famous painters from Rubens to Reynolds and the acclaimed actor David Garrick, there was the celebrated racehorse Eclipse (1764–89), born during the solar eclipse in the year 1764 and undefeated in all his races. His offspring won more than 850 races and his skeleton can be seen to this day in the National Horseracing Museum in Newmarket.[20]

SPORT AND SUSPENSE

If we are to describe the route to the *leisure class*, which the hereditary nobility shared with representatives of the moneyed aristocracy and the bourgeoisie, we should not overlook the third economic aspect of the racecourse alongside the auction of thoroughbreds and the prize money from the race: that third pillar is betting. Since the early modern period, the betting industry had been a shadow that followed every kind of sport that the nobility showed an interest in – above all, horse racing.[21] The high stakes that were placed at the racecourse were another aspect of conspicuous consumption, as described by Thorstein Veblen.[22] Horse racing and betting grew up side by side, carrying each other along, while Britain's more open social structure compared to the Continent played a major role. Since the racecourses were opened up to the middle and lower classes, betting even allowed spectators who could not have their own horse to participate in the gentleman's sport. One commentator towards the end of the nineteenth century described the betting trade as a 'fertilizer' which promoted the staggering growth of horse racing and racehorse breeding.[23]

Moreover, betting on horses, as Max Weber has suggested, was no game of chance like roulette. It was a thrill with a significantly higher proportion of rationality: 'A wager on English sports was seen as one . . . where you could make an informed and reasoned judgement about the probability of the outcome.'[24] You had to weigh up the previous successes of the horses at the starting line against certain other factors: their weight, the jockey's experience, the length and nature of the track. A calculated bet based on these factors and dis-counting uncertainties (a fall, lameness, etc.) was comparable to a capital investment which was never completely without risk. 'As a rational . . . "business", the sporting bet displayed structural similari-ties with the stock exchange and other speculative transactions.'[25] Again and again, cultural anthropologists and sociologists have pointed out that betting on sporting events came to replace the bloody battles and games of earlier times, making sport compatible with the civil codes of modern working life. The horse race – the most sublime form of *agon* involving animals – combined with a speculative financial profit, gave *Fortuna* her contemporary face.

During the seventeenth century in England, the deer hunt gave way to fox hunting as a major aristocratic pursuit. The element of physical force, even cruelty, which was clearly present in deer hunting and which was captured in courtly painting, remained with fox hunting, but was pushed to the background vis-à-vis the pleasure in the dur-ation and speed of the hunt: the agile, persistent and cunning fox was considered a guaranteed 'good sport'.[26] Strict rules for hunters and hounds and self-imposed restrictions allowed new goals to be iso-lated: 'the beautiful race, the suspense, the excitement'.[27] This process of sublimation reached its civilizing ideal form and its historical end-point in horse racing: the element of physical force is completely eliminated and replaced with the abstract form of pure speed. In greyhound racing, the pack rushes after the skin of a hare; in horse racing, nothing and no one is hunted, only the shadows of time.

In the century between the death of Charles II in 1685 and the establishment of five 'classic races' in England,[28] from the St Leger to the Derby in around 1780, the monarchy underwent a curious and momentous shift in coordinates from the vertical axis of transcen-dental sovereignty to the horizontal axis of pure speed. In the new poetics of the racetrack, an art form indifferent to class distinctions, there emerged an alliance of beauty, speed and danger. The bright colours, stripes and checks on the jockeys' jerseys and caps – a system introduced by the Jockey Club – represented a return of heraldry as a semiotic construct for identifying the otherwise indiscernible partici-pants.[29] Whereas in the medieval tournament, the colours, patterns and animal imagery of the coat of arms made it possible to distinguish

who was hiding beneath the armour and helmet, so the modern heraldry of the racecourse made it possible to identify the riders blurred
by the speed of their motion.

The English Puritans did not look kindly on horse racing, as was
the case with all sports associated with betting. That did not of course
prevent their simultaneous, decisive contribution to the renewal of the
cavalry in early modern Europe. Oliver Cromwell – who did not attain
the rank of 'Lieutenant-General of Horse' until the age of forty-three,
but was nevertheless considered the best rider in England[30] – was the
most fervent supporter after Gustavus Adolphus of Sweden of the cavalry as an offensive tool of war. In fact, a comparative study of the use
of horses in war and sport since the Renaissance could unearth some
surprising parallels. The increase in agility and discipline of cavalry
formations, the lightness and speed of the horses, the growing number
of cavalrymen, their differentiation as cuirassiers, dragoons, hussars,
Uhlans, etc., and their tactical use as an offensive weapon[31] corresponds with the promotion and regulation of horse racing, breeding
and betting by the restored English Crown and – from 1750 – the
Jockey Club. The club is, in a way, the civilian General Staff for the
light cavalry of the racecourse.

However, the development of the racing and breeding of racing-fit
thoroughbreds ran on separate tracks to the development of the modern cavalry. Despite all the functional overlaps – the appreciation of
the fast and relatively resilient thoroughbreds, the absolute importance of speed on the racetrack and its relative significance on the
battlefield, improvements to training, the codification of practical
knowledge – and despite all the personal connections, the racecourse
and the battlefield remained systemically distinct. Horse racing might
be a serious game, but unlike a military battle, it is not decided by
blood – at least not that of the rider, usually. Even if it ignored this
fundamental difference, the narrative 'superimposition' of a horse
race and a cavalry attack, which Claude Simon achieves in *The Flanders Road*, belongs to the great, telling depictions of the shared
history of humans and horses – 'as though advancing so to speak
from the depth of time, across the brilliant fields of battle where, in
the space of a sparkling afternoon, of a charge, of a gallop, kingdoms
and the hands of princesses were lost or won'.[32]

1. A raucous bunch – centaurs brawling on a snow-capped mountain:
Battle of the Centaurs, Arnold Böcklin, 1873.

2. Metropolitan beauty: *The Victoria*, Jean Béraud, *c.*1895.

3. The colours of the racetrack: the stands at Deauville.

4. A new tyre, please: *The Centaur at the Village Blacksmith's Shop*, Arnold Böcklin, 1888.

5. For dust thou art, and unto dust shalt thou return:
Ploughing, Giovanni Segantini, 1887–90.

6. *The Polish Rider*, Rembrandt van Rijn, 1655.

7. The artist makes a guest appearance: Frederic Remington (*left*) and
one of his horse portraits, in *Lucky Luke, the Painter*.
 'You're a really good painter. Did you come up with the idea yourself?'
 'No, I always paint from a model.'
 'What a talent! The horse is so life-like!'

8. Pegasus, western
style: rodeo rider
Dixie Lee Reger,
1943.

9. A car collides
with a herd of horses.
Anon., *Car crash*,
video on YouTube.

10. A train journey
with companions:
The Jewish Rider,
R. B. Kitaj, 1984.

11. *The Injured
Jockey*, Edgar Degas,
1896–8.

12. Young men, strong horses: *The Horse Fair*, Rosa Bonheur, 1852–5.

13. *Berbers Horse Races in Rome*, Théodore Géricault, 1817.

14. *The 1821 Derby at Epsom*, Théodore Géricault, 1821.

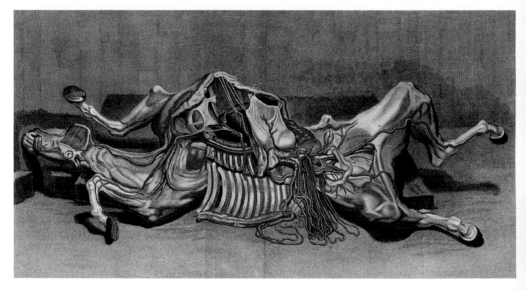

15. The surreal inner world: a plate from the book *Cours d'hippiatrique* by Philippe-Étienne Lafosse, 1772.

16. Riding the waves: *Neptune's Horses*, Walter Crane, 1892.

ZEUS XXIII

I had three godfathers and while two were quite inconspicuous, the third was a man made up entirely of unique qualities, one might even say peculiarities. A dandy and a reactionary, a lawsuit-monger and a womanizer, his moods changed as often as the weather, and – as is usual in that part of Westphalia – storm clouds predominated. Most important, at least in our context, was his foolish love of beautiful horses. Thoroughbreds were de rigueur in his stable, stallions above all. However, I also remember a wonderful grey mare named Attalea which he sold on to the House of Orange. It goes without saying that she had a high proportion of Arab blood. The last of his horses that I met personally before our paths parted forever was a dark bay stallion of immaculate purity of Arabian blood. In stature and temperament he was thoroughly Oriental; he had a family tree that you could trace back, with some goodwill, to the five favourite mares of Muhammad. It was only in the nomenclature that his owner and the apparently long string of predecessors had opted for a different cultural milieu. Over the entrance to his box – a classical pavilion à la Karl Friedrich Schinkel, architect, with an interior upholstered in leather like an English gentleman's club – hung a nameplate on which was inscribed: 'Zeus XXIII, *known as* Bubi'.

Like many members of local equestrian clubs, my godfather also joined a mounted troop of the *Sturmabteilung* (SA) after 1933. It was to his good political contacts that he owed the pleasure of being able to receive Prince August Wilhelm of Prussia, known as 'Auwi', at his summer house. The prince, then Obergruppenführer of the SA had, since joining the Nazi Party in 1929 (member number 24) made himself useful to the party by trawling for votes and new members among the exclusive upper circles of the aristocracy.[33] The same purpose was achieved by the Nazi policy towards equestrian sports in general – as a pseudo aristocratic honey trap to lure in the upper classes – and the SA Cavalry more specifically, even if this was less elitist than the comparable structures of the SS. The more sporty and comradely, one might even say warmer and more welcoming, cavalry of the SA attracted members from the nobility, but also young farmers, and can be seen as a successful tool for the broader integration and diversity of social classes in the new state.[34] Moreover, with instruments like this, the Nazi state managed to bring on side an entire nationwide network of clubs and organizations, together with their officials, equestrian professionals, sportsmen, horse lovers, breeders and veterinary surgeons.

Having developed over centuries, this network encompassed – besides the individuals – a wealth of institutions (associations, clubs, schools and stud farms) and types of knowledge, which were passed on in various ways. Germany had long been a nation of horses, and even if the economic and logistical importance of the horse had already declined sharply by 1930, when the Nazi organizations sought to inherit this culture, the horse was still unique and unrivalled by any other animal in terms of the values, knowledge and social distinction associated with it. Whoever wanted to win over the German people could not fail at the same time to draw in Germany's horse-loving population – even if the Führer himself did not actually ride or like to be photographed on horseback, unlike Mussolini (see p. 245). All political 'co-riders' were welcome on this hunt, be they the decadent scion of the aristocracy, a champion Olympic athlete or a reasonably successful writer. As is typical of Germany, the politicization of equestrian sports and horse breeding was achieved primarily through private clubs; and this also explains the (ultimately unsuccessful) attempt by the SA leadership to take them over en bloc.[35]

The development of equestrian sports clubs experienced a boost with the successful export of British horse racing to Germany in the early 1820s.[36] There is a reason why Germany's first thoroughbred racing event took place in August 1822 in Bad Doberan, a Mecklenburg spa town. After the lifting of the Continental blockade, successful London horse trader and bookmaker Richard Tattersall the younger travelled throughout northern Germany and sold the classic flat race – a competitive and spectator event suited to the English thoroughbred – to the horse-breeding landed gentry to the east of the Elbe. 'The races were intended to serve as a promotional event that would raise the sale price of the horses.'[37] Doberan was the prelude to an amazing success story. Racing spread through Germany

The Godolphin Arabian: when he still lived in obscurity, with only a cat (just out of the picture to the right) for a friend, George Stubbs, 1792.

The Amazon Queen: Elizabeth II riding Surprise on the morning of race day at Ascot, in the mid-1950s.

faster and earlier than any other European country also infected with British racing fever (France, Italy, Russia), taking root along with the associated clubs and racetracks (Berlin, 1829; Wrocław (Breslau), 1833; Hamburg and Königsberg, 1835; Düsseldorf, 1836).[38] Certain German princes also caught the racing bug, following the example of the Stuarts and the Hanoverians, and actively supported horse racing or excelled as breeders.

Thus the Prussian Crown Prince and later King Friedrich Wilhelm IV founded a prize for the Berlin race, the Silver Horse.[39] His counterpart in the south-west, William I of Württemberg, set up at the royal stud farm the most significant Arabian breeding programme on German soil,[40] and although in the 1830s he already possessed an impressive stud – '4 stallions and 18 broodmares of Arabian descent, along with 2 Nubian and 30 other Oriental mares'[41] – he nevertheless sent his equerry Wilhelm von Taubenheim, accompanied by the writer Friedrich Wilhelm Hackländer, to the Orient in 1840 to acquire yet more purebreds.[42] While initially German authors were critical of the goal of breeding specifically for speed, and sceptical about racing as a measure of quality, there were also voices veering over to the other side, such as Count Veltheim[43] of the Duchy of Brunswick, or the Hungarian count and horse connoisseur Stephan Széchenyi, who soon recommended racing as 'a very useful test for investigating the quality and value of each horse'.[44]

Since the establishment of the Union Club in 1867, Germany also had its own national equestrian federation, which took on a similar function to the Jockey Club, although without restricting its membership to the aristocracy, as the English club did. From the beginning, the Union Club was open to representatives of other social classes; its exclusivity was regulated by the membership fee alone. The club was a melting pot of bourgeoisie and aristocratic liberalism, which was significant not only for the sport, but also in political and social terms. In the year of its foundation, Otto von Bismarck joined its ranks – he was a keen fan of English racing.[45] The association maintained two racecourses in Berlin: Hoppegarten from 1868 and Grunewald from 1909. But the Grunewald racetrack had to make way for the sports facilities of the 1936 Olympics and was therefore unceremoniously closed in 1933.

BLOOD AND SPEED

All origins are coloured by legend. Whatever the historical reality of the mythical five mares of Muhammad, the three foundation stallions of English thoroughbred stock were not invented. All the same, their story is entwined with myth. This is especially true of the youngest of the three, Godolphin Arabian, named after his last owner, the Earl of Godolphin. He was a diminutive bay stallion, standing at 15 hands (152 cm) tall, with a beautiful head and an unusually high croup, reminiscent of a wild horse; his features were captured for posterity by George Stubbs (see p. 149). There remains some doubt about his true provenance, and his arrival in England has the gloss of a Latin lover and good old-fashioned machismo. He came from France, from the dust of the road. The story goes that he was a gift from the Bey of Tunis to Louis XV, but did not find favour with the king and found himself outside pulling a water cart.[46] There he was discovered in 1728 by a certain Mr Coke, who in turn sold the stallion to a Mr Roger Williams, who gave him to the Earl of Godolphin. He languished in the stables like a kind of male Cinderella, with only a cat for company, until the moment of his finest hour. This 'strange tale' caught the attention of the German poet and novelist Achim von Arnim, who marvelled at the fact 'that an Arabian stallion, condemned to the life of a carthorse because of his unfavourable appearance, should attract the attention of the most beautiful Arabian mare, one who had resisted all advances until then, and that from this partnership should emerge the most ideal progenitors of all thoroughbreds'.[47] According to other reports, he allegedly bit and killed the intended sire, a lacklustre rival, before leaping upon the beauty named Roxana, who seemed to return his interest: a fervent start to a glittering career as a stud and foundation sire.

At the time when the three 'desert fathers' of the English thoroughbred breed began to work their fertile magic at the turn of eighteenth century, the Arabian horse was already a well-known guest in the British Isles. The first representative of this breed is said to have entered the country during the reign of Alexander I of Scotland (1107–24). Richard the Lionheart (1189–99) bought horses in

Cyprus, while his notoriously penniless brother and successor John Lackland enjoyed receiving elegant animals as gifts.[48] After the English Renaissance, the influx of oriental horses gradually increased, but it was not until the reigns of James I and Charles I that the first imports were made on a grand scale.[49] Their most significant import was that of the 'Royal Mares', a group of forty-three – oriental, Arab, Berber and Turkish – some of which were in foal and were regarded as 'the alpha females of English thoroughbred breeding'.[50] More distinctly than the individual acquisitions of stallions, amidst favourable circumstances and noteworthy coincidences, this systematic acquisition of oriental mares was read as a sign of the start of something historic: with them began a breeding policy which was promoted and driven by a European superpower.

Spain, for a long time home to the most enduring and intense exchanges between Arab and European culture,[51] was also the country where cross-breeding first took place with oriental horses, from the eighth century. The resulting Andalusian or Jennet breeds spread to Italy, especially Naples, and eventually to the entire continent.[52] At the Italian courts of the Renaissance, the possession and exhibition of thoroughbred horses was an integral part of the display of splendour, as described by Jacob Burckhardt. But while these prized horses still resided in the menageries of royal palaces like living jewels alongside rare-breed English dogs, leopards, Indian hens and Syrian long-eared goats, the idea of breeding was developing elsewhere. The experiments carried out at the stud farm at Mantua already had the same goal as those of the English Stuarts at a much later date – namely racing success, based on the speed of animals. 'All interest in, and knowledge of the different breeds of horses,' says Burckhardt, 'is as old, no doubt, as riding itself, and the crossing of the European with the Asiatic must have been common from the time of the Crusades. In Italy, a special inducement to perfect the breed was offered by the prizes at the horse-races held in every considerable town in the peninsula. In the Mantuan stables were found the infallible winners in these contests . . . Gonzaga kept stallions and mares from Spain, Ireland, Africa, Thrace, and Cilicia, and for the sake of the last he cultivated the friendship of the Sultans. All possible experiments were here tried in order to produce the most perfect animals.'[53]

English thoroughbred breeding of the eighteenth century initially did nothing more than what had been done before them by Arabs and Spaniards, Neapolitans and Mantuans: they tried, by crossing two good horses, to create a better third. This better copy could be a good cart- or workhorse, and indeed such animals also attracted the attention of the English breeders. Their main focus, however, was the type of horse whose qualities were proven on the race track – or on the battlefield. England has always bred for both types of horse racing: the *flat race* and the *steeplechase*, but the five famous 'British Classics' (St Leger, Epsom Derby, Epsom Oaks, 2,000 Guineas and 1,000 Guineas for fillies) and other prominent racing events such as Royal Ascot and the Queen Anne Stakes remain flat races as they have always been.

The secret of success in breeding racehorses was therefore to achieve the perfect correlation of the two parameters for racing: blood and speed. In this context, in the eighteenth century, the English developed the 'Newmarket System', which besides the financial components already mentioned (horse sales, prize money, betting) also included two record-keeping systems. The first of these was the *Racing Calendar* which, following a few sporadic precursors, began to be published regularly from 1727, edited by a certain John Cheny in Arundel. In initially annual, later fortnightly, editions, the *Calendar* listed the results and prize money won in recent races and ran announcements of upcoming events. By ranking British racehorses, Cheny codified the aim of thoroughbred breeding: speed. The breeding of thoroughbred horses was consistently subjected to this same goal. The sought-after qualities – build, fitness, health, endurance, character – dominated the agenda of breeder and trainer alike; characteristics such as form and beauty were inherited qualities.

With breeding, another, deeper kind of chronology came into play: the sequence of the generations and the results of each cross. Whereas the needs of the racing and betting systems were met by the short-term memory of the *Racing Calendar*, which recorded the victories and defeats of the past weeks, months and possibly years, breeding on the other hand needed a longer memory. Breeders needed to be able to record the success or failures of each cross along the long line of the generations. Racehorses needed to prove their qualities not only on the racetrack, but also in the covering yard; this is their second touch-stone. Such a record provides a measure not only of their own current form, but that of their descendants. It was for this purpose that the equestrian world acquired its second record-keeping system when the *Stud Book* was established at the end of the eighteenth century.

The *Stud Book*, first published by James Weatherby in 1791 (initially in the form of an *Introduction to a General Stud Book*), is always characterized as a kind of genealogical peerage of the English thoroughbred. Indeed, it is both surprising and somewhat amusing to note that this English register of the nobility of horses preceded that of the nobility of Englishmen – Burke's *Peerage* – by a good thirty-five years.[54] Indeed, the equine aristocracy that was the focus of the *Stud Book* was a nobility based purely on blood, not on merit or success. One might have conceived of a genealogical archive which listed horses of any origin, regardless of whether they came from the Levant or the British Isles, on the condition that they succeeded, either on the racetrack or in breeding successful racers. The *Stud Book*, however, took a different path and stipulated that the provenance of all horses entered had to be traceable to one of the three foundation stallions of English thoroughbred stock.

In other words, the *Stud Book* of English breeding was specifically a *stallion book*. And yet, at the time of the first edition, towards the end of the eighteenth century, all breeders and connoisseurs were quite aware that you did not produce a pure thoroughbred by mating an Arab or oriental stallion with a native mare. The quality of the mother was no less important than that of the father. Mares of oriental provenance were far superior to locally bred mares when it came to producing an English thoroughbred. And secondly, the main thoroughbred breeding lines, as the *Stud Book* revealed, emerged through ongoing *pure breeding* or *inbreeding*. This was what gave the English thoroughbred a high enough proportion of Arab blood (60 per cent and above) and what made these bloodlines sustainable in the long term. It was only by systematic *in-and-in breeding*, that is, repeated pure breeding, that the well-known agriculturalist Robert Bakewell (1725–95) was able to succeed in his selective breeding of sheep, cattle and horses. Charles Darwin, himself from a horse-loving family on his mother's side – the porcelain dynasty of the Wedgwoods[55] – was familiar with the traditional practices of breeders as well as the more experimental approach taken by Bakewell, and referred to both in his *On the Origin of Species*.[56] Charles Darwin's cousin Francis Galton, the founding father of eugenics, went a step further and in 1883 acknowledged the contribution of English horse breeders to his research. Their experiments had shown how suitable breeds or bloodlines could be helped to prevail against the less suitable. The English horse breeders had proved what selection, properly applied, could achieve.[57] Targeted tampering with genetic inheritance in order to improve a breed: this was the great dream of the eugenicists of the late nineteenth and early twentieth centuries. But as they themselves admitted, the birth of this dream came much earlier: in the stables of the eighteenth century.

The eugenicist of racehorses was a contemporary of Galton. He came from Australia, was called Bruce Lowe and died before he managed to publish his theory.[58] His *figure system*, as Lowe referred to his numerological approach, was an attempt, on the basis of the two record-keeping systems, the *Racing Calendar* and the revised *General Stud Book*,[59] to develop a combined analysis that would give future buyers and breeders more reliable knowledge. Lowe started from the assumption that all the horses entered in the *General Stud Book* could be traced through the maternal line to one of the forty-three root mares, which were considered genetically unique and not traceable further back. Lowe organized and ranked the forty-three genealogical lines emanating from these mares according to the number of race-winners produced on that respective line in the three particularly important races (the Epsom Derby, Epsom Oaks and St Leger). Analysis of additional qualities allowed him to split individual lines into *running families* and *sire families*, i.e. families with a race-winner (running) and families who had spawned a winner (sire). With his database, Lowe believed he would be able to forecast successful crosses and produce future race-winners in a planned way. Two German competitors, Hermann Goos and J. P. Frentzel,[60] were simultaneously attempting a similar combination of genealogy, statistics and prognostics, and were later invoked by the numerous critics of Lowe's system.[61] The twentieth century saw renewed attempts, involving calculations, lists and tables (the *Bobinski Tables*, the *Polish Tables*, etc.) to make the breeding of racing champions predictable. None of these systems would defini-tively achieve this goal, and indeed even modern DNA-based genetics cannot, although it can of course explain why none of the precursors succeeded. With genealogy one of the biggest topics on the internet now, besides sex, one can, without being a prophet, predict a brighter future for the study of equine nobility. The internet is already teeming with bloodline charts listing the most famous English, German and American racers since the eighteenth century and their oriental sires and mares.

The Anatomy Lesson

YOUNG MEN, STURDY ANIMALS

The natural gravitational centre of the horse world is the market, the meeting place for everyone whose working life revolves around horses: experts, breeders, buyers and sellers (honest traders and other less honourable types), grooms, stable boys, coachmen, breakers and handlers. The peripheries of the market teem with assorted pedlars hawking their wares: bridle-makers and saddlers, craftsmen and vendors of blankets, grooming combs and whips. Then there are the swarms of customers: farmers, tradesmen, stable masters, carters, employees of the omnibus company and procurers of remounts for the army. And amidst all these representatives of supply and demand stands the true protagonist of the market, shaking its head, snorting and chewing at the bit: the living commodity, the horse. Coldbloods and draught horses, named after the regions of their provenance; thoroughbreds or hotbloods, in whose veins English blood flows; giant steeds, sturdy packhorses, mounts, carriage horses, ponies and mules. Colts and fillies, grand specimens and old nags, all colours, shapes and sizes, groomed, with flicking tails and braided manes. Some you'd suspect would be dragging their hooves, while with others you could imagine yourself soaring from the word go and trotting back home in the morning sun. The horse market is held in the same location, in the middle of city, summer and winter – only in summer you can smell it from a lot further away.

Paris's horse market was not the biggest in the country. Thousands of horses and even greater armies of visitors, buyers and fanciers flocked to the *foires* in Brittany, Poitou or Franche-Comté. But these

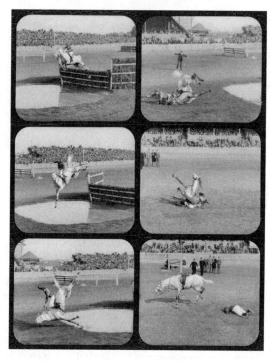

A photo series capturing a horse's fall while jumping over a ditch, 1934.

Victory ride through the history of European art: Parthenon Frieze,
West IX, Phidias.

fairs took place only in spring or summer, once or twice a year, while the Paris market ran all year round, twice a week, on Wednesdays and Saturdays. From 1642 it had a fixed location in Faubourg Saint-Marcel, a stone's throw from the Salpêtrière Hospital. In 1859 it had to make way for Hausmann's construction plans and was relocated to the Porte d'Enfer, while in 1878 it returned to the old site for a last quarter of a century; it closed in 1904. The name of the rue de l'Essai still recalls the track along which the horses were led and shown off by servants and young lads – a catwalk for horses which was by no means restricted to the *haute couture* of the Anglo-Arab thorough-breds. The smart, fashionable district of Faubourg-du-Roule, north of the Champs-Élysées, was home to the handlers of racehorses and top-end animals.[1] The image of the horse market is dominated by the powerful workhorses who came from the west of the country, the *Percherons*, mostly grey and dapple grey, sometimes brown – strong animals, which despite their size move with elegance and, one might even say, with grace.

Like all horse markets, Paris's Marché-aux-Chevaux was also a meeting hub for men. Women, on the other hand, were restricted to serving in the taverns on the edge of the market, where deals were clinched. There was no place for them at the actual market; horse-trading was men's work. Nobody would have noticed the waif-like boy who hung around the Paris horse market for days on end, in 1851 and the following year. Confident that he was unobserved, he scribbled away on the notepad he took everywhere with him, like a painter on his travels. Nobody recognized him as a young woman dressed as a man, pursuing her ambitious plan. She wanted to create a work such as that begun by the revered Théodore Géricault but never completed: a huge, broad canvas that did not simply repeat the famous cavalcade of the Parthenon frieze, but updated it, bringing it into the present day, with a new contemporary interpretation. Rosa Bonheur had already made her name as an animal painter, and now she was thinking big.

The following year, in 1853, it was finished. The Salon where Bonheur displayed her monumental work *The Horse Fair* – five metres long and half as high – was a triumph (Plate 12). The press and public were thrilled, Delacroix feted it in his diary, and the Emperor and Empress bowed to her artistry.[2] At a stroke, she became a household name. She travelled, roaming the wild Pyrenees and enjoying it when Spanish smugglers made eyes at her. In the autumn she returned to Paris where she had a revelatory experience. Her painting was displayed first at Ghent, then it was hung in her home town, Bordeaux; everywhere it evoked unanimous admiration. But no one wanted to buy it, or was in a position to. Her dealer, Ernest Gambart, a big shot in the Victorian art scene, had the painting brought to London. Even two generations after Jacques-Louis David and Antoine-Jean Gros, France could boast the best historical and horse painters of the century: Géricault, Delacroix, Vernet, Fromentin, Regnault, Meissonier; and now Rosa Bonheur was added to the list. But the truly moneyed clientele were in England; a short while later, the money was all to be found on the east coast of the United States. Gambart had Thomas Landseer, the brother of the famous animal painter Edwin Landseer, produce an engraving of *The Horse Fair* and organized an exhibition of French art, managing to lure Queen Victoria and Prince Albert to the grand opening. The horse-loving Queen had the masterpiece brought over for a private viewing at Windsor Castle; now it seemed success would be found in England, after all. And yet, as if the picture were simply too big for Europe, it was eventually sold to an American.[3]

Was Théodore Géricault familiar with the Greeks? Did he have Phidias and the Parthenon frieze in mind when he worked on his Roman horse race? It remains to be proven either way.[4] Whether he had them in mind or not, he also dreamed of a large format canvas, nine or ten metres long.[5] He had allegedly already made a start on such a work when he suddenly left Rome in late September 1817 to return to France.[6] But all that remained after seven months of repeatedly interrupted work on *Course de chevaux libres à Rome* was an abundance of sketches and drawings, now scattered around the museums and private collections of the world, and some oil studies (in Paris, Lille, Rouen, Madrid and Los Angeles) which are among the most perfect works the painter created in his short life (see Plate 13).[7]

In 1645 John Evelyn went to see and described the race of Barbary horses which traditionally took place towards the end of the Carnival along Rome's Via del Corso.[8] Over a century later (1788) Goethe also witnessed this race of riderless and unsaddled, and therefore 'free', Berber horses.[9] Géricault saw it some three decades later, in February 1817, and just as Goethe immediately noted down his impressions, so Géricault began to draw there on the spot. His first drawings – a watercolour study and an oil sketch that followed – breathe the spirit of the street where the race takes place, the suspense and tension among the participants, the speed, the danger and the attempted safety provisions: cordoned-off spectator stands, guards, a trumpeter who will give the start signal any moment now. These are snapshots, instantaneous impressions. Some are so succinct that they come up again and again in later versions, like the detail of a servant boy clinging to a horse's tail, trying to hold it back as it pulls forward. This is not invented; it's something the artist has seen, either on the Corso or somewhere in the Campagna.

As the composition develops and the final painting starts to come into focus, the individual elements within it start to take on a life of their own. The painter isolates distinct groups – a horse, two men – lifting them out of the original story and turning them into building blocks to be experimented with. He inverts the orientation of the scene: the horses no longer run from right to left, but now head in the opposite direction. He changes his position and with it his perspective, letting his audience penetrate deep into the action, thereby increasing the dramatic tension.[10] He draws on his academic training, depicting the servants unclothed, in antique nudity: this is how the race might have looked in Imperial Rome.[11] He draws inspiration from the masters, taking from Raphael the image of a fallen man (Heliodorus, in the *Stanze*, the Raphael Rooms in the Vatican), from Michelangelo the profile of a naked young man (from the ceiling of the Sistine Chapel). His composition gains clarity and simultaneously loses pace, impetuosity.[12] It starts to come too close to Poussin, threatening to become academic in tone: too quiet, too classic, too sublime. The painter corrects himself, steering in the opposite direction. He gives the servants back their colourful trousers and red caps, takes out the fallen man, adds some dramatic spots of light on the horses' flanks, disregarding the rules of how light actually falls.[13] He brings his image back from the realm of an imaginary antiquity. But the present day, where he sets it now, is no longer that of February 1817, it has acquired the form of a timeless present: the contemporariness is in the eye of the beholder.

Perhaps Géricault scholar Lorenz Eitner was right when he remarked that the men leading the horses in the Roman Carnival looked like a gang of Jacobins acting out the Parthenon frieze (see Plate 13).[14]

Géricault has been called a painter of the street, 'the first visual poet of the city'[15] and the precursor to Constantin Guys, whom Baudelaire celebrated as a *painter of modern life*. But while the street gave Géricault his motifs and his impressions, when it came to drafting the eventual painting it was his study of the masters that gave him his architectural and dramaturgical skills. Things were no different three decades later with Rosa Bonheur: she, too, found her motifs on the street and at the marketplace. But when she returned to her studio, she found her role models there waiting for her and foremost of them was Géricault. She owned a few sketches and prints by him, including a lithograph from the series produced in London in 1821, which he sold with the title *Various Subjects drawn from Life and on Stone*. The print in Bonheur's collection was entitled *Horses Going to a Fair* and shows a group of strong horses, Percherons, being driven to market by two men.[16] It is highly likely that Rosa Bonheur had also seen Géricault's drawings and oil studies of the Roman horse race, because certain characters and groups in her painting – such as the horse leader in green trousers to the left – exactly mimic the stance and expressions of Géricault's Roman prints.[17]

Clearly art does not arise only through the artist's engagement with the material that is provided by 'reality' or their social or natural environment. Art is created in dialogue with other art, with precursors, role models, competitors. Art is aware of its own history and its own self-referencing.[18] Horse painting, which might fall within the genre of historical painting, animal painting or as a dramatized segment of social reality, is no exception to this rule. In both Géricault's *Berbers Horse Races in Rome* and Bonheur's *Horse Fair*, we can still make out the outline of the Parthenon frieze procession from the pediment of the Temple of Athena (see p. 158). The comparison with the ancient frieze, of course, also shows just how much the dynamic sculptors among the painters, including Géricault and Bonheur, owed to the study of anatomy (which was unknown to Phidias). Bonheur may have studied horse anatomy from books;[19] of Géricault, it is said that he was in and out of the slaughterhouse and the morgue like anyone else might visit the opera or a brothel. As with Stubbs before him and Adolph Menzel later, hair-raising stories were told of the stench of decay in his studio – the perfume of heroic realism. Such was his reputation that by the late nineteenth century any anatomies without clear attribution in circulation in artists' estates and collections, whether studies of heads, arms or legs, sketches of horse or human skeletons, severed heads or body parts in every stage of decay, were generously ascribed to him.[20] Géricault was considered the painter of the most gruesome realism. In the morgue and in the pathologist's lab, he found a reality without precedent. It seemed as though, in the study of anatomy, the old dream of all realists and materialists of a *prima materia* – a subject free of all artifice – had been fulfilled. In the bloody art of dissection, beautiful art seemed to have gone into an apprenticeship under the tutelage of science, the artist's pen closely following the anatomist's knife.

KEEPER OF THE VOID

Even at seventy, George Stubbs had not lost his appetite for work. The Turf Gallery, which he had opened with his son in 1794 in London's Conduit Street, showed all the signs of becoming a financial success. While their leading and most influential precursor, the Shakespeare Gallery, exhibited paintings by British artists of scenes from Shakespeare's plays, at the establishment of Stubbs *père et fils* you would expect to see the most famous racehorses, painted by Stubbs Senior and made into prints by Stubbs Junior. In other words, the gallery was a semi-official Hall of Fame for British racing and at the same time a private showroom for the uncrowned king of *sporting art* – that sub-genre of painting devoted to the racing and hunting pursuits of the upper classes. It is thought that the heirs of Colonel Dennis O'Kelly, the owner of the legendary racer Eclipse, were behind the enterprise. That the Turf Gallery found itself in the red and had to close after four years was perhaps linked to the devastating effect the war with France had had on the printmaking business.[21] But in the balance sheet of its symbolic capital, the enterprise showed how close the racecourse had shifted towards Mount Parnassus: the day was not far off when a racehorse would achieve legendary status or become, as the writer Robert Musil put it, 'a racehorse of genius'.[22]

George Stubbs had been in the horse painting business for nearly four decades. As a successful artist he had accompanied the phenomenal rise of the English racing scene and had seen this world from every aspect: horses became celebrities and changed owners every year, which meant that they had to be painted every year, whether to be immortalized in effigy or simply to push up the price;[23] races which, like the St Leger, were barely off the ground, but already deemed classic events; the *Racing Calendar* and bloodline records which aimed to elucidate the convoluted family ties and demonstrate a horse's equine nobility; meat traders who had risen through the ranks to become racehorse owners and gentrified estates which came under the hammer because their owners had wagered their assets on the racecourse. Stubbs had closely followed the Formula One of his century and at times lived well from it. As a painter, he was both a parasite in the system and at the same time one of its key players. To this day he epitomizes the lasting image of England's *grandes odalisques*: he was the Ingres of the stable.

By the mid-1750s, he had discovered his niche and had executed an unprecedented coup: for eighteen months he worked in a barn in Horkstow like a man possessed, dissecting around a dozen horses which he bled to death in order to avoid causing any damage to their bones, tendons or veins. He worked for weeks on some of the carcasses, for which he had designed an ingenious hoisting device, seemingly oblivious to the terrible stench and the risk of sepsis. And since he was both anatomist and artist, and both with the same virtuosity, he dissected and sketched ceaselessly, without pause; every layer of muscle that he exposed he at once got down on paper, labelling the sketch in detail; eventually, he boiled the skeleton and charted it too, meticulously recording every individual bone, like an archaeologist working on the remains of an ancient city. These were the heroic years of such archaeology. In his barn in Lincolnshire, George Stubbs excavated the temple of a pagan cult: the anatomy of the horse. Stripping away and exposing layer after layer, he penetrated into the depths of the body; five tiers of muscles, tendons and veins were painstakingly recorded in his drawings. In the uppermost layer, the volumes of flesh are still intact; only the skin has been peeled off. Then scalpel, pen and eye penetrate deeper; the fifth illustration shows the deepest layer of ligaments and tendons directly attached to the skeleton (see p. 167). So as not to disrupt the clarity and beauty of the picture with numbers and labels, for each plate Stubbs provided a corresponding numbered line drawing and legend of muscles, etc., and their functions.[24]

In his methodology, both the layer-by-layer progress from outside inwards and also the way of presenting the reference material in a separate diagram, Stubbs stayed close to the approach taken by Bernhard Siegfried Albinus a decade earlier in his *Atlas of Human Anatomy*.[25] Stubbs followed the German anatomist and the Dutch graphic artist and engraver Jan Wandelaar in the normative aesthetics of representation too. Just as Wandelaar had presented the *écorché*, the flayed human body or skeleton, well proportioned and in an elegant pose, so Stubbs also displayed his dead horses with the elegance and grace of an animated young animal, trotting casually like a dancer. From one look at Stubbs's graceful ideal animal, one can clearly see the breed of horse in question: the Arabian-influenced English thoroughbred. *The Anatomy of the Horse* represents an archaeology of the racehorse. There is one striking way in which Stubbs deviated from the precedent set by Albinus and Wandelaar: he dispensed with the arcadian backdrop. His beautiful and spine-tingling horses do not have idealistic vistas unfolding in the background. Stubbs presented his horses in a void.

Thus, with his *Anatomy*, the masterpiece of a young artist,[26] Stubbs began to reveal the feature of his painting that would secure him a singular position in the history of art: the isolation of the animal body, free of accessories and window dressing, and the suppression of the natural environment. Stubbs, who painted his horses with such photo-realistic precision that each model could be recognized as a distinct individual (which breeders and owners particularly valued), was quietly radical in an abstract approach which was quite ahead of its time: save for the slightest shading beneath the feet, Stubbs did away with everything that was not part of the stallion, mare or foal. These few paintings of beautiful, shimmering horses took on an *iconic* quality, although the gold of these icons was no halo or shimmering background,[27] but a glimmer of light on his subject's brown coat.

There are only a handful of these images in which Stubbs renounced any kind of narrative in the form of landscape, people, accessories or other details. The most famous of the series is the portrait of the riderless stallion Whistlejacket in the levade position, with his head turned ever so slightly to face the viewer. It has been described as 'one of the most significant images of the eighteenth century' and 'the most significant horse portrait ever painted'.[28] There is a theory, a rumour fed by Stubbs himself, that it was a half-finished equestrian portrait of George III, in which, for various reasons, the background and the addition of the king by another artist were never executed.[29] In the case of other similarly abstract or absolute portraits, such as the *Mares and Foals* series from the same year as *Whistlejacket* (1762), it is more difficult to explain the genre: an equine group portrait, a frieze, which, as Werner Busch demonstrates,[30] obeys the laws of the golden ratio, with as much virtuosity in its execution as enigma in its meaning – if, indeed, it has any at all.

Perhaps these radically isolated images with their idiosyncratic auras are something of a secret destination within Stubbs's work. Not in the sense that this painter was only capable of horses and dogs – his *oeuvre* demonstrates that he was also competent at landscapes, although they remained conventional and unoriginal. He would not have entered the pantheon of great painters for their sake alone. More interesting is the way his Newmarket horse and jockey are dressed; here we find the same recurring buildings and details, as though the painter had long since grown weary of such padding. It's amidst this architectural indifference that the emptiness of Stubbs's portraits creeps into view, and with it comes a mood of escapism which foreshadows the twentieth-century realists such as Edward Hopper. For Stubbs, the fullness of life is only to be found in horses and all the more so when we abstract this from all distracting worldly references. The arcadian atmosphere with which the *Mares and Foals* is imbued comes not from an antiquated, idyllic setting, but rather from the fact that they are literally *set free* within the freedom of the empty canvas.

It took a long time for art history to put Stubbs's *Anatomy of the Horse* on a par with Philippe-Étienne Lafosse's *Cours d'Hippiatrique*,[31] although the differences between them are not great. Both works originate in the same period; Stubbs's anatomical drawings were published

A deeper look: *Anatomia del Cavallo*, Carlo Ruini, 1599.

Bone-dry humour: *The Anatomy of the Horse*, George Stubbs, 1766.

in 1766, six years before Lafosse. It is not known whether Lafosse was aware of Stubbs's work. These were the wild years of both equine studies and anatomy, and stacks of literature were being produced on both sides of the Channel, as well as great art. Both authors were experienced, passionate anatomists; both amassed years of anatomical experience in their youth, dissecting dead horses in their teenage years, replacing book knowledge with autopsies. Stubbs had an advantage over his French colleague, who was fourteen years his junior, in terms of his skills as an illustrator and engraver. But Lafosse knew how to buy in from outside; he hired illustrators of the quality of Harguinier and Saullier and a small army of the best engravers and printmakers. The result – sixty-five hand-coloured prints – is as grim as it is startling: it depicts a dead horse as a carcass on the dissecting table or suspended on a hook. Parts of the body are open, revealing the muscles, individual organs or major blood vessels, veins and arteries (Plate 15). The power of this vivid portrayal comes from the position in which the corpse is presented – legs splayed, tongue hanging out – the multiple perspectives of the same image, and the bizarre overall impression of Cubism having arrived around one and a half a centuries too early. Compared with the elegant classicism of Stubbs's portraits, Lafosse's surreal graphics come off worse: the politically correct twenty-first-century critic describes them as an 'irritating aesthetic of sensual and anthropomorphic depiction of violence'.[32]

Was Philippe-Étienne Lafosse a precursor of the splatter film? In fact it seems we're looking at two fundamentally different aesthetics in the visualiztion of the horse. Both Stubbs and Lafosse have their roots in the scientific practice of their time and both satisfy its stringent requirements in terms of precision and detail in how forms are rendered and functional relationships are represented. Both return again and again to autopsy and to a body of knowledge that comes not only from the eye, but also from the hand of the dissector. Both are motivated by the desire to support the practitioner, whether breeder or artist, and to delight the connoisseur, the aspiring veterinary surgeon or farrier. But while Stubbs ultimately lets the aesthete within him prevail and, with his anticipated clientele in mind, shows the dead horse in a graceful prance, Lafosse presents the cadaver as an object of gruesome investigation, as flesh to be dissected. While Stubbs's horses look as though they might yet trot back from the studio to the stable, Lafosse's corpses are not going anywhere.

A GOLGOTHA OF KNOWLEDGE

In Paris, the Bastille fell and with it fell the spirit of despotism, while in Berlin the Brandenburg Gate was erected, which over the next two centuries would become Germany's gateway of destiny. Inspired by the Athenian Propylaea, it became the symbol of the nation and saved its architect from the oblivion into which he – a man of the second tier of German architects behind Andreas Schlüter and Schinkel – would otherwise have easily fallen. The Gate kept Carl Gotthard Langhans's (1732–1808) name alive and recalled an architect who, in helping himself to elements from architectural history like a child rummaging through his box of building bricks, managed to produce some unmissable works. The finest of his *oeuvre* and the most spectacular, for all its external restraint, was built at the same time as the famous Brandenburg Gate and not far from it: the Veterinary School's Anatomical Theatre, which after years of redevelopment has recently been reopened to visitors.

Besides the elements of classical architecture, it is also sculpture which connects the two buildings – the city gate and the anatomical theatre. Johann Gottfried Schadow crowned the Brandenburg Gate with the Quadriga, a group of figures of consummate grace and verisimilitude. The devastation of the Second World War and the conservation efforts of the GDR left nothing intact of Schadow's original besides the monumental plaster cast of a horse's skull. This skull was returned to his birthplace as part of the exhibition on the history of Berlin's veterinary medicine. Like Adolph Menzel after him, Schadow studied and drew not only live horses, but also availed himself of the skulls and skeletons in the equine study collection in the animal anatomy department.[33]

Berlin's Veterinary Anatomical Theatre or 'Zootomie' was commissioned by King Friedrich Wilhelm II and was built in the years 1789–90. Externally reminiscent of Palladio's Villa La Rotonda in Vicenza (see p. 176), on the inside it seems to be following in the footsteps of its precursors: the anatomical theatres of Padua (1594), Leiden (1610) and Bologna (1637).[34] Langhans's originality was evident not only in the transfer of such a venue to the flourishing field of veterinary medicine, but also in the technical features of the auditorium, or perhaps we should say *viditorium* – for it was for watching the proceedings as much as for listening. At its centre stood a dissecting table, which was both rotatable and retractable, making it possible to raise an animal corpse from the depths of the building and to make it visible to the audience from all sides. Unlike his predecessor, Friedrich II, who had been keen to see pets as well as cows and sheep investigated, and sought enlightenment about the rampant rinderpest, or cattle plague, Friedrich Wilhelm II brought the spotlight of veterinary medicine back to its political and military core purpose by focusing mainly on horses.[35] The carcasses which the rotating dissection table raised into the scientific limelight, were, at least in the early years, exclusively those of horses.

In place of the ancient theatre's proscenium, the anatomical theatre of modern times set a more intimate scene: the autopsy table. At the heart of the tragedy were the organs and fibres of a dissected corpse. The drama explored the symptoms that disease had etched into the body's tissue and the indicators which portended that stony guest, death.[36] The amphitheatre's tiers of seats rose in concentric circles, directing the students' perspective onto the fragment of a corpse that had been isolated by the pathologist's scalpel for investigation. The anatomical theatre's dissection table rotated, allowing the audience to examine the object in question from all perspectives; no detail escaped the attention of the spectator. The Anatomical Theatre is a huge apparatus that encompasses the audience and serves the purpose of directing and training the eye: it leads the spectator from merely looking to reading and deciphering signs. This theatre is the stage of modern science, where tokens of death have a systematic, pedagogical purpose.

Langhans's 'zootomical' theatre fits precisely within this tradition of the modern observation apparatus. Its rising table enables the effortless delivery and removal of large and heavy carcasses in the vertical plane. The corpse, prepared in advance by the dissector in the basement, appears to float in and out of the audience's field of vision like an *equus ex machina.* The architect of this extraordinary building won his spurs in the theatre of the performing arts; now another field was benefiting from that theatrical experience. All traces of the slaughterhouse and the knacker's yard are banished to the basement; only sanitized specimens are permitted access to the main floor: the pure phenomenology. But the zootomical theatre's dissection table evokes not only the stage of classical theatre, it also conjures up the altar of an ancient temple. This is what is suggested by the frescoes of garlanded *bucrania* decorating the dome of the theatre and circling its walls, the work of the Berlin painter and engraver Bernhard Rode.[37] But the animals slaughtered in the basement are no longer the sacrifice brought before the old bloodthirsty gods; these animals die for the sake of science.

AT A FLYING GALLOP

In the demonstration hall of the animal anatomical theatre, the inner nature of the horse is laid bare. The audience in the tiered seating observes the architecture of the skeleton, the texture of the muscles, the volume of the chest and the expanse of the lungs; it knows the speed and the endurance of this creature bred for the racetrack. It is, however, only the deceased animal that is seen, not the trotting, galloping, jumping version. The dissection reveals only the musculoskeletal system, the apparatus of movement, but not the motion itself. The gentle trot, suggested by Stubbs's *Anatomy*, is an added aesthetic ingredient like the flowing mane and billowing robe of Jacques-Louis David's *Napoleon Crossing the Alps*; essentially, Stubbs's anatomical drawings were static. The horse, the great mover, here remains unmoved. Even the levade is just another form of stasis; indeed, it is the paradoxical climax of stasis: for a fleeting moment the horse rises to a vertical position, before the sublime figure returns to all fours. Géricault's Berber horses, painted half a century later, are the product of another age, creatures made of light and tempo, metaphors of dynamic motion. In 1821, during his second stay in London, it was suggested to Géricault that he should produce a *Cours d'anatomie cheval à l'usage des peintres et des amateurs,* a textbook for equine painters and connoisseurs.[38] It would be along the lines of Stubbs's work,[39] but for a new era, updated for contemporary tastes. Momentarily, he was on fire and began to draw – not horses in motion, but rather the motion within horses.

The reason for Géricault's visits to London in the early 1820s was unrelated to horses, however: he was motivated by the poor reception of *The Raft of the Medusa* in the Salon of 1819. When Géricault exhibited the painting in London the following year, the crowds rushed to see it and it was warmly received by the critics. He made a second visit to London in 1821 and stayed most of the year, mainly preparing lithographs to sell, but also seeking English customers for his scenes of horses and racing events. He whiled away whole days at the racecourse, where he became friendly with a wealthy horse trader, Adam Elmore, from whom he bought three beautiful animals.[40] The sketches which emerged in this context show the English thoroughbreds and their jockeys with the same dynamics and the same circular swirls of energy that swept through his Roman Berbers. These studies show Géricault at the height of his dynamic, dramatic art. But then something strange happened. The painter became something of a chameleon, blending into his adopted background. From being a pioneer of French Romanticism, he emerged as an English sporting artist. A decorator, a furnisher of manor houses.

Géricault produced an oil painting, which he either gave to Elmore or offered as a down-payment for the racehorses – it's not quite clear. The work is entitled *The 1821 Derby at Epsom* (Plate 14) and may have also been intended as a teaser for the British clientele he hoped to attract, for it corresponded to their tastes exactly. '*The 1821 Derby at Epsom* can only be understood as a deliberate imitation, a pastiche if not a parody, of the most current type of English racing picture, as familiar to the public, and certainly to Mr Elmore, as the Britannia on the penny.'[41] In fact, we can hardly discern the hand of the master: where is the impulsive sensuality of his Berber horses, the erotic flexibility of their limbs, the painful beauty? Géricault had adapted himself so thoroughly to the stiff-legged, roughly hewn horse painting of the English school, it is as though he had just graduated from their ranks. His runners at Epsom look exactly as if they were the work of a popular artist of the day such as Henry Alken or James Pollard. As in their paintings, in Géricault's we even see the horses levitating in a 'flying gallop' with forelegs and hindlegs stretched out straight at the same time, all four animals captured simultaneously in the same flying position. The horses appear to hover, while the jockeys do not crouch in racing position, but sit upright like the pilot of an aircraft, as if clutching a steering wheel. Géricault, a passionate rider who was intimately acquainted with the motion of horses, knew that his picture defied physical reality, that it was anatomically 'incorrect' (the sketches from the same era betray him). But he was also well aware that such were the conventions of English art,[42] which its buyers were used to seeing. This was another kind of cultural 'correctness' to which he needed to adhere, if he was to succeed in London or Newmarket. Beauty was in the eye of the customer.

So, might *The 1821 Derby at Epsom* not have been a crafty move by a versatile artist who was trying his luck in a new market? Indeed, it might have been. It's hard to know for sure, because in December 1821 Géricault gave up and took his English horses with him back to France; in the remaining two years of his life he found other occupations. His Epsom racehorses hadn't provided him with a new formula for representing speed and dynamic motion in pictorial form.[43] This was the formula for which French painting – from Romantic Orientalism via historical painting through to 'scientific realism' – searched over the next few decades, and the pressure intensified with the rise of physiological knowledge and new graphic recording methods.[44] The climax came when officer and anthropologist Émile Duhousset published a work in 1874 in which he criticized numerous previous representations of striding and running horses as inaccurate and corrected them with the aid of schematic drawings.[45] Jean-Louis-Ernest Meissonier, a leading historical painter of his age, was receptive to this critique, and prompted by Duhousset's suggestions he revised a picture in 1888 which he had painted twenty-four years previously – *1814. La Campagne de France* – which at the time had been praised for its historical and hippological accuracy. The following year he corrected another historical painting, which he was still working on: *1807, Friedland*. But the more he fiddled about with his horses' postures, the more he attracted the criticism of experts.[46] He simply could not shake off those annoying critics. Physiology and hippology had taken aesthetic criticism hostage.[47]

Suddenly everyone was claiming to know how to paint a horse and how not to – and the only people who didn't know were the artists. Meissonier came to feel the bitter irony of the whole affair. Paradoxically, it was he – the most scrupulous among French historical painters in the pursuit of verisimilitude – who was singled out by the realism nemesis. The blow was all the harsher, given that he was such an enthusiastic rider; in 1867, Menzel counted eight horses in his stable.[48] He would sit for hours on end on the Champs-Élysées, pencil in hand, watching the spectacle of riders and carriages, unmoved by the scorn of fellow painters such as Degas.[49] In the garden of his studio, he had a track built, along which he could move smoothly on a small, rolling platform (a 'dolly', as they say in the film business) pulled by an employee, as he sketched a horse running alongside him.[50] But even those tracking shots *avant la lettre* did not prevent him from slipping up as he sought to represent a horse's gait. The graphic evidence lay on the table.

This nemesis of realism had a human face and a name: it was Étienne-Jules Marey. His extensive studies of the movements of people, horses and dogs walking and jumping, birds in flight, fish swimming and insects scurrying resulted in 1873 in the sensational work *La Machine animale*, which the following year appeared in English and spread his insights worldwide. Although the *Machine animale* still depended on experiments with electromagnetic, pneumatic and mechanical recording methods, it helped trigger the ingenious series of photographs taken by Eadweard Muybridge from 1877, funded by the railway magnate and horse-breeder Leland Stanford. Their publication, initially in 1878 as *The Horse in Motion* and in the following year as *Attitudes of Animals in Motion*, electrified Marey, encouraging him to establish the photograph as a meaningful recording technique.[51] In 1887, Muybridge in turn marked the culmination of his photographic motion studies with the publication of *Animal Locomotion*, a huge collection with 781 plates in folio format.

The story of chronophotography and its protagonists has been told so often that we can restrict ourselves to a brief mention.[52] However, if, as often happens, we compare Marey and Muybridge's work, we should bear in mind that these were two very different kinds of researcher. On the one hand we have Marey, in Paris: a physiologist of national and international renown, the successor to Claude Bernard at the Collège de France with a corresponding list of publications and academic lectures to his name. On the other hand – in Palo Alto – we have Muybridge, a figure of dubious moral stature, who had to suffer the insult that his powerful patron Leland Stanford described him dismissively in the Preface to *The Horse in Motion* (1882) merely as a hired photographer.[53]

Muybridge must have felt all the more triumphant, then, at his positive reception by the great and good in the scientific world, when he came to Paris in 1881. The reception for him at the home of Marey on 26 September 1881 was attended by the physicists and inventors Gabriel Lippmann, Jacques-Arsène d'Arsonval and Hermann von Helmholtz, besides numerous friends of the host. At a second reception eight weeks later at the home of Meissonier, the crème de la crème of the Paris art scene gathered to honour Muybridge.[54] For Meissonier, chronophotography represented a dream come true: the exact reproduction of motion. But this technique was also a trap that he could not escape. In truth, the series of photographs divided the accuracy of the moment from the fluidity of motion. By aiming for accuracy, Meissonier ended up failing to capture the fluid movement: in his paintings, all action came across as frozen.

Like Meissonier, Degas was also fascinated by Marey's discoveries as they first did the rounds in the early 1870s. Degas, at that time one of the spokesmen of 'scientific realism' and an aficionado of the racetrack, was thrilled by the new perspectives of the horse conveyed by the new *méthode graphique*. Finally, it would be possible to depict horses with scientifically guaranteed accuracy.[55] But as he concerned himself at that time exclusively with the human form, it would be some time before Degas benefited directly from the series of horse chronophotographs. It was only towards the end of the 1880s that he became inspired by one of the equine forms in Muybridge's *Animal Locomotion*. This was followed shortly thereafter by an about-turn as he returned in the 1890s to his youthful errors in the portrayal of motion, 'so much more expressive than flat verisimilitude'.[56] Towards the end of the century, with the image of the *Injured Jockey* (Plate 11), Degas returned to one of his early paintings from the 1860s (*Scène de steeplechase*, 1866). Now he reduced the scene to two figures, the

View of the animal anatomical theatre by Langhans (1789) in Berlin.
Zootomie, August Niegelsson, 1797.

Painter and model: Lord Berners painting a portrait of Penelope Betjeman
and her Arabian pony, 1938.

wooden horse and the jockey who looks like a child's doll carelessly tossed aside. Nothing remains of the realism of the 1870s and 1880s, no trace of the accuracy made possible by Marey and Muybridge, and which Degas's colleague Meissonier still slavishly pursued.[57] Degas had opted for wooden doll-like figures and used them to discover modernity in painting. Perhaps Géricault, the putative opportunist of the English art market, was already on this path when he painted his wooden jack-in-the-box Epsom runners. Or, as Degas used to say: we attain the idea of truth through falsehood.[58]

For Degas, the Parthenon frieze was the first and probably the most important of all horse races: it was a worthwhile endeavour to seek to imitate its artistic truth. Phidias's horses, which Degas copied as an art student in 1855 from plaster casts in Paris and Lyons, opened his eyes to the thoroughbreds at Chantilly and Longchamp, which he studied six or seven years later.[59] The format of the frieze was the obvious choice for depicting the typical broad sweep of the racecourse, the high-relief cavalcades and the spinning rotation of legs as the runners tear along at a terrific pace. It was only late in the painter's life, when increasing blindness made it pointless for Degas to continue striving for a photorealistic reproduction of horses and their motion, that he seems to have turned away from the Greeks. He made his leap into modernity with his jockeys riding in a no man's land of colour, on horses whose excessively long legs remind us of models on the catwalk, and with the help of archaic depictions of horses like those that survive in wooden toys and on fairground carousels.

Connoisseurs and Conmen

THE FOX AS EDUCATOR

Twenty-three is a dangerous age in a man's life. At twenty-three, you can get swept up by a passion that you won't shake off for your entire life. One young American fell victim to Anglophilia when he was studying history at Cambridge in 1930, but that was not all. Along with his love of England, the country's history and its way of life, his enthusiasm also grew for English culture to the exclusion of almost nothing that had been generated by an English quill or brush. When this Anglophilia made the leap to the most important art form engendered by modern England, his fate was sealed.

This art is not the stuff of exhibitions and museums; it is rooted in the life of a nation and its upper classes. It is an organic, polychrome sculpture, moving agilely with its many parts. The art form in question is horse racing and its wild sister, fox hunting. As picturesque as an English fox hunt may seem with its green meadows and hedges, babbling brooks, glistening horses, the riders' gleaming bright coats and the frenzied, bustling dogs, it is in fact the work of an artist who has combined all these elements into a lively composite piece which, thanks to the movement of its parts, is in constant metamorphosis.

Anyone who has seen the hunt can sense the vibrant pulse of English rural culture, the epitome of all that is fine, fast and furious. And he will know the small demon who keeps the whole dance in motion, the tutor of the English nobility and the dancing master of the nation: the fox. More inconspicuous than the Spanish bull – that black mass of force and unbridled savagery, the threatening incarnation of the dark principle – by contrast, the fox is a diminutive embodiment of guile. The swiftest of the smart and the smartest of the swift, the fox is a practical philosopher and a teacher of earthly wisdom. Nations are formed not only by saints and heroes. They are also raised by animals; they need a totem in which they can find themselves. England was brought up by the fox, and almost every trick the wily British have up their sleeves, they have learned from this master of deceit. In Newmarket, the second capital of this horse-obsessed country, there is even a monument to the fox, housed in a roofed temple with four Ionic pillars.[1]

Unlike the children of the British upper classes, the young American was not born in the saddle. Initially, he encountered the great outdoors only in art and literature. Like many young people in the western hemisphere, especially those from well-to-do homes, sheltered and shielded against the hardships of social reality, for a long time Paul Mellon knew the world of meadows, forests and horses only from books. He spent hours on end as a child, rifling through old bound editions of *Punch*, the forefather of all comics. It was in the satirical cartoons that he first encountered the English upper classes and what seemed to be their natural environment and companions: hedges, ditches, horses and dogs, and of course the fox. As an undergraduate in Cambridge, he set foot in this world and skipped lectures in order to ride with the hunt. At the same time, he began to indulge the artistic impulse of aristocratic culture to start a collection, starting with engravings and prints of traditional British sporting art, along with specimens of the abundant literature about horses, race meetings, hunting and breeding. The hunt and the racecourse reflected everything he saw and read, from the characters of Samuel Alken and Thomas Rowlandson to the shimmering runners of Stubbs and Benjamin Marshall.[2] What other young Americans of his time found in Venice or Paris, Paul Mellon experienced on the turf of Newmarket: the coalescence of art and life.

It was several years later that Mellon became a collector on a grand scale, after he had married and settled in Virginia.[3] In 1936, he bought his first English painting, a Stubbs (*Pumpkin with a Stable-lad*), and it would not be his last. The great horse painter of the eighteenth century was the secret focal point of Mellon's continuously growing collection which, thirty years later, when Mellon bequeathed his paintings and books to Yale University, had become the most significant collection of English painting outside Britain. Mellon had acquired his first racehorse in 1933, soon after returning from England. Not long after that, he started to breed horses himself, initially steeplechasers, and later, after the war, thoroughbreds for classic flat racing. His most famous horse was Mill Reef, who as a three-year-old won all the major European races – Epsom, Ascot and Longchamp – in a single year, 1971, and to this day ranks among the ten greatest racers of the twentieth century.

When Paul Mellon was promoted to the Racing Hall of Fame, he was described by the equestrian journalist Terry Conway as the Renaissance prince of horse racing. This was not only an allusion to Mellon's accomplishments as a breeder and the dazzling success of his racing team, the Rokeby Stables, but also to his humanist inclinations and his princely generosity. Mellon gave funds to Yale, his first alma mater, like no patron before or after him, and he patronized Clare College and the Fitzwilliam Museum in Cambridge in a similar way. In conjunction with the foundation named after his father, Andrew Mellon, and with the help of his sister, he expanded the National Gallery of Art in Washington, as well as putting huge sums into other museums and collections (Virginia Museum of Fine Arts, the Tate Gallery, the Pierpont Morgan Library) and scholarly foundations such as the Bollingen Foundation. He also funded research which promised to promote the life, health and safety of racehorses. Philanthropy and human welfare came away empty-handed.

The Bollingen Foundation, founded in 1945, was intended to act in the spirit of C. G. Jung – a figure revered by Mellon and his first wife, Mary. Its history goes back to a number of encounters with the psychiatrist from October 1937. The Mellons were in the audience when Carl Jung lectured at Yale and New York. Mary hoped to find relief from her asthma from the inspired doctor, while Paul hoped to be liberated from the shadow of his overpowering father, Andrew Mellon, who had died a few weeks before. In the spring of the following year, 1938, the Mellons travelled to Switzerland for two months, first to Zurich, then to Ascona. On their last day in Europe, Jung granted them each a fifteen-minute appointment. He taught Paul Mellon that his wife was suffering from an over-active *animus*: it was the horse in her that was wildly kicking and fighting for more space to run.[4] Her husband was over the moon.

Besides English art and the paintings of the Impressionists, Mellon collected works of equine literature from medieval times up the twentieth century. As an Anglophile he focused on English literature and the themes of hunting and racing. In this way, his friend the fox was naturally given pride of place in his literary collection.[5] Classics of hippology originally in Latin, Italian and French, such as Giordano Ruffo's *Liber Equorum* or La Guérinière's *École de Cavalerie*, amounted to a mere fraction of the total collection. In most cases it was their first translations into English which paved the way for them to enter Mellon's collection. One example is Federico Grisone's *Ordini di Cavalcare*, originally published in 1550, which Mellon acquired in its first English translation (*The Rules of Riding*) of 1560.

The collection was first made publicly visible in a large format and richly illustrated catalogue in 1981, under the authorship of John B. Podeschi, while Mellon himself selected the volumes and illustrations to be included. It was the very personal directory of a private collection, 'the record of the household library' of a passionate rider, breeder and racehorse owner, as Podeschi put it in the preface. Many of the works listed, he wrote, emerged from a similar background. They were not written for the sake of profit or for scholarly motives, but from the desire to express a passion and to share it with others of the same disposition. 'It was not for the sake of earning money that these works were written, but because the author wished to share with others his sheer enjoyment of the subject matter.'[6]

This short, easily overlooked sentence sums up the essence of the connoisseur as writer: someone who writes for the sake of his love of the subject. Or rather, for the sake of his sheer *delight* in the subject matter. Mere enjoyment might be enough for the plebs, but the connoisseur seeks to indulge his pure delight. Whether one sees oneself as a devotee, an aficionado or a connoisseur, what is certainly absent is the motive of making money. The motivation is rooted in passion and passion alone. In the catalogue of Mellon's collection, the immeasurable wealth of the collector lies discreetly in the background. What brings together devoted writers and readers is the intimacy of the 'household library'. At its heart is the special breed of horse that was the focus of Mellon's passion: the classic English thoroughbred race-horse with an Arabian streak. The thoroughbred is the true protagonist of this polyphonic equestrian narrative stretching over six centuries. Mellon's catalogue is a poor bibliography, yet it is a grandiosely book-ish homage to the noblest creature brought forth by England in modern times.

COMÉDIE HIPPIQUE

If Paul Mellon had indeed intended his collection and its catalogue to be a tribute to the horse as such, then he would have started not with the fifteenth century, but with antiquity, something attempted in a comprehensive form by Frederick H. Huth. His bibliography, *Works on Horses and Equitation*, published in London in 1887 and reprinted a hundred years later by Germany's most hippophile publisher,[7] stretches back to 430 BCE with the inclusion of surviving fragments of a treatise by Simon of Athens on horsemanship and veterinary arts. Huth's bibliography also emerged from the catalogue of a collection. But unlike Mellon's directory it includes many curious and rare titles and narratives about other members of the family Equidae besides the horse, such as the donkey and the mule. Thanks to the bibliographer's thoroughness, Huth's work is still used as a reference work by antiquarians and specialists in hippological literature. As it also included German-language books, it provides a first impression of the development of a very specific European market, which in the seventeenth century and well into the next would stretch far beyond England, France and Italy. While England as the leading European horse-loving nation also dominated the associated book market, the Italian influence soon declined, making French the second language of the hippophile world. From the last third of the eighteenth century, German authors and publishers of equine literature pushed relent-lessly forward, to the point that in the next century they would dominate the European market.

But if we want to gain a broad overview of the world of equestrian literature, we can do no better than to reach for the work of a French general. Mennessier de la Lance, author of the two-volume *Essai de bibliographie hippique*, published between 1915 and 1917, was, as the title page notes, '*ancien commandant de la 3e division de cavalerie*'. In keeping with his background as a cavalry officer, this bibliographer sought to catalogue works 'relating to the horse and the cavalry'. Anyone interested in such mundane objects as coaches and carriages would do well to consult the work of Gérard de Contades, *Le driving en France*.[8] Mennessier represents a familiar type with only a slight change in appearance: he is a connoisseur in uniform. For every even vaguely significant work, he lists not only a short biography of the author, but also a concise summary of the text itself. If he cannot precisely identify the author or the publisher, he makes do with conjecture. He assesses the content and style of the text in question, restrained with neither his praise nor his criticism. He particularly gets into his stride when it comes to discussing the teaching methods of the famous riding schools and riding masters (*école allemande, école de Versailles*).

Mennessier approaches other connoisseurs and collectors with especial warmth, including, for example, Charles Louis Adélaïde Henri Mathevon, Baron de Curnieu, born around 1811, died 1871, editor of Xenophon and author of a major work of equine studies.[9] He joined the General Staff after training as a Hellenist, but left military service soon after to dedicate himself to *études chevalines*. His considerable wealth allowed him to travel extensively, especially to England, where he broadened his expert knowledge. His library of equestrian literature includes many treasures acquired from Huzard's library, in his time the richest in the world.

This brings us to Jean-Baptiste Huzard, a French veterinarian (1755–1838), graduate of Alfort veterinary school – one of the first of its kind – and architect of French veterinary medicine and military remount procurement. Huzard organized the supply and training of horses for the armies of the Revolution and of Napoleonic France. A second Talleyrand, he survived all the regime changes, became a Knight of the Legion of Honour, introduced the merino sheep to France together with his colleague Daubenton, and built up the largest hippological library of his time, with almost 40,000 volumes. The catalogue of this great collection, published in 1842 by Edward LeBlanc in three volumes, was, according to Mennessier, 'a precious resource in spite of certain errors because, with only a few rare exceptions, Huzard possessed *everything* that had been written on the subject up to 1837'.[10]

Bibliographies don't have readers so much as users. But Mennessier's bibliography makes for an unusually enjoyable read. You can take a leisurely stroll through this equestrian landscape. One biography of a rider and collector leads to another; one aristocratic stable greets another. The world of connoisseurship is a continuum, a network of names, provenances and possessions. It is only in its external form that Mennessier's book is a bibliography. Inside it is a rich, sprawling *comédie hippique* of Balzacian proportions. He who knows how to read it will make the most astonishing discoveries. Before the reader's eyes unfurl the secrets of connoisseurs and traders, the races and the stands. New breeds of horses entered the arena, new fashions, diseases and cures, as well as new types of people, known as *hommes à chevaux*, not yet known to the society of the *Ancien Régime*. The wanderer through this text can experience *en passant* how the French developed their sense of the equine from the eighteenth century and how they mastered riding and driving, like learning to walk a second time. A trip through Mennessier's text opens up the strata of society in all their fathomable depths, accompanied by the functional layers of knowledge that rewrote the centaurian existence of modern society, the sluggish tempo of the country, the fast trot of the cities, the entire hippo-ontology of the French world. How strange and how regrettable that Bouvard and Pécuchet, those Flaubertian heroes of useless and hypertrophic knowledge, dipped their toes into every conceivable topic of study in their endless quest and yet sauntered obliviously past the mighty hippological scholarly community of their time.

THE SCIENCE OF HORSES

Towards the end of the eighteenth century, the first works of hippological literature appeared on the market with titles asserting a *scientific* claim. What kind of a strange constellation of knowledge is this that suddenly claims to be a *science*? What does it comprise of and where do its component parts come from? We are familiar with the era around 1780, referred to by Reinhart Koselleck as the 'saddle period', when a number of disciplines emerged which would come to play a defining role for modernity. Suddenly, there they were, mingling with the old concert of sciences, these new formations of biology, economics, philology, geography and history. From the confused magma of baroque tableaux and histories, of relationships, allegories and anecdotes, these new disciplines suddenly surfaced before us, young sciences of life, of people, their languages and their history.

In fact, their birth certificates reveal a lengthier provenance than we might think, looking back. Hippology, an old science with its origins in antiquity, was no exception. It was within the traditional mass of riding lessons, hippiatry and manuals for grooms and stable masters that this new Faustian desire for knowledge emerged towards the end of the eighteenth century. On the eve of industrialization, urbanization and the large-scale, fast-paced wars of the Napoleonic era, the horse – as the most important supplier of kinetic energy – moved into the spotlight of research, politics and national administration. But a modern equine science did not rise suddenly from the traditional mixture of dogmatism and empiricism as a counterpart to human sciences. The development of knowledge of the Equidae family took a different path: as tortuous and full of surprises as an English steeplechase, winding cross-country over ditches and hedges.

A vigilant, market-focused publisher like Johann Friedrich Cotta could not fail to notice these trends. As with other genres – women's literature, horticulture – he responded with the publication of an annual almanac. Unlike a journal, which tended to be highly specialized and highly strung, this welcoming and chatty medium was well suited to the task of carefully luring in new readers and testing out the field's still uncertain requirements. So Cotta set to publishing an almanac of all things equestrian. The 'Handbook for Horse Lovers, Riders, Breeders, Veterinary Surgeons and Supervisors of Large Stables', as its full title ran, was published every year on 11 November, St Martin's Day. The first edition in 1792 was self-published by its editor, the Equerry for the State of Württemberg, Franz Maximilian Friedrich Freiherr Bouwinghausen von Wallmerode, but from the following year, the shrewd businessman Cotta took over and published

Fall from the bridge: Bouwinghausen von Wallmerode's 'Handbook for Horse Lovers', 1802 edition.

The levade of the flayed: Philippe-Étienne Lafosse, *Cours d'hippiatrique*, 1772.

it in an almost unchanging format, with an annual print run of 1,500, until he put it to rest ten years later.

Bouwinghausen's literary output was otherwise limited to short treatises on veterinary medicine, practical guidance for farmers on the treatment of horse hoof conditions and other animal diseases. In 1796 he published an 'Ordinance of the Duke of Württemberg's Studs'. With his 'Handbook for Horse Lovers', however, he spread his net wider and offered instructive and entertaining titbits from the field of horse husbandry as well as news from the worlds of fashion, the nobility and the professional classes. He rounded off his content with anecdotes and references to hippological innovations. With this broad range of topics, Bouwinghausen stood at the centre of a ragged field of knowledge, which from the 1780s liked to refer to itself as 'equine science'. In his 'Letter to the Public' in the almanac's first edition, i.e. the editorial, he consciously described himself as part of this new discipline.[11]

The third and most substantial part of the annual publication consisted of a 'Genealogical Directory of the Noblest Living Potentates, Princes and Princesses, Secular and Ecclesiastical'. The long list of names in the vein of the *Almanach de Gotha*,[12] a registry of aristocratic families similar to *Burke's Peerage*, made it clear who was the publisher's target audience: the well-educated, horse-owning and horse-breeding aristocracy who needed to be au fait with all matters hippological. Both the equine almanac and the courtly one, two intimately related documents, were at that time, towards the end of the eighteenth century, still in search of their definitive, systematic format. The *Stud Book* – the register of recognized breeding animals – and Gotha's Almanac – the directory of European royalty and nobility – were two genealogical projects both in need of a uniform, controlled format, an 'official' version. The era of the many competing genealogical narratives, when every house and stud farm told its own story, was coming to an end. The bloodlines were being conclusively mapped.

This was true for the English in a particularly clear, conspicuous way. As already mentioned,[13] in Britain, the land of thoroughbred breeding, the registry of noble horses was already more established than that of human nobility. In Germany, national fragmentation, a pluralized and decentralized equestrian culture and the relatively late arrival of the fashion for Arabian-influenced thoroughbred horses all stood in the way of the creation of a comparable national stud book. On the other hand, the genealogical record of human nobility was established earlier in Germany: the *Almanach de Gotha* was first published in 1763. In the early days, the *Gotha* – like Cotta's almanac later on – consisted only partially of a registry of European nobility, while the rest was devoted to diplomatic relations and historical background. Bouwinghausen's hippological almanac included, first, reports on stud farms, racehorses and their offspring, followed by an excerpt from the *Gotha*, thus bringing together two strands which at the time felt closely related: the two great narratives of pure bloodlines.

Despite its name, 'equine science', as it explicitly appeared in the last third of the eighteenth century,[14] was not exactly a systematic and academically rigorous discipline, but rather a heterogeneous mix of branches of knowledge of varying status and repute. Anecdotal evidence was still deemed legitimate. 'Science' in the late eighteenth century was not a protected or certified term. It had prestige, but no exclusivity. Unlike the contemporaneously emergent study of the diseases of horses,[15] equine science was not limited to the study of the horse diseases and their treatment, but included other practical spheres of knowledge relating to horse husbandry and to the breeding, acquisition and treatment of horses. Slowly and gradually the old knowledge of the nature of horses, their illnesses and how to treat them – a body of wisdom collected and handed down throughout the era when the *stable master*, or *equerry*, was the keeper of such insights – was reorganized around the domains of the *veterinary physician* and the professional horse *expert* or *connoisseur*.

The 'equerry era' is a term used to refer to the half millennium from 1250 to 1762. It is an epoch ushered in by a text on the work of the groom or stable master, *De medicina equorum* (thus giving a name to 500 years of equine medicine) by Jordanus Ruffus or Giordano Ruffo, marshal to Friedrich II, which was published in 1250, the year of the death of this Holy Roman Emperor. The 'equerry era' comes to a close with the foundation of the *École vétérinaire*, the first veterinary school, in 1762 by Claude Bourgelat, also the director of the Riding Academy in Lyons.

This period, commonly delineated in the history of veterinary medicine, has a certain asymmetry to it: its inception is marked by a literary publication, while its end is heralded by an institutional event. In fact, it was some time before Lyons's new institution truly made an impact on the hippiatric literature. In the book market, the firm favourites were still the traditional manuals conveying the handed-down medical wisdom of the stable masters in ever new variations. The original thirty-six simple recipes of Master Albrant (also known as Albrecht or Hildebrandt), a blacksmith who lived and wrote at the same time as Ruffo, were reissued with ever-increasing circulation and added appendices. In 1797, the German publisher Cotta issued a 'new and revised edition' – the fourth – of *Nachrichters nüzliches und aufrichtiges Pferd- oder Roß-Arzneybuch* ('A Handbook of practical and genuine veterinary cures'), the work of Johann Deigendesch, an executioner, first published in 1716. Until well into the nineteenth century, there was a steady flow of hippiatric tracts of this kind, which could be traced back to ancient times, well beyond Ruffo. Their authors were on the whole not academically trained physicians, but practitioners: blacksmiths, stable masters, executioners, riding instructors, huntsmen and troopers.

Other elements of equine science were also of a practical nature. Alongside hippiatrics and the complex of horse *husbandry* (horse care, diet, stabling), the two main branches were the *exploitation* and reliable *selection* of horses. The use of horses was dominated for a long time, from the sixteenth to the eighteenth century, by the riding schools and the cavalry; driving with horses, as important as its logistical contribution was, sees relatively little reflection in the literature. Montaigne's elegant essay on carriages, *Des coches*, stands out as an exception.

The main goal of the baroque riding schools from Antoine de Pluvinel ('La maneige royal', 1623) through to François Robichon de La Guérinière (*L'École de Cavalerie*, 1733) was not merely bending the animal's will to that of the rider. It was the mastery of two integrated moving bodies with the aim of conveying a picture of harmony and grace. The doctrine of baroque riding schools carried the aesthetics of grace from the ballroom into the manège and from there into the theatre of war.[16] It was only towards the end of the eighteenth century that the manuals for the military use of horses broke free of this influence. It was no coincidence that it was an Englishman, the Earl of Pembroke, who first developed a special training technique for the cavalry in his work *Military Equitation* (1778).[17] It was at this point that ballroom and battlefield began to go their separate ways.

Under an attractive title for the time around 1800, 'equine science' tied together a somewhat incoherent bundle of literary and practical strands of knowledge from different ages and of varied provenance. It included an ensemble of knowledge, which though easily overlooked in fact was characteristic of and indeed central to the hippological expertise of the era: the safe *selection* of a good horse. If one is to make the right choice at the horse market, one must be able to identify the properties by which a healthy and vigorous animal can be distinguished from a diseased and defective specimen. From antiquity, the handed-down wisdom pertaining to horses encompassed advice on the criteria for assessing their quality, accompanied by references to a charlatan's machinations. There is therefore an ancient tradition of written counsel on the matter, aimed at making horses easier to judge and safer to buy. When Jacques de Solleysel published his influential text on the work of the stable master in 1664, he made this intention clear in the title: *Le Parfait Maréchal, qui enseigne à connoistre la beauté, la bonté et les défauts des chevaux.* No textbook of equine studies, no treatise in the vein of *On Horsemanship*, no *Parfaite connoisance des chevaux* was complete without guidance in identifying the tell-tale signs. Instruction on the 'beauty and flaws of horses' (Solleysel) stands at the very core of hippological know-how. 'A flawless horse with only good qualities would be perfect, but alas is very rare,' writes La Guérinière in *L'École de cavalerie.* 'All this I have repeated, *because an expert must know it all.*'[18]

THE NEW SCHOOLS

Claude Bourgelat (1712–79) is considered the founder of modern veterinary education. In 1762 he opened the École vétérinaire in Lyons; four years later, the veterinary school at Alfort near Paris was opened. By 1763, the Prussian King Friedrich II had already sent two 'surgeons' off to study in Lyons. But the king's hopes that they would bring back a cure for his country's rampant Rinderpest (cattle plague) were dashed; in Lyons, the surgeons reported on their return, there was talk only of horses.[19] That did not stop the two French schools from prompting a wave of similar establishments being founded throughout Europe over the following few decades: in 1767, Vienna saw the opening of the K. K. Pferdekuren- und Operationsschule (Imperial Royal School for Horse Cures and Operations) while similar institutions opened in Turin and Göttingen in 1771, Copenhagen in 1773, Skara (Sweden) and Dresden in 1774, Hanover in 1778, Freiburg in 1783, Budapest in 1786, Marburg in 1789, Berlin and Munich in 1790, and London and Milan in 1791. And so it went on.

Bourgelat, a lawyer by training, wished to be seen not only as an administrator but also as an authority on veterinary medicine. He based his *Éléments d'hippiatrique* on older hippological works such as those by Jacques de Solleysel and William Cavendish, 1st Duke of Newcastle. The three volumes of this much larger work were published between 1750 and 1753. A friend of Jean le Rond d'Alembert, Bourgelat also contributed more than 200 entries to volumes 5 to 7 of d'Alembert's *Encyclopédie*. Even after setting up his veterinary school, he continued to publish widely on equine medicine and on practical aspects of horse husbandry, care and selection, without being able to silence his critics, who saw him as a dilettante.

The most important of these was Philippe-Étienne Lafosse (1738–1820). The son of a horse doctor, he had even as a youth performed dissections of horses for the purpose of teaching the cavalry. Because his rival Bourgelat's school was off limits for him, he taught between 1767 and 1770 at an anatomical theatre in Paris, established at his own expense. Also out of his own pocket, in 1772 he published a large-format and magnificently illustrated work, *Cours d'hippiatrique*. While, as an autodidact, Bourgelat was still following the episteme of classical mechanics and describing the horse's anatomy as a collection of levers, forces and loads, Lafosse structured his anatomy according to the system of organs, adhering thereby 'to the classification that is more usual nowadays', as it was put in a recent history of veterinary medicine.[20] While Bourgelat may have created the practical framework of veterinary education with his school in 1762, it was Lafosse, the experienced pathologist, who ten years later laid the foundations for the systematic classification and autopsy of veterinary medicine.

It would, of course, still be decades before the real birth of such a system. Neither Bourgelat's schools nor the courses given by his rival Lafosse brought forth truly scientifically trained physicians. The majority of the 'veterinarians' who graduated from their school were blacksmiths with an advanced knowledge of a horse's anatomy. State and private stud farms, the growing market for horses and the army all called for efficient practitioners with specific knowledge limited to certain applications. Even in Lafosse's opulently illustrated folio work, the last and by no means least significant chapter deals with farriery and the requisite procedures and equipment for shoeing a horse. Bourgelat's first schools were criticized for imparting purely book knowledge and not having their own forge.[21] Until the end of the century, the farrier's anvil and irons remained the core utensils for teaching.

A GLOSSY GLOW

Like the vet's clinic, connoisseurship also requires a well-trained eye. But the curriculums of the two faculties are quite different. The success of a professional expert on horses, a connoisseur, relies on his ability to discern the relationship of the visible and the invisible. The hippological connoisseur does not read the symptoms of disease or study the semiotics of hidden infections. This branch of expertise looks out for characteristics of health and beauty; it is a school that trains the *ability to judge* a horse by external signs. But this skill that the connoisseur has to hone is not an expression of disinterested admiration, it is aimed at imparting practical advice, helping a buyer make an informed choice, and providing buying recommendations. The connoisseur's perspective is firmly focused on the market. Like any branch of expertise that is combined with a practical application, equine expertise is put on the spot at the moment of truth. The expert's know-how and his skills are put to the test the moment he chooses one particular horse to be bought over another, be it for sport, breeding, war or work. The act of procurement is the crisis moment of equine science.[22]

Only a few years after the establishment of the veterinary schools in Lyons and Alfort, Claude Bourgelat published his *Traité de la conformation extérieure du cheval*, a treatise on the good form and appearance of a horse.[23] With the exception of the last third of the work, which is devoted to the care and maintenance of horses, the treatise is a handbook for the education of future connoisseurs.[24] The budding aficionado of horses needed to learn to judge the inner nature of the horse from the external evidence, and to see the external in the context of the whole. This was the basis on which the savant could tap into the correlation between the horse's external beauty and inner well-being. Beauty, according to Bourgelat, rested on 'the equilibrium and harmony of the parts'.[25] The horse specialist was indebted to the theory of proportions, a tradition which harked back to Leonardo da Vinci and which was transferred from the human condition to that of the animal.[26] The basic dimension, against which everything else was measured, was the length of the horse's head. There was nothing subjective about the proportional measurements extrapolated from the length of the head; these were objective rules or 'mechanical truths'.[27] They guaranteed that a fine horse was also a healthy, strong and fast animal, and that it would pass on its good qualities to its progeny.[28] For decades, equine science was trapped under the spell of the classical concept of proportions until, in the wake of Romanticism, the first wave of resistance rose up against this orthodoxy.

Beauty comes about only through the free and equal play of the limbs, argued Friedrich Schiller.[29] The expert judge of a horse approached this principle from the opposite direction: from the beauty of the animal he infers that there is free play of the limbs and swift movement. The connoisseur would formulate a judgement of taste in order to make a simultaneous value judgement of the quality of the animal, its predicted performance on the turf or in the regiment, and its anticipated progeny. The semiotic approach[30] of the connoisseur was to seek in evidence of beauty an indication of a horse's good health, strength, speed and breeding success. The connoisseur strikes a balance between two contrasting poles: personal or anecdotal experience on the one hand, and clinical expertise on the other. The foundation of horse science, writes one 'equine Doctor and Professor' in the early nineteenth century, 'is the accurate knowledge of a horse's state of good health'.[31]

However, this wisdom is not without its dark side, its opposing power, its nemesis: skulduggery and *horse-trading* in the underhand sense of the word. 'In my opinion,' proclaimed the Hungarian politician and cavalryman Count István Széchenyi, 'nothing makes us wiser about horses than the pain of being swindled.'[32]

Connoisseurs and conmen share in the same knowledge, but they use it in different ways. Both are keenly aware of the tokens of beauty, the marks of affliction and the signs of age. The connoisseur seeks to discover them, making them the object of *perception*. The swindler, on the other hand, strives to bring one to the fore and to conceal the other, making them the object of his *deception*. It's a dichotomy with classical roots: Xenophon included in his book *On Horsemanship* a chapter on selecting a horse that has already been ridden, which included suggestions about 'information a buyer needs to avoid being swindled when buying such a horse'.[33] Since the mid-eighteenth century, there has been a proliferation of literature explicitly warning against the stratagems of the horse-trader. One book which might be considered canonical is Baron d'Eisenberg's *Anti-Maquignonage pour éviter la surprise*, published in 1764 in Amsterdam, which shortly thereafter also appeared in German: *Entdeckte Rostäuscherkünste zur Vermeidung der Betrügereyen bey den Pferdekaufen* ('Horse-trading wiles revealed for the avoidance of deceit when buying horses').[34] This magnificently illustrated work demonstrates all the physical defects of horses and all the moral shortcomings in humans, giving carte blanche to the hermeneutics of suspicion.

It is perhaps no surprise that in the pages of a literature that so intently investigates the abyss of human baseness we see resentment thriving – and, with it, anti-Semitism. The year 1824 saw the publication of a work, edited and revised by Dr C. F. Lentin, purporting to reveal the 'secrets of all commercial gains made through the art of horse beautification by horse dealers. From the papers of the late Israelite horse dealer Abraham Mortgen in Dessau, for the benefit of all those seeking to buy and sell horses at a profit but without harm or deceit'.[35]

The late Mortgen was alleged to have pushed back the limits. He skilfully negotiated the fine line that divides experienced, shrewd horse dealers from common charlatans, commercial aptitude from downright fraud. No other item of trade, no other artefact on the goods and chattels market was as prone as the horse to being manipulated by

To horse! French soldiers mount their steeds at a riding school during the Great War.

Austrian veterinary surgeons removing shrapnel at a field hospital on the Italian front, First World War.

beautifying stratagems. It is precisely with the weaker or inferior specimens that the horse trader's art is manifest: 'A faulty horse is of the least value to the connoisseur but of the dearest value to the savvy trader. You can dress up a bad cloth with a good finish, but you can't make a good one look better than it really is.'[36]

Where is the dividing line between legitimate profit and common deceit? Is someone who attempts to make a horse look better than it truly is necessarily a con artist? Is he not just doing what we all do when we use the artifices of toiletries and hairstyling to appear a little fresher and younger? Which resources are acceptable in the realm of beautification and which are forbidden? Does the blame often not fall – if there is to be talk of blame at all – on the buyer who, like a fool in love, is ready and willing to be deceived? A horse should never be put on display, writes Mortgen, which has not previously been washed and groomed to a glossy glow, be it through exercise, use of the brush or other more cunning means: 'For it is in the cleaning and grooming of horses that the main commercial profit is to be made, just as with a tasteful . . . toilet the ageing woman knows how to defy the passage of time, how to raise a flat bosom, refresh the complexion, soften the skin, make the hair brown and curly, yes, even conceal a hunched back, make a plump figure look slender and give a lean figure a certain *embonpoint*: so must the horse dealer by the art of toiletry . . . seek to beautify the horses he wishes to trade and to conceal their shortcomings and flaws . . .'[37]

Even the trained eye of the connoisseur can be outwitted. It is, of course, not only a matter of the proportions of its body and the gloss and glow of its coat that can give a horse a favourable, attractive appearance, or leave it looking plain and ungainly. No less important are the buoyancy of its gait and vigour in its movement. Practically all methods were permitted to make a lazy horse seem awake and lively – the use of the carrot as much as the whip. But one method is recommended above all others: the use of pepper. 'For pepper is the true spirit, the true life of horse trading; it turns old to young, sluggish to fiery, dull to keen-witted, clumsy to light-footed . . .' Just before the horse is presented, it must have 'some peppercorns . . . inserted by the stable lad by sleight of hand into the anus, by which means the finishing touches of the horse's toilet is completed'.[38]

Could someone who was unfamiliar with such ruses deserve to call himself a consummate expert? 'Whoever is unaware of . . . the effect of pepper, remains quite inexperienced in the knowledge of horse trading and will view a great number of expressions as natural properties which are in fact artificial talents brought on by the pepper.' But the horse trader can be betrayed by his own devices, his ruse undone by the dialectic of the horse's behind: the initial advantage is soon lost 'by the horse's frequent defecation, and betrayed by the trembling of the tail. The animal must be peppered anew, whereby a genuine inflammation of the rectum can sometimes occur.'[39]

An initially curious-looking work of equine literature, published in 1790 by Cotta, emerged from the pen of William D. Gottfried Ploucquet, 'the Medical Science Professor'. Entitled *Über die Hauptmängel der Pferde* ('On the Main Defects in Horses'), it hints at the purpose and value of its practical training only in the subtitle: 'For horse lovers and dealers, and above all legal scholars, with consideration of relevant lawsuits'. The physician offered lawyers information and expertise. In both cases, the focus is on eliminating manipulative horse-trading and on the enforcement of warranty claims by victims. Experience suggests, as the author explains in the preface, 'that there is as much controversy and misunderstanding about the perceived main defects in horses as that which prevails about the darkest matter . . .'[40] The six main defects which should be identified before it is too late, are 1) 'glanders';[41] 2) 'the staggers';[42] 3) 'incurable infestations'[43] (such as scabies); 4) 'pounding heart', i.e. a heart condition or asthma;[44] 5) 'prone to the falling sickness', i.e. epileptic,[45] and 6) 'moon blindness' (i.e. cyclically recurring eye diseases).[46]

As the chapter on 'pounding heart' shows, semantics and symptoms can stray so far apart that the defects of a horse risk being concealed behind the defects of the classification system. But we would be wronging the author if we blamed him for the shortcomings of the taxonomy of his time. The work of Dr Ploucquet is more than a guide, it is a handbook for a hunting party. Three types of knowledge are collated in its pages, which in the modern division of labour are rarely if ever seen together: the knowledge of the horse expert, of the veterinary surgeon and of the lawyer. They have taken up their positions in perfect harmony on the periphery of the horse market. The enemy, for whom they lie in wait, is the duplicitous horse dealer. They recognize him and hunt him down, by all means in their power; their skills lined up against his schemes, their wisdom against his wiles. But secretly they fear his cunning, his unexpected subterfuges. In the face of the organized formations of Connoisseurship, Science and Jurisprudence, the sly horse dealer is like the fox in the face of the mounted aristocrats of England and their packs of dogs: he rises to the challenge with guileful sophistry. An entire sporting world is kept in business by the fox's cunning; likewise, an army of experts is kept in business by the ruses of the horse trader.

Researchers

AN ANIMAL OF DUST

It is mid-May 1879, south-east of the Dzungarian Basin, near Lake Goshun Nur in northern China. Somewhere on this tawny lunar surface of the Gobi Desert, nearly a hundred years later, Perry Rhodan, 'The Heir to the Universe' of the eponymous German science fiction series, will land and found the capital Terrania. His spaceship will be called *Stardust*, as if there wasn't already enough of the volatile fine matter down here. Every morning when the wind rises, it carries masses of sand and dust swirling up into the air, dashing it against the rocks, the sparse shrubs and anything found moving along the parched ground. The expedition's caravan stumbles along, half blind: the leader and his assistants, a painter and illustrator, seven Cossacks who take care of the animals and food, twenty-three camels, and behind them a flock of sheep forming the mobile fresh-meat counter. The equipment is extensive and includes a wide array of instruments, tents, crates of sugar, tea and dried fruit, 20 litres of alcohol, 1,500 sheets of blotting paper for the preservation of fauna and flora, huge quantities of weapons and ammunition, as well as heaps of gifts for the natives: guns, mirrors, magnets and coloured prints of Russian actresses, the pin-ups of the Russian Empire, which were particularly gladly received.[1]

It is the third expedition carried out by Nikolai Mikhailovich Przhevalsky (Przewalski in Polish) and this time the company is luxuriously well equipped. The success of his first two expeditions of 1870–73 and 1876–8, their booty (the word has the smack of truth to it) in terms of geographic, botanical and zoological findings and specimens was so impressive that it was much easier to finance the third expedition. The party was saved from the cumbersome necessity of going cap in hand to potential donors like the Academy of Sciences, the Geographical Society, the War Office, and an endless round of lectures and banquets, by direct backing from the Tsar. The potential gains of the expedition, whose goal was the unattainable Lhasa, were clear to St Petersburg: certainly it would bring a wealth of data, animal furs and rock samples, but above all it was about Russian hegemony over Central Asia. This covert objective brought other operations into the compass of the expedition; the researchers were tasked to gather intelligence as well as scientific data. Przewalski was the right man for the mission: a desire for knowledge was as much a part of his personality as a desire for power.

Even before he set off in the spring of 1879, Kyrgyz hunters had brought him the skin of a wild horse such as he had never clapped eyes on before. The Kyrgyz name for it was *Kurtag*, while the Mongols called it *Takhi*. It was the pelt of a young animal, about the size of a Mongolian pony, but more sturdily built and with a short, bushy mane like a punk's Mohican. The shaggy pelt with a white mouth and white belly was a mottled mix of the colours of Dzungaria: brown, yellow and grey. Przewalski examined the powerful hooves, the relatively large head with its deep-set eyes and unusually strong jaw and became convinced that before him lay the remains of the ancestral *ur-horse*, the ancient progenitor that roamed the steppes of Central Asia. Even if it would turn out in the course of time that his suspicions were only partially correct,[2] it was nevertheless perhaps the most significant discovery of his life. The explorer may not have given his name to a continent, but he managed to pass it on to a good number of plants and creatures,[3] including this dying breed, a small, tough desert horse that resembled a cave painting come to life. But it was this dust-coloured beast that would make his name immortal.[4]

The name varies, or at least its spelling, depending on whether the family were resident in Russia (Przhevalsky) or Poland (Przewalski). It became obvious early on that he was destined for a life of adventure, and for that the career of an officer was the ideal choice. Keenly intelligent, or rather gifted with a capacity to learn effortlessly, no matter what institutional framework he found himself in, be it school or the military academy, he approached life with such radical laxity and indifference that he was always on the verge of being expelled or sacked. He began as a geographer, making his name with a dissertation on the military and statistical status of the Amur region and set himself up as – or found himself becoming – one of the most knowledgeable botanists and zoologists and especially ornithologists of his time; au fait, too, with the art of taxidermy. His role model was David Livingstone, and he had long dreamed of making a journey like his to the Dark Continent. As a teacher at the Corps of Cadets in Warsaw, he read not only Alexander von Humboldt's travels but also Carl Ritter's geographical research, and came to realize that his inner Africa lay to the east. On the maps of the time, Central Asia was still largely terra incognita. Geopolitically, it had long been a theatre of conflict between the major European powers, the home of the Great Game. It was also the focal point of increasingly intense intra-Asian rivalries between Russia and the 'Middle Kingdom', China.[5]

For a researcher of the conquistador mould such as Przewalski, political tension just made matters more interesting. His passion for shooting targeted countless birds and mammals, which landed alternately in the cooking pot or in the crate to be taken back and stuffed. The expedition turned into a kind of scientific war machine that hunted, trapped, picked and plucked its way through the wild steppes and deserts of Central Asia. Przewalski belonged to the type of trigger-happy explorer who shot first and asked questions later; as he trawled for specimens, whatever his eye fell on was destined for a brutal end. He took it as a personal humiliation that he never managed to strike the wild horse from his hit list. Recluses like him, glad to avoid human company and of mysterious, perhaps deviant, sexuality, carried death with them in the wilderness, seeking it out and of course often finding it.[6] Przewalski saw the Asians, and particularly the Chinese, as an unclean species, the subjugation of whom by Russian colonial rule was a simple matter, indeed, almost a cultural obligation. In his 1886 secret memorandum on China policy, commissioned by the Russian government, the geographer allied himself wholeheartedly with the colonial strategists.[7]

The wild horses, meanwhile, which Przewalski finally came across in May 1879 on the south-east edge of Dzungaria, managed to survive the encounter. The hunters had almost come within firing range, but before they could shoot, the horses had got wind of them and fled. There were two groups, each with a stallion and six or seven mares – harems, as are common with this type of wild horse. Przewalski's successors also had to be content with individual skins and remains; it was not until the turn of the twentieth century that the first living specimens were caught and either passed on to the Falz-Fein family's zoological reserve in the Ukrainian steppe or sold on to entrepreneurs like Carl Hagenbeck.[8] Most of the Przewalski's horses found in captivity today stem from five mares originally bred in Ukraine.[9] *The International Studbook for the Przewalski's Horse*, edited by Erna Mohr of Hamburg Zoo, was first published in 1959, although it is now under the aegis of Prague Zoo. Thanks to several successful reintroductions in the last twenty years, Przewalski's horse has returned from the brink of extinction in the wild, and has been reclassified as a merely endangered species.[10] One of the areas of reintroduction, incidentally, is a region no longer inhabited by people: the Chernobyl exclusion zone.

AN ANIMAL OF WORDS

A session of the Berlin Reichstag, 4 March 1899. There's a serious matter on the agenda: 'funding for the troops'. Nevertheless, the transcript logs multiple outbursts of merriment during an intervention by a certain Hoffmann, a member of the house. The deputy calls for better recognition for army veterinary surgeons, not stopping at financial remuneration, but also turning to the question of nomenclature. The official titles of the staff vets, he argued, required urgent attention. Hoffmann: 'The titles read: *Unterroßarzt* [Junior Horse Doctor], *Roßarzt* [Horse Doctor], *Oberroßarzt* [Senior Horse Doctor], *Korpsroßarzt* [Corps Horse Doctor]. Yes, gentlemen, the horse is indeed in itself a noble animal (laughter), Pegasus was also a horse (loud laughter), but I wish you could travel around the world for ten years with such a title (loud laughter), and then you would see what a reaction you get. You have to twitch when you introduce yourself or else you'll have everyone in stitches when they hear your title (laughter). To get a sense of how people generally perceive the difference between *Pferd* ['horse' in northern Germany] and *Ross* ['horse' in southern Germany], let me tell you a story: on a manoeuvre down in Swabia, a Prussian gunner, a driver, comes to the billets with his two horses. The Prussian says to his host, who greets him kindly, "Now you take your *Rosse* out of the stable and make space for these *Pferde*!" (riotous laughter) I would ask the Minister of War to kindly follow my suggestions, or else I shall, as often as the opportunity arises, keep returning to the topic (laughter).'[11]

Franz Boas, who a decade later would be responsible for disseminating the myth about the wealth of terms in the Eskimo language for 'snow',[12] would have enjoyed this Reichstag debate, which conveys something of the linguistic complications surrounding the German words for 'horse'. Like mankind, our closest and most important companion is also a phantasm of the dictionary, a being conjured up by words. Since antiquity, hippological literature has spelled out its subject in endless tracts: the art of taming and breeding the horse, of assessing its form and curing its suffering. In belles-lettres, too, we find celebrations of this fabulous being: 'The words summon up an animal, a perfect one of unsurpassable beauty,'[13] writes Ellen Strittmatter of a description of a palfrey in Hartmann von Aue's medieval narrative poem *Erec*, which throughout its over 500 verses builds up an image of Enite's light, piebald horse: a Song of Songs to the horse in early German literature. Hartmann's artistry is clear in the way the imagination is kindled. 'The description opens with a verb of seeing and observing, which serves as a signal for the listener or reader to conjure up the image of the horse in the mind's eye.'[14] More than seven centuries after Hartmann forced open the wellsprings of the imagination, Guillaume Apollinaire moved in the opposite direction in his *Calligrammes*, letting the lines of his verse physically draw the outline of a horse (p. 362).

The palfrey, a riding horse that walks at a gentle trot, called a *Zelter* or *Tölt* in German, is a term that has disappeared from modern usage. Even the German word *Ross* has long seen a decline in usage, but unlike its medieval counterpart, palfrey, *Ross* has not retreated altogether into the dust of obscurity. Until well into the nineteenth century, the words *Ross* and *Pferd* divided the German-speaking territory: the north had the *Pferd*, while the south had the *Ross*. The language barrier ran along the route of the Roman *limes*, the boundary between

Long in the tooth: *Equus przewalskii* skulls from the collection of the
Natural History Museum in Berlin.

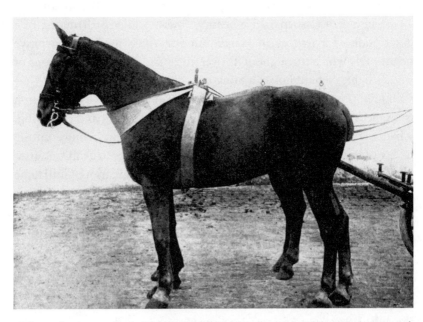

'The unfortunate necktie' (Marc Bloch): the experimental reproduction of
an Ancient Greek-style harness by Lefebvre des Noëttes showed how it
would have strangled the classical beast of burden, Paris, 1910.

provinces of the Roman Empire, and the occasional vocabulary difference in provincial dialects is reflected in the North German riddle: 'Which state has no *Pferde* (horses)?' To which the answer was: 'Swabia: there they have *Rosse* (horses)!'[15]

The historical etymologies take us back to different provenances – Latin for *Pferd* (*parafredus*), and Old Norse (*Rasa*), possibly Hebrew (*ruz*) or Latin (*Ruere*) for *Ross* – but common to all these forms is the inclination to trot and to canter. Max Jähns, who collected the names for 'horse' and boiled down their morphemes and etymologies like Stubbs did with his skeletons, found hints of motion everywhere: as if there was a hidden arrow, a linguistic vector running through all European languages. As if all linguistic expressions and fragments of kinetic energy were concentrated in the name of this one animal; as if the dynamics at play within the languages themselves had assumed the shapes and names of the animal now known in German by its household name *Pferd*.

Take, for example, the ancient word for a horse – *Märhe* – which Jähns suggests also 'harks back to a description of movement'.[16] Indeed, he finds cognates in the Irish Gaelic *markayim*, Low Breton *markat* and Scots *to merk* – 'to ride'. Hearing the resonance with the verbs 'march, marcher, marciare, marchar', he concludes that 'we might then with reasonable certainty speak of the element of motion as being highly characteristic of the horse and therefore as the source of the name *märhe*'.[17] Besides the more contemporary *Mähre* ('old horse') Jähns lists *Pfage, Hess, Hangt* and *Maiden* as German words for a horse in general; *Hengst, Beschäler, Schwaiger, Stöter, Renner* and *Klepper* for the male horse (stallion); *Stute, Kobbel, Wilde, Fähe, Fole, Taete, Gurre, Zöre, Strenze, Strute, Strucke* and *Motsche* for the female (mare); and for the young animal, he gives *Füllen* (compare with the English *filly*), *Burdi, Bickartlein, Kuder, Heinsz, Wuschel, Watte* and *Schleichle*. Added together with all the other local dialect variants such as *Kracke, Zagge, Vulz, Nickel, Schnack, Grämlein, Kofer* (Southern German for a bad-tempered horse, Jähns suggests from the verb *keifen* 'to bicker'[18]) and finally *Hoppe* ('a word which clearly originates in the horse's motion'[19]), he comes to a total of sixty-three different German names for a horse.[20]

These names and their origins are just the beginning. Taking them as the starting point, Jähns sets off on a voyage of discovery through the entire linguistic world of horses and riders, collecting words, say-ings, songs, rhymes, poetry, everyday language, specialist vocabulary, myths and legend, and the realm of what the German writer Peter Rühmkorf described as the 'national wealth': satire and wit, jokes and ditties both erudite and smutty. Just as for the Grimm Brothers – the trailblazers for this lexicographer and collector of linguistic antiquities – for Jähns no unearthed treasure is too bizarre, no turn of speech too trivial and no joke too coarse to be admitted into his archive of hippological idiom.[21] Unlike the Grimms, though, he does not limit himself to the German-speaking literature of recent cent-uries, but draws from all sources available, including Graeco-Roman and Norse mythology.

In the 1860s, when he was amassing his huge collection of material for his lexical encyclopaedia *Ross und Reiter in Leben und Sprache, Glauben und Geschichte der Deutschen* ('Horse and horsemen in the life, language, beliefs and history of the Germans'), Jähns was himself an officer and a rider; he taught at the Military Academy and worked at various headquarters. All of this experience benefited his book: as an expert, the author lifted countless details of real life from stables and blacksmiths, including diseases, horse-drawn vehicles, tack and riding equipment. He even found room for 'antiquated legal terminol-ogy' in the chapter on 'Horses and Riders in Worship and Law'.[22] The reader cannot but admire Jähns's encyclopaedic thoroughness: as a cultural history of the centaurian 'double-being'[23] of horse and rider, it is unparalleled.[24] The second volume of the work goes deeper into the historical context and offers an overview of the sweep of German history from a hippological perspective. Towards the end we observe a shift to a more patriotic turn of phrase with increasing hints of nationalist ideology: an aversion to England, 'the land of racing and betting',[25] and to the 'alarming influence of Englishness on our own horse breeding'.[26]

The racehorse was, according to Jähns, 'an artificial product, an artefact, which was excessively "trained" for a single, moreover illu-sory, role'.[27] The English had not only invented the merry dance around this golden artefact, but, to top it all, had desecrated it through the association with gambling. Mammon had spoiled everything, he argued, even the horse: 'Bit by bit . . . wealth, luxury and passion have reduced the noble steed to a mere plaything . . . The race has become a mighty sport for money, where the horse as a harmonious entity has completely receded from sight, and the element of speed is hot-housed and intensified to the exclusion of all else.'[28]

With their passion for flat races, inbred racehorses and betting, the gift the Englishmen had brought across the Channel turned out to be a Trojan horse, argued Jähns, 'infesting our German language with the plague of English'.[29] The examples of 'vile jargon' proffered by the author capture the spirit of the racecourse and its love of casual expression: when the talk is of a horse's 'pace', of a 'handicap' or when a race ends with a 'match'. There is nothing that would make a modern German reader shudder, accustomed as we are to anglicisms, but Jähns's audience may well have responded differently at the time. For the author himself, the debate about linguistic purism, which first stirred around 1872, would over the years become a *force majeure*: in 1896, Jähns assumed the presidency of the Allgemeiner Deutscher Sprachverein (the General Association for the German Language), a national body which applied itself to the purity of the German language with such intransigence that not only liberals like Hans Delbrück, but even conservatives like Gustav Freytag and Heinrich von Treitschke turned their backs on it.

Ross und Reiter ends with a consideration of the practical value of the cavalry in present-day warfare, drawing on the lessons of the American Civil War, as well as the wars of Prussia against Austria and France: the hippological lexicon even branches into offering tactical tips.[30] In his own specialist area, military history, Jähns remained an early representative of a modern perspective on war that recognized not only conflicts and large personalities, but also the economic and social structures within which wars and battles were waged.[31] His linguistic chauvinism, however, meant that with time he was increasingly tempted by nationalist thinkers. His 1872 publication was dedicated to 'His Serene Highness, the Chancellor of the German Empire, Otto Prince von Bismarck-Schönhausen, Major General *à la suite* of the Magdeburg Cuirassier Regiment', which was perhaps a nod to Bismarck's 1867 pronouncement in the North German Reichstag: 'Let us put Germany in the saddle! She will know well enough how to ride!'[32] Reading the 800-plus pages that follow certainly gives one the impression that this cavalier detachment of German liberalism might well have proved its worth in the saddle, but had nevertheless lost its way in the mists of legend.

AN ANIMAL OF LIGHT

A Parisian soirée in the prestigious 16th Arrrondissement, 26 September 1881: Étienne-Jules Marey is hosting a reception in honour of Eadweard Muybridge, the famous American pioneer of chronophotography who has just arrived in Paris. Marey has invited a number of important colleagues from France and abroad,[33] including several from his close circle. Two are in the dress uniform of the Army of the Republic. Raabe and Bonnal are cavalry captains who collaborated with Marey in the lab and at the recently opened 'experimental station' at Auteuil. The well-known physiologist Charles Raabe was engaged in military research. Or rather, he was doing research whose value was recognized by the army, which was providing personnel and funding. The topic was as significant an issue as the gait of a horse.

Despite the strategic importance of the railway, something the French Army's General Staff had been wise to since the war against the Germans ten years ago, the horse remained the most significant means of traction and transport. Unrivalled in terms of speed, horses remained indispensable. In contrast to the historical painters and the amateurs of equestrian sport, the main concern of the army was not what happened to a horse's legs when it galloped, but the question of how animate military resources could be used most cautiously and efficiently. Two doctrines had developed within the cavalry: one that placed more emphasis on the will of the rider, and another that preferred to emphasize the nature of the horse; the two schools of thought had long been at loggerheads.[34] Military horsemanship doesn't come cheap, after all. By the late nineteenth century, the focus was not on the grace of the horse and rider as in the Baroque riding schools. Now the main concerns were expenditure and sustaining vital energy so as to avoid premature exhaustion.[35] Wars depended not only on rifles and grenades; they would also be won by muscles and tendons. Or lost.

Charles Raabe died in May 1889, and in the following year his younger colleague Guillaume Bonnal published their collaborative work, *Équitation*,[36] the result of fifteen years of research combined with experimental physiology. The appendix contains seven tables of film strip, shot at twenty-five frames per second, showing the horse in all its gaits. According to Bonnal, the recordings were made in summer 1889 at Auteuil. The author describes the *défilé* of the long-legged models: 'The subject of the experiments – with the exception of the normal trot and jumping – was a pure Arab blood mare called Fanfreluche, born at the Pompadour stud on 1 April 1878. This horse, a dapple grey, walked along in various gaits in front of a curtain of black velvet, while being captured on film by a photochronographic apparatus. For trotting and jumping, the curtain was replaced by a white wall. The mare Sylphide provided the images for the trot.'[37]

He was searching, as Marey wrote in 1886 in a letter to his assistant Georges Demenÿ, for 'a way to see the invisible'.[38] This desire was shared by others at the time; nine years later, Wilhelm Conrad Röntgen would find his own way of making the invisible visible. Marey's most famous method, which was also practised by Muybridge, consisted of photographically forcing open the fleeting moment, invisible in its swiftness, and thus making it visible.[39] The movements of a trotting horse (see pp. 222, 270) or a woman running, dissected into slices almost twenty-five times per second with a scalpel of light. Leonardo da Vinci had undertaken a similar analysis[40] – albeit with a draughtsman's stylus – of people in rapid motion, and in his commentary of 1940 Erwin Panofsky remarks on how da Vinci's drawings reminded him of the cinematographer's art.[41] Marey and Muybridge were doing nothing different to Leonardo when they used continuous photographic technology – the immediate precursor to the film camera – to get inside the infinitesimally small detail of the moment to break apart a second of time like nuclear fission. Where else would time's invisible details be hiding if not in its smallest components?

Historians know that there is also a certain invisibility within periods of longer duration. History, the embodiment of protracted time periods, is suffused with this kind of obscurity. Only a few years after Marey and Muybridge, long-duration chronographers began trying to visualize the invisible in history. Aby Warburg was the most prominent among them. Using a long iconographic range, he attempted to trace the evolution of forms – Warburg spoke of 'formulae' – by which the artists of ancient and modern times had sought to express strong inner motion, or emotion. The constancy as well as the mutability in these formulae was only captured when a series of images was used to span a long historical time period and compress its contents, just as Marey and Muybridge's photographs had stretched apart the fractions of a moment. Of course, it is not the same thing to dissect the bending of a horse's knee into 100 frames and to line up 100 works of varied artists to trace an expression of sadness, anger or joy over two millennia from ancient times to the Renaissance. The analogy lies in the technique of sequencing time by slicing it into images, whether the time period being carved up is a second or a millennium. Seen as a technical process, Warburg's iconographic analysis was an extremely slowed-down form of chronography – and vice versa.

Shortly after the turn of the century, the history of horses would find its own Warburg. Richard Lefebvre des Noëttes was a retired cavalry officer, the son of a cavalry captain who had served in the Franco-Prussian war of 1870, and great-nephew of a general of the Empire. Even while he was still on active service, in the 1890s, he had started to carry out and publish research into the history of the horseshoe. A serious riding accident in April 1904 forced his resignation, after which he devoted himself entirely to his historical and antiquarian hippological studies. He became an iconographer, spending an eternity in the museums of Paris and collecting whatever equine representations he could get his hands on, be it artefacts from archaeology and art history or contemporary publications. Over the years, he amassed an enormous iconographic library on all aspects of historical horse art. Like his comrades Raabe and Bonnal, for Lefebvre it was also a question of an animal's potential energy and how to put it to optimal use. But unlike theirs, his work was not the synchronous fragmentation of minuscule units of time into images, but rather the use of his own diachronic method to carve up millennia.

With the informed perspective of an *homme de cheval*, Lefebvre noticed details in the representations from the ancient world that had escaped archaeologists and art historians. Briefly, they concerned the posture of the horses' heads and certain details in the apparatus by which the strength of the animals was transmitted to the wagons – in other words, the harness. Starting by comparing images and relics, Lefebvre began digging around in the testimonies of ancient literature, which he learned about from lectures at Paris's school of historical sciences, the École des Chartes: he attended for two years after leaving the service. When he reached a dead end on this path, he returned to his practical knowledge. Borrowing some draught horses and wagons from the Parisian *Compagnie des petites-voitures* that were similar to those of the era in question, he began to experiment. With the help of some skilled craftsmen, he constructed a classical harness such as he had seen represented in the ancient Greek sources. He placed this somewhat comical item on Paris hackney horses of the year 1910 and had them pull a wagon (see p. 204). The tests confirmed his theory.

The ancient method of harnessing a horse consisted of placing a belt or collar around the neck, which applied pressure at the exact point on the neck where the carotid artery runs particularly close under the skin. Once the animal had to pull harder, this 'unfortunate necktie'[42] pressed against the artery, robbing the animal of oxygen and restricting its performance. Horses harnessed in this way could draw a maximum load of 500 kilograms. With a modern harness, the same team of horses pulled four or five times what was possible with the antique apparatus. In other words, the ancients had used only a fraction of the potential strength of the horse. Why did the harness remain like that, and why was it not until the Middle Ages, from the tenth century, that the technical innovations (horseshoes, stirrups, harness) were made that allowed the animal's potential energy to be exploited more efficiently? Why had antiquity not developed this practical understanding of horses?

Lefebvre's answer was because they had not needed to. They were not dependent on horses for power. And why not? Because they had slaves to provide manpower – and more than enough of it. This kinetic economic theory with its historical and sociological consequences was developed by Lefebvre in passing as he worked on the first edition of his book of 1924.[43] In the extended edition of 1931,[44] he included it in the subtitle of his work, thus lending it the necessary emphasis.[45] Lefebvre argued that not only were the ancients' exploitation of slaves and their woeful energy economy (their inadequate use of animal *force motrice*) interdependent issues, but also that the stagnant climate for technological innovation caused by slavery held up other inventions in the energy sector. For example, without transport capacity the water mills of the West would have been unfeasible.[46] It was only under the French Capetians that the knot was unravelled that had so long linked the exploitation of the human energy machine with the lack of advances in alternative energy provision, whether based on animal power or hydropower. It was not antiquity, so lauded by classicists of the nineteenth century as the exemplary age, but rather the 'Dark Ages' that saw the release of the enormous potential of kinetic energy, so fundamental to the rise and dominance of the West.[47]

The classical world lagged behind technically,[48] because the surplus of manpower meant there was little need of innovation. It was the substitution theory, one very well established in the history of technology – man invents the means to exploit nature in order to preserve his own strength – that backed up Lefebvre's assertions and had the historians spellbound. Of course, Lefebvre was not entirely without critics; in 1926, Marc Bloch pulled his autodidact colleague up on what he saw as his basic misunderstandings about bondage and slavery under the Merovingians.[49] But while the ancient historians and philologists tore Lefebvre's work to shreds, demonstrating where he had simplified and misinterpreted evidence from archaeology and art history,[50] his assessment of the technically innovative Middle Ages has naturally been highly rated by medievalists. Even in the 1960s, Lynn White, Jr., medievalist and doyen of American technological history, described the French cavalryman and antiquarian as 'very nearly a genius'.[51]

Nowadays, Lefebvre's analysis of the history of the horse's harness has been proved wrong in both its archaeological premises and in its sociological implications (the question of slavery), and for authors such as Judith Weller the sole interesting aspect of his work is how it was possible that the abstruse views of an officer and amateur researcher could bewitch critical readers for half a century.[52] To focus on such a question is to underestimate the charm of Lefebvre's method and the intriguing evidence brought about by his curious combination of iconography and technical reconstruction. Was it not more fun to err with Lefebvre des Noëttes than to be right with his critics?

AN ANIMAL OF SPIRIT

A Berlin courtyard, 12 August 1904. Firewalls, staircases, sheds and a coach house used as a stable: this is the setting of a gathering of the great and the good from the local scientific institutions, including the Privy Councillor and the Prussian Minister of Education Dr Konrad von Studt. The motive for this outing and the object of their scholarly curiosity is a horse and recent celebrity, named after the Grimm Brothers' fairy tale 'Clever Hans'. Hans is a stallion with, as the prominent Africa scholar Carl Georg Schillings personally testifies, very unusual abilities. 'The animal can read perfectly, can perform arithmetic, has mastered simple fractions and can raise numbers to the power of three. He can distinguish between a large range of colours, knows the value of German coins and the value of playing cards. He recognizes people from photographs, even very small ones and where the similarity is not very great. He understands the German language and has acquired a vocabulary of terms and ideas that in no way corresponds to assessments made heretofore about the psyche of the Equidae . . . So I am today, along with a number of friendly scholars, completely convinced that the stallion is capable of independent thought, deduction and negotiation.'[53]

In Berlin's hot summer of 1904, Clever Hans was the talk of the town. A godsend for the press, he was the mythical creature of the not yet invented silly season. As pundits crowded around the smart black horse and news of his feats spread far and wide (after all, this was a militarily useful commodity: just imagine what an interactive, independently thinking hack could do for Emperor and Fatherland), new and ever greater achievements of the horse became well known. Not only could Hans read and count, had a perfect command of German and even understood a little French – but now he could solve mathematical problems that no one had even asked him out loud. In other words, the animal could read your mind. Had it not always been said that we should leave the thinking to the horses, as they have the larger heads? It's little wonder this miracle horse found his way onto the cabaret stage, providing endless comedy gold.[54]

But it was still early days for the celebrity of the wonder stallion. The year before, scholars had got wind of the case and had started to carry out experiments on the animal. Hans had been obediently going to school for three years up to this point. His owner and sole teacher was a nobleman from the region to the east of the Elbe, Wilhelm von Osten. He acquired the animal in 1900 and immediately got down to business with his education. No time to lose – after all, you can't teach an old dog new tricks. In fact, 'Clever Hans' was actually Hans II; before him was Hans I, who could count to five when he died in 1895 of a bowel obstruction. The teaching methods pursued by the passionate educator von Osten were photographed and documented by his successor and heir Karl Krall,[55] and combined a range of methods, from the kindergarten style ('Good boy, Hans, that's right!') to the more rigorous grammar-school approach involving square roots and elementary geometry. But as capable as von Osten seemed, he was in fact blessed with very little pedagogic talent. 'Despite the year of daily contact, he lacked a compassionate understanding of his pupil's emotional responses and did not recognize the signs of boredom which were clear in Hans when he attended the hours of mostly monotonous lessons.'[56]

Communicating with animals and being understood by them is one of the oldest and most cherished dreams we have as humans; it's an idea that has inspired countless myths and stories. From the talking horse head in the Grimm Brothers' fairy tale 'The Goose Girl' to *Lucky Luke*'s brainy white and brown stallion Jolly Jumper and Mister Ed, the talking horse. Children once stayed up late in the stables on Christmas Eve and could not be persuaded to go to bed, because they had been told that on the stroke of midnight on Holy Night the animals could speak like humans. The twentieth-century German author Peter Kurzeck describes falling asleep as a child and hearing his two wooden horses on the windowsill chatting 'in a quiet, human language'.[57] This childlike faith was evidently alive and well in the adult Wilhelm von Osten, who was trying to bring the dream to life with the obstinacy of the lord of the manor. For him there was no doubt that Hans could reason independently, even if he – still – lacked the power of speech. But as impressive as the stallion's performance was, opinion remained divided: only some of the scholars, circus

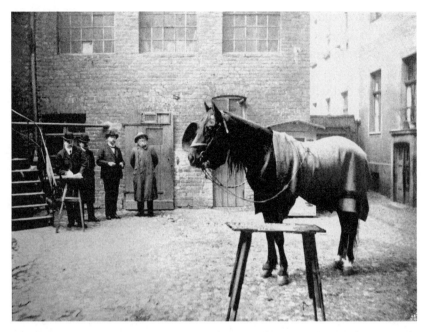

Clever Hans being put to the test. His teacher, von Osten, is on the right and the evaluation team on the left. Berlin, 1907.

Zarif, one of the Elberfeld horses, learning to spell. Elberfeld, 1909.

people and zoologists watching the spectacle in the Griebenowstrasse courtyard in the summer of 1904 were convinced of the stallion's capacity for independent thought.

To cut a long story short: the sceptics were convinced that Clever Hans only did what was somehow hinted to him externally, whether it was by means of a barely noticeable signal or by 'suggestion'. Whatever these minuscule signals were, perhaps slight nods of the head by the horse's teacher, the experts were willing to concede that these clues may have been 'involuntary'.[58] Von Osten and his colleagues were not being accused of underhand behaviour or deception, especially as it was not money that was at stake, but rather the 'mere' matter of scientific truth, and the only party being deceived appeared to be the horse, which of course lent new meaning to the expression 'horse-trading'. The critics' stance was published in a succinct appraisal by the student Oskar Pfungst in a 1907 work translated shortly thereafter into English.[59] The naysayers' review sharply dismissed the assertion of the independently reasoning animal[60] and sought to explain its purported achievements as being the result of gestures or movements by his teacher or the interviewer, which were very slight and yet perceptible by the sharp-eyed stallion, as suggested by third parties present at the numerous examinations.

Reluctant to let his animal be dismissed from the ranks of independent thinkers, von Osten complained that it was the researchers Oskar Pfungst and Carl Stumpf[61] who had corrupted his horse by training him to respond to signals.[62] Von Osten had long had a backer in the form of the imaginative jeweller Karl Krall from Elberfeld, who set out with new experiments to prove the thesis of the independently reasoning animal, not influenced by any external cues. Krall went on to broaden the scope of animal–human communication far beyond the narrow academic sphere von Osten had defined (reading, counting, arithmetic . . .) to include aesthetic judgement, that is, Kant's 'Third Critique'. His conclusion was that one can also communicate with horses on matters of taste and, more generally, matters involving sensitivity and feeling.[63] He attempted to familiarize Hans with the difference between beautiful and ugly, but eventually gave up when he realized that the education based on awarding treats was only consolidating the association between love and aesthetic preferences and the desire for food.[64] Like many horses, the way to his heart was through his stomach.

After the death of von Osten in June 1909, Karl Krall inherited Clever Hans and took him back with him to Elberfeld. At his own expense he set up a research station where two more bright horses, the stallions Muhamed and Zarif, would have the opportunity to enjoy his reformed ('simplified', 'abbreviated, time-saving') teaching approach.[65] The main impact of his report, published in 1912,[66] summarizing von Osten's Berlin experiments and his own work at Elberfeld, ensured that Hans and his classmates remained in the public eye. Elberfeld, like Berlin, saw a constant coming and going of scientific committees.

Hans, incidentally, came to an inglorious end. When Maurice Maeterlinck, the famous composer and researcher into the souls of animals, visited Elberfeld in September 1913, he demanded to see 'the great ancestor, the Clever Hans'.[67] The old boy, however, was a mere shadow of his former self and led a life of forced obscurity: 'Hans has degenerated and we speak of him only reluctantly.' He, who had led 'a puritanical, monastic existence, devoted to celibacy, scholarship and arithmetic',[68] had allegedly been so inflamed at the sight of a beautiful mare that he had bounded over hedges and fences, ripping the underside of his body so badly that the vet had had to come and stuff his entrails back inside and sew him up. Ostracized, he eked out the rest of his days in shame. Clearly, the hour of sexual liberation for stallions had not yet come.

Maeterlinck described the phenomenon of the Elberfelder horses (meanwhile, another pony and a blind stallion had been squeezed into the classroom), and suggested an explanation which one might call dialectic, because it transcended the two antagonistic positions – that of *independent thought* and that of *involuntary signalling* – although it did so in a way that would make it hard for any dialectician to follow. The author, rapt by the idea of a 'first dawning of an unexpected intelligence that suddenly manifests itself as human-like',[69] imagined a kind of spiritual ether or 'subliminal' spiritual force, 'that lurks under the veil of our mind and . . . surprises, dominates and controls it'.[70] Putatively drawing on psychoanalysis, Maeterlinck had no qualms about describing this spiritual force as 'subconscious'[71] and then in the next breath identifying it in terms of the Hegelian 'world spirit'.[72] With a few exceptions,[73] scholarship has not pursued Maeterlinck's 'mediumistic' approach to solving the problem of the thinking horses.[74]

Franz Kafka, meanwhile, sent an ambitious student off on the trail of the Elberfeld horses.[75] His fictional student is forced by his unfavourable financial situation to work nights. He tries to make a virtue of adversity and to put to good use the capacity for concentration that night gives him: 'The sensitivity that comes over man and beast both waking and working at night was an integral feature of his plan. Unlike other experts, he had no fear of the wildness of the animal, he positively encouraged it – yes, he sought to produce it, not through the whip admittedly, but by the irritation of his constant presence and constant teaching.'[76] It is possible that here, as elsewhere in Kafka's notes, imagery of horses, riding and dressage stand as metaphors for writing and the self-education of the writer.[77] Seen in this way, the student's strategy is to rediscover the ferocity and savagery of writing, in place of prudence and obedience. In view of the high value associated with the concept of savagery since Rousseau's time, it is no surprise that this motif was a source of fascination to inspired commentators on Kafka's work, such as Gilles Deleuze[78] and Durs Grünbein.[79]

THE JUMPING POINT

Münster in Westphalia on 18 July 2003. Reinhart Koselleck receives the city's historian prize and gives an unusual acceptance speech. After years studying the history of equestrian statues he had found the blind spot of history: not the rider and not the pedestal, but the object in between. It was in this speech that he coined the concept of 'the age of the horse'[80] and outlined the past achievements of horses. He paid tribute to their mythological and symbolic roles and stressed their military importance – up to the tragic finale in the Wehrmacht's Russian campaign, emphasizing that 'It could not be won with horses, and certainly not without them.'[81] Koselleck was among those who had, with horses, *not* won the war. As a member of the horse-drawn artillery, he had suffered alongside the animals.[82] A horse-related accident, quite typical of his troop, had left a lifelong memory of pain: exhausted, he had leant against the carriage and a wheel of an oncoming vehicle had rolled over and crushed his foot.

Koselleck was not the only one of his 'circle' who had taken part in the end of the horse era as a kind of 'embedded historian'. The historian Andreas Alföldi, son of a Hungarian country doctor, had served in the cavalry in the First World War. Many of his observations in his later studies of cavalry and chivalry among the early Romans clearly owed something to his own experience as a trooper in war.[83] The same was true of his colleague later on at the Institute for Advanced Study, James Frank Gilliam, himself a specialist in Roman military history: 'his many encounters with the Cossacks gave an opportunity to study their tactics and to prepare him later to understand the horsemen of Northern Asia. He acknowledged readily that when the muscular small horses of the Cossacks were captured, he was regularly thrown through the air when he tried to ride one.'[84]

In an even more direct manner than Alföldi, the American medievalist and technical historian Lynn White, Jr. seized upon his practical experience in the United States cavalry when he wrote, decades later, on the history of medieval inventions. 'From 1918 to 1924,' wrote White, 'I was badly schooled in a California military academy that operated at the technological level of the Spanish-American war. I learned to ride bareback and have detested horses ever since. My enthusiasm for the stirrup was confirmed by the more advanced stages of cavalry training.' He was, he continued ironically, 'probably the only living American medievalist who has ever taken part in a charge at full gallop by a line of cavalry with sabers bared. We yelled like Comanches less to terrify the hypothetical foe than to encourage ourselves in the face of the possibility that a horse might stumble. Our stirrups were a notable consolation. Those who doubt that the coming of the stirrup opened new possibilities in mounted warfare ... are invited to ride stirrupless in strenuous cavalry maneuvers.'[85]

In 1962, White published a work which is still widely read today, *Medieval Technology and Social Change*. It would bring him not only vehement criticism from his colleagues, but also praise from Marshall McLuhan.[86] With the eagle eyes of a trailblazer, McLuhan recognized the milestone the medievalist White had pinpointed. The invention of the stirrup had revolutionized medieval life: a key step on the road towards man's ability to harness energy through technology. Like White, McLuhan had an eye for the simple things that could harness energy and thereby bring about an enhancement of man's limited strength. Something as simple as a metal ring, used in the appropriate position in a mechanism, could produce a massive increase in power – that is, of energy and strength.

The particular metal ring of interest to these scholars – the *stirrup*, or *Stegreif* as it was called in Old German – worked not as a prosthesis directly attached to the person, but by usefully complementing the entire environmental ensemble of human, animal, tool and weapon. This ring consolidated the potential of the various component parts and combined them, thereby increasing the impact of the vector. The consequences for the military utility of the horse were clear to see: in combat, the cavalry relied much on their speed, but also on their compact formation, to act like a projectile that pierces the wall of the enemy infantry.

The problem of how a relatively small animal like a human should go about mounting a relatively large animal like a horse is one that has troubled us since ancient times.[87] Among the practical solutions – stone steps, ladders, lances and servants – the stirrup emerged relatively late, after the decline of the Roman Empire. As we find so often in the older technological history, it was not Europe that was in the lead but the Orient.[88] Archaeologists, iconographers and philologists have long asked themselves where precisely the stirrup and its precursors such as leather ropes, footrests, and the tiny stirrup for the big toe only originated. White, the medievalist, collated their findings[89] in the hope of answering a different question: what happens when a technical innovation and social context come together in a set of reciprocal conditions?

History shows how the stirrup took on new roles in line with changes to its design and its stability: from a simple aid for mounting the horse, it became an indispensable support for the rider and especially for mounted combatants. Over the course of centuries of evolution, the stirrup came to be the central point of a complex moving system: a stable central node, a kind of static connecting point that enabled the energy of the system to be concentrated and turned outwards, without destabilizing the entire system. Within the moving system of horse, rider and technical objects or weapons, the stirrup provided a kind of internal core strength, which had previously been absent; it gave the system a singular and historically unprecedented efficiency. It was the Franks who were the first in history to realize the profit enabled by this system. 'While semi-feudal relationships and institutions had long been scattered thickly over the civilized world, it was the Franks alone . . . who fully grasped the possibilities inherent in the stirrup and created in terms of it a new type of warfare supported by a novel structure of society which we call feudalism.'[90]

The stirrup, according to White, was a unique device in the history of technology that was cheap and easy to produce, but of remarkable efficiency under the foot of a mounted warrior: 'As long as a man is clinging to his horse by pressure of his knees, he can wield a spear only with the strength of his arms. But when the lateral support of stirrups is added to the fore-and-aft buttressing of the pommel and cantle of a heavy saddle, horse and rider become one. Now the fighter is enabled . . . to lay his spear at rest between his upper arm and body. The blow is struck no longer with the strength of a man's muscles but rather by the impetus of a charging stallion and rider. The stirrup thus made possible the substitution of animal power for human power. It was the technological basis for mounted shock combat, the typical Western medieval mode of fighting.'[91]

The summation of energy made possible by the stirrup,[92] concentrated at the tip of the lance, had technological consequences, including the increased demand for heavier armour and more powerful horses. It also had a social impact: the split of society into a mounted warrior aristocracy, the knights, and the great mass of peasantry who could not afford to take part in the knights' warfare.[93] The close association between feudalism and military combat drew the connection between horse and rider into the centre of the feudal system and influenced its ethical code. 'The new mode of combat, with its high mobility and fearful impact, opened fresh fields for deeds of individual prowess. The old days were gone of standing in formation in the shield-wall and thrusting and hacking.'[94]

The stirrup had become the *punctum Archimedis*, the vantage point from which Lynn White, Jr., reconstructed the history of feudalism.

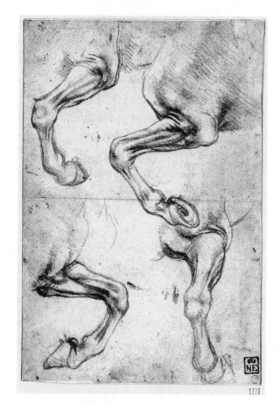

Studies in movement, Leonardo da Vinci.

Ballet moderne: Étienne-Jules Marey, 1890.

What White demonstrated still exerts a kind of magic, even after synthetic approaches such as his have fallen out of favour.[95] Even when his book was published in the early 1960s, the author was charged with claims of technological determinism and excessive speculation.[96] But the criticism could not shake the old cavalryman; he was inspired by a revelation that came to him in the mid-1930s when he discovered the French *Annales* school of historiography. It was reading the work of Marc Bloch that led him to stumble across the wondrous hippologist Lefebvre des Noëttes, whom he later referred to as 'an eccentric of genius'.[97] It had dawned on him that there could be a place for the history of technology other than in the back seat of history and the humanities.

PART III

The Living Metaphor
PATHOS

At some point, Lev Nikolayevich, you must have been a horse.
Turgenev to Tolstoy (in *Lev Tolstoy* by Viktor Shklovsky, 1974)

For 6,000 years, the horse has been man's dependable beast of burden, an essential part of the livestock of the farm. As an agricultural product, the horse is not alone: other animals have supplied man with food and clothing. Pigs and sheep have filled his plate, geese have warmed his bed with their feathers, dogs have guarded his house and his herd. Oxen have pulled his plough, mules have carried his grain to the mill, cats have kept the army of parasites at bay. Rarely had any had their services acknowledged in their lifetime. 'We're sure to find something better than death,' as the donkey muses in the Grimm Brothers' fairy tale, 'Town Musicians of Bremen'. The horse has also fed man, like the cow, pulled his plough like the ox, carried his wares like the mule, and become his friend like the dog. And in the idiom of symbols created by man, in his myths and fairy tales, his philosophical allegories, the horse has always been one of the stars of the show. But unlike the lion and the eagle, the beasts of heraldry, unlike the snake, the owl, the pelican and other creatures of myth, and unlike the thieves and parasites like the wolf, the mouse and the rat, the architectural ants and the burrowing mole, as a symbolic beast the horse has never lost its practical role in its relationship with man. Even when the horse is tasked with carrying symbolic meaning, it still remains a physical carrier of man, his transporter, his beast of burden – and the opposite is also true. Its closest relative, not only in genetic terms, has always been the ass.[1] Philosophically speaking, the donkey, or ass, is undoubtedly the more significant colleague, but when, other than Jesus' triumphal ride into Jerusalem, has the 'Jerusalem pony' played a politically significant role? The donkey might have ranked alongside the horse in literary and philosophical terms, but when it came to politics, the horse was in a whole different league.

It is thanks mainly to its velocity as a vector of animal power that the horse came to be a key political ally and fellow traveller of *Homo sapiens*. His steed has helped man rule over all other species and especially his own kind. 'The rider appears on the stage of history,' writes the economist Alexander Rüstow, 'like a new breed of man, marked by a powerful superiority: he is over two metres in height and moves several times faster than a walking human.'[2] The animal's symbolic value corresponds with its practical use. The horse has tended to be both a functional creature and a living metaphor in the same breath. It has spread terror and also given terror a face. It has given man the capacity to seize power and to secure it, at the same time lending mankind an appropriate image of sovereignty. There has never been a need for the symbol of hegemony to switch saddles: the horse is by nature, as it were, the absolute political metaphor.

The combination of horse and rider is a powerful symbol of domination and one of the oldest in the book. It has been astonishing in its impact. It almost does not matter whether a man has already been anointed and crowned as a monarch; when he sits atop his steed, his physical elevation gives the impression in the people's eyes that he holds the reins of power. It works in other ways too: the affirmation of a prince as regent and leader of men and state lies in the manner in which he sits on his steed. The legitimacy of the *princeps*'s power was encapsulated in the grace and lightness with which he steered his mount.[3] Until well into the twilight of the age of the horse, equestrianism maintained its power as metaphor, as when Sigmund Freud in 1923 compared the ego with a horse rider 'who has to hold in check the superior strength of the horse', the difference being that 'the rider tries to do so with his own strength, while the ego uses borrowed forces'.[4]

The word 'metaphor' comes from the Greek *metaphorein*, meaning *to carry, to transport*, which refers, in this sense, to the act of transferring something from here to there; for example, the transference of meaning from what is literally said to what is actually meant. In other words, the wealth of a metaphor consists in an intellectual shuttle service between contexts that are sufficiently vaguely defined to allow such an excursion to be made.[5] Among all the historical protagonists who were capable of taking on this transportation role, the horse had an idiosyncratic double talent to offer. Indeed, it was already distinguished in the real world by being able to carry something and, secondly, to transport this 'something' elsewhere, to another place or another level. It was not to be outdone by any other living thing in this functional duality; no other creature carried out the services of transporting, and raising to another level, with anything like the same reliability, speed and grace.

Added to this was the metaphorical power of the horse in the symbolic realm, that is, its capacity to lend a tangible, memorable form to ideas and feelings. The horse could carry not only humans and other loads, but also abstract signs and symbols; it was, in the words of Polish philosopher and historian Krzysztof Pomian, not only a *phoros*, a carrier of something, but also a *semiophoros*, a semaphore, a carrier of signs.[6] The king, to continue with this example, is not just any rider or a physical burden in human form; he is a figure charged with symbols and legends, a much-*inscribed* man. His horse – and in this respect it belongs to a special class of semaphores – not only carries the entire ensemble of symbolism and narratives that bears the label 'king', but is also itself an integral part of the semiotics that makes the king a king: *Le roi n'est pas roi sans son cheval.*[7] The horse is a visible, living component of the concept of royalty, while also being the real, practical embodiment of the dynamic power of royalty. Richard III, whose horse sank in the mire at Bosworth Field, sees himself as robbed of not only a decisive part of his competitive potency, namely his ability to escape at speed; he also experiences the physical undoing of his kingship. His *kingdom*, which at this moment he would be willing to exchange for a horse, is reduced to a secondary, static aspect of monarchy.

The practical history-making capacity of the horse is therefore balanced with a corresponding literary story-telling capacity. Both capacities are reflected in one another and mutually augment the singular metaphoric strength of the horse, to transcend real and imaginary contexts with a leap or to bring something to collapse, as if with a thwack of its hoof. And therefore we cannot go wrong if we describe the horse as the metaphorical animal par excellence, though we must stress that the metaphorical animal, the figurative animal and the signifying animal always remain an inalienable part of the tangible, material reality. And the physical can always rematerialize when you least expect it, just like the metaphorical lion that appears one night to the philosopher and metaphorologist Hans Blumenberg in Sibylle Lewitscharoff's eponymous novel *Blumenberg*: 'tactile, furry, yellow'.[8] The horse, for all its sublimations and projections, remains a snorting, nodding, hoof-scraping, warmly fragrant reality. You can criticize a metaphor or an image, but how do you criticize a rich, composite natural phenomenon?[9]

A peasant stands in a field – so the riddle goes – and a horse comes towards him. The next moment, the peasant disappears from the face of the earth. What happened? The answer: the field was a chessboard; the peasant was a Pawn, taken by a Knight. All the animals went on board the ark, but only one made it onto the chessboard; only the horse became part of the royal game. Along with two other figures, the Bishop and the Castle, the Knight belongs to the middle ranks, the officer class, distinguished by a greater degree of mobility than the common infantry or Pawns. And the Knight has the greatest mobility of them all; he can be moved forwards, backwards and to the side, and indeed can jump over another piece. It is this that makes him so dangerous and so prepossessing.

Napoleon

To rule is to ride.

Carl Schmitt

REFLECTED IN A PUDDLE OF EXCREMENT

Few authors of European literature have made use of the idiosyncratic dual nature of the horse as artfully as Heinrich von Kleist in his narrative of the undeserved fate of the horse dealer Michael Kohlhaas and his formidable quest for justice. Early in the story, when all was still well in the horse trader's world, the two blacks that he is forced to submit as a surety that he would obtain the requisite travel permit are still smooth and lustrous; the knights who admire them, and Kohlhaas's other animals, all agree 'that the horses were like stags and none finer had been reared in the entire country'.[10] However, when Kohlhaas returns to collect his steeds, he finds them in a pigsty, haggard and broken from maltreatment in the field.[11] Denied justice and resorting instead to violence to obtain his rights, Kohlhaas, in desperation, calls on Martin Luther, who appears as a stern man of books and paper, a hard-hearted priest and an upright jurist.

The lowest point of humiliation for Kohlhaas is when he sees his blacks, or rather a shadow of them, again in Dresden. There, where his rights are finally trampled into the ground, he finds his blacks, racked up to the cart of a knacker who shamelessly relieves himself right beside them. The following scene, in which the dealer recognizes the animals as his own – although by the association with the *dishonourable* profession of the knacker they had had their own honour tarnished – plays out in the town market which he sees as if reflected in a great puddle of shit (mentioned twice by Kleist in one passage), just as if it were his reality. The true measure of the moral condition of the country is not the scheming members of the Junker camarilla or the vengeful horse dealer, but the two black horses: all the world's injustice is visible in their ill-treated bodies. They take on this function again at the end of the story, just before Kohlhaas's execution and after we hear of his adversary getting his just deserts, when justice and honour are reinstated: we see them again as 'the pair of black horses, now shining with health and pawing the ground with their hooves'.[12]

Kleist is clearly straying off the beaten track of the traditional iconography of power in his novella *Michael Kohlhaas*, when he uses the horse as a metaphor or a moral dipstick. The key metaphor for sovereignty and authority is traditionally the act of *riding*, not the *horse* itself. Kleist, however, aimed to express something different from the conventional function of the portrait of a ruler. His black horses were not intended to reflect the good governance, authority or military competence of a prince, but to bring to the fore something that is more difficult to grasp: the dangerous relativity of the legal system in a state like the Electorate of Saxony. The horse is well suited to the role of physical indicator of abstract circumstances, because it can so quickly descend to being as skinny as one of the Pharaoh's cattle, and just as quickly rise from the Elbe, plump and shiny with good health. Unlike traditional embodiments of justice, such as *Justitia*, these horses do not personify the state of justice; they lay it open to scrutiny.

Kleist's use of the horse as a metaphor goes further, however, and does not shy from inversion. In the Western tradition, the *white horse* carries the burden of a particular allegorical and eschatological significance. The solar importance of the Horses of Helios harks back to Greek mythology, while in Christian eschatology we find the White Horse of the Apocalypse bearing Christ the Lord. The horse as a symbol of the sun is to be found 'in almost all cultures', as the art historian Jörg Traeger summarily notes, including in the most radiant equestrian figures of the Christian Middle Ages and the modern period: 'St George and the Christian emperors on horseback are the iconographic

Survivor of an iconoclastic history: equestrian statue of Marcus Aurelius, Giovanni Piranesi, 1785.

Up above, down below, horses everywhere one looks: the nineteenth-century city square. Equestrian statue of Field Marshal Radetzky at the Platz am Hof in Vienna.

successors to the steeds of the Sun God.'[13] Even Napoleon was portrayed by the painters of his time firmly within this tradition, seated almost exclusively on greys, usually stallions. It is therefore as a substitution for this absolute metaphor that Kleist, in an act of double negation, replaces the white horse with a pair of blacks. He sends this pair plummeting in a *descensio ad infernos*, which reaches its lowest point at the marketplace in Dresden, the lake of hellfire reflected in the sloppy puddle of excrement (which is more liquid in the original German than it comes across in the English translation by D. Luke). In the final scene, immediately prior to the execution and death of Kohlhaas, the reappearance of the blacks, believed until this point to be dead and buried, but now completely restored to health, represents an *ascensio* from the underworld, a return from the dead. The horses are blessed with this miraculous reincarnation; whether such a fate also awaits the human sinner is something Kleist leaves open to speculation.[14]

The chronological moment at which Kleist writes his novella based on the true story of a humiliated and indignant horse dealer – 1808 – provides a good vantage point from which to look both forward and backwards in history. Looking forward into the future, we glance over the final century of horses: one hundred years later, motorized cabs would be driving back and forth through the Brandenburg Gate; and shortly before, on 27 October 1806, Napoleon had led his victorious troops through it – Napoleon, the mounted *heros*, the great reviver of the old formula of sovereignty. A few years earlier still, in 1797, Immanuel Kant grumbled about the new King of Prussia, Friedrich Wilhelm III, travelling to Königsberg in a carriage rather than presenting himself to his people on horseback. Kant might also have thought that a king was not a king without his horse, or rather that a king was only a king while he was *riding*. After all, he had, albeit from a safe distance, followed how the Parisian revolutionaries had toppled the four equestrian statues of the Bourbon kings on 11 and 12 August 1792, and three days later the statue of the mounted Henry IV of France. As contemporary engravings make clear, the revolutionaries were not content with dragging the hated kings off their horses: they also knocked their steeds to the ground.[15] Those who could read the symbolism knew that the king's head was no longer worth the *sou* it was embossed on: a king was only king when he was on horseback. Whoever could lay a hand on the sovereign's steed could also bring the monarch to the ground. Even if this time it was only in effigy.

Kant's concern was not unfounded. When, on 15 February 1798, French Jacobins in Rome proclaimed the revived Roman Republic, there was much to make the last equestrian statue of a ruler of the old world tremble. The tumult of revolution was unleashed precisely here on Rome's Capitoline Hill, by the statue of Marcus Aurelius on horseback, in front of which the French planted a 'Liberty Tree'.[16] As if by a miracle, this statue has remained standing, the last link in a chain of antiquity. We must imagine the cities of the Roman Empire as being full of these equestrian monuments; indeed, Cicero scoffed at the 'swarm' of such statues filling the Capitol in his lifetime, and with time, or more precisely in the course of the era of empire, they increased both in number and scope. The two main types of equestrian statue – the *striding* steed, as with Marcus Aurelius, and the *rearing* steed (standing on its hind legs in the position referred to later as the levade) – were at that point already fully developed tropes.[17] However, with the exception of this one statue on the Piazza del Campidoglio, Capitol Hill, none of these larger-than-life effigies have survived.[18]

Ever since, with the creation of the first equestrian portraits and statues of the modern era in Florence, Padua, Venice and Piacenza, this ancient representational scheme was revived and broadened in scope to include the princes and generals of the Renaissance;[19] painters have tended to seize upon the dynamic formula of the levade, while sculptors, for gravitational reasons, have preferred the pose of the striding horse – rhetorically emphasizing the great strides made by the ruler in question. One famous exception is Bernini's equestrian statue of Louis XIV, which was not looked on kindly by the supreme sovereign and was banished to a far-flung corner of the royal palace gardens at Versailles.[20] In the course of the seventeenth and eighteenth centuries, the levade became so ingrained as the peerless 'King formula' of painted equestrian portraits that a riderless horse captured in this stance – as in the case of Stubbs's *Whistlejacket* (see p. 166) – was enough to convince the world that this was an unfinished picture waiting for the English king to be painted in.[21] The

English king at that time was George III – the same monarch whose equestrian statue was brought down on 9 July 1776, together with the horse, by the people of New York after hearing the Declaration of Independence (Plate 18).[22]

Napoleon may well have had the fate of all these royal monuments in mind when he persistently rejected all proposals for decorating a prominent square in the city with a sculpture of himself on horseback. It's possible, as historian Volker Hunecke suspected, he was 'conscious that the equestrian monument, symbol of dynastic princely rule par excellence, did not suit him',[23] parvenu and usurper that he was. He was far more willing, on the other hand, to allow himself to be painted by artists such as David, Gros, the two Vernets and other painters of his time as a mounted hero and strategist.[24] When, in 1800, David painted the first of five versions of Napoleon's celebrated crossing of the Alps (*Bonaparte franchissant le Grand-Saint-Bernard*),[25] probably neither the painter nor his model would have guessed that this equestrian portrait would become an icon of the century, one that would be mimicked and parodied a hundred times and would lend lasting, emblematic expression to the nineteenth century's *idée fixe* of the great man and legend of world history. With unerring instinct, Napoleon refused the attribute of an unsheathed sabre David wanted to include in his portrait: 'No, my dear David, battles are not won by the sword. I wish to be painted sitting calmly on a spirited horse.'[26]

The ultimate attribute of the new type of ruler was not the field commander's staff or his weapon, but his cool confidence amidst the raging energies of war. In the painter's pictographic interpretation, this meant that, amidst the vortex of the tempest blowing through the props and accoutrements, billowing fabric and animal alike (the toga of the First Consul and the tail, mane and limbs of the horse), with a cool head, the hero controls his fiery horse and together they both ride out the storm. David painted Napoleon as a god of wind and speed (Plate 20). With this iconic image – riding as a metaphor – that old trope of domination had been lent its specifically modern facet: the aspect of *velocity*. Whoever wanted to prevail in the future had above all to be swift.

The sessions in the studio were preceded by events in which

Napoleon had dazzlingly demonstrated his intuitive understanding of the political significance of riding in the troubled reality of post-revolutionary Paris and its shaky power relations. To understand Napoleon's successful tactics in autumn 1799, one needs to remember the failure of the greatest and most fearsome of his predecessors in the summer of 1794.

THE EIGHTEENTH BRUMAIRE

It is the 27th of July 1794, or rather the 9th of Thermidor, the date on which the fall of Robespierre brings an end to the Reign of Terror. That morning, Robespierre and his friend and confidant Couthon are on the way from the Mairie to the Hôtel de Ville. Paris is restless, the crowds are agitated and in every fibre of his crippled body Couthon feels the passion directed against the man behind the Terror. 'Robespierre,' says he, 'this is the time to get on a horse! Lead the people against the Convention!' 'That's not going to happen,' says Robespierre, 'I don't know how to ride. We shall respect the Convention and win by force of words.'[27] Although a lawyer like Robespierre, Couthon knows the signals that need to be sent. But Robespierre refuses; he is lawyer and will remain one. Even at this hour, he trusts in the power of argument: the word and not the sword! *'Je ne sais pas monter à cheval,'* he says. 'I don't know how to ride,' and maybe he does not want to either.[28] Robespierre's weapon was always the word, and few knew how to wield it as skilfully as the lawyer from Arras. But today he will lose the game, and when he senses that it is lost, he reaches for his pistol to shoot himself. Yet even this soldierly gesture misfires – he cannot kill himself either.

Five years later, in autumn 1799, the Abbé Sieyès's plots for a coup against the Directoire are nearing completion. On 30 October, an alliance is forged with the cordially detested General Bonaparte. Now Sieyès has the right man for the job; ten days later, the two will strike. What does the Abbé do in these autumn weeks when he is not spinning his web of intrigue? He takes riding lessons. 'Sieyès is learning to ride at a time like this!' notes Jacob Burckhardt, also recalling that, 'Robespierre never learned.'[29] Sieyès, the cleric and theorist, also a man of words more than of action, has learned from the lawyer's mistakes. On the day of the coup, the eighteenth of Brumaire or 9 November, his accomplice, the lionized General Bonaparte, makes just about every mistake going – at least when it comes to rhetoric. He makes nonsensical speeches, reveals the intentions of the conspirators, declares his desire for power and his violent disposition. It is only thanks to the parliamentary experience and the eloquence of his brother Lucien that fate did not turn against the putschists. It is in just one aspect, that of symbolic, political conduct, that the General's instincts do not abandon him: whenever he needs to bring the troops behind him or impress the masses, he mounts his steed.[30] At first he comes across as inept: when he is cursed and beaten black and blue in the council (he will claim to have received dagger wounds) and knocked out for a moment, he is pale and shaky; outside, his horse, frightened by the commotion, shies and rears up, but soon the rider is himself again, parading around and cursing the alleged assailants and enemies of the fatherland.[31]

With the unbroken force of the symbol of hegemony, his confidence returns. That night, with Ducos and Sieyès at his side, Napoleon is appointed First Consul of France – a late republican descendant of Clovis, the Frankish king of whom Gregory of Tours reported that as he mounted his steed dressed in diadem and purple, the jubilant masses cheered him as 'Consul' and 'Augustus'.[32] When they head eastwards, back to Paris in the early hours – Sieyès, Lucien, General Gardanne, Napoleon and his private secretary – Napoleon turns to the latter: 'Bourrienne, I said many ridiculous things?' 'Not so very bad, General.' 'I prefer to speak to soldiers than to lawyers.'[33]

This will change, as Napoleon is quick to add. He will learn how to talk to lawyers; one day a famous civil code will carry his name. But he would remain the man on the horse until the very end, even when he was long past being the young god of war that David's paintbrush made him out to be, rather than the short, fat man with a bad temper and bad manners that he actually was. He would let himself be painted like Jupiter on the throne, remaining for posterity the mounted soldier-emperor, the ruler on horseback. Nietzsche, who did not think in historical but typological terms, saw in him the last hero of antiquity and willingly accepted Napoleon's self-styling as a born-again Alexander. Hegel, who saw him ride through Jena as a 'world-soul' on horseback,[34] expressed his admiration of him in his lectures on the philosophy of world history, as a man who knew how to clear the decks and impose his rule: 'He chased out whoever was left of the lawyers, ideologists and men of principle, and instead of mistrust it was respect and fear that prevailed.'[35]

Where the hero and genuine ruler appeared, the lawyer had also played a role. Perhaps this also explains the lawyers' hatred of the heroic image: had it not, after all, been two lawyers, Thuriot and Albitte, who in August 1792 had proposed in the National Assembly that the monuments of despotism be destroyed? Of course, the only one *recognized* as a ruler was he who sat on horseback and knew how to ride. This was basic semiotics, as Couthon reminded his friend in vain. The image of the hero is a simple icon, a pictogram consisting of two components: man on top and horse below. As simple as a road sign: Caution, riders! Since ancient times this is how a ruler has looked. Whether or not he's legitimate is not the first question we ask; the key thing is that he instils fear.

Certainly, the horse-riding formula does not say anything about the legitimacy of a modern ruler, as Robespierre notes when he stresses that they should respect the Convention, the legitimacy of the written text, the rule of law. The man on the horse has a higher seat, but no greater legitimacy. And yet it is specifically his exalted seat, as a rider, that explains his superiority in political semantics. Thermidor was a tragedy for the lawyers, while 18th Brumaire was a comedy for the heroes.

PRIZED LITTLE ARABIANS

If we consider the works of the painters who accompanied Napoleon's rise, we cannot avoid the impression that the man was constantly riding on stallions from one battle to the next: the horseman of world history, a gentleman who prefers blondes. This is clearly the impact of the representational tradition with its tropes of political portraiture. A world ruler such as Napoleon simply had to sit on a white steed; he owed this tribute to the apocalyptic tradition. In this, the iconography created by David, Gros and their artistic contemporaries obeyed a different truth to that of the historian. In the reality this side of the artist's studio, Napoleon seems indeed to have had a penchant for light-coloured horses (although he also possessed some beautiful blacks, bays and sorrels), but most of these were of a light grey colouring, as was common in purebred Arabian and Berber breeds. This provenance was the decisive factor for Napoleon: it appears from everything we know of him as a rider and horse owner that he had a definite soft spot for Arabian horses or, more precisely, Arabian stallions.

This predilection for the rather spindly limbed and not particularly large animals from the Orient has been linked to his diminutive build, and it has been suggested that he would have been well aware of how ridiculous he would have looked on a larger horse. But apart from the fact that rumours of his alleged shortness can be traced to the malice of hostile contemporaries and English sources (with a recently calculated height of five feet five inches, he was in fact average for a man of his time), his esteem for the Arabian horse had other motives. It was partly to do with the animal's nature and partly with his riding style.

Long before he set foot on Egyptian soil for the first time on 1 July 1798, Napoleon seems to have developed a preference for elegant, fast horses of French, Austrian and Andalusian origin. The encounter with the horsemanship of the Mamelukes and the rich introduction to the qualities of the oriental horse that his stay in Egypt and Syria gave him was an eye-opening experience. From that point on he would consider no horse other than an Arabian. The speed, the resilience and especially the manoeuvrability of the Arabian horse, not to mention the beauty of its lean, 'dry' head and the fineness and elegance of its limbs, entranced the strong-willed military man, who harboured a secret aesthetic side. He was particularly impressed by the ability of the well-trained Arabian horse to stop abruptly or instantly change direction at full gallop. This kind of agility and manoeuvrability appealed to the impatient strategist with his tendency towards abrupt changes of direction. In fact, Napoleon did not ride at all like a cavalry trooper (which he had never been) or a horse lover or connoisseur, but as an impetuous madman, who was accustomed to imposing his will on others, whether soldiers, horses or women.[36]

He began with what motorists call a racing start. He would mount one of the horses that stood in the field equipped, saddled and harnessed twenty-four hours a day, constantly ready for him to ride, and the second he was mounted he would bring his steed immediately to a full gallop, so that his retinue had trouble keeping up with him.[37] He always wanted to be the fastest. He would work his horses to death with his fierce, impulsive riding style, and on long, relentless rides he would often come crashing down with his exhausted steed, something which had to be kept quiet at all costs.[38] He was just the same in the driver's seat and on occasion he would cause the entire carriage to keel over, complete with passengers, because of his insistence on getting his own way; once he was a hair's breadth from a fatal accident.[39] It is clear from many depictions of the time that his attitude to horses in no way corresponded to the protocol of ideal horsemanship. Throughout his life he retained his casual Corsican riding style in which, in the absence of a bridle, the horse is steered like a motorcycle, mainly by shifting the body weight from side to side, which, on a horse, is not particularly elegant.[40] The older and heavier he became, the more ungainly was his equestrian stature, as shown in contemporary iconography.

Napoleon, who had gone to Egypt to chase after Alexander the Great's glory and to liberate the country from the Ottomans just as Alexander had expelled the Persians; Napoleon, who wanted to make Egypt French, returned to Paris and in the following years proceeded to orientalize France and the whole world with his infectious Egyptomania. Thanks to the help of artists and scholars such as Vivant Denon, he succeeded in making 'Egyptian' the style of the Empire, and with the support of furious cavalry commanders such as Joachim Murat, he taught his cavalry to ride as fluidly and to fight as recklessly as the Mamelukes – only with much more discipline.[41] For fifteen years, the Napoleonic cavalry was the best-run and most fearsome military unit of all European armies. It's true the English cavalrymen, all trained in the wild, rustic steeplechase style, were as fearless as the devil, but when it came to rapid, orderly manoeuvres, the French, with their heady mix of oriental furore and Gallic discipline, were far superior.[42]

Refined by his Egyptian adventure and fired up by visions of the Orient, Napoleon's initially naive preference for the small, elegant Arab horses grew into a genuine antidote to the rampant anglomania that was still widespread throughout the *Ancien Régime* among French riders and in the French studs.[43] For the aristocracy of the Empire, the fashionable creatures from the East, from the Nile and from Kabylia, whose endless genealogical charts stretched back to the mares of Muhammad, trumped the English thoroughbred as the ultimate must-have.[44] Meanwhile, the orientalist streak in French Romanticism which emerged in Napoleon's day would go on to survive its patron by a good half-century.

WHITE HORSES, BLACK BOXES

In *Washington Rallying the Americans at the Battle of Princeton* (1848), attributed to the American painter William T. Ranney (Plate 19),[45] George Washington is depicted hurling himself into battle to rally together his scattered troops. It is looking bad for the Americans, who have just lost their General Mercer to the Hessian mercenaries' bayonets. Washington, so it is said, leapt onto his horse, broke into the fray and saved the day. With the double battle of Trenton and Princeton, the tide was turning in the Revolutionary War. Ranney's image, composed seventy years after the Battle of Princeton, may have been based on historical sources, but the concept it portrays certainly digresses. Even the aesthetic truth needs its advocates, and Ranney's most important witness was Jacques-Louis David.

Ranney's representation of Washington's campaign clearly harks back to David's painting of Napoleon crossing the Alps. David's portrait quickly became famous; shortly after its completion in 1800, it was being copied by German painters.[46] The grey horse rearing up onto its hindquarters, the posture of the rider, the windswept trappings (the horse's tail and mane, Napoleon's robe in one, Washington's flag in the other), the entire colour palette of the painting with its sandy and ochre tones and its various greys and blues (the dust around Washington can be read as a reference to Zeus as a cloud) – the combination of these elements creates a visual formula that is oblivious to any differences in detail. Anyone looking at it can discern the silhouette of Bonaparte.

Although David's painting came hot on the heels of the historic event, Napoleon's crossing of the Alps in May 1800, the artist paid not the slightest attention to the question of historical accuracy. David represented Napoleon's Alpine crossing as the work of a youthful hero. He points the way with right arm outstretched, indicating a path that had been trodden before by two heavyweights of world history, as indicated by the inscription on the rocks: Hannibal and Charlemagne. In reality, Napoleon's campaign was much less spectacular in its execution. Riding on a mule, he lagged a few days behind the bulk of the army. In 1848, Paul Delaroche painted a version of events which came much closer to the historical reality. But by this time David's vision was already ingrained as the popular choice and no denial of it, in writing or painting, would change that. It was the image of Napoleon that had gained currency and which soon rose to the status of a major icon. Washington, the hero of Princeton, would not be the only one transferred into this particular formula.

There is, of course, a particular irony to the iconographic afterlife of these two great men. Washington had, after all, been a guiding light throughout the entire period of the French Revolution. He was revered as a *Cincinnatus moderne*, a man who combined both military glory and republican virtue. He was the citizen who had refused to be king.[47] The young Bonaparte must have felt flattered when, in the years of his rise to influence, he was described as a *Washington français* or a *jeune Washington*.[48] Conversely, the image of the young Washington left those who witnessed his ascent with the reassuring hope that Bonaparte would, when the time came, also reject dictatorship and monarchy, and embrace republican values.[49]

With the events of 18th Brumaire that hope was shattered. From this point on, Bonaparte came to be seen as a second Caesar or Cromwell in the eyes of his critical contemporaries. With his coronation, wrote François Furet, 'Bonaparte bid farewell to the world of Washington, to place himself instead within the tradition of monarchs.'[50] Yet the prisoner of St Helena clung onto the comparison with Washington and presented himself as *Washington couronné*: for him, there was never any other choice.[51] It would only be three decades before the tide turned again. Now it was Washington who, captured in oils by Ranney, was brought under Napoleon's iconographic schema: in 1848, the artist's brush transformed Washington into a *Bonaparte américain*.

Washington was not the first and nor would he be the last military leader who at times needed to jump on a horse to prevent the dispersal or even escape of his troops. In the Russian civil war, the commander-in-chief of the Red Army would find he had no other choice. 'At one point he even mounted a horse, rounded up the retreating troops and led them back into battle,' says Orlando Figes of Leon Trotsky.[52] However, there was no revolutionary David, nor even a Soviet Ranney to capture his heroic action in this seasoned pictorial format. The civil war was not the environment for historical portraiture, and a few years after its end Trotsky fell into *damnatio memoriae* and disappeared from the official iconography. He had in fact always underestimated the value of the horse, or rather of the cavalry, until a successful raid by the Red Cavalry against the White Cossacks in October 1918 taught him better:[53] 'Proletarians, on your horses!' went the slogan from then on. It had the ring of Schiller's *Reiterlied* ('Cavalry Song') from the play *Wallensteins Lager* (*Wallenstein's Camp*), perhaps echoing a similar revolutionary context: when the common man sits on horseback, the coup is only a hoofstep away.

In the picture gallery of dictators and despots of the twentieth century, the white horse makes a rare appearance, to say nothing of the levade. Unlike Mussolini – who willingly raided the wardrobe of antiquity, particularly of Rome, to don the imperial iconographic formulae of dominance and blessing in the guise of Caesar on horseback – Hitler could not and would not ride, detested horses and looked on approvingly as the army's cavalry regiments were dissolved. The third ruler in the Axis powers' alliance, the Japanese Emperor, loved to appear on a grey horse, riding ahead of his generals. Apparently, this image also struck his enemy, the Americans: in John Ford's film *December 7th* about the attack on Pearl Harbor and the USA's entry into the war, a shadowy Tenno rides into the dreamscape of a sleeping Uncle Sam (p. 253).

Revolutionary Russia, on the other hand, as the case of Trotsky

The revolution on horseback: a mounted Emiliano Zapata.

Fascism on horseback: a mounted Mussolini.

shows, had a more complicated relationship with the horse and with the associated leadership formula. Lenin, it seems, was happy to draw a line under the horse age and its symbolism. When his train from Zurich via Berlin pulled into the Finland Station in Petrograd shortly before midnight on 3 April 1917, to address the waiting crowds he climbed not onto the back of a horse, but the roof of a car, before being driven off in an armoured vehicle. But that was not the end of the matter. Even Stalin, who had ridden in his youth, had no time for horses and troopers in visual propaganda in his later years as red Tsar, though he remained conscious of the power of equestrian imagery. When, in June 1945, the popular Russian commander-in-chief, Marshal Zhukov – who had previously fought in Budyonny's Red Cavalry – rode a white horse in the Victory Day parade, leading Soviet troops across Red Square (p. 253), and was subsequently portrayed as the victor over Nazi Berlin in an adaptation, or a travesty, of David's *Napoleon* (Plate 21), this was perceived as a bold grab at the old monarchical formula and contributed to his falling out of favour with Stalin. Zhukov vanished into political oblivion and was only reinstated much later by Stalin's successors.

Nietzsche was seeking to deconstruct another irrepressible formula – the opposition of military men and lawyers – when, quoting French historian Hippolyte Taine, he sought to uncover Napoleon's lawyerly side: 'For Napoleon, the lawyer is as significant as the general and the administrator. The essence of this skill is never to submit to the truth . . .'[54] It was not until years later that the cliché of man-of-law versus man-of-action was truly ridden to death.[55] In his short story 'The New Advocate', Kafka combines in one protagonist the contrasting duality of jurist and military hero – the steed of Alexander the Great is reincarnated as the eponymous lawyer, once and for all closing this allegorical chapter of world history. 'In his outward appearance,' it is said of the new lawyer Dr Bucephalus, 'there is little to recall the time when he was still the war-horse of Alexander of Macedon'.[56] But a simple court usher 'with the expert eye of the regular racegoer' sees the truth when he watches the lawyer, as he walks up the steps to the court, 'climbing up with a high-stepping tread that made each of his steps ring out on the marble'. Bucephalus is approved indulgently, deserving 'on account of his historical importance, at least a sympathetic reception'. The era when someone knew how to lead an army to India was long gone, and so the best one could do was 'what Bucephalus has done, and immerse oneself into the books of law', leafing through the pages of our ancient tomes 'in the still light of the lamp, far from the din of the Battle of Issus'. The time of heroes is over and with it that of warhorses. All that remains is a lawyer who bears the name of a legendary horse, who brushes the dust off the dossiers with his mane: a silent, virtuous draught horse.

When Ulrich, the protagonist of *The Man Without Qualities* – the novel which Robert Musil began in 1921, four years after Kafka's short story – recalls his youthful desire to become an important man, he notes the connection between his former admiration of Napoleon and his decision to enter a cavalry regiment. But when, shortly thereafter, he reads in the newspaper of a 'genius' racehorse, the knowledge dawns on him that the horse has beaten him to the glory and that 'sports and strictly objective criteria have deservedly come to the forefront, displacing such obsolete concepts as genius and human greatness'.[57]

The Fourth Rider

Wrapped in the flag of the United States, the coffin of the President rested on a gun carriage drawn by six grey horses. A single standard bearer followed the funeral carriage, a member of the Marine Corps, the branch of the army to which the President himself had formerly belonged. What followed next in the third position was for most viewers the most puzzling element in the long procession. Led by a soldier in parade uniform, walked a dark-brown riderless horse, restlessly prancing (p. 260). The animal was fully saddled and carrying a pair of riding boots reversed in the stirrups, as though its rider had been facing backwards before dismounting. As John F. Kennedy had at no point been a cavalryman, it could not be seen as a reference to his military origins. But even if the meaning and origin of the symbol remained obscure to most witnesses of the ceremony on 25 November 1963, no one was left untouched by the power of the strange spectacle. The riderless horse with boots reversed – a nervous, prancing and snorting sculpture – evoked nothing less than death.

The 'caparisoned horse' is a ceremonial element of the American state funeral. Appearing for the first time at the funeral of George Washington in 1799, this symbolic horse then walked behind Abraham Lincoln's coffin in 1865, before later appearing in the funeral processions of Franklin D. Roosevelt (1945), Herbert Hoover (1964), Lyndon B. Johnson (1973) and Ronald Reagan (2004). The word 'caparison' (from the French *caparaçon*) refers to the ornamental covering worn by a horse, which was typical of medieval tournaments and baroque funeral horses. Despite the name, the caparisoned horse of the US military wears only a bridle, saddle and an elegant black saddle blanket with a white trim. This sobriety makes the backward-facing boots all the more arresting. Through simple reduction, by omitting the full cover and decorative accoutrements and adding just one detail – the boots – the military ceremony established its distinct formula for pathos, which can barely be outdone in terms of austerity and intensity. Unlike its baroque predecessors, it does not speak grandiloquently of the transience of earthly things, the vanity of human existence and the perpetuity of glory; it gives voice to Death itself. And yet the great reverser of all things does not speak; only the clatter of the horse's hooves breaks the silence.

The popular interpretations that accompany the ritual and promise details of its historical origins in fact amount to little more than references to figures such as Genghis Khan, Buddha and certain Native American chiefs, who were buried along with their horses. Instead of dispersing the fog that obscures its origins, they make it denser.[1] There's an unintentionally comic ring to the explanation that the upturned boots represent the fallen leader, who turns one final time to his troops[2] – as though he had spun around like a gymnast on the horse and had sat down in the opposite direction to that of the procession. The strength of the image is matched by the futility of the interpretations of it: what makes great iconography and strong symbolism is the fact that anyone can feel the impact, even if very few can analyse it.

However, the formula of *reversal* – for example, of weapons or shields – has belonged since the Middle Ages to the ritual of the princely and military funeral cortège,[3] as does the custom of having the coffin of the deceased person followed by his favourite horse.[4] This ceremony was witnessed by the young Hermann Heimpel in Munich before the First World War, on the occasion of the funeral of Prince Regent Luitpold: 'Erhard watched the funeral procession from a balcony in the Arcisstrasse, opposite the garden of the Glyptothek. The Royal tack room was teeming with life: so many horses, saddle cloths, grooms. The men in cowls proceeded like a gloomy mummers' play before the coffin. This rested on a cart pulled by twelve horses, swathed in black cloth, led by handlers; high up on the box of the hearse sat the coachman in his three-cornered hat, the immense reins in his fists. The deceased was followed by his favourite horse – "Spanish-Burgundian court ceremony" Erhard heard someone behind him mutter.'[5]

In contrast to the origins of the ritual, the identity of the American funeral horse is well known. The fidgety horse that followed Kennedy's coffin, constantly prancing about, was called Black Jack. Born in 1947, Black Jack had been in the service of the army since 1953, serving as the military funeral horse in over 1,000 funeral processions, although he was considered uncontrollable and would constantly disturb the solemn tranquillity of the occasion. After twenty years in service, he retired in June 1973, and after his death (by veterinary euthanasia) in 1976, he was cremated and interred with full military honours in Fort Myer, Virginia, not far from Arlington Cemetery where John F. Kennedy is buried. With hindsight, what in the eyes of his military superiors constituted Black Jack's biggest weakness – his stubborn disobedience and tendency to fidget nervously – came to be seen as his symbolic strength: after all, in countless myths and folk legends of old Europe, a horse starting with fright and snorting is taken as a harbinger of death in the vicinity.[6]

EASILY SPOOKED

Popular belief – dubbed by doubters as superstition – and the myths of Northern and Eastern Europe are full of horses. When these timid animals are particularly nervous and jumpy, this is taken to suggest the proximity of the realm of spirits or a manifestation of the horses' special divining abilities. A horse's twitchy behaviour suggests either that spirits are unsettlingly close at hand or that the horse itself is in league with the spirit world and therefore has prophetic gifts. No other animal, except the cat, is as strongly affected by the otherworldly. Horses are said to be particularly affected by the ghosts of the dead after dark; at night, spirits and spectres like to go for a ride, after all. The many different versions of the legend of Leonora, a maiden who returns from the grave, best known in the form of Gottfried August Bürger's Gothic ballad *Lenore* (1774), are eloquent testimony to this midnight riding club whose tradition continues to this day in the genres of trashy horror and zombie movies such as *Tombs of the Blind Dead* (1972), with its horse-riding skeletons of blinded Spanish knights. The prose narratives of the nineteenth century also saw the horse as an ally of the spirit empire or as messengers of death, as we see in Theodor Storm's novella *Der Schimmelreiter* (1888) (*The Dykemaster*) or Hugo von Hofmannsthal's 'The Tale of the 672nd Night' (1895). Neither should we forget the talking horse's head of the Grimm Brothers' 'The Goose Girl'; it is hard to imagine a German childhood in the nineteenth or twentieth century without its memorable mantra 'Oh Falada, dost thou hangest there!'

Naturally, the historian has a more sober perspective and looks for what it is that links these ideas together: why is it that the image of the horse has such a close, almost brotherly, association with the idea of impending death? From the historian's perspective, Reinhart Koselleck proposed a very specific answer, developing a political anthropology based on five categories. The first of these categories speaks of death, or rather of killing: 'Heidegger's central provision of the march towards death must, in order to make histories possible, be complemented by the corresponding category of the ability to kill.'[7] Part of the human condition, as the historian knows well, is the thoroughly political 'threat of the death of others or at the hands of others'.[8] The example Koselleck uses to demonstrate this general point is that of the cavalry charge at Omdurman, as described by Winston Churchill (see pp. 99–101), which the talented British author endows with a timeless quality. Thus Churchill contrasts the situation of someone sitting strong and ready on their horse with that of another fighter who, whether wounded or thrown from their horse, becomes the victim of an attack. In a similar vein, Koselleck himself at times contrasts the status of mounted soldiers with that of infantrymen or wounded soldiers, who face the threat of being trodden under hoof.[9] In fact, the very real – and not merely mythological or literary – representation of the horse as a messenger of death may well have been forged on the battlefields of Asia and Europe, where an onrushing cavalry would scatter the army of foot soldiers into flight, if it did not simply trample them to death.

Or rather, it would threaten to trample them to death. Real power, in sociologist Niklas Luhmann's theory, is not in the stark fact of doing something, but in the subtle possibility of doing it and the demonstration of hypothetical behaviour.[10] The exercise of power has a theatrical aspect to it: it is not necessarily the act of violence, but the threat of it. Carried over to the example of the cavalry, the power lies not in the *factum brutum* of the infantry being overrun, or overridden, but in the threat of such a fate that the infantry internalizes. Before it touches the integrity of the body in the form of violence, power is a theatre of fear.

The horse is the main protagonist on the stage of this theatre, because over the course of evolution it has perfected its expression of terror. As Charles Darwin identified, this expressiveness prompts a simultaneous response of mimicry in the beholder and gives a practical trigger to flee a dangerous situation: 'The actions of a horse when much startled are highly expressive. One day my horse was much frightened . . . His eyes and ears were directed intently forwards; and I could feel through the saddle the palpitations of his heart. With red dilated nostrils he snorted violently, and whirling round, would have dashed off at full speed, had I not prevented him . . . This expansion of the nostrils, as well as the snorting, and the palpitations of the heart, are actions which have become firmly associated during a long series of generations with the emotion of terror; for terror has habitually led the horse to the most violent exertion in dashing away at full speed from the cause of danger.'[11]

Nobody has better grasped the theatrical show of power and its embodiment in the horse and represented it in a more resplendent manner than Peter Paul Rubens in his charging horsemen and savage scenes of boar, lion and tiger hunts. As Jacob Burckhardt puts it, Rubens 'paints, as no one did before him, the horse sharing in the general tumult and, already swift and wild, bearing its rider into battle. He knows the animal in danger and in rage, and it is to the horse that he gives the expression of great and terrible moments in the conflicts of men or beasts.'[12] Rubens and several of his students who followed his example recognized wherein lay the unique quality of the horse in the representation of power: not in the power of his physique, however much the sheer size of the horse's body dominated the canvas. The horse was not powerful because it was a large and strong animal – for that would be a trivial conclusion – but because it was a uniquely expressive subject of fear. The horse could spread terror while, or rather *because*, it was itself imbued with terror and expressed this like no other creature. The place where a horse's active and passive nervousness is concentrated is in its large, expressive eye.[13] The

Tenno rides into the dreamscape of a sleeping Uncle Sam (Walter Huston):
film still from John Ford and Gregg Toland's propaganda film,
December 7th (1943).

Pale Rider of the Red Army: Marshal Zhukov at the
Victory Day parade in Moscow, 24 June 1945.

look that emanates from this eye is not the petrifying stare of Medusa; this eye does not turn a man to stone, but certainly conveys the fear that the stare reflects: the panic, the sheer terror. In the horse's eye, painters found the most concentrated, concise formula for the horror confronted by man and beast alike on the battlefield or at the bloody climax of a hunt.

In all the cavalry battles and hunting scenes drawn and painted by Rubens, the eye of the horse (or horses), upon which this particular iconic task fell, is consistently located at the central focal point of the entire composition. The glances of the other protagonists – the men, animals or monsters – all remain trapped within the picture; they do not break out and make eye contact with the observer. One single eye pierces the observer directly – the chilling stare of a horse. As we consider *The Lion Hunt* (Plate 23), we feel constantly pierced by this stare with its unmistakable expression of terror. The wide-open eye becomes the crux of the composition and the mirror of its power. It is a simultaneously passive and active mirror: the horse embodies power precisely because it is able to sense fear, express it and pass it on. The light beam of power is concentrated in this rolling prism, this bulging eyeball, to be refracted outwards, towards the viewer, the witness, the enemy.

The dialectic of this gaze, whose inner contradictions Rubens captures with such clarity and exploits at the fulcrum of his composition is, of course, the dialectic of the animal itself, which – easily spooked and inclined by nature to flight – has been, as it were, recoded by mankind and converted into a vehicle of terrifying power. When a horse carrying a rider is spooked, it starts and wants to bolt – these are all characteristics of its original nature and have, as Darwin demonstrated, a practical purpose. However, as the poet Albrecht Schaeffer writes, 'through its beautiful . . . form, the effect on the spectator is as though these features reflected an inner boldness, and as though the terrified eye was in fact burning with a bellicose rage'.[14] This is what Rubens saw: inside the perfect incarnation of power is the expression of sheer terror.

Sigmund Freud would also encounter this dual nature of *equine fear* in the course of his analysis of infantile sexuality. It was Little Hans's phobia about horses[15] that brought to his attention the ambivalent relationship between an anxiety *about* something and a fear *of* something. In the first conversations recorded by his father, five-year-old Hans initially expressed his fear of horses suddenly dashing off, adding 'that the horses will fall down when the cart turns'. But a short while later he added that he was afraid that a horse might 'fall over and bite' him and thrash around with its legs and make a 'racket'.[16] Here Freud discerned the ambivalence of the phobia which made Hans fear alternately that the horse might bite him and that something might happen to the horse. Freud noted that 'the biting and the falling horse, had been shown to represent his father, who was going to punish him for the evil wishes he was nourishing against him'.[17]

More than the apparently 'classic' reduction of the father, Freud seems, however, to have been interested in the surprising phase transition within the phobia: 'It is especially interesting, however, to observe the way in which the transformation of Hans's libido into anxiety was projected on to the principal object of his phobia, on to horses. Horses interested him the most of all the large animals; playing at horses was his favourite game with the other children . . . When repression had set in and brought a revulsion of feeling along with it, horses, which had till then been associated with so much pleasure, were necessarily turned into objects of fear.'[18] The phobic process, wrote Freud, was responsible for raising the horse to become 'a symbol of terror'[19] and thus represented the preliminary result of a phase transition, which painters had already recognized and exploited for its visual impact: the fleeting transition of the horse from the object of fear to its subject.

THE GREAT COLLECTIONS

The nameless stranger played by Clint Eastwood in *Pale Rider*, a late Western from 1985, is a wandering, or rather a horse-riding, preacher. In a previous life, he might have been a gunslinger, maybe an outlaw, a desperado.[20] Like all Western heroes, he has a fixed abode of a kind: he comes from nowhere. His back bears the scars of bullet wounds – the sort of wounds after which you would think he'd be left for dead. Indeed, perhaps he had been, for no normal person could survive such injuries. Whether he holds the Bible in his hands or a Colt, he is always surrounded by a stony, cool vibe, through which blows the icy breeze of death. The pale rider on his pale horse is one who has returned from the other side. The gloomy aura of death lingers around him and his beautiful horse, whose head shape betrays its thoroughbred provenance. Like many Westerns, *Pale Rider* is a cinematic ghost story. The character who calls himself 'Marshal', the cynical leader of a band of hitmen, ends up being gunned down by the Pale Rider; his gunshot wounds reveal a similar pattern to that of the preacher's. The mill of repetition turns, as in all ghost stories: the burned-out hero makes a comeback as *revenant*.

When revenants make their return on horseback, and indeed many do seem to, their mythological and iconological origins lie either in the misty climes of the north or in the balmy coves of the Aegean. Their screenplays were originally composed by John of Patmos and the anonymous army of creators of myths, legends and figures of the pre and sub-Christian Europa: St John's Apocalypse and Norse mythology with their popular apocrypha, and the broad field of superstition, all make up the fictional horse markets where the spirits of the dead come to procure their mounts.

The Apocalypse of St John the Apostle (Rev. 6: 1–8) brought us the *four horsemen of the apocalypse*: the first, on a white horse, carries a bow, wears a crown and is called Conquest. Traditionally interpreted as a ruler, he was identified with the victorious returning Christ. The second, on a red horse, carries a great sword and represents War and Violence. The third, on a black steed, brandishes a pair of scales in the air as he announces Famine. And the fourth, riding a pale horse, brings Death by plague, war and wild beasts.[21] He is the pallid rider on an ashen horse, whose colourlessness recalls the pallor of one who is dying. This fourth horseman dominates the cultural imagination of North America, so influenced by Protestant ideology that finds its way even into the film scripts of Hollywood.

Nordic and continental Germanic mythology is also characterized by an enormous cavalry, stretching back to Odin and his eight-legged steed Sleipnir. Since Jacob Grimm's anthology of *Teutonic Mythology*, first published in 1835, the folklorists, mythologists and philologists of the nineteenth and twentieth centuries have never tired of collating all the local variants and sub-variants of horseman legends, of sacred steeds and devilish nags – a boundless hippo-mythology, which has never been granted its own grammar or theory of evolution. For literary narrators and authors of theoretical texts alike, this wealth of ethnographic positivism has provided an overflowing fount of material, helping to tip realistic stories into the realm of fantasy and drawing theoretical constructions into the quicksand of ethnological sources. Any lover of theories could find what he was looking for in the gigantic and chaotic treasure trove of the great anthologies.

When, in 1886, Theodor Storm began his last great novella, *Der Schimmelreiter (The Dykemaster)*, he made liberal, if not excessive, use of the trappings of sagas and folklore to furnish the dramatic story of dykemaster Hauke Haien. The tale is conceived as a ghost story and there can be no doubt with whom the Faustian protagonist – the technically and mathematically talented, zealously modernizing dykemaster – is in league, at least in the eyes of his suspicious fellow villagers and dyke workers. We lose count of the thinly veiled hints at the diabolical and the undead, nocturnal apparitions, skeletons roaming in the moonlight, mermaids, monkfish (known in German as *Seeteufel*, 'sea devils'), a seagull trampled under a horse's hooves, an animal sacrifice and the last words of a dying man – the North German fantastical realm seems inexhaustible. We only encounter deeper and more subtle contours to the dykemaster when the narrator holds up the mirror to reflect his grey horse.

The mare that Hauke Haien buys from a suspicious-looking fellow, a Slovak whose brown hand 'looked almost like a claw', turns out after a few weeks of tender nurturing to be a noble thoroughbred. The rough hairs disappear, a 'shiny, bluish-grey speckled coat' comes to light; above all, it has 'what an Arab horse should have: a thin fleshless face, from which blazed two fiery brown eyes'. In other words, the dykemaster has been sold an oriental pedigree, probably the only Arabian mare to have reached the stables of North German realism. For the dykemaster's superstitious neighbours, the 'fleshless' or sunken face of the Arabian only confirms their suspicion that the horse is as closely affiliated to the devil as his master and rider. Where he recognizes the signs of equine beauty, they see only a portentous skull. Moreover, with time, the master comes more and more to resemble his sinister mount, with 'his eyes staring from his gaunt face'. The horse will not tolerate another rider besides his master, and responds to the pressure of his thighs like a lover. 'No sooner had he mounted,' we read in Storm's narrative, which calibrates the chaste eroticism of married love by the pressure of the touch of a hand and the strength of colour of a blush, 'than the animal uttered a neigh like a shout of delight'. It would be the only shout of delight that, for generations, this set text brought to the classrooms of the nation.

But if the dykemaster is the Pale Rider of Norse mythology, then what does his horse represent? His curious 'existence' develops in three phases. In the first stage, he stands on the beach of the coastal island, a skeleton that rises and roams at night; in the second phase, he is the dykemaster's diabolically elegant riding horse; and in the third, after their common ruin, he reappears as the spirited skeleton. There's no doubt that his pale dapple-grey represents the undead, a creature of terror tasked by the author to convey what remains unnamed in this novella: the death-wish of a man who can no longer be helped on this earth. As the vital pendulum of the undead animal swings between the underworld and the world of the living, between stony chill and lustful heat, this beast bears the burden of horror.

In Henry Fuseli's most famous painting, *The Nightmare*, of 1781–2 (p. 270), the horse also appears as the embodiment of horror in both guise and function. The picture shows a curvaceous sleeping beauty, lightly clothed and half tumbling from the bed, with a demonically grinning incubus crouching on her chest – presumably the *'alb'* ('demon') from the German word *'Albtraum'* or *'Alptraum'* ('nightmare') – while behind him an eerily glowing horse head peers through the curtains into the murky midnight room. In another painting produced a few years later, around 1793, Fuseli delves into the dream world, making clearer the relationship between the two tormentors, the animal-like goblin and the horse. Entitled *The Nightmare Leaves Two Sleeping Girls*, the painting captures the *alb*, the demon, riding away through the open window, leaving behind the two girls he has just afflicted. It is unclear, though, who or what is intended by the word 'nightmare': the monkey-like sprite, his mount or both together.

The phonetic correspondence in English between 'night*mare*' and '*mare*' as in a 'horse' has meant that in the English-speaking world, including North America, the idea of a nightmare is intimately associated with the idea of the horse.

Ernest Jones, student and biographer of Freud, included Fuseli's *Nightmare* as the frontispiece to his 1949 study *On the Nightmare*[22] and dedicated an entire chapter to the interpretation of the sinister horse's head.[23] He begins by noting that to ascribe the same etymology to both kinds of 'mare' is a misconception arising from the confusing similarity of the two words, and that in fact the second part of 'nightmare' derives from the Anglo-Saxon word *mara*, which was more like an *incubus* or *succubus* – that is, an erotic intruder at night. But, as Jones continued, it is possible that within this linguistic confusion lies another deeper, dormant truth in the realm accessible by psychoanalysts. Philology might sleep calmly on its certainties, but suspicious psychoanalysis lies wide awake. And what if there was something in the mistaken correlation of the sexual demon and the horse; if the two acquaintances really were in fact related, as the English terms suggest? Jones is confident that when human beings and animals are put on an equal footing in a dream there is always one underlying meaning: 'In a word, therefore, the presence of an animal in such contexts always denotes the action of an incest complex.'[24] This, in short, means, for Jones, that if a dream takes a person's breath away, and if it involves horses, that person must harbour incestuous desires.

To start with, Jones stays in a similar territory to Max Jähns,[25] mentioned above, who sums up his impressive collection of Nordic-Germanic equine terms and idioms with the remark: 'Quite peculiar and without example is the intimate *juxtaposition of horse and woman* in poetry, proverbial wisdom and sayings . . . This juxtaposition is primeval.'[26] He describes a witch riding on a broom and the pole of a hobby horse in terms of animal worship within a phallic religion, which in turn would reveal much to deep psychoanalytic investigation. 'We have insensibly glided from the theme *mara = mare* to that of the horse as a phallic animal, but this illustrates the remarkable interchangeability of the sexes in this whole group of myths . . . The explanation of this state of affairs is that the forbidden wishes that furnish the driving force behind all these beliefs and myths are

Funeral procession for John F. Kennedy, Washington, 25 November 1963.

Death on a Pale Horse,
John Hamilton Mortimer,
c.1775.

the repressed sexual desires of incest, and one of the most characteristic defences against the becoming conscious of such desires is to
repudiate them and conceal them through the mechanism of identification with the opposite sex.'[27]

With the determination of someone foraging for mushrooms in a
forest, Jones rummages through the wealth of literature and reaps the
following gems: Odin and his nocturnal army (Jones, *On the Nightmare*, p. 263), death as a horseman (p. 265), the horse and the Sun (p.
278), Zeus as miller (p. 281), the significance of the horse skull (p. 287),
horses, water and urine (p. 291), storm gods (p. 293), the significance
the horse's hoof (p. 297), the horseshoe (p. 301), horse theft (p. 304),
horse manure (p. 305), sex and neighing (p. 311), the horse as oracle
(p. 312), the mare's shiny coat (p. 314), the Teutonic magic steed (p. 323),
and so on. Behind all of these legends and metamorphoses, he argues,
lurks the repressed desire for incest.[28] Seen through Jones's interpretation, these great collections of folklore, which just a few years earlier
had also served the purposes of Aryan research, with different intentions but in a similar way, are turned into an evidence room bearing
witness to the process of sexual repression. The entire stable of Nordic,
Germanic and even Mediterranean mythology is seen as a wardrobe of
masks and costumes disguising a latent desire for incest. If you want an
example of how a tenuous theory can be dressed up with a persuasive
explanation, look no further than Ernest Jones's interpretation of the
nightmare.

ERUPTING VIOLENCE

The interpretation of Fuseli's *Nightmare* formulated a quarter of a
century after Jones by the Swiss physician and literary scholar Jean
Starobinski is only superficially psychological.[29] Starobinski follows
the lines and figures of the famous painting before placing Fuseli, with
a glance at his artistic *oeuvre* and biography, within the ideological
and emblematic history of the revolutionary age. He describes the
atmosphere of an oppressive, claustrophobic fear that imbues Fuseli's
painting, but views it not as an expression of an inner psychic
mechanism, rather as the painter's historical and moral philosophical

statement. For Fuseli, there was no escape from this world of brutal violence: 'He cares nothing for the great day of history . . . sin and death rule the world, and it is these that Fuseli's questions always address.'[30] Although Fuseli does not disguise the sexual possession of his subjects, the viewer of his works is not entering an intimate erotic theatre. Fuseli dreams up the state of the world after the revolution, but unlike David, whose work takes a diametrically opposite stance, he formulates his response not in classical drapery or in the future tense; Fuseli spells out the timeless ontology of evil in the philosophy of the boudoir.

Starting from a close examination of the painting, Starobinski refuses to be led back to the theme of incestuous desire: if this had been the correct interpretation, Fuseli would have deliberately chosen to depict a nightmare.[31] However, it does not seem as though the artist intended to portray a gallery of 'cases', in the vein of Jean-Martin Charcot's iconography of hysteria. As Starobinski sees it, the painter is not penetrating into the pathology of fear, but is making a curiosity of anguish: 'He sees suffering; he evokes suffering. He observes the disintegration of the shrewd artifices manufactured by the beautiful temptress before the mirror for the purpose of conquest. He sees her in despair, an urgent state close to death . . .'[32] Unlike the Fuseli researcher Nicolas Powell, who had published a tome on the iconographic interpretation of Fuseli's *Nightmare* the year before,[33] Starobinski did not enquire into the possible precedents for elements of the composition – in the case of the horse, perhaps Hans Baldung Grien, Veronese's *Venus and Mars with Cupid and a Horse* (Plate 24) or the statues of Castor and Pollux with their horses at the Dioscuri fountain in Rome's Piazza del Quirinale – but rather he tracked down the *literary* sources behind the imagery: 'It is a visionary *mise-en-scène*, and it does what it wants with its dramatic and epic precedents . . . Fuseli performs the work he is reading with a pencil in his hand, and develops his graphic representation of the literary piece, intensively filling in his sketch, exploring its most hidden aspects.'[34]

But despite this literary interpretation Starobinski did not overlook the idiosyncrasies of the representation. These were evident not only in the shapely lines of the sleeping woman, but also in the attention the painter pays to the third participant, the horse. Starobinski notes the sudden violence of his intrusion: 'The appearance of the head and long neck in the gap between the curtains represents a violation. The body of the horse remains outside in the night.'[35] He also comments on the luminescence of the horse ('as though it were a source of light'[36]) and specifically its eyes that shine like light bulbs: 'in the face of the horse we encounter the paroxystic expression of an over-presence corresponding with the over-absence of the sleeping subject'.[37] He pointed to the forced opening of the space by the horse's intrusion: 'the room of the nightmare is forced open by the penetration of the horse bursting in from a distance'.[38] While the other two protagonists of the painting and the interior surrounding them are all calculated to convey an atmosphere of oppressive, weighty fear, the horse, on the other hand, embodies the sudden onset of sheer terror. Fuseli's drawings and paintings, writes Starobinski, 'were always dominated by passionate violence: the night, murder, erotic seduction and the singularity of evil are fixed values for him'.[39]

The appearance of the horse, or rather of its head, in the scene of *The Nightmare* delivers a powerful formula to express the presence of violence in that it establishes a connection with the dynamics of penetration. The horse head represents the moment of erupting violence and conveys to the viewer, as the only appropriate form of response, the sensation of horror.

On 23 December 2002, the historian Reinhart Koselleck put into words for the first time an image which he had harboured in his memory for sixty years. It was the image of a severely injured horse that he had witnessed in the summer of 1942. 'I saw corpses whose skulls were half blown away – in Barysaw[40] after the reconquest – but the corpses were dead. Then I saw this horse whose skull was half blown away and the horse was alive, galloping along at full pelt through the marching column, deathly despair itself – and no one could deliver the horse from its fate, because there was no racehorse there that could catch up with it – and because a shot from a standing position would have posed a fatal risk to the marching soldiers. And so the horse raced on with its half a skull – an inversion of the Apocalypse. The horse did not carry an omen of death – it was the incarnation of human self-destruction that dragged everything along with it.'[41]

The wounded horse seemed to have emerged from the Apocalypse itself, but Koselleck knew it was not of *literary* provenance. There had been no script for this scene, no artistic precedent. The sinister event, too absurd to have been invented,[42] had actually happened; he had seen it with his own eyes. How many times since then had the memory flashed back? When had he last seen the horse? Why did he only now pick up a pen to capture the memory? Was it only now that he recognized its full emblematic significance? It was like an invasion of the surreal into the reality of war, and was almost more horrific than the Apocalypse: precisely because there was no longer a rider. Because all that remained was the horse, its gaping wound and its *fatal despair.* The Apocalypse had descended upon the world, not from the outside but as an occurrence 'of human self-destruction that dragged everything along with it'. Sixty years later, just before Christmas, Koselleck sat at his desk and wrote down what his memory gave him, suppressing the rising pathos. It cannot have been easy for him to capture in words the horror of the image that had accompanied him for so long. But he recognized what it boiled down to: the absence of a rider. It was that absence that made the scene absolutely unbearable. Even Fuseli's scenes had had literary or iconographic precursors. For the *inversion* of the Apocalypse, there had been no script.

The Whip

The man shall have his mare again, and all shall be well.
William Shakespeare, *A Midsummer Night's Dream*

What once only the rural population knew from first-hand experience is now for everyone just a mouse click away. The next moment you find yourself in a large hot zoo full of copulating animals, while their keepers clearly don't object. And we've all seen it on TV: 'You and me baby ain't nothin' but mammals / So let's do it like they do on the Discovery Channel.'[1] Among all the animals in the zoo, it is the horses that appear to enjoy the most popularity. This may be down to their size and beauty, but may also be linked to other reasons, such as the idea that horses are particularly noble animals and therefore chaster than others or as untouchable as Brahmins. But then there's the opposite view – one expressed by Aristotle – that horses have the strongest sex drive of all creatures after humans. Anyway, if you look up mating horses in your search-machine zoo, you'll be offered an extensive list of options, including examples of the 'hardcore' variety and contemporary variants on Greek mythology, where, as with the ancients, the species barrier between human and animal is casually skipped over.[2]

So, too, in the 2013 Icelandic film *Of Horses and Men*, where one of the high points is a scene of love-making between two horses, while throughout the entire procedure a man sits, somewhat perplexed and flustered, on the female horse – and remains sitting there quietly because the stallion, far from embarrassed by his presence, takes not the slightest notice. Somewhat more dramatic is the scene in the play *Medea* (1926) that Hans Henny Jahnn has the older of Jason's two boys experience and recount: finding himself sandwiched between two copulating horses, he is almost crushed to death. Narrowly escaping danger, he falls in love with the rider of the stallion in question, 'an Amazon girl, full of laughter', and suddenly feeling like a man, he begins to long for the young woman. But instead of seeing her again, he falls victim to his mother's hunger for revenge. In retrospect, the horse scene seems like a garishly ominous portent for the violence of sexuality, a force that destroys the life of the family and even rips to shreds the bonds of filial love.

Since ancient times, sex has been considered a dangerous force, hazardous for the house and household as well as for the cohesion of the community, especially when it expresses itself in forms that move beyond the broad realm of interpersonal relationships. Hans Baldung Grien's famous engraving of *The Bewitched Groom* stands out from the iconography of the Renaissance, looming like a dramatic warning sign admonishing against the lure of bestiality, a sexual urge to which a human male can succumb. With extreme and humbling foreshortening, the composition shows a stable boy lying supine on the ground, while behind him, in the central axis of the picture, we see the vulva of the mare whose buttocks shimmer in the light. For Pia F. Cuneo, Professor of Art History at the University of Arizona and herself a keen rider, the tangible misogynistic allusions in the picture are unmissable, especially for an educated audience that is intimately familiar with the equine literature of the time: 'In some of the hippological literature, discussion of ideal equine conformation often includes comparison between a well-shaped horse and a beautiful woman. According to this comparison, both horse and woman should possess a shapely posterior ... a desire to be "ridden", and the ability to make pleasant movements underneath their "riders".'[3]

Cuneo interprets the engraving, completed a year before the artist's death, as a warning to the humanistically educated, wealthy and noble horse-owning layer of the society of his time against the consequences of an excessive love for the beautiful animal.[4] Bestiality is something, albeit rare, to which the eroticism between men and horses can lead; literature has certainly known of it since the reference by the Roman writer Aelian to a case recounted by Eudemus concerning the stable boy who fell in love with a mare. The other apex of the erotic pendulum is the latent sexuality of endless waves of young girls, who throughout the generations have transformed the riding school into a pleasure ground of pubescent and teenage nymphs. Somewhere in between – but where? – there is the confusing terrain of the pleasures of torment and obedience, and the associated toys, poses and whips; these pleasures cannot dispense with images of riding and pulling without the imagery of equine love.

Leaving aside the reality of bestiality, in which the times and places where people such as shepherds or grooms coexisted in close quarters with the animals in their care may indeed have played a certain role,[5] we are still left with the imagery, metaphors and cultural coding – a whole phenomenology of sexuality between men and horses in the hypothetical. But only very few of those things that we commonly refer to as 'images' exist without a connection to the supposedly other, imageless 'reality'. And, vice versa, this is intimately asserted with images, signs and symbols, and would probably not be perceived without their existence, and thus the images and symbols are associated with reality through countless threads and particles and can only unfurl as a result of their impact. Sexuality, as banal as it seems, is the 'reality' most mediated and punctuated by images; some even assert that it consists of nothing other than images and discourse. If, for example, we wanted to understand the phenomenon of the 'horse girls', it is not enough to speak of projections and cultural codes, unless we consider where they are directed, namely at these large, characterful animals of outstanding beauty, with their own behaviour and their special smell. Horses are not teddy bears or smartphones, but very special living creatures, which we do not only project ourselves onto, but which we can also fall in love with: they are a kind of *living metaphor*.

But the 'horse girls' are a special case, a world unto themselves. The other phenomenon which also falls within this chapter is the riding and driving school of desire to which we were introduced by the novelists of the nineteenth century. Pretty much all the well-known nineteenth-century novels of love and adultery turn out on closer inspection to be equine novels that could not exist without the large, warm body of this odd-toed ungulate. The literature shows how people toy with animal imagery, picture themselves as animals, and are able, when dressing up or hiding behind an equine mask, to say what otherwise can only be left ambiguously unspoken.

TRIAD IN BRONZE

Close to one another at Berlin's Alte Nationalgalerie stand three large bronze sculptures in which horses play a supporting role. Chronologically they are also close to one other; the oldest originated in the years after the unification of Germany, the most recent in 1900. Here the similarities are exhausted, and the list begins of their differences. A comparison of the three sculptures seems to circumscribe the realm of erotic possibilities that opens up between men, women and horses – be they literary, graphic, sculptural, or whatever. Since we cannot have all three sculptures in our field of vision at one time, a synopsis is not possible in the strictest sense, so let us examine them in turn. One tends to begin with the largest of the three sculptures, the most mighty, although not necessarily the most beautiful: the equestrian statue of Friedrich Wilhelm IV, which towers above the viewer on its high plinth in front of the entrance to the gallery.

Based on a design by Gustav Bläser, the work was executed by the Berlin sculptor Alexander Calandrelli between 1875 and 1886, the date of its installation at the gallery. It shows the King of Prussia and patron of the arts riding his steed in a southerly direction, not, as all the clues in the monument might lead us to expect, in a westerly direction towards France. The king has a thoroughly martial presence. The horse, a stallion of strong physique and ostentatious masculinity, strides with vigour and yet with restraint. It carries its rider, a man of powerful build, energetically towards an invisible opposition. Everything about this pre-eminent dual entity, from the horse's flared nostrils to its strikingly bushy tail, represents a dynamic expression of strength.

The contrast with the *Amazon on a Horse* by Louis Tuaillon, which stands to the right of the regal horseman on the long side of the New Museum in Berlin, could not be greater. The youthful warrior, riding bareback, with a small, only slightly menacing axe in her hand, is draped in a light chiton which accentuates her dainty figure rather than veiling it, leaving her upper thigh uncovered. Where she touches the horse, the Amazon is completely naked. Unlike the statue of the Prussian king, which emphasizes the sense of distance, Tuaillon's Amazon invites empathy. Not in the sense that she turns the viewer into a rider, who feels the horse's every movement – in fact, the animal stands still and holds its head slightly turned to the left – but in the way she conveys to the viewer the warmth of the horse's body, the beat of its heart and the pulsing of its blood. The serene grace, the lightness of the sculpture, makes it quite possible for the viewer to assimilate the pair entirely and to empathize with the eroticism that is discernible in the contact between the two bodies. For a brief moment, the viewer *becomes* an Amazon, whose bronze eyes scan the broad square.

The third sculpture, *Centaur and Nymph*, installed in front of the colonnade on the other side of the National Gallery, is the work of the neo-baroque sculptor Reinhold Begas, a student of the Rauchschule. It shows an elderly, bearded centaur, not dissimilar to the artist himself, helping a young, naked nymph up to sit side-saddle on his back. In his younger years, Begas had lived and studied for a time in Rome, where he met the artists Anselm Feuerbach and Arnold Böcklin, whose sometimes crudely sensual art seems to have been an inspiration behind this portrait of a gallant centaur. Although the sculpture of the two mythical beings, both handsomely built and erotically charged, is clearly intended to charm the viewer, the latter nevertheless remains at a safe remove: the narrative of the sculpture reduces its seductive power. It does nevertheless open up the associations of a centaurian love-life, where often enough seduction pairs with abduction and the threat of violence can tilt the game of love between the sexes into something darker.

The horse, which one might think would play the strongest role in this third sculpture, with it having a more active part to play as a centaur, is in fact cheated of some of its phenomenal impact, because of sharing a hybrid body with the bearded human. Unlike the statue of the Prussian king, where the horse provides the entire dynamic spectacle of the show of power, and unlike the mare's quiet serenity in the Amazonian sculpture, the centaur is not a real horse. He cannot parade the horse's distinctive strengths, but rather, as a four-legged

The Nightmare and the 'night mare': Henry Fuseli
(Johann Heinrich Füssli), 1781.

The Parthenon frieze of modernity: the chronophotography of
Étienne-Jules Marey, 1886.

old man of legend, he draws the erotic scene back into the realm of the text.

Until the twentieth century, the game of seduction and ravishment which constantly threatened to tip over into violence was often depicted by means of the centaur; it was a symbol that German painter and illustrator Max Slevogt also drew on. Although lustful ruffians by nature, centaurs can age into gentler, wiser veterans, above such lascivious horseplay. We see this in the example of the ancient educator of princes, the senior centaur Chiron. Moreover, such bawdy behaviour clearly occurs in art without any centaurs being involved; quite 'ordinary' horses also appear as a dynamizing element foreshadowing the sexual act, as we see in *The Rape of the Daughters of Leucippus* by Rubens (Plate 22). Another example is *The Abduction of a Young Girl* by the late-baroque godfather of Impressionism Franz Anton Maulbertsch. While the young woman, in the arms of her abductor, looks back in horror at the body of her decapitated companion, the horse appears in the role of seducer and throws the beautiful, unfortunate maiden a look of compassion mixed with desire. Maulbertsch, the sensitive colourist, lets everything else be said in the colours: the milky white skin of the young woman and the same tone in the shimmering coat of the white stallion hint that these bodies will soon become one flesh.

Goya's etching *El caballo raptor* (*The Horse-Abductor*) reveals the disturbing power that can emanate from an image, where we see the inversion as described by Koselleck. It is one of the *Los disparates* or *Proverbios* series of prints produced by the Spanish artist between 1815 and 1823. One could translate 'raptor' differently, and more harshly, and label the horse a robber or a rapist. There is violence in the air of this scene, no doubt, and any critic who, like Robert Hughes, interprets the woman's expression as nothing but an orgasm, is projecting rather than truly looking at the picture. What prompts the horse, rearing up in the levade position, to bite at the woman, as she stares at him, frozen? Does he want to steal her away, kidnap her, seduce her, harm her, or does he intend to carry her to safety from God knows what other danger? Is the 'raptor' perhaps a diligent rescuer, who has snatched the woman from greater harm? Perhaps from the threat of being devoured by the beasts in the background of the image? What kind of beasts are these that seem to live in water like oversized beavers or rats? When we look more closely, we notice that the horse is also standing with its hind legs in the flood water, so that its wet tail is sticking to its legs. Suppose now that the animals in the picture represent the might of land and sea, the plump rats stand for the Leviathan, and the horse for the Behemoth, the long-toothed monster, the ruler of the land – what would the message of the engraving be then? And what would the woman represent?

The iconographic tradition to which Goya's picture tips its hat is the same one that shows through in Reinhold Begas's work: the compositional formula of the centaur carrying away a nymph on his back. But at the crucial point, referred to in Koselleck's concept of *inversion*, Goya departs from the well-trodden path of tradition. He grants the horse and the horse alone certain attributes which were previously associated with the centaur. Or with violent men mounted on horses. *El caballo*, by contrast, is very much a horse, not a centaur. Rather than playing in the well-lit theme park of Greek mythology, Goya digs down to subvert the political menagerie. What does the woman see behind her closed eyes: the violence facing her or the violence that lurks behind her?

BRIGHT YOUNG AMAZONS

With her low-budget production *Of Girls and Horses* (2014), Monika Treut was returning to her roots as a film-maker, as she writes in the press release for her equestrian 'coming-of-age movie'. 'Horses were my best friends during my difficult adolescent years. I was fascinated by the community of girls and horses, a community without boys and men, the bond between the animals and the girls and women . . . The physicality and energy of riding, grooming and taming these shy and strong prey animals had its own eroticism that enthralled us girls and kept us grounded. From this innocent, energetic perspective I wanted to tell a simple story from my own experience: how a troubled teenager can slowly, through contact with the horses, build a relationship with herself and build trust in others.'[6]

Pubescent girls and horses. Like all great love stories, this one remains an enigma. Psychologists have, of course, sought to explain it. As a rule, their conceptions of sexual development are oriented towards the model of heterosexuality. In these theories, the horse is presented as the last substitute before choosing a male partner – a kind of *transfer object*. 'Somewhere between a doll and a real-life partner, the horse is the ultimate soft toy. It's the largest, most beautiful and final plaything before the transition from home and family to a new relationship with a sexual partner.'[7] In contrast, Monika Treut depicts a world outside of this teleology. Horses and girls establish a world unto itself, based on the 'bond between the animals and the girls and women'. In this world, the horse is more than a mere cargo ship slowly but surely carrying the libido of the teenage girl to the shores of heterosexual attachment. Its *physis*, its vitality, its strong, animated body, and its *dynamis*, expressed in the energy of the ride, give rise, in connection with the physical care for the horse, to an erotic charge that for a certain period gives contentment in the relationship and the bond. How long this lasts, how durable the communities of girls and horses are, is something the author doesn't dwell on. But the 'energetic perspective' makes it possible to see these mini female republics as temporary symbioses in their own right: girls and horses are islands in the flowing river of time.

For a few years, the riding school is a counter-existence remote from the world of school and family life, an adventure that offers girls the opportunity to discover a certain ferocity within themselves – something which there is little provision for outside of the stamping ground of the Amazons. 'Here, a girl can be not only a girl but also a boy: not just loving, but also hating; not only defensive, but also aggressive; not just tender, but also violent; not only gentle, but also demanding; not only modest, but also dominant. It offers a female rider a place and an object of gender transgression.'[8]

Girls and horses: both swift and shy, difficult to tame, always ready to flee. Young girls, write Gilles Deleuze and Félix Guattari, quoting Marcel Proust, are 'fugitive beings'. By their nature, they are 'pure relations of speed and slowness and nothing else. A girl is late on account of her speed: she did too many things, crossed too many spaces in relation to the relative time of the person waiting for her. Thus her apparent slowness is transformed into the breakneck speed of our waiting.'[9]

Herodotus tells the story of how the Scythians 'broke in' the Amazons.[10] After the victorious battle of Thermodon, the Hellenes sailed homeward with the captured Amazons divided between three ships. On the way, the Amazons rose up and slaughtered all the men and sailed on alone. Unfamiliar with the art of sailing, they drifted about until they finally landed 'on Lake Maeëtis, at Cremni, which stands in the land of the Free Scythians'. They stole a herd of horses and went rampaging through Scythia, again on horseback. When the Scythians realized, astonished, that it was not a band of young men attacking them, but women, they rallied their youngest men, about as many as they assumed there were Amazons. They were instructed to live in the vicinity of these women, to flee if they were attacked by them and when the women desisted, to return and live alongside them. When the Amazons accepted that the men meant them no harm, they left them alone. The young men began to imitate the Amazons, hunting and pillaging like them, and day by day the two camps came closer together. Around noon the Amazons would go off alone or in pairs to relieve themselves, and the young Scythians did the same, until eventually one of them waylaid an Amazon on her own. She did not resist him, but communicated to him by signs that he should come back the next day and bring a companion, and that she would also bring a friend. The four met each other, liked each other, and the rest is history. 'Then the remainder of the young men, when they learned what had happened,' writes Herodotus, 'came and broke in the remainder of the Amazons.'[11]

That was not the end of the story, of course, because now it was important for the women to secure some financial security from the young men and set up something of a mobile household with their new partners. The Amazons feared the vengeance of the Scythians from whom they had stolen their sons, and could not conceive of living together with their Scythian in-laws. ' "We have no customs in common with them. We have never learned to do women's work. We shoot arrows, throw javelins, ride horses. But what do your women do? None of the things we just listed. They only ever do women's work! . . . So you can see, it would be quite impossible for us to get along." '[12] Again, the young men acquiesce, and the *partially* broken-in horsewomen and their men move together to a new territory where they live a wild life as mounted hunters and predators.

To this day, the image of the Amazons is marked by Greek myth-making, the curious mixture of shock and awe, horror and fascination, that these wild riding women inspired in each of the legendary heroes who had to grapple with them – Hercules, Theseus, Achilles – as captured in verse and painted on vases. It is to the fertile imagination of the Greeks that we owe the sensational attributes of the Amazons, such as their supposed lack of breasts or having only one, it being suggested that the warrior women improved their ability to shoot a bow by burning off their right breast. Since Greek culture had no prototype for the femme fatale, the source of this danger was located far away from the homeland of the Greeks, off in remote Scythia, to the north-east of the Black Sea and the Caspian Sea. Were the Amazons just a Greek male fantasy? That's what has long been surmised. Recent archaeological findings suggest otherwise, though, as historian Adrienne Mayor notes: 'recent and ongoing discoveries do offer astonishing evidence of the existence of authentic women warriors whose lives matched the descriptions of Amazons in Greek myths, art, and classical histories, geographies, ethnographies, and other writings. Scythian graves do contain battle-scarred skeletons of women buried with their weapons, horses, and other possessions. Scientific bone analysis proves that women rode, hunted, and engaged in combat in the very regions where Greco-Roman mythographers and historians once located "Amazons".' [13]

Incidentally, the Greeks were not the only ones who dreamed and spun yarns about the legendary Amazons; in all literary cultures of the Middle and Far East (Egypt, Persia, India, China) we come across the notion of the female horseback warrior, whose actual sphere of life would most likely have been located among the nomadic steppe peoples of Eurasia. Among such equestrian populations, it was customary for a girl to ride and learn to shoot with the bow, just as boys did, and to take part in hunts, battles and looting. Frequently, they were the ones who chose their male partners or only allowed themselves to be 'conquered' after a ritual duel. As Mayor puts it, 'Amazons were enthusiastic lovers of men of their own choosing.' [14] They tended towards casual sex, but as Herodotus suggests, they also entered into strong monogamous bonds.

The coexistence of the warrior girls and women with their horses

Blazon of death: horse cadavers in a narrow pass on the Somme, from Ernst Jünger's photograph collection: *The Face of the World War*, 1930.

There is a reaper whose name is Death: from Jünger's Great War photograph collection (as above).

is thought to have been particularly close. The girls learned from the horses and vice versa. Indeed, this was common not only with Amazons. Early on, practically since the beginning of their alliance, nomadic tribes had closely studied their horses' behaviour. They knew, for example, of the authority mares enjoyed within a herd: 'Mares can be as strong and fast as stallions, and they can fight ferociously. An alpha female horse dominates the other members of the herd and physically disciplines the young male horses, while the stallions help defend the herd and await the mares' sexual interest.'[15] Admittedly, the ancient female riders were not the first to realize that there was something to learn from horses. Among the tribes of nomads and their horses there have always been learning processes, going both ways, touching on all common areas of life: migrationary movement, rest periods, sexual behaviour, methods of fighting and avoiding danger, models of alertness and understanding body language. In these learning processes, the important thing was to develop common rhythms and a fast, sensitive, mutual understanding.[16]

Certainly no one would think of trading our traditional psychology – which clings to its cuddly toys and life-phase models – wholesale for the reading of Herodotus or the results of archaeology and cultural cognition research: no one would think in such an anachronistic way. But perhaps we do still need to accept, in all modesty, that when it comes to young girls and horses, and the deeper reasons underlying their close affinity, we have not yet heard the last word.

RIDING AND DRAWING

More than half a millennium has passed since Hans Baldung Grien compared a shapely horse with a beautiful woman, but his comparison is by no means confined to the past. And neither do the semantics of riding and being ridden belong to the department of ancient literature and art. In 2013, a commercial for the Honda CBR1000RR superbike was taken off air following criticism that it was sexist. It showed the transformation of a beautiful woman, the Spanish model Angela Lobato, into a shapely motorbike, with the suggestion that a male driver would get a thrill leaning into the curves. This metamorphosis, which Ovid might well have admired, was accompanied by the beginning of the song 'Smack my bitch up' by the Prodigy. Besides this one line from the song, the ad had no text; to add any more in English, where the verb 'to ride' retains a perfectly vivid memory of the *original* motorbike ride, would have led to inevitable redundancy. In any case, without the need for words, the advert showed that the light metonymic shift from the act of riding to the sexual act and back is familiar to many cultures where the bridge to the age of horses was thought to be long gone.

We're on slippery ground here: it can be difficult to assert innocence in this context. Whoever paints, draws or films people in the position of the horse, whoever treats a man or woman like a mount, has poor grounds to claim ignorance. Playing horses is not the same as playing doctors – when someone is being ridden, clearly comparisons are drawn. The potential is there, at least, for equality to be thrown out of the window, with no hope of reversing roles. 'Humiliation,' writes American essayist Wayne Koestenbaum, 'is an observable lowering of status and position,'[17] whereby the visibility is of as much importance as the reduction in status and position. It's a trite observation, perhaps, but humiliation creates a triangular relationship: the victim, the abuser, i.e. the perpetrator, and a witness.[18]

One need not necessarily mount another individual to humiliate them; draught animals are just as badly off, after all. The Roman emperors, for example, were, as Montaigne describes, extremely given to experimentation when it came to having their carriages pulled. 'Mark Antony was the first to be drawn through Rome – with a minstrel-girl beside him – by lions harnessed to a coach. Heliogabalus did the same somewhat later, claiming to be Cybele the Mother of the gods; then, drawn by tigers, he pretended to be the god Bacchus. On other occasions he harnessed two stags to his coach; once it was four dogs; then he stripped naked and was drawn in solemn procession by four naked girls.'[19]

A common motif frequently reworked by artists of the Renaissance and the baroque is that of an old man being ridden by a young woman. Most depictions show the woman sitting side-saddle, holding the whip in her right hand and the reins in her left hand, with which she steers the old man. Hans Baldung Grien also produced a woodcut of this motif in 1513 and, as with most erotic themes, his work is more vivid than that of his contemporaries. In Baldung's woodcut, both participants are naked, and the rider holds up the little finger of her right hand which holds the whip, as if to suggest the exquisite pleasure she is deriving from her erotic abuse of power. The old man, her mount, is not just anyone. The story that Baldung is illustrating is that of Aristotle being enslaved by Phyllis, a well-known fable at the time, thanks to a popular medieval verse narrative.[20]

The story goes that the venerable old philosopher, the teacher of Alexander the Great, falls in love with his pupil's consort Phyllis. Aristotle teaches his disciple to show restraint and resist her, and then Phyllis seeks her revenge. With the lure of erotic favours, she compels Aristotle to let her ride on his back, with Alexander as witness, watching his tutor in this degrading position. The artist lets us observe this scene of humiliation through his eyes, putting us, the viewer, in the position of Alexander.

The young woman who turned the head of a lascivious old man and led him to this humbling act was and remains stock satire material; in German theatre, we think of Kleist's comedy *The Broken Jug*. What's significant about the legend of Phyllis and Aristotle is that the old man is an important philosopher; indeed, the Stagirite was for a long time known only as '*the* Philosopher'. This sharp drop in status is all the more degrading since he is treated not as a bear or a mighty stallion, like something from modern advertising, but as a simple, plodding hack. The contemplative, philosophical thinker was now paraded about on all fours, *à quatre pattes,* as Rousseau was accused of calling on others to do. The consequence of Aristotle's uncontrolled lust was that he was pushed down to the basic level of animals; he found himself literally debased.

From the point of view of technological history, we can see from the prints and drawings of Baldung and his contemporaries that in the sixteenth century there was not yet any differentiation between whip and riding crop. Phyllis and her cruel cousins handled their old nags, as was typical at that time, with a small whip with a short handle and a short cord. It's not unlike the toy whip with which Friedrich Nietzsche furnished his adored friend Lou Salomé, for a famous photograph taken in Lucerne by Swiss photographer Jules Bonnet in which she rides a wagon, pulled by Nietzsche and Paul Rée. Fifty years later, in May 1882, Salomé described in her memoirs the scene in Bonnet's studio that day. Nietzsche, she writes, 'arranged a photograph of the three of us, in spite of strong objections on the part of Paul Rée, who suffered throughout his life from a pathological aversion to the reproduction of his features. Nietzsche, who was in a playful mood, not only insisted on the photo, but took a personal hand in the details – for example the little (far too little!) cart, and even the touch of kitsch with the sprig of lilacs on the whip, etc.'[21]

Rée's alleged reluctance is not discernible in the photograph. On the contrary, none of the three looks into the camera more comfortably: he is the very picture of bonhomie. At the geometric centre of the image, the thumb of his right hand is tucked into his waistcoat, while his other fingers rest on his stomach, halfway between the top button of his open frock coat and the top of his trousers; no bold Napoleonic gesture, but the perfect expression of a contented bourgeois. The second horse in the team could not look more different. Nietzsche, the older man here, a mature thirty-eight, takes his part in the studio masquerade before the background image of the snowy Jungfrau Mountain (the 'Maiden'), looking astonishingly serious. With his prophetic expression, the pastor's son seems to focus on something vague in the distance, as if he had already seen Zarathustra striding down to the valley.

Finally, the young beauty riding in the cart: crouching like a cat, she tilts slightly forwards and to the right, holding the reins in her left hand (like Phyllis) as she steers the philosophers, with a knotted child's whip in her right. The young Russian lends the image what Roland Barthes would have called *punctum*: she is the only one who truly stares at the camera – and therefore at the viewer – with a strong, clear look as severe as her breathlessly tight-laced wasp waist. The fourth figure is the only one not to be seen in the picture, although in fact he's the main character. The horse does not make a personal appearance, represented only by his job description. The absent figure is located both in the cart that its deputies are pulling, and in the whip that they are supposed to fear. The horse's strongest representation *in absentia*, though, are the two understudies, the men who are harnessed in his place.

The main thrust of the critique of womankind that Nietzsche formulated in *Thus Spoke Zarathustra*, only a few months after the
practical joke photo shoot at Lucerne, considers the fundamental difference in positions of power: 'The happiness of a man is "I want", of
a woman it is "he wants".'[22] In his notes, Nietzsche goes a step further and suggests oriental origins to this erotic despotism: 'By virtue
of love, man searches for the absolute slave, the woman the absolute
slavery. Love is the desire for a past culture and society – it harks
back to the Orient.'[23] His infamous line about not forgetting your
whip if you're 'visiting women' stands out in this regard.[24] In his posthumously published fragments, the sentence is unabashed,[25] while in
Zarathustra it is veiled in a literary device, uttered within quotation
marks: it is not Zarathustra that says this, prompted by the author,
but rather it's a little piece of advice offered to him by an 'old
woman',[26] a literary trick intended to hide the author from the line of
fire and lend the text a level of mystique. As a strategy against interpretation, it might have been helpful – but what Jacques Derrida
called the 'climate' of a text cannot be saved with a dodge like this.
The first book of *Zarathustra* shows how Nietzsche started to gain
authority as a writer the further he roamed from the marshy territory
of gender psychology. He did not succeed in turning this boggy
ground into something fruitful. He did not become an Ibsen, a
Schnitzler, Wedekind, Weininger or a Freud ahead of his time. He
merely glimpsed the land of gender understanding from a distance;
he did not set foot and explore.

In formal terms, the Lucerne group photograph parodies a childhood scene, such as that painted by Philipp Otto Runge in *The
Hülsenbeck Children* (1805). The iconographer might, of course, be
unimpressed by the comparison, because Runge's little girl in the cart
makes no attempt to steer and is not the one wielding the whip –
that's in the hand of the younger of her brothers. Chronologically
closer to the Lucerne staging is *The Courtesan* (1873) by French Salon
painter Thomas Couture (Plate 26). Here we see two young artists – a
poet and a painter, flanked by a knight and the god of drunken rev-
elry, Silenus – before the carriage of a scantily clad allegory of beauty
lashing her whip at them, while behind her sits a crooked old lady, a
reminder of the transience of youth and beauty. Unlike the wagon in

the Lucerne studio, the vehicle is here no mere toy but a full-size carriage, the typical Parisian cab of the era. With this canvas, Couture is
calling on a tradition entrusted to him as an academic teacher: the
iconography of Apollo in his Sun Chariot. It is quite conceivable that
the classical philologist Nietzsche had the idea of the unequal brother
gods Dionysus and Apollo in mind when he choreographed the scene
in Bonnet's studio.

However, we can't help wondering about the atypical draught animals. In classical mythology we would rather expect to see animals,
usually horses. In both the Lucerne photograph and in Couture's
painting, we have men in the harness and women wielding the whip.
Man is no longer asked to give a ride, as with Aristotle and Phyllis;
now he's called upon to replace the horse as a draught animal too.
Considering references in cultural history at this point, we recall the
dark Romanticism of the era, the cult of the femme fatale and the
literary tradition of masochism. The late nineteenth century, shortly
before the *fin de siècle*, sees an explosion in the realm of sexuality,
with ever greater differentiation, especially at the margins where
domination, violence and inequality of roles all loom. Seen in this
context, the two philosophers harnessed to the wagon of a young
Russian lady in Lucerne in 1882 are nothing but the protagonists of
a *grand récit*, which we might – were it not for the risk of confusion
with the Nazi ideologue Alfred Rosenberg's eponymous book – call
the myth of the twentieth century.

These *male* draught animals may have been a product of the nervous
age, but *human* draught horses of both sexes are a much older trope.
The Romans were no stranger to the infamous yoke that those they
defeated were made to pass beneath (*missio sub iugum*); indeed, twice
they had to undergo this humiliation themselves.[27] A painting by the
Flemish artist Paolo Fiammingo, *Castigo d'amore* (c.1585), from his
four-part *Amori* series shows what it means to be under the yoke of
God's love: a couple is hooked up with a suggestion of a harness to a
carriage driven by an ungracious charioteer (Plate 25). Their cruel
slave-driver is a diminutive Eros, threatening his draught animals not
with a whip, but with the flaming sword of expulsion from Paradise.
Indeed, the draught animals here are a human couple being chastised
by the God of Love and expelled from the Garden of Eden. Cursed

therefore are not the men who are made to act as horses, and not the women who ride them; cursed are both sexes because of their differentiation by gender. Cursed be the sex that drives them from Paradise and chains them eternally to the carriage of the vengeful Eros.

Perhaps this was the message Nietzsche intended to convey in that curious, uptight studio shot in Lucerne: never mind the whip – with or without it, love is as good as hopeless. It's irrelevant who's sitting up top and who's pulling the cart down below; either way, love always results in humiliation for both parties. That's why love always longs to return to the Orient: because while it seeks exaltation, it brings only debasement. In the metropolis of the late nineteenth century, teeming with cabs parked in the shadow of cavalry monuments, horses and carriages act as a simple index of social inequality. One sits up above; the other pulls and sweats down below. Sex is one of the generators of social inequality, placing one up above, the other down below, and yet it is also a great perverter of hierarchy: it debases those who were previously exalted. When we speak of sex, we are also speaking of humiliation, and neither sex is invulnerable.

Nietzsche's topicality lies in this message. It resonated with the playwrights and sexologists who followed him over the next couple of decades, and it is the link to the experiences and the visual memory of the people of the twentieth and twenty-first centuries. The severest whip scene in twentieth- century cinema, incidentally, was in a film by John Huston. In his 1967 *Reflections in a Golden Eye*, an adaptation of a novel of the same name by Carson McCullers, Marlon Brando – playing a US Army Major with homophilic inclinations – injures his wife Leonora's horse when riding it, for which she (played by Elizabeth Taylor) lashes him several times across his face with the riding crop, in the presence of their guests. The melodramatic, erotically charged movie, possibly too baroque for the late 1960s, was a box office flop.

EMMA, ANNA, EFFI AND CO.

The focus of a considerable number of the major social novels of the nineteenth century is on illegitimate love and broken marriage. In the subtitle of Wolfgang Matz's subtle study of the three most famous adulteresses – Emma Bovary, Anna Karenina and Effi Briest – he adds the phrase 'and their men'.[28] Is it too much to claim that the subtitle could also have been 'Emma, Anna, Effi *and their horses*'? Indeed, these celebrity romances, like those of many of their fictional contemporaries, are shot through with haunting horse-riding and carriage scenes. It's when riding and driving that the intrigue unfurls; it's when driving and riding that intimate relations unfold. Love finds its way into the hidden space of a closed cab; fate finds its messenger on horseback; death finds its pale steed.

In itself, this is no sensational discovery. After all, horses and carriages were the transport mode of the time, and if we consider the importance of the automobile in the novel and especially in the cinema of the twentieth century, then we might see the presence of horses and carriages in the narrative work of the nineteenth century as trivial. Yet, what is less trivial is observing *how* writers like Flaubert, Tolstoy and Hardy made use of the horse. They exploited horses deliberately as a symbol and a substitute for something that simultaneously called for discussion and for silence, as a veiled reference to the unspoken element at the heart of their novels. The horse therefore stands between amorous women and their husbands as a living metaphor of love and death. In this world of corsets and muslin, the horse is the only being that can represent the moment of nudity: '*tout nerveusement nu dans sa robe de soie*' ('nervously nude in her dress of silk'), as Degas put it in a sonnet to a thoroughbred mare.[29] The horses reveal what the people do not voice. They are the means of expressing the inner emotion of lovers and the guide that leads them around the perilous bends of the novel, the *chevaux fatals* of the nineteenth century.

The manner in which a person sits on horseback and moves with the animal says everything about his inner sensitivity, his sense of his body, his skills and qualities as a lover or a loved one. Charles Bovary may have completed his intellectual studies as well as 'any dressage horse', but when it comes to riding and driving, the clumsy fellow cuts a poor figure. When he first visits Les Bertaux, the estate of his future father-in-law, his horse slips on the wet grass, shies and effects 'a great leap'. His first, accidental physical contact with Emma comes when he is looking for something that he has mislaid. *Comme il faut,*

The cruelty continues: animals are tortured, a child is run over.
Second Stage of Cruelty, William Hogarth, 1751.

No one sees us in the dark: a pit pony at the smithy,
Saint-Éloy-les-Mines, Auvergne, 1912.

it's his riding crop, and as both bend down to look for it at the same time, his chest brushes against her back. 'She straightened up, red-faced, and looked at him over her shoulder, handing him his riding crop.'[30] Bovary's life's journey through the awkwardness that begins at a Norman prep school leads him eventually to the market at Argueil where, rapidly falling apart after the death of his wife, he sells his horse, 'the last resource'.[31]

The girl on horseback observed by the farmer Gabriel Oak, protagonist of Thomas Hardy's *Far from the Madding Crowd*, looks as though she must have grown up with her horse. When she rides under the low hanging branches of a tree, she drops weightlessly backwards 'flat upon the pony's back, her head over its tail, her feet against its shoulders, and her eyes to the sky. The rapidity of her glide into this position was that of a kingfisher – its noiselessness that of a hawk . . . The performer seemed quite at home anywhere between a horse's head and its tail, and the necessity for this abnormal attitude having ceased with the passage of the plantation, she began to adopt another . . . Springing to her accustomed perpendicular like a bowed sapling, and satisfying herself that nobody was in sight, she seated herself in the manner demanded by the saddle, though hardly expected of the woman, and trotted off in the direction of Tewnell Mill.'[32] Bathsheba Everdene, as the young woman – in fact still a girl – is called, does not only ride like an Amazon, she also speaks like a horseback warrior from Herodotus, when she says to the love-struck farmer: ' "It wouldn't do, Mr Oak. I want somebody to tame me; I am too independent; and you would never be able to, I know." '[33] Indeed, the rest of the novel turns out to be the long, painful story of the domestication of an unruly woman, who breaks two strong, tough men, until at last she finds her way to Mr Oak, who is flexible, contrary to what his name would suggest, and is always waiting nearby for her. This scene with the acrobatic Amazon on horseback not only opens his eyes to her, but also opens up an unusual way into the sphere of the narrative.

What is bright and fiery in this story – and indeed the novel includes a great fire and a storm scene – and seems to take place in a major key, is reflected in *Tess of the d'Urbervilles* too, although this time the drama unfolds in a sombre minor key. In the horse-themed opening of the novel, we see the night-time accident involving the stallion

Prince. 'The pointed shaft of the cart had entered the breast of the unhappy Prince like a sword' and Tess is forced to witness his death in helpless despair. It is from her attempts to make good her debt-ridden misfortune that the entire tragic love story unfolds. Tess, a 'pure woman', ends up on the scaffold after stabbing Alec, the false d'Urberville, in the heart with a knife, after he has ruined her life, leaving him to bleed to death like the horse on the country road. The equine scene at the start of this novel thus provides not only the trigger for ensuing events, but also the leitmotif foreshadowing the conclusion of the story – the stab in the chest and the unstoppable, growing pool of blood. As in *Far from the Madding Crowd*, in *Tess*, too, the horse's body represents the man's body, or rather its vital, natural, animalistic aspect, as opposed to its social existence that is so entangled in stories and intrigues.

In contrast, the author of *Anna Karenina* draws a correlation between the body of a coveted woman and that of a mare. Against the advice of the English groom, Vronsky goes in to see the nervous Frou-Frou in her stall just before their big race: ' "Oh, you beauty, you!" said Vronsky, moving up to the mare and trying to soothe her. But the nearer he came, the more excited she grew ... The mare's excitement had infected Vronsky. He felt the blood rushing to his heart and that, like the horse, he, too, wanted to move about and attack.'[34] The link is further reinforced when after this visit to see his racehorse, and just before his big race, Vronsky goes to see Anna on the terrace at her house, where she is awaiting the return of her son. Anna confesses that she is pregnant. He leaves her, 'looking at her with ecstasy', having just caught her 'rapturous smile of love', both of them having agreed in a whisper to meet again that night, and returns to the stable where his mare excites him in just as sensual a way as his lover shortly before. 'Vronsky cast another look at the exquisite lines of his favourite mare, who was quivering all over, and tearing himself with an effort from the sight of her, he went out of the stable.'[35]

Flaubert, Tolstoy and Fontane all emphasize the contrast between the dull (Bovary), cold (Karenin) or strict (Innstetten) husbands and their wives' dashing, charming and bold lovers (Rodolphe/Léon, Vronsky and Crampas[36]) through a portrait of these men's skills at riding and driving carriages. Granted, Bovary appears as mediocre on horseback and Fontane's Innstetten might even be described as a good rider, yet they both belong firmly in the plodding world of the sturdy coach, where Bovary inevitably makes an unfortunate impression.[37] As a piece of rolling architecture, a kind of wooden house or dacha on wheels, the coach represents the established world of marriage and family, which is thoughtlessly overrun and smashed to bits by the cavalry of free love. The arrow has already hit the target when Emma and Effi consent to ride out with their respective seducers (albeit, in Effi's case, under the suspicious eye of her husband). Effi is seduced in a carriage; Emma, in her second affair, succumbs in a carriage; and Tess, after a long night ride with Alec and, in one edition of the novel, after being drugged by him, is raped by him in her sleep. When Anna is seen riding a 'small, sturdy English cob with cropped mane and short tail',[38] it appears for one brief, happy moment as though, having been excluded from the beau monde of St Petersburg and Moscow, she might at least be granted entry into the circles of the provincial landed gentry.

Both Tolstoy, who once calculated that he had spent about seven years of his life in the saddle,[39] and Hardy had strong links to the countryside. In their depictions of country life, both writers emphasize a second contrast: they demonstrate the penetration of machinery into the provinces, presented as a kind of pastoral idyll for all its bleakness (Hardy) and stifling monotony (Tolstoy). In Tolstoy, it is the classic example of the railways, the 'machine in the garden'[40] which forces itself into the bucolic realm. With Hardy (in Tess), it is initially the horse-drawn mechanical reaper[41] and later the steam threshing machine[42] whose relentlessly whirling wheels allow no respite and seem to drive Tess far over the edge of physical exhaustion into mental despair. While, at first glance, technology seems to play a lesser part in Tolstoy's vision of the apocalypse, in truth the role it is given is even more sinister. To appreciate the power of this narrative device, we must return to the famous steeplechase scene.[43]

Vronsky's rise 'with a powerful, agile movement' onto the 'supple back' of his mare, again described as excited and jumpy, is the prelude to an event depicted as an act of perfect love-making between man and mare, over the three-mile steeplechase course, accompanied by Vronsky's inner exclamations – ' "Oh, you beauty!" thought

Vronsky' – until the vivid moment when the rider seems so sure of his success: 'His excitement, his happiness, and his affection for Frou-Frou grew keener and keener.'[44] It is shortly after this that the fatal moment comes, when Vronsky makes a jockey's error. The mare falls and is unable to get up again, 'fluttering on the ground at his feet like a wounded bird. Vronsky's clumsy movement had broken her back.'[45] Anna, following the action from the stands, is unable to retain her composure and unconsciously reflects the desperate movements of the mare: 'She began fluttering like a caged bird, at one point getting up to go, at the next turning to Betsy.'[46]

Karenin, witness to his wife's despair, comprehends at this moment how things stand between her and the officer. The carriage ride home brings confrontation and Anna's passionate confession. And so fate takes its course. In the stands at the racecourse, Anna meets her social death; she simply does not know it yet. The following months will reveal it to her, slowly and bitterly. It will be several hundred pages before Tolstoy, towards the end of the novel, describes Anna's suicide under the wheels of an oncoming freight car. Her real death replicates the fate of the unfortunate racehorse. Anna, 'looking in the shadow of the truck at the mixture of sand and coal dust which covered the sleepers,' misses the first opportunity, but then, before the next comes, she 'threw aside the red bag and drawing her head down between her shoulders dropped on her hands under the truck, and with a light movement, as though she would rise again at once, sank onto her knees'.[47] As she crouches on her knees, in an animal pose, the truck's wheel hits her and breaks her back.

The author does not say this explicitly, but this is the conclusion we are invited to draw, when Vronsky sees his dead mistress, 'her mangled body, still warm with recent life, stretched out on a table shamelessly exposed to the gaze of all'. Her body is shattered, but her head and face are intact. 'The head, which had escape hurt, with its heavy plaits and the curls about the temples, was thrown back, and the lovely face with its half-open red lips had frozen into a strange expression – pitiful on the lips and horrible in the fixed open eyes . . .'[48] The manner in which Vronsky recalls the autopsy in the railway shed makes his fatal fall on the racetrack seem like a prefiguration of Anna's cruel end. The death of the beautiful mare foreshadows that of the beloved woman – the difference being that in the former case, the lethal injury to the spine is caused by a human rider and in the latter case by a train.

The railway accident at the beginning of the novel, where a guard is hit by a train and killed, has a deep emptional impact on Anna and has been interpreted as a blueprint for the heroine's demise. ' "It is a bad omen," she said.'[49] Yet this accident, as striking as it is, provides only a sort of abstract model for Anna's eventual suicide. It is not until Vronsky's accident on the racetrack that we see a true 'omen' complete with blood and pulsing with life. The beautiful mare is the novel's living metaphor; her death is a glimpse, a preliminary sketch, of the fate that awaits Anna at the end of her journey.

To rule is to ride, noted Carl Schmitt. This concise and apodictic expression conveys the idea that riding is much more than a figurative or a symbolic action. Indeed, riding can be described, among other things, as an elementary practice of steering. It is a method of driving and controlling; it entails mastery over the will of another being. Somewhat like a precursor to cybernetics, only more direct: a neuro-navigation between interrelated natures. Two moving, loosely coupled systems, circumnavigating the lengthy route of thought, exchanging information directly via the short cut of touching nerves and tendons, thermal and metabolic systems. The act of riding means that command data is transferred in the form of physical data, in a direct exchange of sensory messages. Riding is the connection of two warm, breathing, pulsating bodies, mediated only by a saddle, a blanket or mere bare skin. Humans enter into similar informational connections when they dance together, wrestle or embrace. Darwin wrote about feeling the heartbeat of his frightened horse's heart through the saddle. Horse and man: one detects the pulse of the other, senses the nervousness, smells the sweat. Even beyond all its symbolic and metaphorical transformations, riding is an articulation of two living bodies, and as with sex, there comes an irreducible moment of pure physics.

Wherever he may have gained this awareness, Gustave Flaubert *knew* of this physical truth innate to living bodies. The fate of the young woman who marries a pedantic country doctor and now in turn, with pedantic thoroughness, proceeds through every literary

17. Pausanias describes a ghostly echo of neighing on the former battlefield at night: *Marathon*, Carl Rottmann, 1847.

18. *Pulling Down the Statue of King George III, New York City*, Johannes Oertel, 1852–3.

19. Turning point in the battle: *Washington Rallying the Americans at the Battle of Princeton*, William T. Ranney, 1848.

20. A landmark moment of world history in art: *Napoleon Crossing the Alps* or *Bonaparte at the St Bernard Pass*, Jacques Louis David, *c.*1801.

21. Marshal Zhukov in triumph over fascist Berlin: *Portrait of Georgy Zhukov*, Vasily Yakovlev, 1946.

22. *The Rape of the Daughters of Leucippus*, Peter Paul Rubens, c.1618.

23. *The Lion Hunt*, Peter Paul Rubens, 1621.

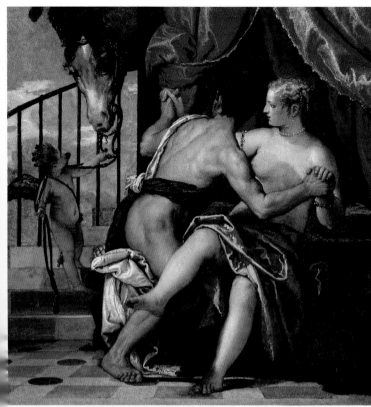

24. Liaisons with onlookers: *Venus and Mars with Cupid and a Horse*, Paolo Veronese, 1570.

25. The capricious god Eros drives the chariot: *Castigo d'amore*, or *Punishment of Love*, Paolo Fiammingo, c.1585–9.

26. A carriage drawn by men: *The Courtesan*, Thomas Couture, 1873.

27. Detail from the *Bourbaki Panorama*, Lucerne, Edouard Castres, 1881.

28. Unbridled youth:
Boy Leading a Horse,
Pablo Picasso, 1905–6.

29. Siesta time for man and horse: *The Tarascon Diligence (Stagecoach)*,
Vincent van Gogh, 1888.

30. Rider without a bridle:
Don Quixote, Honoré Daumier,
c.1868.

31. The subject as critic: *Lucian Freud and Grey Gelding*,
photograph by David Dawson, 2003.

cliché of romantic love, is measured against a scale of body temperatures, a scale that captures all expressions of life and desire and all
stages of their slow, cruel death. [50] The author closely tracks the pulse
of his characters, in a very literal sense. 'Today, for example,' Flaubert wrote to Louise Colet in December 1853, when he was working
on *Madame Bovary*, 'as a man and as a woman, as lover and mistress
both, I have been out riding in a forest'.[51] Both as an author and as a
rider, he is able to cross the shadowy line between metaphor and
metamorphosis. Before Rodolphe becomes Emma's lover, she has
already given herself fully to the rhythm of the ride and allowed herself to be seduced by the sway of the animal; arriving at the edge of
the forest, she has already become one with the horse. Like somnam-
bulists, Flaubert and Tolstoy have unconsciously found the zone
where two nervous, flighty animals – a woman in love and an excited
horse – exchange their natures. Through narrative means, they produce an unprecedented, breathtaking fluidity between the two
species. They are not alone on this path: someone is there on the road
ahead. When Werther, the forerunner of all great lovers in the world
of the European novel, confesses he has seized a knife a hundred
times to relieve his aching heart, he suddenly pictures the image of
the horse and the heat of its body: 'People tell of a noble breed of
horses that instinctively bite open a vein when they are exhausted and
feverish, in order to breathe more freely. I often feel the same, and am
tempted to open a vein and so find eternal freedom.'[52]

Turin: A Winter's Tale

THE TRIANGLE OF CRUELTY

It is more than ten years since the end of the First World War. Through-out this time, Ernst Jünger has not stopped expressing the terror of the war, but also a certain fascination with its power. He follows up *In Stahlgewittern* (*Storm of Steel*) with *Der Kampf als inneres Erlebnis* ('Battle as an inner experience'), *Feuer und Blut* ('Fire and Blood') and finally *Das Wäldchen 125* (*Copse 125*). At this point, twelve years after the armistice, the author changes register. He swaps the literary record for the photographic, switching from the written memory of the war to its picture archive. Jünger publishes a collection of photo-graphs with the title *Das Antlitz des Weltkrieges* ('The Face of the World War'), a selection of the many thousands of wartime photos taken between 1914 to 1918, including propaganda images, reportage and photographs from private collections both official and personal. The author does not entirely efface himself, admittedly. Instead, he doubles his role, adding photomontage to his ability to write graph-ically. Jünger selects pictures, groups them into stories, pens narratives and introductory short essays. The tone of these texts is audible: the cold, objective quality for which the author is famous. Just as typical is the moment of the war that particularly interests him: the moment of the assault, when the seemingly empty battlefield suddenly fills with movement, that *dangerous moment*[1] when the paralysis of the trenches gives way to the explosive dynamics of the attack.[2]

In the shadow of this particular dynamic is a small group of photos. It is easy to overlook their importance, given their dispersal through-out the entire anthology. These are the images of *negative energy*, photos of the dead and their remains on the battlefield. Among them is a not inconsiderable number of shots of dead horses. At first glance they do not seem to fit the author's rakishly detached stance: what could be less dashing and stylish than dead horses, their bloated bellies and frozen legs sticking out of the mud of the Flanders wasteland? The photographs of destroyed military equipment, especially of heavy weapons, shattered tanks and downed fliers, can be more easily explained. This selection of pictures hints at the future author of *Der Arbeiter* (1932) (*The Worker*), which portrays the war as a part of the titanic work of technology. But why the dead horses?

Horses are not usually the focus of Jünger's attention. Of course, he had to learn to ride in the course of his officer training. Thereafter he did not have much to do with the animals, as he served in the infantry. When he flirted with another branch of the army, it was with the air force. Why, when he composed the picture anthology in around 1930, is he suddenly interested in dead horses? Jünger's particular brand of post-heroic heroism, one could argue, has changed its bearer. The new man of mechanized warfare has dismounted from his steed and withdrawn into the steel casing of technological war. This is why Jünger shows the dead horses; they are the losers of international modernity. But the dead horses are not particularly suitable as illustrations of the stark dynamics of historical displacement – at least not those presented by Jünger. They are too complex, too aesthetic, too emblematic. Take, for example, the photograph of the horse corpses, described in Jünger's caption as 'horse cadavers in a narrow pass on the Somme' (p. 276). It could hardly be said in a more sober, tight-lipped way. In a landscape sparingly furnished with scrub, rubble and telegraph poles, this existentialist stage for the theatre of war, we see two dead animals, a pale grey horse and a dapple-grey. The dapple-grey on the left is more badly maimed – grenade shrapnel has torn off its foreleg, lacerated its chest and blown apart its muzzle – while the coat of the grey on the right has two bullet holes. It is the parallelism of the bodies and heads that lends this gruesome image its macabre beauty. The juxtaposition of the bodies of two dead horses creates a heraldic totality, like the lions and the griffins in the coats of arms of ancient clans. The images of the dead horses always retain something of Jünger's aesthetic composition – the stage director in the theatre of war. But in the background, concealed, as it were, in the backdrop and in the wings, and within the stage direction itself, the images of the dead horse carry a different message, one of an emotional nature.

Contrary to war author Jünger's typical air as a cold *flaneur* wandering through the arena of mechanized warfare, these images of dead horses convey a faint but unmistakable flow of warmth: how casually they create a narrow, clear pathway to pity. What the text author Jünger does not want to say, the picture author Jünger is able to *show*: the silent suffering and death of the creature. It is not through the photos of fallen soldiers, but the sight of dead horses that Jünger cracks open a chink in the work's hermetic seal for pity to shine through. In this respect the experience of the war participant and the viewer of war photos agree on one thing: pictures of dead soldiers arouse horror, but images of dead horses evoke pity.[3] Even in interviews with German officers, prisoners of war in the Second World War, the same unchanged motif comes up repeatedly. One pilot describes how they were attacking columns, with all guns blazing. 'Everywhere we looked, we saw horses fleeing.' His interlocutor is shocked: 'Oh God, the horses . . . how awful!' The narrator softens his tone. 'I felt sorry for the horses, not the people. But I felt sorry for the horses till the very last day.'[4]

Sympathy for the war horse is a widespread motif in literature, with a peculiar twist for the twentieth century: the horse in combat has irrevocably shifted to the side of the victims. Unlike in the nineteenth century, indeed unlike all eras of the past, the horse was no longer on the side of the historic perpetrators – as part of the mighty machine that rides and rolls roughshod over everything – but itself ended up trampled under the wheels of progress. The literature of the Great War sees the horse almost exclusively as an animal dying, dead or decaying. Thus we have the old horse perishing in the ditch in Joseph Roth's poem 'Der sterbende Gaul' ('The Dying Nag') while the horse-drawn artillery drags on by, paying no heed.[5] Thus we have the horses frozen overnight and trapped in the ice of a Finnish lake in Curzio Malaparte's novel *La Pelle* (1949) (*The Skin*, 1952). Thus we have the mud-drenched, rotting horse corpses in the repeated narrative of the decline of the French cavalry in the novels of Claude Simon.[6] It is

Death in the afternoon: bullfighting, Málaga, *c*.1900.

End of the road: *The Knacker's Yard, or the Horses last home!*,
George Cruikshank, 1831.

as if, in the literature of twentieth century, the dying or dead horse had superseded the nineteenth century's whipped horse as an emblem. Indeed, the horse of the nineteenth century still maintained certain reserves of ferocity and terror, while the horse of the twentieth century functions above all as a tolling bell, a death notice.[7]

This is not to say that the savagely beaten or tormented horse disappeared from the moral canvas of the twentieth century without a trace. Austrian writer Karl Kraus was still pursuing the subject in the 1920s, or perhaps more precisely, the issue was pursuing him,[8] and German poet and playwright Else Lasker-Schüler in 1913 described the suffering of horses on the bridleways of Berlin's Kurfürstendamm, where sweating and bleeding animals were flogged half to death by boorish carters without awaking the slightest spark of compassion in 'the ladies' new-fangled, heaving bosoms'.[9] However, that there were bosoms around the turn of the century in which pity did indeed thrive was proved by a remark, recorded by art historian Colin Rowe, and made by an old lady of Swedish descent, whose father, the Dean of Uppsala Cathedral, had once intended her to marry a young man of Prussian origin. The daughter had categorically refused his proposal: 'But, my dear Colin, I could never have married Kurt von Beckenrath! He was so cruel to his horses!' [10]

At the demise of the era of the horse, Else Lasker-Schüler's depiction is another grim triangle of cruelty to horses, chalked on the Ethics class blackboard: brutish, often drunken coachmen, indifferent passers-by and the silently suffering creature. The pair reflecting the original barbarism – the coachman and the horse – are constantly replicated before the eyes of the spectator or witness who does nothing to deliver the animal from the torment and put a stop to the perpetrator. Often enough it is the unfeeling passer-by who is the actual target of the accusation of moral failure and lack of empathy. Because, after all, the coachman is a coarse, uneducated person, drunk or mad, closer to the beaten animal than to the unmoved, onlooking bourgeoisie. From the eighteenth century, the description of the triangle of cruelty spread throughout the literature of cities and of travel; in his *Tableau de Paris* of 1781, Louis-Sébastien Mercier dedicated a solid monument of paper to the idea.[11]

In the late eighteenth century, a European debate took this triangle as its starting point, a discussion that outwardly revolved around the widespread cruelty to animals and how it could be avoided. Besides this, however, and perhaps this is the true essence of the matter, it was about the redefinition of the human; about the emergence of a new type of man. In the shadow of the old *heroic man*, for whom, in the nineteenth century, wreaths were still being plaited and monuments erected, emerged a new type: the *man of compassion*.

FIGURES OF EMPATHY

The nineteenth century invented not only dynamite, the automobile and the World's Fair, it also brought moral innovations. The most important was undoubtedly compassion, not in the sense of an admirable virtue in others, but as the basis of humane moral feeling and behaviour. Of course, the nineteenth century did not bring compassion into the world, but it perhaps gave it a new fundamental value, to which two of the best writers in the German language testify: one in the mode of praise (Schopenhauer) and the other in the form of criticism (Nietzsche).[12] Like any new way of feeling, this innovation also needed figures around whom it could crystallize – that is, become visible and intelligible. They were personifications of a calamity, which witnesses found so awful, so unbearable – a misery that literally cried out to the heavens. But since no help came from the dead heavens of the nineteenth century, earthly wheels had to set themselves in motion, turning the cogs of editorial offices, pulpits and Cabinets, to transform acute shock or outrage into social and legal protection and regulation.

Of the numbers of suffering individuals from which the societies of the nineteenth century formed their experiences, and which permanently changed their moral system, four stand out in particular.[13] One is the whipped horse, the tortured animal. The others are the working child, the wounded soldier and the orphan. Together they wander through the nightmares of a tough century – the humiliated and the flayed – a quartet of secular misfortune. The fallen, bleeding to death on the battlefields of war; the young, their youth sacrificed in the factories of capitalism; the fatherless and motherless child; and the animal tormented before the cold eyes of men. Four incarnations of *miseria hominis* revealing the depths to which the rage of nations, the pillage of capitalism and the savagery of the human heart can lead.

Not until Henri Dunant's account in *A Memory of Solferino* had there ever been such a relentless, yet compassionate description of the suffering on the battlefield. His text, published three years after the 1859 battle between the Austrians and the French, contributed to the foundation of the Red Cross and is cited to this day as a model of humanist literary intervention.[14] His text, though, is a relatively late beacon. Since the Napoleonic wars, since the debacle in Russia in 1812, there had been a mounting body of writing speaking in a similar spirit, descriptions that seek to say the unspeakable. Where they fall silent – in a reversal of Gotthold Ephraim Lessing's *Laocoön* – the mute speech of painting instead gives expression to the horror: J. M. W. Turner's painting *The Field of Waterloo*, first exhibited in 1818, showed the gruesome reality of the night after the battle: masses of dead, dying and wounded men, distraught women, and in the darkness the hordes of dogs and rats. Dunant bears witness to the same reality half a century later. But unlike Turner's picture, his account is not met by closed eyes and ears. The sensitivities have changed.

When one twenty-four-year-old published his most famous book in the summer of 1845, the phenomena he described were considerably older than himself. But Friedrich Engels grew up with the misery of the workers and especially of their children; he came from a dynasty of textile industrialists who built schoolhouses alongside their factories. If there is a common thread that pervades *The Condition of the Working Class in England*, it is capitalist society's theft of the spirit and life of its youngest and most vulnerable members. Depriving children of their elementary education meant robbing them of their future. In Engels's eyes, this is a sinful crime that weighs even more heavily than the physical stunting that the brutal exploitation of the working child entails. In the half century from 1780, the level of social violence against children was continuously on the rise; it was not until around 1830 that there was the first sporadic rumble of resistance.[15] As E. P. Thompson put it in his 1963 study of *The Making of the English Working Class*, 'the exploitation of little children, on this scale and with this intensity, was one of the most shameful events in our history'.[16]

The social reality of the century's high infant mortality rate is countered with an even higher parent mortality rate in the era's novels and short stories. 'The literature abounds with orphans, half orphans, social outcasts, foundlings, stepchildren; characters of shady or secretive, if not incestuous, parentage.'[17] As obscure as their provenance is the fate of their parents, whose disappearance is rarely explained, and if so, usually in a few sparse, fragmented lines. Rarer still is the reappearance of one of the parents, as in the case of Huck's violent father, Pap, in *The Adventures of Huckleberry Finn* – granted, he reappears only as a meddlesome ghost that returns to the other side at daybreak. The ranks of orphans and foundlings begin with Goethe's Mignon (*Wilhelm Meister's Appenticeship*) and Ottilie (*Elective Affinities*), continues through Oliver Twist, Quasimodo, Little Meret in Gottfried Keller's *Green Henry*, Hans Christian Andersen's *The Little Match Girl* and Dostoevsky's Smerdyakov in *The Brothers Karamazov*, until we get to the large fairy-tale orphanage where Cinderella, Snow White, the Seven Ravens and the Twelve Swans all sit and await deliverance. Perhaps the most sublime orphanage of the era was that constructed by the 'Sorcerer of Bayreuth', Richard Wagner: 'He gave the orphans and the outcasts . . . the unforgettable language of music.'[18]

The fundamental right, protected these days by our constitutional courts, of the individual to know the names of his or her parents, was unknown in the nineteenth century. The period's literature laments the plight of orphans and uses it to play furtively with the motifs of patricide and incestuous liaison whose fruit is the child with the murky past.[19]

Historically speaking, none of these four figures of pity is new. European societies did not need to cross the threshold into the nineteenth century to be confronted by the sight of dying soldiers, neglected children and abused animals. These images have been part of their history for centuries. But battles between armies of tens of thousands which, within a matter of hours, leave legions of corpses and abandoned, dying men in their wake; children who wander through life without parents, or toil under heavy machinery and in narrow shafts, and are literally worked to death; horses that are beaten on the street until they're lame – these are the totems of a new era. These victims who are caught under the wheels of accelerated history – the injured soldiers, the exposed and emaciated children, the animals that fall and are flogged to within an inch of their lives – all have something else in common. They do not have the strength to stand up alone. They are the oppressed, the humiliated – thrown to the ground by an inhumane society.

It was Rousseau who extended the horizon of compassion to encompass animals. Schopenhauer then went a step further and made sympathy with a suffering creature the truest proof of human compassion. But it is one thing to feel compassion for animals, another to look on as humans are reduced by their own kind to the level of animals. Rousseau stood accused of wanting to make people return to nature and become animals crawling about *à quatre pattes*, on all fours. But a person who is tossed to the ground by the violence of war or by early capitalist production, and to whom no helping hand is offered, is indeed reduced to the status of quadruped: they are forced to crawl. To witness such a sight is intolerable; it is a sight that stirs indignation in onlookers. It is unbearable to see someone, lying on the ground, for whom nothing is possible but to eke out a demeaning existence on hands and knees like an animal. It was this ubiquitous sight of the intolerable that fostered the outrage and the rebellion, initially of individuals, then gradually of larger groups and societies, of the nineteenth century – a growing social discontent until finally the hour came when the journalists, reformers and lawmakers campaigned for change.

CAN THEY SUFFER?

The Englishmen whose queen declared in 1868 that her subjects 'are inclined to be more cruel to animals than some other civilized nations are'[20] were, however, the first to confer legal status on the protection of animals. True, the Bill proposed by William Pulteney in April 1800, whose aim was to abolish bull-running and bull-baiting, failed to get passed and a subsequent attempt in 1809 by the eloquent Lord Erskine to pass legislation aimed at protecting animals stalled in the lower house. It was only in June 1822 that Martin's Act, named after Richard Martin ('Humanity Dick') and aimed at banning cruelty to animals, was passed by both Houses of Parliament.[21] Two years later, the Society for the Prevention of Cruelty to Animals (SPCA, from 1840 the RSPCA), the world's first animal protection league, was founded in London. As in other countries which followed suit, the roots of the movement lay in religious and philosophical strata which were significantly older.[22] In England, this was mainly denominations such as the Quakers, founded in 1650, which generally assumed that animals had a soul. Many writers who were early proponents of vegetarianism in the eighteenth century appeared in their ranks, including radical representatives of the Romantic generation such as Percy Bysshe Shelley (with his essay 'On the Vegetable System of Diet', 1814). Vivisection, justified as it was on scientific grounds, still met with resistance from prominent early opponents such as Samuel Johnson, who in 1758 declared his hatred for all those whose favourite pastime it was to 'nail dogs to tables and open them alive'.[23] William Hogarth expressed himself in a similar vein, albeit in a different art form, when, in his 1751 work *Four Stages of Cruelty*, he depicted a brutal coachman beating his horse after it had toppled over, along with the heavy carriage, and broken a foreleg (p. 285).

This scene of cruelty finds a natural counterpart in the image of the founder of the Methodist Church, John Wesley, who spent his life on horseback on the road and who made it his principle to ride with loose reins, reading, while the horse walked along of its own accord. Allegedly his horse never foundered, which Wesley, who also proved himself a proselytizer in this regard, attributed to the fact that his animal was never forced nor had to endure pain.[24] Besides religious motives, with the English Enlightenment genuinely philosophical arguments came into play, as when Jeremy Bentham, the founder of Utilitarianism, stopped the familiar debate about whether animals were capable of rational thought or speech in its tracks and replaced it with the question, still valid to this day, of their capacity to feel pain. 'The question is not, can they reason? Nor, can they talk? But, can they suffer?'[25]

As might be expected in the homeland of horse racing, the authors associated with the SCPA were particularly vocal about the hard lot of racehorses. After a few strenuous years at Newmarket, they retired to a dreary afterlife as a carthorse or a hack.[26] Vehement attacks on those who tormented horses, such Henry Curling's *A Lashing for the*

Searching for food in the ruins of Stalingrad, 1943.

Not just the Scythian kings: the Gauls also shared their graves with their
horses. Excavation at Évreux, 2007.

Lashers (1851) and popular titles such as John Mills's *The Life of a Racehorse* (1854), which opened up the genre of equine biography, or autobiography, were seconded by the graphic arts, where Hogarth's tradition of criticizing cruelty lived on. In the 1820s, the animal painter and Royal Academician Sir Edwin Landseer, whose fame was still to come, explored the fate of horses and donkeys in London; in 1830, George Cruikshank ('the Hogarth of the present age') shocked his audience with his unflinching depiction of *The Knacker's Yard* (p. 295) – a dreadful sight no one wanted see.[27] But even animal welfare had its dark side. Lewis Gompertz, one of the leading thinkers and authors associated with the British animal welfare movement,[28] assumed the chair of the SPCA in 1826, but had to resign six years later, after the Society's board decided to admit only Christian members, effectively excluding Gompertz, who was of Jewish origin. Anti-Semitic tendencies that dogged vegetarianism, the fight against vivisection and the protection of animals from early on would become loyal companions following in the shadow of these movements.[29]

The most prominent among the early friends and protectors of animals in Germany was not motivated by religion. From early on, Frederick the Great treasured the company of his horses and dogs; if he did not prefer them to humans, he at least put them on an equal footing. He rejected the use of spurs and whips and, particularly in his later years, adopted a very relaxed and rather unconventional riding style. He used to give names to the horses of his unusually large royal stables that at first alluded to their particular attributes and later drew on historical sources (Caesar, Pitt, Brühl). The last of the king's favourite horses, a piebald gelding, was named after the French prince Louis Henri de Bourbon-Condé, a prominent seventeenth-century commander and a great patron of the arts, of Molière in particular. Condé followed his master like a dog and nibbled the figs, melons and oranges which the king loved and grew in the orangery at Sans Souci. Condé was given such freedom to roam that he would help himself to the contents of his royal friend's pockets when he was deep in conversation.[30] The resourceful animal survived the king by eighteen years, and reached the grand age of thirty-eight – a biblical age for horses. His skeleton is preserved in the collection of Berlin's Humboldt University. It is exhibited in front of the Department of

Art History, a very apt location: his skeleton might belong to the zoologists, but the image he represents is the domain of the art historians.[31]

As in England, the animal welfare movement in Germany grew from religious roots. The first German association for the protection of animals was founded in Stuttgart in 1837. Its founders were two Württemberg pastors, Christian Adam Dann, who passed away the same year, and Albert Knapp. Dann had previously attempted as an author to galvanize the conscience of his contemporaries with his fiery rhetoric.[32] Both pastors were deeply influenced by Pietism and stood firmly in the tradition of the Moravian revival movement.[33] Dann's impassioned appeal would enumerate a constantly growing list of acts of violence by barbaric gentlemen, coachmen and children, which dogs, oxen, and above all horses ('the most greatly tormented animal') had to suffer, and to which the public were blind and deaf. Dann was convinced that humans would face retribution for all crimes committed against a 'fellow creature' and that children who were cruel to animals and went unpunished would grow up to be cruel adults. He contrasted the bleak perspectives of this 'old earth' with the comforting hope of 'a new heaven and a new earth',[34] where wise and just men would live with animals in blissful peace. The editor of Dann's writings rightly suggests that the concept of animal welfare within Württemberg Pietism fed from deep sources, which included, among others, the millenarianism of Johann Albrecht Bengel and Friedrich Christoph Oetinger. Dann quoted the 'blessed Bengel' himself in the context of his notion of the eschatological liberation of the animal. In this respect, Dann's notion of animal welfare is, as Martin Jung puts it, 'closely linked to the worldly eschatology of Württemberg Pietism',[35] which spread throughout Germany in the early nineteenth century inspired by the first Stuttgart Animal Protection Association.[36]

Friedrich Theodor Vischer, the German author who most ambitiously and zealously engaged with the issue of maltreated animals in the mid-nineteenth century, rose from the same intellectual soil. In 1838, the philosopher, commentator and novelist became co-founder of the Association against Animal Torment in Tübingen. With his first public intervention, a long, three-part newspaper article in 1847, he set the tone that would ring in the ears of his contemporaries for more than a quarter of a century. His was the voice of a philosophically deeply grounded individual given to spirited invective. In the opening to his article, Vischer launches into a diatribe about the abuse of horses in Italy.[37] Following Vischer's portrayal of them, the Italians would share with the brutish coach men of Württemberg the dubious distinction of being the most savage barbarians in the civilized world: 'The Italians' cruelty towards animals is most atrocious . . .'[38]

It was not without pride that Vischer reported, in another letter from Italy, of a run-in with a coach driver, which he just managed to settle to his advantage: 'On the return journey, and during the course of a six-hour ride, and a four-hour rest stop at Paestum, the barbarian had not given the horses a single drop to drink. It was impossible to go on, since they were sweating again. I gave him a stern piece of my mind . . . When I got out, he demanded a tip for a drink. I told him he was the last one who needed a drink and that he should try going thirsty just as he had let his poor horses languish. He replied in coarse language that I did not understand the ways of horses and that giving them a drink would have been harmful to them; I called him a beast, he accused me of being soft, while I, inclined neither to engage in this slanging match nor to put up with his insults, punched him in the mouth. He turned silent and pale, and as he grabbed the hilt of his knife in his pocket, I took two steps back, reached into mine and cocked my pistol, at which point he thought better of it, got up and drove away.'[39]

Certain subjects that had triggered an emotional response in the English animal protection movement were of course absent in Vischer's diatribes: Germany did not have the blood sports which were popular among all classes of English society. The citizens of Württemberg, whom Vischer so loved to flagellate, were at least not guilty of engaging in bull-baiting, cock fights or dog fights. The Italians, too, definitely in Vischer's second league of scapegoats, stood accused of different offences from the British. Although the critic Vischer liked to travel, had crossed the Alps several times to visit the South and enjoyed Italy's variety of landscapes, his perception was still very much that of a typical city-dweller, the classical objects of whose compassion were horses and dogs which laboured under the severe conditions of everyday urban life, tormented by tough transport work and morally deficient coachmen. It was not bloody mass sports or the cruel popular amusements such as one encountered in England that upset him, it was the ubiquity of individual cases of violent human–animal relationships. This violence spilled out over precisely those beings that were the truest and noblest companions of mankind. These were man's closest friends and in better moments they were those with whom man could most easily empathize: 'Empathy with the suffering of an animal relies on a way of thinking that can visualize the inner state of another creature,' wrote Vischer,[40] revealing himself as a rationalist of empathy. This ability to empathize was evident in 'wise' horses and dogs and was directed at their preferred objects – while conversely, the phenomenon of total lack of empathy among mankind dumbfounded the philosopher, to the extent that the only way he knew how to respond was with his fist.

Vischer had a plausible explanation for this, as he saw it, peculiarly Italian cruelty. He blamed 'the priests for the growth of this dark aspect to the Italian national character, because they nourish it rather than fighting it, namely by way of the Catholic Church doctrine that says that animals have no soul.'[41] All that is important for the Catholic Church, Vischer asserts, is to tout 'its magic as the only effective means' and thus to capture its followers' souls. To preach the 'preservation of animals does not help the church rule over its subjects . . . a being that does not confess and cannot receive absolution, that is indifferent to holy water and holy oil must therefore have no soul'.[42] Now, wrote Vischer in 1875, Italy was waking up, it lived and breathed honour. The deplorable character trait he had previously described belonged to the old Italy, for which he felt only contempt. The new Italy, he declared, was different. 'Before the time of the resurrection of Italy, we saw in the flayers of animals the grandsons of the mobs that once celebrated animal fights and gladiatorial carnage. We saw the late fruit of the decay of the old imperial Rome and the toxic corruption of priestly Rome.'[43]

What the Roman clergy was for Vischer's Württemberg Protestants, Irish Catholicism was for the British protestant animal welfare movement. British animal activists registered countless acts of cruelty towards animals in other Catholic countries such as Italy, Spain and France, but especially in Ireland, the focus of constant suspicion. And they also found that the underlying cause was the denial of the existence of a soul in animals.[44]

MY BROTHER

Friedrich Theodor Vischer was not the only German in Italy who made himself conspicuous because of his outrage over the mistreatment of a horse. More famous than Vischer's story is that involving Nietzsche. His descent into madness became evident when, in Turin on a winter's day in early January 1889, he witnessed a fairly common street scene: a brutal coachman was beating his lame cab horse. The scene, taking place under the ironical aegis of fate, in the shadow of a monumental equestrian statue, was so commonplace that the average passer-by, blind to such ubiquitous brutality, would not notice it. In contrast, Nietzsche, so legend has it, felt such a stirring of pity that he tearfully threw himself around the neck of the flogged animal, refusing to let go and calling the horse his 'brother'. People stopped in the street and gathered around to watch, it was written later of the event. Nietzsche's landlord passed by, recognized the professor and led him home.

This much-embellished tale of Nietzsche's response has become one of the most famous anecdotes in German intellectual history. It's so touching that it barely seems to matter whether or not the details are true. It was passed from one biography to another, from one film to the next, a little wandering wench of literature. The story's truth has long since broken away from history and become fused to art instead. Now it has become a precious gem, like an aria in a language you do not understand.

Of course Nietzsche knew the term 'animal cruelty'; anyone who read the newspaper in the second half of the nineteenth century would certainly have come across it. Nietzsche even used the phrase, but not in its original sense. He mocked the new term, using it ironically, perhaps metaphorically, as he sat at his desk in 1882, struggling with his new typewriter. To attempt to write anything with this treacherous instrument was nothing but 'animal cruelty'. Nietzsche, the victim of technology, was the tormented animal. Elsewhere, as a genealogist of morality, he criticizes modern man's pathology of conscience, and likewise speaks of 'self-inflicted animal cruelty'.[45] Beyond such contexts, animals mean very little to him.[46] It is true that *Zarathustra* has its own menagerie presided over by eagle and snake, referred to by Zarathustra as 'my animals', but they are extras in a lesson on wisdom, the acolytes of a new religion; they are not real animals. Nietzsche does not tend to waste his time on animals.[47] In this respect, he differs considerably from his compatriot Vischer who loves animals, real animals, even if it is only the cat and dog that share his room with him and his afternoon snack.

Different, too, are the two philosophers' responses to the phenomenon of violence perpetrated against an animal by a thuggish individual – Vischer's *vetturino* and Nietzsche's Turin cab driver. Neither are indifferent passers-by or indolent onlookers. But in each case the scene of the creature's distress that unfurls before their eyes develops in a different way and prompts a different emotional reaction on the part of the two philosophers. Vischer, the Hegelian, behaves like a dialectician: over the course of several hours, he notes the latent violence, as it were captured in the *thesis* of the act of letting the horses go thirsty. Then, as the dispute with the *vetturino* escalates, his wrath lays the fuse to the powder keg and explodes in the *antithesis* of his punch. Nietzsche's reaction is quite different. He has hardly left the house[48] before he is witness to an overt act of violence and translates it immediately into an inner state of compassion. Or rather, he tries to restrain the already exploding violence in the form of despairing empathy – not realizing that this was the single drop that would cause the barrel of sorrow within him – already full to the brim – to overflow.

For a long time, the origin of the story of Nietzsche's nervous breakdown was obscure. Most retellers and biographers, as well as poets like Gottfried Benn,[49] adhered to the apparently accurate and reliable spin put on it by Erich Friedrich Podach in 1930: 'On January 3, when Nietzsche has just left his house, he sees, at a carriage stand in the Piazza Carlo Alberto, a tired old nag being tormented by a brutal coachman. Pity overcomes him. Sobbing, he throws himself protectively around the neck of the tortured animal. He collapses. Fortunately, at that moment Fino appears, attracted to the scene by

The Sleep of the Author produces Horses: Countess Mechtilde Lichnowsky's doodles in the manuscript of her autobiographical novel, *Der Lauf der Asdur* ('The course of the A flat major'), 1936.

It's all in the stroke: the secret to grooming and sketching a horse. *Petit cheval*, Picasso.

the gathering crowds.[50] He recognizes his tenant and leads him with great difficulty back up to his apartment.'[51]

Forty years after Podach, and eighty years after Nietzsche's breakdown in Turin, the philosopher and writer Anacleto Verrecchia looked into the origins of the story of the poor horse, the aggressive coachman and the compassionate philosopher.[52] He tracked down the first written account in an anonymous article in the *Nuova Antologia*, 16 September 1900. This was shortly followed by other articles in other Italian media; it seems Nietzsche's death on 25 August 1900 got people talking in Italy. That first text, which Verrecchia ascribes to a Piedmontese journalist named Giovanni Cena, contains a range of information about the philosopher that, for whatever reason, did not appear elsewhere (Franz Overbeck, Carl Bernoulli, Elisabeth Förster-Nietzsche). Verrecchia suspects that the source is a conversation with Davide Fino,[53] including the episode with the horse, which makes its literary debut here. Fino, writes the anonymous journalist, rescued his tenant from the hands of two city police officers, who 'reported that they had found the foreigner by the arcades of the University clinging tightly to the neck of a horse and refusing to let go'.[54] The subsequent texts mentioned above contribute further details, partly from conversations with Davide's son, Ernesto Fino, and partly from the imagination of the authors: this category of apocrypha includes the detail of Nietzsche kissing the old nag and calling him his brother.[55]

Nietzschean philologists have identified other possible origins of the Turin horse story.[56] There is a letter to von Seydlitz, in which Nietzsche himself describes a scene 'of a *moralité larmoyante*, as Diderot would say ... Winter Landscape. An old coachman, who with an expression of brutal cynicism, harsher even than the winter all around, relieves himself against his own horse. The horse – a poor, maltreated creature – looks around gratefully, very gratefully.'[57] This distinctive correspondence – Nietzsche biographer Curt Paul Janz speaks of a 'cringe-worthy scene' – highlights three things. First, it demonstrates the currency of the unholy pair of the harsh coachman and the ill-treated horse, united *in dolore*, in the imagination of the nineteenth century. Secondly, it points to Kleist's *Michael Kohlhaas* as a possible source of inspiration, as that novella has a knacker relieving himself, perhaps not *against* his horses, but in the immediate vicinity.[58] And thirdly, it shows Nietzsche all but penning his own finale, an act of conscious authorship which is thoroughly consistent with the logic of his megalomania.

The other set of philological tracks lead to Raskolnikov's grisly dream in Dostoevsky's *Crime and Punishment*, in which a horse is slain and Raskolnikov, still a child, goes up to the maltreated old nag, throws himself around its neck and kisses the dying animal.[59] However, so far no one has conclusively proved that Nietzsche knew the scene or that he was following the Russian cue when he embraced the Turin cab horse. It remains a mystery why an animal was invoked at the demise of two of the greatest philosophers of old Europe – Socrates and Nietzsche. Socrates' last utterance was alleged to have been about the rooster that he owed to Asclepius, and in the case of a Nietzsche it was a horse, to which he gave the gift of his compassion.

The style and staging of each philosopher's demise is reflected in the different animal species. Socrates' death occurred at the intimate venue of his own home, while Nietzsche's spiritual death, marking the onset of dementia that plagued the final decade of his life, occurred on the very public stage of a city, a city which – at least for Nietzsche in those last days – was representative of old Europe. Again, the horse represented the whole of history, which Nietzsche, who was in the process of identifying with every figure in European history, could embrace in no form other than that of a battered animal: the hurting animal to the hurting man, whose last letters were signed from Dionysus or Christ, 'the crucified one'.

THE TRIANGLE AGAIN

The grim triangle of horse cruelty – harsh coachmen, unfeeling passers-by and silently suffering creatures – still exists. The only differences are the locations where it occurs and the media used to record it. It's the horse dealer in place of the coach driver, and the indifferent passer-by or curious spectator might not watch in the street, but online, for example on YouTube. Under search terms such as 'horse market hell' we find the same old brutal scenes: half-dead horses going mad from thirst, maltreated by their cursing, apparently intoxicated dealers and handlers in horse markets in Poland (Skaryszew) and Austria (Maishofen). They're dragged into trucks, buffeted about, dragged into another truck, beaten and transported on again. If they do survive the trip, for many, if not most, their destination is the slaughterhouse and the sausage factory.

Another arena of horse cruelty is in the same part of the world that brought equestrian culture to its zenith and from where it spread over half the world: the Arabian Peninsula. The Emirate of Dubai in particular and the United Emirates in general have gained a reputation for harsh endurance rides in the desert at high temperatures which have risked or indeed caused the deaths of countless horses.[60] Here, too, the curious can take on the role of passer-by, watching online as horses are so badly flayed and severely injured that they collapse and have to be 'put out of their misery' by a vet.

And, of course, there is a new actor in the role of the one who steps in and dismantles this triangle of indifference and cruelty – like the philosopher who has lost his mind, who throws himself around the neck of the tormented nag and calls out, 'My brother!' These days it's young activists in raincoats and beanies, and animal rights campaigners who use a range of approaches – including posters, flyers, films, petitions, flash mobs, protests and even the emergency purchase of individual animals – to counter the maltreatment of horses and to campaign for the closure of horse markets. Will they have more success in the long term than Nietzsche in Turin? *Speriamo.*

PART IV

The Forgotten Player
HISTORIES

To describe the separation of man and horse is one thing. To seek to find meaning and purpose in their former cohabitation is something else entirely. What did man gain when he allied himself with the horse? What could the horse do that other beings could not? The first answer is provided by physics. Horses were able to generate energy, so physics tells us, by converting energy. They were able to turn the inconspicuous potential energy of tough prairie grasses, inedible to almost all other animals, into the spectacular energy of a fast endurance runner. Thanks to its natural properties as a converter of energy, the horse could bear kings, knights, female lovers and rural doctors, draw carriages and cannons, transport hordes of workers and employees, and mobilize entire nations. This is the first answer.

The second answer is that the horse was also able to create knowledge and convey experience. As the most important and closest animal partner of symbol-forming and history-making mankind, the horse became the privileged object of human research and cognition. So thorough was this that horses threatened to disappear behind all discourse, had it not been for the painters and sculptors who helped bring them to a second life in art: until they finally faced the threat of disappearing behind all the images. The horse was part of a complex economy of various knowledge areas (medical, agrarian, military, artistic) and types of knowledge (empirical, experiential, scientific), as well as a long literary tradition founded in antiquity. That this knowledge economy is today largely forgotten does not diminish its former weight, which would have been at its greatest in the eighteenth and nineteenth centuries.

The third response concerns the wealth of emotions associated with horses, such as pride and admiration, desire for power and lust for freedom, fear, joy and compassion. In its capacity as bearer of signs and symbols, in its role as a *semiophore*, the horse has always been a significant carrier and transmitter of human emotions, moods and passions. Beside its functions as converter of energy and object of knowledge, the horse is also a converter of pathos. This is the third economy in which the horse has played a central role as an object and an actor: through the images it conveyed, and by virtue of the passionate attributes that were ascribed to it, the horse came to play a role in the fate of human passions.

Within these three economies – *energy, knowledge, pathos* – the history of man and that of the horse became intimately combined and intertwined. But are these three economies not governed by quite different laws? To what extent should they be mutually convertible? 'Material causes', wrote Thomas Hardy, 'and emotional effects are not to be arranged in regular equation. The result from capital employed in the production of any movement of a mental nature is sometimes as tremendous as the cause itself is absurdly minute.'[1] But given such different spheres – *energy, knowledge, pathos* – who would expect regular equations? To start with, a great deal has already been achieved when we consider the wealth of phenomena: the abundance and variety of images, texts and objects left behind by the common history of men and horses.

Eventually other questions arise. We will no longer ask, what do we know of equine and human history? What did the horse mean to us? What evidence did its history leave behind? What was learned and which institutions administrated that knowledge? In which literatures does it live on and in which archives is it languishing forgotten? Instead of asking what we know of the horse, what we did know or what we have forgotten, we will ask what horses *can teach us*, in the present and in the short period of time we can foresee, which we endow with the grand title of 'the future'. What will the equine species teach us in future? How will we speak about it? What form will we give to our knowledge? These are the questions at the heart of the last section of this book, subtitled *Histories* (in the very Greek and literal sense of the word: explorations and investigations) and which might equally be called *Aesthetics*, that is, historical aesthetics.

Some books end with a kind of symphonic close, while others fail to come to any conclusion at all. Well, this last section is no classic fourth movement. Instead of closing in with a summary or a synthesis, it moves out towards the opposite effect: an open end. The *Histories* will be something like a market: various techniques and styles of telling horse stories will be paraded around the ring: historical and philosophical narratives, research reports, literary texts, fragments of theories, memoirs, pictures, anecdotes and quotes. Nothing that might look like a whole, nothing that rounds itself off coherently. No conclusion, but rather a collection: a loose anthology of possibilities and ways of narrating the history of horses and people, of reflecting on it, of committing it to memory. Like a rug, the text comes to an end in the countless tassels of the fringed edge. An essay can grant itself that freedom. It enjoys certain privileges that more strictly scholarly writing is denied. Its stated method has just three words: *search and find*. An essay cannot and will not do more than that. Or perhaps it should do just one more thing: *show*. And share its discoveries with others.

Teeth and Time

GREAT ADVANCES, GREAT POLITICS

In September 1528, the people of Regensburg nominate the artist Albrecht Altdorfer as their mayor. He declines. He has more important things to do: he's working on a large painting for Duke Wilhelm IV of Bavaria. It's a huge canvas filled with thousands of characters, portraying the entire Battle of Issus in 333 BCE, with subtle references to contemporary times and the resistance against the Turks. Sociologist Georg Simmel will one day ask himself how a historian of the twentieth century should go about narrating a major event such as the Battle of Marathon in all its detail. Altdorfer shows how a painter of the sixteenth century solves the problem: by composing a scene teeming with activity. The broad battlefield, the plain of Issus, beyond it the mountains, the sea and the celestial expanses – all that can be taken in at a glance. But as soon as the viewer loses sight of the broader picture and wanders through the countless dramatic details of the event, he gets hopelessly lost. He only finds himself again at the centre of the action, at the point where world history has just turned a corner: Darius, King of Persia, turns his chariot drawn by three horses and takes flight; Alexander, the young hero, pursues him on Bucephalus, his favourite, glorious steed. The outcome of the battle is foretold by this fleeting constellation of protagonists: victory will fall to the horseback rider. The new military technique of the cavalry asserts itself spectacularly against the outdated chariot warfare; the young god of war has triumphed over the hegemon of the old world.

A reader of the German historian Reinhart Koselleck might wonder whether he had this picture in mind when he coined the term *saddle period* for the transitional, or threshold, period from pre-modernity to modernity – one of his most significant contributions to conceptual history. While we do not know the source of the theoretical concept, we do know what Koselleck meant by the evocative term: in the late eighteenth century, in around 1780, there was a turning point in the concept of history. This era saw a shift from a diversity of differing histories towards a more unified *world history*: a shift from the teeming canvas of multiple narrations towards a singular narrative of a unified period. For the historian, this was the moment when modernity began. Whoever wanted to set out a vision of the future as a series of expectations would need to be able to look back on the past as a coherent set of experiences.

The success of the term 'saddle period' (also known as *saddle time* or *threshold time*) rests on the fact that the evidence supporting it was hardly ever questioned. A casual investigation into the origin and sense of the word brings us to a geological reference: the 'saddle' of a mountain range is the high ridge between two peaks, at once *separating* and *connecting* them. The 'saddle period', seen in this way, was a kind of temporal watershed. But no one ever seems to ask who it was that first put topography into the proverbial saddle. Besides, looking at how a saddle rests on a horse's back is enough to make sense of the metaphor. But what has to happen for the geological term to become commonly used enough for it then to take on a figurative meaning as a temporal notion of history? For the facts on the ground to be saddled up as a perception of time? This was the work of a historian and temporal structuralist.

It is not unreasonable to suspect that Koselleck was being polemical and intended his coinage to be seen as an antithesis or a response to another concept of historical theory. One of his academic tutors in Heidelberg in the late 1940s was the philosopher Karl Jaspers, after all. In 1949, the latter published his historico-philosophical work *The Origin and Goal of History*, a phenomenology of historical consciousness.[2] In it, Jaspers explores the question: when did the populations of the great cultural realms that he focuses on – Western/Greek, Indian and Chinese – begin to develop an historical awareness of themselves, their way of life and their artefacts? When, the philosopher asks, did they start to transcend their innerworldly horizon and begin to consciously think about this transcendence? Jaspers's answer: in the period between the eighth and the second century BCE. With astonishing simultaneity, in each of these high cultures there occurred a shift towards reflexive thinking, which expanded the finiteness of their consciousness, but also brought about an increasing awareness of its transcendability. For this decisive time in terms of historical awareness, Jaspers developed the concept of the *axial age*.[3]

Of course, when Koselleck coined the term 'saddle period', it was not his intention to provide a mirror-image antonym to Jaspers's term. He was not particularly interested in precisely where and when the earliest awareness of historicity had developed – palaeohistoriography was not really his thing. He wanted to identify the *caesura*, the moment when modernity entered into a reflective relationship with itself, when it contrived a unified realm of what lay in the past: its history. What interested Koselleck were the dynamic concepts of modernity, not the holistic concepts of the metaphysics of history. So was it a question of the brave new world mutinying in a bold cavalry attack against the chariot culture of the old school? Had conceptual history saddled up to ride out against a spiritual history borne by axial chariots? This clash of the conceptualizations would certainly make for a good sword and sandal movie: Alexander against Darius, the Saddle Period v. the Axial Age, conceptual history pitted against the philosophy of history, and from the outset it would be clear which would triumph.

A historical pun? Perhaps a touch more. Jaspers had himself laid the track which leads to the historic hippodrome. In the run-up to his theory of the axial powers of consciousness, he asks what might have motivated the new way of thinking. In response to the question 'Why the simultaneity?', Jaspers argues that there is only one hypothesis worth discussing and that is Alfred Weber's. 'The penetration of the nations of charioteers and horsemen from Central Asia . . . had, so he argues, analogous consequences in all three regions. The men of these equestrian peoples came to experience, thanks to the horse, the limitless vastness of the world. They took over the ancient civilizations by conquest. In hazards and disasters they experienced the problematic character of existence, as master-peoples they developed an heroicotragic consciousness that found expression in the epic.'[4]

It was no coincidence that Alfred Weber's book, to which Jaspers

Straight from the horse's mouth: horse teeth in papier mâché, taken by French physician Louis Auzoux, late nineteenth century.

The artist as a young Native American: pencil drawing by the ten-year-old Paul Klee.

referred – *Das Tragische und die Geschichte* ('The Tragic and History') – was published in the year of Stalingrad and that it intoned the current 'tragic existence view' which the Germans famously shared with the Greeks, and also approvingly cited the émigré scholar Heinrich Zimmer.[5] Weber responds to the question of how the sense of the tragic had come to be in the world – and not only in that of the Greeks – by pointing to the two waves of conquest since 2000 BCE against the European and Asian 'pre-cultures': first, one based on chariot technology and then, from 1200 BCE, a cavalry-led conquest. This second, in particular, triggered a major process of cultural dynamism. 'This cavalry wave is like a huge swell, the greatest that has ever flooded Eurasia in any temporal context . . . With the nations riding the crest of this wave bringing, along with their social and political structure, their spiritual character and the masterly quality and atmosphere of their warfare . . . this was the dawn of a new world era, a period of spiritual upheaval . . . Everywhere there was the clash of the masculine perspective and attitude of the nomadic master-peoples with the originally matriarchal "Mother Earth" way of life, rooted in the earth and in agriculture . . .'[6]

The stooge behind the monumental military men and epic heroes is not Friedrich Nietzsche, but Oswald Spengler. Even if the colours Spengler uses to paint his historical prospectus are derived from Nietzsche, it is nevertheless Spengler alone – the history teacher and zoologist who graduated with a thesis on 'The Development of the Organ of Sight in the Higher Realms of the Animal Kingdom' (1904) – who clearly perceived the revolutionary role of the horse and its military use in history. With a slight technological shift: Spengler's interest in art lets him move the gun into the foreground and the horse slightly into the background. His enthusiasm is less for the chronologically later horseback warriors than for the earlier chariots; the cavalry appears to him therefore as a derivative, secondary phenomenon. 'No weapon has been so world-transforming as the chariot, not even firearms. It is the key to the world history of the second millennium BCE, which changed the world more than any period in history . . . Above all, *speed as a tactical instrument* makes its first entry into world history. The emergence of the cavalry . . . is only the consequence of chariot warfare.'[7]

322

As Spengler delivered his lecture in February 1934 to the Munich Society of Friends of Asian Art and Culture, he sounded as if he was speaking as a prophet of an impending new kind of chariot-borne *Blitzkrieg*, as though he were writing the screenplay for Heinz Guderian's Panzer units. The author cited even greater anthropological consequences emerging from the large-scale roll-out of the chariot: '*Speed as a weapon* enters into the history of war, and with it the idea that the weapons-trained professional soldier has a status, indeed enjoys the most lofty status among the population. In this form of warfare we find a new kind of man. ... New classes of nobility emerge that regard war as a *raison d'être* and look down on farmers with pride and contempt. Here, in the second millennium, a form of manhood declares itself which was not there previously. A new kind of soul is born. From this point on, there is conscious heroism ... The impact on world history is tremendous. It acquires a whole new style and feeling.'[8]

Nobles, heroes, warriors and a new man. Three years after the Second World War, Hans Freyer, with the publication in 1948 of his two-volume *World History of Europe*, is still walking in Spengler's footsteps. He also identifies 'one of the greatest revolutions of warfare in the history of mankind'[9] in the combination of horse and chariot. Freyer is even more direct and apodictic when he links the new driving and fighting technique with a monumentalizing anthropology and a metaphysics of will: 'it is a question of natural eruptions of military will ... their appearance (signifies) a new era; because it means that a new will to conquer – as a very specific ethos, namely as a genuine weapon at certain points – breaks through the existing power topography with the violence of a volcano breaking through the earth. ... It is only now that there is conscious heroism ... It is only now that the *epic* is possible.'[10]

But it was not only the epic that found its way into history once humans started to fight one another with the weapon of speed. 'From this spirit is born a new world reality that did not exist in the first millennium of the ancient cultures: politics ... It is only now that we see the real drama of political history; no longer simply the typical actions of rulers, judgements and pacifications in the old Chronicle style, but sudden falls from grace, sudden switches from grandeur to downfall, where it is states themselves that are at stake.'[11] It seems like fate that politics now enters the stage of history, inexplicable and looming large, and yet it is only the result of a technological breakthrough.

Even Jaspers, whose words in the late 1940s resound with nobility and fate, steers us directly towards this new type of man. He does not lose sight, however, of the animal catalyst for this technical revolution. The rise of the horse changes the position of the people – the 'cavalier perspective' – and along with it their view of the world around them: 'it (the horse) furnished him with a new and superior battle-technique and brought with it a spirit of mastery that is bound up with the taming and curbing of the horse, the courage of the rider and conqueror and the feeling for the beauty of the animal'.[12]

It is now high time to bid farewell to the illusory analogy between the axial age and the war-chariot culture: *adieu*, false friend. Jaspers did not drive through history as a philosophical charioteer; the author whose tracks he was following was not Oswald Spengler, but Alfred Weber. As far as they were concerned, the only historical protagonists to have unleashed the epochal phase-change of the axial age were 'the Indo-European nations of *horsemen*' who burst onto the scene in around 1200 BCE with 'a great new thrust' that took them on to Iran and India.[13] In all other respects, the authors writing after 1939 – be they Weber, Jaspers or Freyer – carry the same small catechism of archaeo-hippology in their pocket: Joseph Wiesner's text *Fahren und Reiten in Alteuropa und im Alten Orient* ('Charioteering and Horse-riding in Old Europe and the Old Orient').[14] In a manner that remains astonishing, Wiesner brings both strands together: historical knowledge as it stood in 1940 and the colours of ideological narrative.

The historian and archaeologist Wiesner forgoes the thunderbolt characters and fateful eruptions that are so dear to the Nietzscheans (Spengler, Freyer) in favour of a consistent historicizing of the early equestrian age. But, like them, he cannot renounce the idea that it was only with the emergence of the war horse and the chariot in ancient Europe and the Near East that a period of *great politics* ('*die große Politik*') could begin.[15] This large-scale politics needed to be borne along somehow; it needed new historical subjects: 'a knightly, propertied nobility ... with the irrepressible desire to have their deeds represented and thus to have a narrative that would not live on in obscurity'.[16] This 'desire to eternalize one's dominance' is, as Wiesner tirelessly asserts, an *Aryan mentality*. It is characteristic, he argues, of the entire Orient from Iran to Assyria, while in other cultures, such as the Egyptian, it is non-existent: clearly, the old world was also familiar with the dichotomy of heroes and merchants.[17]

Warring by chariot was a good half a millennium ahead of warring on horseback: 'in the Near East, riding is rare ... It has no military application; neither is there the notion of the exalted horseman ... There is little trace of the ethos of riding. There are therefore no horse-riding gods.'[18] Archaeology leaves no room for doubt: riding for military purposes, as a cavalry, is a late invention compared to charioteering. The perspective of the cavalry, as Fontane captures in the words of General Bamme in *Before the Storm*[19] – a perspective in which the entirety of history is perceived as equestrian history – turns out to be a retrospective illusion. The fascination with the speed of conquest was not, incidentally, limited to the Nazis and their preferred authors or the ones influenced by them. Neoliberalist and co-founder of the social market economy Alexander Rüstow spoke in 1950 of the 'speed rush' and the 'completely altered sense of oneself with respect to space and distance' that the 'new locomotive technology of high-speed driving and riding' must have created.[20]

Elias Canetti also recognized the considerable impact on world history of the horsemen thanks to their speed: 'the taming of the horse and the perfecting of mounted armies led to the great invasions from the east. In every contemporary account of the Mongols, great stress is laid on their *speed*: suddenly they were there, only to vanish again and appear somewhere else even more suddenly.'[21] Even the 'schizo-analysis' of heroic post-structuralism could not dispense with the clichéd cigarette-card image of the brisk cavalrymen: ' "They come like fate ... they appear as lightning appears, too terrible, too sudden," ' write Deleuze and Guattari, quoting Nietzsche, and continuing with Kafka: 'Like a cloud blown in from the desert, the conquerors are there: "In some way that is incomprehensible to me they have pushed right into the capital, although it is a long way from the frontier. At any rate, here they are; it seems that every morning there are more of them."'[22]

THE NARROW GATE

In the six decades since Jaspers's coinage of the term 'axial age', research into the early stages of the equestrian age has come a long way. It has thrown off the ideological ballast and bid farewell to the Aryan spirit along with the heroic and noble horseman clichés. Archaeology and archaeozoology have finally freed themselves from *'Ariomania'* as historian Peter Raulwing puts it,[23] the fascination with the Aryans who allegedly domesticated the first horse and thereafter invented the chariot. In general, the pattern of interpretation is no longer of the macro perspective, or the cavalier perspective, looking down and across over the sweep of the philosophy of history, but is aligned with the micro perspectives of archaeological findings.[24] This does not mean, however, that archaeologists across the vast Euro-Asian realm between the Black Sea and Central Asia, digging for testimonies of the connection between man and horse, refrain from all traditional forms of interpretation. Thus in recent years, the figure of the Eurasian nomadic warrior, that 'natural-born' combatant, who, as tough and austere as his resilient horse, emerged as the terror of the sedentary populations of Europe and the Orient, has been the focus of a boom in research.[25] The fact that the steppe warriors no longer crash onto the scene with new political ideas like lightning from heaven does not mean they are exhausted in terms of historical research; what has changed, however, is their *raison d'être*. It is no longer the politics that is our destiny, but ecology. 'The nomads', wrote John Fairbank, an explorer of Chinese military history, in 1974, 'were by necessity horsemen and hunters specialized in mounted archery, the most natural warriors ever produced by ecological circumstance'.[26]

From the perspective of archaeology, the concept of the *warrior* has been problematized. As David Anthony, the author of a comprehensive study of the Eurasian horsemen of the Bronze Age, reminds us, horses are ideal for use in herding livestock, but equally useful when stealing and driving away cattle, and moreover are prone to being stolen themselves. 'When American Indians in the North American Plains first began to ride, chronic horse-stealing raids soured relationships even between tribes that had been friendly.'[27] The use of horses created new combat situations and gave rise to new styles of conflict, making it difficult to clearly distinguish between riding and warring. 'Many experts have suggested that horses were not ridden in warfare until after about 1500–1000 BCE, but they failed to differentiate between *mounted raiding*, which probably is very old, and *cavalry*, which was invented in the Iron Age after about 1000 BCE.'[28]

Because these age-old conflicts between Eastern European and Asian nomads did not threaten the major cities of Mesopotamia and the Near East, they remained outside the spotlight of history. To enter into the spotlight, they had to improve not only their warriors' weaponry (shorter, stronger bows and iron arrowheads), but also their organized cooperation and their discipline: tribal warriors had to become warrior states. This transformation seems to have played out from 1000–900 BCE. 'Cavalry soon swept chariotry from the battlefield, and a new era in warfare began.'[29] In other words, in the incipient stages of Jaspers's axial age, around 800 BCE, military history had long ago trumpeted the arrival of the 'saddle period'.

For those digging for the roots of the association between man and horse, saddles and axles are poor indicators: both come much too late, historically speaking. If we're looking for the early history of the domestication of the horse – not as consumable livestock, but as a load-drawing and carrying work animal – then we need to look for teeth marks. Long before it was customary among horse traders to look a horse in the mouth, horses have twice bared their teeth to history, first in the early days of their evolution and again in the era of their early domestication.

To investigate the history of domestication, archaeology has joined forces with both iconography and osteology. While the field of archaeology that bases its arguments predominantly on depictions of ridden horses (or horse-like animals) and relevant written sources came to the conclusion that 'there is no reliable textual or artistic evidence for horse-riding earlier than the end of the second millennium [BCE]',[30] the alliance of osteology and palaeohippology could push this date back another two or three millennia. For a long time, the most effective instrument here has been radiocarbon dating. With the help of this technique, horse bones found first at Dereivka on the River Dneiper in Ukraine and then at Botai in northern Kazakhstan, both Chalcolithic period (Copper Age) settlements, could be dated to the end of the fourth and beginning of the third millennium. But this finding gave no answer to the crucial question: calories or kinetics? The bones said nothing about the purpose of these animal populations. However, beside the bones at both sites, snaffle bits were found carved from stags' antlers. These suggested that the horses were not intended exclusively for consumption, but were either used for riding with bridles or as draught animals.[31]

Archaeology was able to go a step further when it came to examining the animals' teeth. Whatever kind of bit had been used and whatever material it was made from, whether hardwood, leather or textile fibres such as hemp, it had left marks and signs of wear on the tooth enamel of a horse that had been steered using such an item.[32] This evidence enabled the earliest use of the horse as a draught animal or mount to be dated to 4200–3700 BCE.[33] This is also supported by the herding of domesticated animals (horses, cattle, sheep), for which there is also evidence dating to this period. While it's possible to herd cattle and sheep on foot, in the long term this is impossible with horses. In order to keep horses permanently in herds, the herdsman needs to be mounted.[34]

Despite all the advances made in archaeology, the precise cultural and moral achievement of domestication is still veiled in obscurity: no text, no picture and no material evidence testifies to the courage of the man who first mounted a wild horse and coaxed it into tolerating its rider and obeying his will. Historian Ann Hyland is not wrong when she describes this moment with words that, almost five decades before, accompanied the steps of the first man on the moon: 'It was a small step, albeit a brave one, for man to mount a horse.'[35] The comparison with the moon landing is certainly not exaggerated. The moment when man began, by domestication and breeding, to connect his fate with the horse – not with a *nutritional* intention, but with a *vectorial* aim – may have been, before the invention of writing, the narrow gate through which man entered the realm of history.

TOUGH GRASS

With the horse, man not only had a particularly fast and agile companion whose strength, endurance and speed gave him new, unheard-of means to wage war and engage in 'macro-politics'. The horse was also a comparatively undemanding and robust partner that was almost as adaptable as man himself. This is particularly the case with respect to the horse's nutritional needs and digestive system. Horses feed on grass that no cattle would be able to eat: its cellulose structure is too tough and because of its low protein content it offer insufficient nutrition for cows and most even-toed ungulates. Moreover, ruminants such as cows need long rest periods to chew the cud, while a horse with its simple stomach can digest as it carries on walking. But the primary precondition for the horse's resilience and frugal nutritional needs is, of course, its pearly whites. Thanks to their particularly high and hard-crowned teeth, horses can graze on and break down the tough grass of the prairies, steppes and savannah with its high proportion of silicon in the cell walls. As teeth evolved in the horse's precursors, these early animals would have become able to move away from softer leafy fare and exchange their former habitat, the forest, for the steppe.[36]

In order to provide sufficient nutrition, this new, less protein-rich feed needed to be consumed in larger quantities. This in turn required the newcomers to the steppes and the semi-arid zones to roam freely, covering large ranges and living in small groups. It was this combination of circumstances – physical constitution and lifestyle – which made the horse the ideal partner for man, who longed to expand the radius of his sphere of life and of influence. In addition to these attributes, there was the inherent domesticability of the horse (or of specific types of proto-horse, including perhaps Przewalski's horse, although not the tarpan, an extinct subspecies of wild horse). Once 'broken' out of its wild state, the horse proved to be a reliable and sensitive companion for man. While the philosophy of history and the theory of power in the schools of Nietzsche and Spengler directed their macro-historical focus solely on the effect of *speed* and its impact (war, macro-politics), historical ecology has focused more closely on the processes that played out between animals and their environment, and the significant consequences on the energy balance.

The horse, writes Jürgen Osterhammel, in the context of the nineteenth-century North American Wild West, 'functioned as an energy transformer, converting the energy stored in grassland into muscle power obedient to human command'.[37] Indeed, not only the North American prairies, but all large grassland and semi-arid areas of the world represented gigantic energy stores that could be put to use by domesticable animals such as horses. These animals were capable of taking in the potential energy of the steppe grasses and transforming it into kinetic energy, which could be used for a range of purposes, from war to buffalo hunting.

This theory of the animal organism as an energy transformer, as Osterhammel puts it, or *converter*, the term used in English, harks back to the engineers and physicists of the late nineteenth century, who, in an effort to increase the energy efficiency of machines, studied the animal as a *living combustion engine*. Robert Henry Thurston should certainly be mentioned in this context (whose reflections also reached a German readership, thanks to the translation by German mechanical engineer Franz Reuleaux).[38] The transfer of this energy into historical human societies was the focus of the work of Chicago sociologist Fred Cottrell.[39] According to him, the first and most important converter is man himself, because of his inventiveness. Man understands how to harness the different types of potential energy and put them to use. But man, says Cottrell, 'also makes use of converters other than his own body to achieve his ends, and the energy these converters make available to him is also measurable. Thus wherever other converters can be used to replace or supplement the energies of man, the relative advantage, in energy terms, of using them over using his own physical effort can be calculated.'[40]

The horse's metabolism enables the transformation, or conversion, of energy: it absorbs the energy stored in plants and converts it into energy that can be exploited as kinetic energy (for moving, pulling and carrying). This assumes, of course, that the conversion of plant matter into the horse's flesh is used not just once – i.e. when it is eaten – but that the horse is recognized and exploited as a sustainable, renewable producer of kinetic energy. The tack and riding equipment used (reins,

Shadowing the chase: filming *The Misfits*,
directed by John Huston, 1961.

To ride is to rule:
Barbara Klemm, view
from the Neues
Museum of the Alte
Nationalgalerie and
an equestrian statue,
Berlin, 2000.

saddles, spurs, etc.) harness the energy derived through this conver-sion process and steer it in the direction desired by the respective historical group.

Man is also a converter, as Cottrell demonstrates, and a particu-larly sophisticated one at that. He has learnt to make use of other energy converters and to harness them for his own purposes. This harnessing is to be understood in both a literal and in a more compre-hensive way. Man expands his range not only by harnessing the power of his own muscles, but by exploiting other converters to his own advantage, initially only as suppliers of food but later, at a higher stage of development, as *vectors*, that is, suppliers of kinetic energy. 'The domestication of *draft* animals greatly increases the *mechanical energy* available to those who possess them.'[41]

A historical ecology, seen in this way, involves various actors from animals, plants, microbes, viruses, through to technology, water and wind, not to mention the dust and sand that clog up the gears. Since we live in enlightened times, we can round off the list without includ-ing ghosts, devils and assorted otherworldly fauna, but we can't escape natural disasters. Of course, people are also subjects of their own historical ecology, but that seems to play a lesser role here than in classical political history, because they are now perceived more and more in connection with and in contrast to natural processes. The further we move into the twenty-first century, the more clearly we see what is at the heart of an historical ecology: the history of *energy*, the transformation of its forms and its carriers, the challenge of its distribution. It is true that in the foreseeable future, the core of the narrative is still dominated by the ensemble of political ideas and actions: war and peace, law, administration and the realm of free-dom. But all political attitudes, actions and concepts will in future be re-examined and re-evaluated in the light of the balance of energies. In contrast to the concept of history that came before, this history of energy no longer divides the historical world into two separate halves: human and non-human history. And it is in the horse that this history of energy has one of its most significant index fossils.

Conquest

BECOMING AN INDIAN

When the comedian Myron Cohen delivered his stand-up act on the club circuit of North America in the 1950s and 1960s, his repertoire included several jokes with an unmistakable foreign flavour. Some gags were 'immigrants' from Italy, others came from Ireland or Poland, while most were of Jewish origin. But even Cohen's apparently indigenous American numbers wavered somewhere between cultures. Among them was the one about the man who was driving in the wrong direction down a one-way street and was stopped by a police officer. The officer asks, 'Didn't you see the arrow?' The man replies, 'What? I didn't even see the Indian.'

Cohen's joke is distinguished not only by its brevity, but also by its universality. Someone from Austria or China can laugh at it as much as an American. Perhaps the Americans were tickled most of all by it, because the confusion between the two kinds of arrow amounts to a reversal of two centuries of American culture and way of life. In other words, for Americans, the joke is not just a matter of semiotics, it's also about history. From the world of cars and arrow-shaped graphics on road signs, the quip takes us back to the world of mounted natives and their arrows – too quick to see.

However, this alliance between horses and the arrow is anything but a purely American invention. First forged by the Asiatic nomads, the residents of the steppes, it was later reinforced by Arab horsemen. The arrow, wrote Elias Canetti, 'was the Mongols' main weapon. They killed from a distance, and they also killed while moving, from the backs of their horses.'[1] The American popular imagination, of course, only pictures the Native Americans; that's the direction they look historically, down the cultural one-way street. The connection between horses and bows and arrows is, in this respect, real in nature; it is 'historic', if by history we imagine events that actually took place and things that actually existed. But we also know there to exist besides these things, and in the folds between them, many other connections between horse and arrow, conjectures and conjunctures that have formed in the realm of the imagination. Why should they be any less real than the things made of wood, iron, flesh and blood? Ideas are also facts, as Jacob Burckhardt put it.

In Cohen's joke, we see two images in close contact, a glimpse of a horse and one of an arrow, two indicators of fast motion in space. The fleet-footed animal combines with the speeding projectile, the technical object, the man-made artefact (as, too, is the domesticated horse). The Native American in turn is their liaison officer, the point of contact between the two; he is horse-man and arrow-man in one form, master of two types of speed: the animal speed of the horse and the technical velocity of the arrow. He is the agent who coordinates their interaction, steering and adding, the helmsman who brings the two parts together. He is the *arrownaut* in the airspace over the prairie.

In a short piece of flash fiction, as fast as the wind, consisting of one single sentence, with the title 'Longing to be a Red Indian',[2] Franz Kafka portrays in staccato, lightning-quick bolts of consecutive phrases a complete metamorphosis from rider to arrow or perhaps to a simple, matterless rushing motion.

> Oh to be a Red Indian, instantly prepared, and astride one's galloping mount, leaning into the wind, to skim with each fleeting quivering touch over the quivering ground, till one shed the spurs, for there were no spurs, till one flung off the reins, for there were no reins, and could barely see the land unfurl as a smooth-shorn heath before one, now that horse's neck and horse's head were gone.

Taking a closer look, we see what is actually happening in the Indian's ride or dream ride: it's a single, breathless process of dropping and discarding, throwing off reins, spurs and tack, a process that devours even the horse in the end. Nothing remains of the rushing ensemble as the rider leans 'into the wind', and eventually nothing remains of him besides his perspective and a quivering and a dashing motion that sends this perspective racing over the 'smooth-shorn heath' into the void. And then it is the sentence itself, this single sentence, that flies on over the horse's head, like the vista opening up or like a bolt of lightning, while the reader is carried away by the dynamic momentum, hurtling over something bald or closely shaved like the bare heath – or it could be the prairie. And as the sentence dismantles everything, discarding whatever comes to hand – spurs, reins, the horse's neck and head – it calls up other ideas and images, forcing the reader's imagination to finish saying what it – the galloping sentence – needs not say explicitly.

It is in the double beat of homonyms or repeated phrases, words and syllables (*quivering/quivering, till/till, for/for, horse's neck/ horse's head*), that we hear the clip-clopping of galloping hooves. It is with the replacement of the expected subjunctive verb by the indicative imperfect 'there were no . . .' that we feel the quivering, shaken-up structure of the sentence. It finds no syntactic completion, but is left dangling, giving readers the impression that they are there on the back of the horse, clinging on behind the author, peering over his shoulder. Or even that the readers are alone on the horse, that they are themselves the rider, being shaken and jolted, so that they can barely hear or see. And the reader becomes this arrow of pure kinetic energy, hurtling west, in the direction of the marching American frontier, the same direction underlying Kafka's novel *America*, which begins on the east coast and moves ever westward to Oklahoma.

With a single, relatively short sentence construction, which is grammatically and syntactically defunct and threatens at every moment to disintegrate into its component parts like a stagecoach ransacked and ravaged, Kafka conveys the essence of a narrative that unfurls in the mind of the reader, a story that plays with a stock of cultural images the author knew he could rely on: cowboys, Indians, horses, riders, the prairie, the Wild West – just as Myron Cohen could be sure that his audience was familiar with a one-way street, a car, a driver, a policeman, an arrow and a road sign. The sentence plays with what Flaubert called *idées reçues* – received ideas – commonly held conceptions, common goods, shared by every reader participating in the wordplay of his time. Except here it is perhaps *objets reçus*, shared objects, the semantics and usage of which are familiar to everyone. It is only on the surface level that it appears Kafka has written a passage of sixty-one words (seventy-one in Malcolm Pasley's English translation), ten commas and one full stop on white paper, perhaps yellowing with the passage of time; in fact, what he has written in this text, which is incomparably expansive and diffuse, is the sediment of cultural vestiges, the particles of dust kicked up by the hoof beats of the prose, the soil in which we etch out our last will and testament, the soldier marking his dying wishes in the sand, as described by the German lexicographer Johann Heinrich Zedler.[3]

In other words, as they read, readers experiences Kafka's sentence decomposing 'over the quivering ground', disintegrating into its component parts, not building or welling up into a narrative whole, but – on the contrary – crumbling into one. Kafka's sentence is like the beginning of a firework display, sparks bursting out over the ground, before fizzling and fading out. At the same time, this passage is like the microscopically small film script to the shortest Western in movie history, a miniature screenplay for the only scene ever to be filmed from the perspective of the mounted native – the 'cavalier perspective' – replicating the disorientating filmic effect of the tracking shot through the means of linguistic mimesis: first the camera tracks over the neck of the galloping animal, then out over its head, zooming out into the distance over the endlessly sprawling prairie, a land that is nothing more than 'quivering ground' and, a little later, 'smooth-shorn heath'.

Kafka, like many artists of his time, is known for his repeated treatment of the phenomenon of speed. He was fascinated by Zeno's paradox about the impossibility of motion: everything is in motion except one thing, the flying arrow. Rest is found only in the absolute motion liberated from all friction. Does Kafka's piece, 'Longing to be a Red Indian', also experience this paradoxical moment of rest? The longing is directed unmistakably at the desire to dispense with and throw off all riding tack, all accessories, such as spurs and reins, to end up as pure movement, a vector in empty space. *Being* a "Red Indian" therefore means eliminating all accoutrements to minimize friction, or even more than that, and more radically, dispensing with the horse itself, the physical medium of transport, to become entirely disembodied.

Seen in this way, Kafka's miniature undertakes a journey of abstraction. With every phrase the galloping steed throws off another civilizing element with which mankind had sought to dominate and steer the horse: first the spurs, then the reins. There's no mention of a saddle or of any stirrups; the items that Kafka dispenses with are the instruments of steering and spurring on, the bridle and the goad. These are the most visible, most acute instruments of domestication: domination as expressed in the possibility of inflicting pain and exercising control. Unlike any other animal in history, the horse has been girdled by a wreath of technical objects aimed at making it easier to exploit the beast, to drive and steer it in mankind's desired direction. All these items served the same purpose of incorporating the horse more intimately into our civilization, making the animal a significant element of our human world, turning it into what was for a very long time our most important source of energy. This history disintegrates before our eyes under the power of Kafka's pen. Just a few more hoof beats and it will be gone forever: *there were no spurs, there were no reins.*

As the instruments of domination fall away, so there emerges the negative arrow of motion: pure, absolute, *abstract*. Kafka's 'Longing to be a Red Indian' gallops away, leaving the realm of history in its wake. Every civilization of the past headed in the opposite direction: with their tools and tack, their reins and spurs, they domesticated this wild conveyor of animal energy and perfected the use or transformation of its energy. It is not the act of dispensing with spurs and reins that releases the positive arrow of energy, but its systematic application, or the way it is coupled or networked with other instruments (carts, harnesses, roads, etc.). Technical innovations have led to improvements in the man–horse system's energy efficiency and its steerability. Kafka's "Red Indian", however, traverses this one-way street in the opposite direction, his arrow pointing into the civilizational void. Discarding the reins and spurs, the instruments of domination, the rider-author establishes himself as the sovereign master. But this overthrow of hegemony accomplished by the Native American or which his *Being a "Red Indian"* accomplishes for him, is not associated with a dramatic fall

Roman chariot races *à la russe*: victory parade by units of the Soviet 5th
Shock Army in front of the Altes Museum, Berlin, 4 May 1945.

20. La Grande Guerre 1914-15 — *Une bonne prise - Officier de Uhlans
conduit à la prison d'AMIENS*   « Phot-Express »

A good catch: French infantrymen lead a captured German
Uhlan officer to Amiens jail, 1915.

from a horse. Kafka's protagonist is not Saul of Damascus. He deserts his horse not by falling from it, but rather by leaving it under or behind him; he transcends it, releases himself and the horse into a condition of wildness.

Kafka's 'Longed-to-be' Native American has abandoned the realm of history. What has been the object of history if not to permeate and occupy land, to conquer territory, to annex soil into one's own dominion? He does not occupy the land and mark out his frontiers; he flies over the land without describing it or even referring to it. It's as though he does not even perceive it. He *barely* sees it, but he hears it: the rhythmic pounding of the horse's hooves that set the ground quivering. The earth is the rider's echo chamber, a tautly skinned drum, and on it the hooves beat out their dry rhythm of the Wild West. The rider does not stop to describe the ground, to occupy it; no, he merely grazes it with the drumsticks of the horse's hooves, conjuring up sound, Hegel's 'mechanical light': the thud of hoof fall on the prairie or the smooth-shorn heath. There is no text, there are no signs, no territory, no history, no space; there is only the rhythmic knocking and bumping on the drumhead of the prairie and the whirr of the arrow accelerating from the bowstring. Kafka's protagonist does not *make history*; he does not *make anything*, in the strictest sense, but he *evokes something*, something dormant in the earth, in the hooves and in the air: the possibility that matter can tremble, can quiver, can be knocked, banged, rubbed and given sound; the possibility of the sound and the vibration. He is not creating history; it is *physics* that he summons up, creating resonance in the earth, friction in the air, sound waves all around.

WIDE OPEN SPACE

In the 1840s the Munich landscape artist Carl Rottmann produced a series of twenty-three paintings of Greece for Ludwig I of Bavaria, scenes of historical sites he had visited and sketched during a long tour of the country. One of these paintings, perhaps the most famous, shows the plain at Marathon, over which a violent thunderstorm is brewing – an unmistakable reference to the fateful battle of the

Athenians and the Plataeans against the army of the Persians led by Darius I. Rather less usually in terms of symbolic meteorology, the artist included another, this time four-legged, historical icon. In the centre of the large canvas, which hangs in Munich's Neue Pinakothek art gallery (see Plate 17), we see a riderless horse crossing the plain at breakneck speed, dragging a red cloth fluttering behind it. The source for this detail may well have been the esteemed Greek tour guide Pausanias, who reported the nightly echo on the one-time battlefield of the battle cry and the neighing of horses.[4] Herodotus, the chief source for the Battle of Marathon, on the other hand, says nothing of horses and cavalry.[5] But since the legendary runner who sacrificed himself for the sake of his victory message was an apocryphal addition from a later period, so too might the riderless galloping steed be granted its lofty, poetic truth as a historical beacon. Given emphasis by the signal colour of the cloth, the horse motif provides a concise, pithy encapsulation of the sum of historical violence that exploded at this location. The horse as a dynamic symbol, a vector as swift as an arrow, turns this open space into a specific location, the open plains into the field of battle where, on a late summer's day in 490 BCE, the West was saved.

Franz Kafka, Carl Rottmann, Carl von Clausewitz: there are not many artists and writers we can rely on for a dynamic conception of space. Most philosophical, political and sociological theories of space are devoid of that genuine human or non-human vector that crosses the space and opens it up. Space, much encumbered since academia's *spatial turn* in recent decades (an approach to scholarship that considers place and space in social science and the humanities), is generally presented as a kind of stable, pre-existing vessel in which movements can be registered.[6] Only a few authors have recognized that a space is not present until there is motion within it; indeed, it is only constituted by the action carried out within it: it is from this motion that spatial relationships develop. It is the battle that creates the battlefield, just as the sailor creates the headland, the rider the bridleway, the climber the ascent, and pedestrians the pedestrian zone. A space results not from the static juxtaposition of various items, but from the movement that brings these various elements into a relationship with one another.[7] 'A space exists,' writes Michel de Certeau, 'when one takes into consideration vectors of direction, velocities, and time variables. Thus space is composed of intersections of mobile elements. . . . In short, *space is a practised place.*'[8]

We fail to recognize movement by considering it in a spatial and segmented way – that is the thrust of Henri Bergson's critique of metaphysics. Kant's transcendental aesthetics sees space as 'a ready-made form of our perceptive faculty';[9] like a *deus ex machina*, no one quite knows where it comes from. Bergson also sees Kant as attributing to space an existence that is independent of its contents;[10] in other words, according to Bergson, Kant is closer to the generally accepted perspective than his adherents claim and thinks of space as a vessel. Bergson sends his readers back to the school of phenomena, to learn how to think of space as arising from movement – and to conceive of it in relation to duration of time. In this sense, Zeno's paradox of the flying arrow is rejected as meaningless, based as it is on the false premise that an ongoing movement consists of a series of infinitesimal moments of rest, while the flight of the arrow is in fact a continuum. 'Suppose an elastic stretched from A to B, could you divide its extension? The course of the arrow is this very extension; it is equally simple and equally undivided. It is a single and unique bound.'[11]

If one wished to carry Bergson's theories over to the spatial realm of history, one need only follow the horse's hoofprints. To see history from the horse's perspective means to conceive of it as a *mover*, as a *vector*. As Rottmann exemplifies in his Marathon landscape, it is only the galloping horse that enables the viewer to see the plain as an historical space – a sphere of combat, of remembrance.[12] Conceiving of history in a vectorial sense does not mean it must be understood as being unidirectional, like the arrow of time or a one-way street. Space, as de Certeau asserted, is made up of intersections of movable elements: 'It is in a sense actuated by the ensemble of movements deployed within it.'[13] The space of history, or rather the *spaces* of history, arise out a diversity of human, animal and technological movements; concrete movements at various tempos, from the lightning quick to the apparent non-movement of the sclerotic. Even a ship bound by ice is in motion, because the elements are still at work: the wind, the frost and the wood. The horse, according to the Arabs, is a creature of the wind: it can help us to perceive movements in space and to understand things from the perspective of that movement.

The vector may be a mounted messenger, a lone hunter or an entire army; its movement makes the land it crosses tangible and recognizable. *Landnahme* ('conquest' or 'land grab') – a term Carl Schmitt places at the centre of his geopolitical theory ('appropriation, distribution, production', or in more prosaic terms, 'grab, divide, graze')[14] – is a legal term to describe the successive acts of taking possession of territory. If we were to put it to the test for historical veracity, it would quickly become apparent that such an appropriation would never be practically possible without horses (other than in parts of the Orient, where Bactrian camels and dromedaries take the place of the Equidae family). Before the conqueror can go from appropriation to distribution and eventually to production (i.e. from seizing land to sharing it out and finally turning it to pasture), he must first have traversed the territory, i.e. *ridden through* and secured it. If 'appropriation' is to lead to genuine retention and administration of the land, then surveying and mapping must be followed by the implementation of a network of communication channels and inspection points (paths, roads, fortifications, depots, customs offices, post offices). The operation of such a network again relies on the availability of animal vectors (messenger and post horses, remounts, draught animals) in sufficient numbers and adequate distribution.

In the example of the Spanish *conquista* of America, these procedures can be seen as prototypical. 'It is possible to imagine the conquistador without his pig,' writes Alfred W. Crosby, Jr., 'but who can imagine him without his horse?'[15] Initially a primary instrument of military conquest (*appropriation*), the horse later became indispensable in terms of control of the land and guaranteeing its exploitation (*distribution, production*). 'The conquistador would never have been able to keep the vast sullen Indian populations under control if the horse had not enabled him to transfer information, orders and soldiers from one point to another swiftly . . . The horse made possible the great cattle industry of colonial America, which, in the final analysis, affected much larger areas of the New World than did any other European endeavor in that period. A swineherd can operate effectively on foot; a *vaquero*, or cowboy, needs a horse.'[16]

Another historical example – that of south-west Africa in the nineteenth century – was recently a hot topic in German-language human–animal studies. The evolution of political power by means of territorial control has proved to be linked to the presence and the use of horses in Africa too – a continent not usually at the heart of equine history. Horses were instrumental not only in establishing and securing power structures, but also in expanding the territory of acts of violence, such as armed raids and cattle theft. In this sense, as Felix Schürmann was able to demonstrate, horses genuinely did 'radically change the conditions and possibilities of domination and its spatial spread, as well as the character of violent confrontations'.[17]

The most spectacular acts of conquest in recent times, however, were seen in the Midwest of the United States. The Oklahoma Land Rush (or Land Run) of 1889 and the pursuant 'runs' of 1893–1906 saw tens of thousands of settlers pour into the state of Oklahoma, originally designated as native territory. One run that enjoyed particular fame, or infamy, was the first land run on Easter Monday, 22 April 1889, not least because of the colourful reportage that accompanied this act of mass land appropriation (or perhaps, land *theft*). The correspondents observing the event could not fail to notice how this 'land run' was in essence indistinguishable from a gigantic horse race, as reported by William Willard Howard, later famous for documenting the plight of the Armenians,[18] in his feature for *Harper's Weekly*: 'At the time fixed, thousands of hungry home-seekers ... were arranged in line along the border, ready to lash their horses into furious speed in the race for fertile spots in the beautiful land before them.'[19] One eyewitness to the second race of 1893 was even more receptive to the racecourse aspect of the land run: 'First in the line was a solid bank of horses; some had riders, some were hitched to gigs, buckboards, carts, and wagons, but to the eye there were only the two miles of tossing heads, shiny chests, and restless front legs of horses.' The starting shot is fired and they're off. 'That one thundering moment of horseflesh by the mile quivering in its first leap forward was a gift of the gods, and its like will never come again.'[20]

Franz Kafka, who leads the protagonist of his first novel, *Amerika: The Man Who Disappeared*, precisely to Oklahoma, must have known of the land runs. News of them was spreading like wildfire throughout the international daily newspapers at that time.[21] Of course, instead of reproducing events in a 'realistic' way, Kafka merged or blended images of the land rush with those of a real horse race, something he had seen in October 1909 when he and Max Brod paid a spellbinding visit to Longchamp Racecourse in the Bois de Boulogne, Paris.[22] However, the *aim* of the Oklahoma Land Rush, the staking of a claim, seems to have interested Kafka less than the run towards it. One suspects – and his 'Longing to be a Red Indian' attests to this – that Kafka was less intrigued by the processes of territorialization than in the opposite: becoming landless, free of the land, becoming the arrow and the native. Perhaps he is therefore only partially useful as a companion for historians. For the latter must, of course, take as much interest in Taking, Doing and Having as they do in Giving Away, Shedding and Leaving Behind. And in the catastrophic impact that the loss of their land spelled out for the Native Americans.

AN ANIMAL AND A ROPE

'The old man sat at the table and drank his cool, fresh wine.'[23] So begins the legend of the giants of Castle Nideck in the nineteenth-century poem by Adelbert von Chamisso. This relaxing evening drink comes to an abrupt end when the giant's daughter comes home from playing amidst the humans down on the plains of Alsace. When he sees what his daughter has brought home wrapped in her handkerchief, the lord of the castle is not amused. The child has plucked a farmer from his field, together with his plough and horses, and brought them home in her hankie. But farmers and horses are not for picking, the old man reprimands her: 'The farmer's no plaything; what were you thinking?'

The giants of theory might also have found the young girl's behaviour a little disconcerting. None of them would have come up with the idea of laying the entire agricultural network out on their desk: realism is fine, but please, only as a principle. The reason for this was the usual professional distortions in the division of labour. Anthropologists see the man, historians see the farmer, technologists see the plough and perhaps someone will even be interested in the harness, whereas nobody feels responsible for the horse. Ernst Bloch once

A mobile accessory, or: what's a cowboy without his horse?

Saddle up for the civil war: fighting near the Alcázar in Tòledo, 1936.
Photo: Hans Namuth, *Barricade, Toledo*, 1936.

remarked that an anthropology that focused only on people did not go far enough. But this design feature – or should we say this structural defect? – forms the basis of most writing on history: it puts man at the centre and isolates him from his animate and inanimate team mates and opponents in nature. How else to explain the fact that it has overlooked man's chief zoological partner in the business that philosophers like to call the 'making' of history?

So far, the exceptions to the rule of widespread hippophobia among historians, sociologists and anthropologists are rare: some examples include historians of technology such as Lynn White, Jr.,[24] early modern period specialists such as Peter Edwards,[25] urban historians such as Clay McShane and Joel Tarr[26] and military historians like Gene Marie Tempest.[27] Global history, both in its earlier incarnation (Arnold J. Toynbee) and in its more recent, contemporary version, has thus far developed very little horse sense. In the era of global electrification, it used the metaphor of the 'conductibility' of cultures and territories (Toynbee), while today, in the digital age, it speaks of the 'connectivity' of cultures (Jürgen Osterhammel and Akira Iriye). But all of these historians pay little attention to the central vector of every historical land power, the horse – the charge and the hardware of history. Even historians and theorists of communication such as Harold A. Innis (who grew up on a farm in Ontario), Marshall McLuhan and their followers have tended to overlook – together with the human messenger – the most important envoy and courier of such messages. Similarly, the history of communications, sublimated to the history of speed, prefers to interpret in terms of networks and systems,[28] which, of course, unlike van Gogh's *Tarascon Diligence (Stagecoach)* (Plate 29), can get by perfectly well without horses,[29] as if communications over large expanses could ever have been possible without fast and well-rested mounts (by regularly changing horses at post-houses). Weren't the numerous mounted messengers in Kafka's stories precisely this: *mounted* messengers?

But this die-hard anthropocentrism clings on. Even in the case of the newer, empirically minded theory of history, informed by Bruno Latour's 'symmetrical anthropology', which calls for the inclusion of non-human actors, we rarely find the most historically significant among those non-human actors being given the slightest credit.

Indeed, it seems as though even Latour himself, someone from whom equine history has much to learn, prefers to speak of *things* when he means non-human actors, although they appear in his comments on clouds, gods, spirits, ancestors and other beings,[30] mostly left un-categorized and unnamed. Hailing from Burgundy, Latour was a child of rural France. Nevertheless, he was not a farmer's child who grew up with ploughs and draught horses, but a son of the vineyards. His interest was not in animal breeding, but the cultivation of yeasts and microbes; it was not the cavalry school at Saumur that caught his attention, but the laboratory of Pasteur.

Nevertheless, Latour's symmetrical anthropology remains one of the best schools for the history of horses and mankind today. His teaching does indeed deal with the great divide in Western thought and how this trend should be reversed. What he means by this is 'the total separation of humans and non-humans' which is accompanied by the radical distinction between relative cultures and what is per-ceived as a universal culture. 'But', argues Latour, 'the *very notion of culture is an artifact created by bracketing Nature off.*'[31]

It is only when we calmly leave behind the artificial separation of the realm of culture (that which we understand as the domain of signs and meanings) from the realm of nature (the domain of beings and matter), and recognize that reality is always mixed, and that we open the way up to a historically and ecologically informed anthro-pology, one that no longer describes people in isolation from the other beings with whom they interact and counteract. 'All natures-cultures [sic] are similar in that they simultaneously construct humans, divinities and nonhumans. None of them inhabits a world of signs or symbols arbitrarily imposed on an external Nature known to us alone. None of them – and especially not our own – lives in a world of things. All of them sort out what will bear signs and what will not. If there is one thing we all do, it is surely that we construct both our human collectives and the nonhumans that surround them . . . No one has ever heard of a collective that did not mobilize heaven and earth in its composition, along with bodies and souls, property and law, gods and ancestors, powers and beliefs, beasts and fictional beings . . . Such is the ancient anthropological matrix, the one we have never abandoned.'[32]

The ancient anthropological matrix. This should not only include the other beings with whom humans interact – the gods, spirits, ancestors, animals – but also the tools, instruments and artefacts, the technological objects man uses to assert himself in the world and to stand up to the world, from the most basic combinations such as an animal and a rope through to the MRI scanner. Technology, wrote one of the most important students of Marc Bloch and Marcel Mauss, the agronomist, linguist and ethnologist André-Georges Haudricourt, 'is not a mechanical or physical science, it is a human science'.[33] It resonates like an echo in a remark made half a century later by Bruno Latour: 'The strange notion that society is formed only of human relations is a reflection of that other, no less strange, notion that technology consists entirely of non-human relationships.'[34]

As Haudricourt puts it, a technical object such as a vehicle is 'the result of human work, and human work is an interaction of movements; in this respect, technology represents a system of traditional, (i.e. neither natural nor instinctive) muscular movements. To investigate a device in a technical respect therefore means locating it within a certain number of such systems and then explaining how the object produced fulfils its practical function. A device is subject to two technical registers, a technology of making and one of usage.'[35] Before Haudricourt goes on to outline a typology of the combination of horse and carriage and its geographical distribution, he notes the two fundamental principles underlying the forms of transport involving horses and carts, namely *soutien* and *déplacement*,[36] or carrying and traction, as pack animal or draught animal. The distinction applies not only to the connection between horse and carriage, but also to the connection between horse and rider. The horse *carries* the rider, it raises him above the ground (or similar), and it carries him *away*, that is to say it *transports* him from here to there.

By reducing things to first principles in this way, we take the initial step towards effectively overcoming the *Great Divide* of culture and nature, symbols and things. If we take the beginning of the history of horses (which is in fact nothing more than a historical *anthro-hippology* – the history of humans expanded to include the history of the Equidae), where was its origin if not in the moment when for the first time a simple connection was made between a human and two non-human actors? The two non-human actors in this case were a rope and a horse. The affair between *Homo sapiens* and the Equidae began at the moment when, for the first time, a human being placed a rope or a belt between a horse's soft lips, slotting it into that space between the teeth – in which gap rests the potential of another entire history. At this moment, a technical connection was made, the fundamental step that paved the way for countless other technical, political, symbolic and emotional connections. In other words, a technical connection whose existence would form the basis for countless historical collectives (Latour) – and of all animal-human-technical connections it is surely the one that has most effectively pushed open the door to the realm of history (Spengler).

In his obituary of the scholar, who died in August 1996, Antoine de Gaudemar wrote that it was with astonishing candour that Haudricourt continued to ask himself during the course of his lifetime, 'if it was not the other creatures who had essentially educated mankind; if it were not the horses that had taught man to run, the frogs that had taught him to jump, and the plants that had taught him patience'.[37] Certainly, very few thinkers had posed the question of the emergence and transmission of knowledge in such radical terms. Haudricourt had managed to demonstrate the obligatory causal web that is spun from an 'invention' such as the connection between an animal and a rope. One first practical application of being able to catch and tame an animal is hunting: suddenly, man was equipped with a much faster, more effective and more resourceful hunting partner. The second practical application was traction. 'If one can catch an animal and put it on a leash, it is not difficult to use it to pull something. Of course, prior to the use of animal traction there existed virtually no object or land vehicle to be pulled. The history of harnessing animals is linked inseparably with the history of these vehicles and other objects pulled by draught animals'[38] In other words, this knowledge spreads and evolves dynamically in networks of technologies and technical devices which are causally inspired by that original knowledge. And vice versa, seemingly elementary technical objects can only be used effectively in the context of the accompany-ing practical knowledge – handling instructions as it were, as we see in Heidegger's analysis of the 'readiness-to-hand' of a hammer in *Being and Time*.[39] Indeed, the phenomena that we call 'things' are in fact form-mediated syntheses of knowledge and matter, or knowl-edge networks with an object-like physical appearance.

Out of the Picture

CONSPICUOUS BY ITS ABSENCE

A joke from old Eastern Europe. A Jew comes out of the railway station and a carter gives him a lift to the nearby shtetl. The road is steep and after a while the driver climbs down and walks alongside his cart. Eventually he even takes the Jew's suitcase down and starts carrying it. A short stretch later, he says to the passenger, 'The hill is very steep and my horse is old. It's hard for him. Would you mind walking for the last stretch?' The passenger dismounts and walks along beside the driver, deep in thought. Finally he says, 'I don't get it. I am here because I need to go to the shtetl. You are here because you, *nebbich*, want to earn some money. But why is the horse here?'[1]

Why is the horse there? Indeed, it may be that the passenger already fears the carter's next request: might he have to pull the cart himself the rest of the way? With Beckett, this would be the next logical step. The sensitive carter's horse is present, and yet also eerily absent. A horse that is not carrying or pulling anything, that is just walking alongside – what is the point of that? Is it even a real horse? But the horse is not simply walking along; it is, after all, still drawing the cart. Its harness, its bridle, the cart – all that is still there. It is only its idiosyncratic purpose that has vanished into thin air, its logistic function between the station and the shtetl. Its being a carthorse is lost somewhere along the way, its *meaning*. Two helpless men follow a cart, in front of which walks a weary horse, and one of them carries a suitcase.

In the late nineteenth century, the horse starts disappearing from paintings, slowly at first and in instalments. Historical painting clings on tenaciously. First it is just the tack that starts to disappear – the harness or the bridle. More than in other genres, this omission of physical objects is tangible. The images start to feel empty. Painting trains itself in the art of omission, in a way that has not been seen since Stubbs; and hot on its heels is photography. Daumier sets the ball rolling: his 1868 painting of Don Quixote (Plate 30) depicts the knight as a faceless figure on an old nag, which has a saddle but no reins. In one hand he holds his shield like a palette, in the other he clutches a lance like a brush. How is he going to hold onto the horse as well?

When, forty years later, Picasso paints a boy leading a horse (Plate 28), he leaves out the elements which would indicate the act of *leading*: his horse has neither reins nor bridle. And yet the position of the boy's hand seems to suggest their presence. The lone Castor – or is it Pollux? – still has the age-old stance of a man leading a horse in his desired direction. But the device, the technical instrument, for steering is omitted, and the viewer of the image experiences how his perception and stored cultural knowledge involuntarily replaces the missing part.

We also find images where the horse itself is absent, but can be inferred from its attributes like a historical casting mould. Things are only the limits of man, says Nietzsche, but things set a limit on domestic animals too. In the *Tarascon Diligence (Stagecoach)*, painted by Vincent van Gogh in 1888, we find a stagecoach in the deserted midday heat of a southern French marketplace (Plate 29). The horses have been unharnessed, presumably led to a water trough by the driver or someone from the post-house. They're out of view, but we still have a presentiment of their presence, we can feel it with all our senses: their smell still lingers in the air. Their presence remains tangible as long as we can see the garland of limiting things that turn an animal without properties into an old coach-horse.

Then we come to photography, which flaunts its sovereignty in the art of omission. What might have become of the horse of the German Uhlan officer who is being led by the French infantry as a prisoner of war to Amiens prison (see p. 338)? A lost, riderless animal with reins chafing? A bloated corpse with stiff legs and a blood-encrusted coat swarming with flies? Amidst the heavy tread of the *poilus*, the cavalryman prances lightly like a jockey in sleek boots; the slight injury to the head does not seem to trouble him. His gaze is bright, almost cheerful; for him the war is over. The sabre is gone from his side, all rank insignia *perdu*, tunic half-open – he could almost be on his way out for an aperitif or a rendezvous. But no, he is the infantry's trophy in their triumphal procession. He has made their day: the infantry have caught their old mounted nemesis like a rabbit and are parading their booty through the streets. There's no horse anywhere to be seen, and yet the animal's presence is unmistakable: we can almost see the horse between the bowed legs of the rider; the form is clearly outlined in this hollow mould.

The next photo, taken by Hans Namuth in 1936 (see p. 345), is from the Spanish Civil War. A Republican brigade has entrenched itself by the Alcázar of Toledo. Behind a huge barricade of saddles, bits of carts and wheels, a light infantry troop is in operation; one aims, another smokes. But where have they got all these saddles that they're using as a bullet trap? Where are the horses that are missing their saddles and have lost their carts? Are they tied up loosely around the next corner, because they are useless when it comes to street combat? Or are they lying somewhere with bloated bellies, dead in the sun, devoured by the catastrophe of one last, unsuccessful cavalry charge? Are the militants in the picture dismounted cavalrymen or are they irregulars who have plundered the arsenal next door? Again the horse is the great absentee, inferred from the symbols of its erstwhile presence, from the relics of its tack.

Even more telling is its tacit presence in the film still from a Western (see p. 345). A lone ranger crosses the desert, the mountains loom in the background, clouds gather above. The man drags his load pitifully: a bag or a saddle blanket in his left hand, a saddle and bridle in his right. He was a cowboy until very recently. Where is his horse now? What can have become of him? Stolen, run away, killed? The lonely portrait is silent on the matter. This enhances the eloquence with which the absent friend, the missing mount, is brought into the game. 'The spur, the bit, the whip: more than any other animal,' writes historian Reviel Netz, 'the horse was surrounded by human tools.'[2] And just as we once saw the insignia of a king in his riding regalia, so too can we infer from this tack the presence of its wearer and object: the horse. Now it's the dismounted cowboy who has to haul it along, and is made a fool of in the process. A cultural artefact of equestrian accessories refined over centuries is reduced to a heap of scrap in his weighted-down arms. At the same time, the heap of scrap betrays his hope of finding another horse that would raise his status from the laughable pedestrian in the Hollywood desert to rise again as the king of the prairie.

The horse in these examples is replaced by an ellipsis, a suggestion of an animal in the space left intentionally blank. The network is there; only the central protagonist is missing. Omitted as a subject, the horse can be inferred from the margins, from the context of the objects that define it, be it saddles or a stagecoach. In other cases, the horse is present only in the form of an abstract proxy. This brings us to the hobby horse, a stick with a wooden horse's head which served to provide the equestrian socialization of young boys until well into the twentieth century. The repository of proxy steeds also includes the abstract horse's torso, a wooden barrel with a diameter corresponding to the girth of a fully-grown riding horse, which throughout the nineteenth century furnished the studios of painters who specialized in equestrian portraits: a mount that now slumbers in the archives of historical museums.

What might Goethe have had in mind when he acquired the tall, saddle-shaped writing stool for his Weimar Garden House (see p. 355)? Did he have such fond memories of composing verse while on horseback or on long carriage rides that he sought to recreate the riding posture, perhaps to summon poetic inspiration? One might indeed speculate that it was 'not in vain' that Goethe ordered a custom-built 'saddle-like pedestal for sitting at his tall writing desk in the summer house'.[3] This four-legged wooden stool with an upholstered seat was unmistakably a riding chair, on which, as Friedrich Justin Bertuch wrote, 'one would sit with legs astride as though on a saddle'.[4] To the modern-day spectator, Goethe's writing/riding stool expresses a degree of abstraction that seems like a rather crude and yet insightful anticipation of Bauhaus furniture. 'The poet as a tour guide through the German classics,' writes the critic Walter Benjamin of a book by Max Kommerell, had taught him 'how much time the

Riding as literary inspiration: Goethe's writing stool in his Garden House.

'The *coup de grâce*': Ernst Jünger's caption to this photo
from the First World War.

writers spent on horseback'.[5] It's a sentence that remains a mystery until you see Goethe's riding stool.

Another, historically later and indeed apocalyptic, version of the proxy horse is offered by Stanley Kubrick in *Dr. Strangelove or: How I Learned to Stop Worrying and Love the Bomb* (1964). Shortly before the end of the film, the fatal B-52 bomber pilot (for whom there is no recall code) appears dressed as a Texan cowboy, waving his hat, riding his nuclear warhead into Armageddon. His horse, already on the way to becoming an arrow, a mere symbol, rematerializes again briefly in the shape of a missile. It is the hobby horse of the nuclear age, whose warhead is about to pulverize the Soviet Union, triggering the doomsday device.

How durable is an entry in our collective memory? For how long after the end of the horse era will people be able to discern the contour of a horse in unprepossessing relics and references? What remains when the creeping amnesia of the virtual era deletes the traces of our former shared memory? An afterlife can be long, and the imaginary has a different viscosity to that of the real. But must it not have consequences for people's lives and their feelings when the most important non-human body, their former companion, in whom they have so long recognized themselves and misunderstood themselves, is no longer there? Their old friend with whom they had been through thick and thin, who had comforted and rescued them, kicked and bitten them: who in future would show these people what it means to have a body, a rhythm and a world? 'This desire', writes Paul Virilio, 'for a *foreign body* following as it does the desire for the *different body* of heterosexuality seems to me a major event on a number of points, comparable to the invention of fire, but an innovation that has been lost in the obscurity that surrounds animality.'[6]

DRAGGING ONWARDS

The journey to the shtetl drags on and on. The dry timber of the roughly built cart groans, the axles squeak, two men trudge behind, sweating. Even the horse up front is exhausted, but it keeps plodding on, hauling its absurd fare. What else can it do? It's not as if it has its

own travel plans these days, after all. In earlier times, when it still
knew its own mind, it would run off for a little jaunt from time to
time, stopping to hide around the corner and soak up the sun while
its people were out looking for it, cursing. But those good times are
over. Alone among all animals, writes the poet Albrecht Schaeffer,
the horse 'is tragic in its appearance':[7] tragic because it has completely
dispensed with its freedom and its free will. The dog may have done
the same, but at least that animal knows its purpose: to serve its master. The horse, on the other hand, knows 'that it would like to be
free . . . but the burden is neverending, and it is rarely allowed to run
and has to stand there even when it is frightened and when it is seized
by the urge to return to its nature, to flee . . . It is trapped in eternal
captivity, always overshadowed by an inescapable will to which it
resigns itself without ever realizing.'[8]

In Schaeffer's eyes, the horse is torn like the hero of a Greek tragedy,
trapped in a timeless bondage that forces it to defy its nature: its desire
to escape and run. The will of the horse is broken, and not only its
will. There may still be mares and occasionally genuine stallions but,
argues Schaeffer, the real incarnation of the domesticated horse is the
gelding, the stunted eunuch, in whom 'defiance and stubbornness,
freedom and volatility are no longer essentially active characteristics,
but merely a memory'.[9] The dialectic at work here is certainly that of
master and slave, but the horse is a servant whose master has no need
to fear resistance or treachery. And yet, Schaeffer continues, this animal held in perpetual captivity is seen by us as the epitome of all in
nature that embodies nobility and magnanimity, stature, pride and
courage.

The paradox that Schaeffer puzzles over, seeing it as nothing other
than tragic, lies in the situation of the domesticated animal that is so
often put to work in contexts that are contrary to its nature and its
natural instincts; but is also linked to the horse's double talent as
bearer of both physical and metaphorical burdens, the object of
countless historical tributes and attributes. This includes, not least,
the countless predicates of nobility with which the horse is credited
(beauty, purity, pride . . .), attributes which have a certain hold on us,
and this author is no exception. Nor did these qualities escape the
many authors who contributed in their own small ways to give equine

literature and iconography a veneer of glory and to make the horse a prominent object in the display case of our visual memory. Man has given dazzling roles to other animals in his worlds of desire and delusion; the lion can sing a throaty desert song or two about that.[10] Instead of giving the dove the role of sexual maniac in the Garden of Eden,[11] mankind has entrusted that naturally dense bird with a peace mission; conversely, we have associated the often harmless, non-venomous, albeit vole-guzzling snake with the Old Testament's general suspicion of malice.

The horse, this creature with an infinite capacity for being sentimentalized, has long occupied an established position in the Almanach de Gotha of the animal kingdom. A supposedly peace-loving vegetarian with an attractive build and pleasant scent, its faeces included, the horse stands for everything people see as beautiful, good and noble, qualities which they like to imagine pervade their own nature. The horse has always embodied man's nobler side, his better self; for that reason, we cannot bear to see a horse suffer. This ennobling instinct has also erased from man's memory the fact that there can be bad-tempered horses. Indeed, this was common knowledge to horse connoisseurs such as Hans Baldung Grien, Hugo von Hofmannsthal and John Wayne, as well as to that new recruit to the English cavalry who wrote to his bride that at the front and the back the horse was a very dangerous animal and in the middle it was uncomfortable. In contrast, given the horse's constant nodding of the head, philosopher Otto Weininger reached the conclusion that an animal with such a penchant for saying yes must represent insanity. After a short comparison of the supposedly insane animal with the dog, though, Weininger was ready to concede that the horse was an intrinsically *aristocratic* animal, since it was 'very selective in its choice of sexual partners'.[12]

The nineteenth century witnessed not only the starkest increase in the number of actual used-up and worn-down horses in history, but also strong growth in metaphorically weary animals. There was hardly a single idea that moved the century that was not in some way connected with horses. It began with an obsession of historic proportions, the worship of 'world-historical individuals' (Hegel) and the whole range of ideas associated with sovereignty and heroes on horseback. It continued through the notions of freedom and progress up to images of fear and passion – not forgetting compassion, of course. It seemed as though horses could and would have to carry every kind of emotional burden: man's hopes and fears, his elation and his lamentation. The horse is probably, after the human being, by far the most vividly described creature and the one ascribed with an ever-growing list of qualities – the re-semanticized being par excellence. And then there was always the enigmatic form that remained unmerged with all the written emphasis and paraphrasis, the creature of flesh and blood, the living metaphor, that wants to be loved, cherished and cared for, and that we cannot bear to see die. The metaphor that can give us comfort or rip us apart with anguish. 'Tactile, furry, yellow' – as tangible as the lion that appears in the flesh to the philosopher Blumenberg one night.[13]

In Florence in the late nineteenth century there lived a man who was particularly sensitive to the enormous impact of very slight details, such as the minutiae in a painting. Throughout his research career he sought to make sense of the economics of human passions, insofar as it formed the idiosyncratic stuff of art. Aby Warburg, to whom art history owes the concept of the *pathos formula*, recognized even as a student that the painters and sculptors of the early Renaissance had harvested from the ancient world, particularly from sculptures and reliefs on sarcophagi, triumphal arches and pillars, those idiosyncratic formulae of body language with which antiquity conveyed such emotions as sadness, anger or rage. Without concerning themselves with the archaeological origins or the ancient significance of the sculptures, the Florentine artists of the Renaissance interpreted them with a new vital and emotional dynamic, by which they often transformed a theatrically exaggerated and intentional pathos into a laboured, 'mannered' rhetoric.[14] Touched, or even infected, by the excitement of the ancient formulae, artists such as Botticelli, Pollaiuolo and Donatello translated them into modern characters and contexts such as elegant interiors. Reframing these formulae, they granted themselves all the licence of a contemporary sovereign. They treated the ancient formulae, gestures and means of expression as malleable morphemes with which new languages could be constructed. While the artists were translating the ancient inventory of emotional modes of expression (the pathos formulae) into a language of the present, they *processed the stimulus*, as Niklas Luhmann might have put it. And the horse frequently played a supporting role as the privileged 'second'.

Because the majority of the classical images that Warburg considered stemmed either from sarcophagi or triumphal arches and pillars, they were dominated by articulations of sorrow, of struggle and of victory. Besides these, Warburg collected expressions of violence and sexual frenzy, in mythical poses modelled by centaurs and maenads. In most of these scenes, especially those of struggle and triumph, the horse plays a key supporting role in carrying and conveying the 'tragic pathos of Greek mythology'. The central figures are often, especially when it comes to the depiction of battles, composite figures of humans and animals (as mounts), while male-dominated scenes of violence have centaurs appearing as single-person hybrids and energetic ciphers ('primordial symbols of female-ravishing animality').[15]

Even Warburg's first seminar paper as a student of art history and classical architecture focused on the representations at Olympia and the Parthenon of battles between centaurs and Lapiths, where the fascinated young student noted the 'animal strength' with which the 'centaur grips his victim and the savage desire which even approaching death cannot stifle . . .'[16] Along with all the honorary titles awarded to him, Warburg can justifiably be credited not only with discovering a troubled, strife-torn, passion-filled antiquity, but also with rediscovering the horse as a privileged conveyor of the formulae of passion.

Energy, knowledge, pathos – the three economies. Is it legitimate to explore them in isolation from one another? If it's a heuristic approach or perhaps a simplification that we're after, then yes. But reality does not respect such divisions. Whichever way we look at it, we don't inhabit the world theoretically in the same way that we *somehow* cope with it in practical terms. Perhaps it's because we tend to underestimate the gravity of the *somehow*. When equine history is investigated in isolation and in all its contexts and connections, we see a constant overlap and intersection of economies and categories which we might prefer, for the sake of theoretical convenience, to keep separate. But why should the connoisseurship of horse owners and breeders be any less dominated by passion than that of people who love beautiful women, operas or collecting autographs? Are the practices of horse breeding not objects of the history of ideas as much as they are an expression of traditional empiricism? What are the artefacts of horse history such as saddles, harnesses and types of carriage if not objects of cultural and anatomical knowledge in material form?

As long as we go about trading, assessing, appraising and comparing, in the immanence of equine knowledge, in stables, market halls and libraries, it does not occur to us to divide up and classify the phenomena that are revealed to us fleetingly. There's a pattern here: we say this is a fact, a scientifically tested one, and that over there, that's just ideas or images or feelings. Instead, we process emotions and experience the charge of what we encounter as reality in very imprecise categories. We experience this flowing charge as here and now, a present tense that is at every moment shaded with values and tempered with emotions. Our ability to orient ourselves is based largely on instinct and our practical sense of the 'somehow or other'.[17] This does not amount to what the Marxists called 'false consciousness'. On the contrary, we falsify reality the moment we shift to the mode that we consider 'theoretical' and switch to the great distinctions such as *res extensae* v. *intensae*, things in themselves v. things for our sake, hardware v. software. But the astonishing thing about the history of horses lies precisely in the fact that it familiarizes us with an object or rather a rich phenomenon heavily laden with tradition that constantly circumvents the great distinctions, or – as befits the species – jumps over them. This means that equine history reminds us, again and again, in a gentle manner, and sometimes in a not so gentle manner ('Horses will be horses . . .') of the initial stage of recognition: astonishment.

Astonishment not least about how heteroclite an entire, huge body of knowledge based on centuries of empirical research and tradition can be, how impure and how true. For those who believe that knowledge is truer the purer it is, and the less emotional impulses are involved in the 'cognitive subject', equine history offers a lesson in realism. The idea of a pure science, Michel Serres once said, is pure myth. Readers and devotees of the Old Testament know that love and

An animal of dust: Poland, 1939, a horse in the inferno.

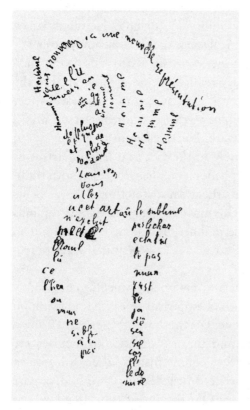

An animal of words:
Calligrammes, Apollinaire,
1918.

knowledge are not mutually exclusive – on the contrary. The same applies to the history of the horse; it, too, is full of impure knowledge mixed with love. Objectivity, the ascetic switching off of that which is sentient, touched or excited, comes up against its natural limit, passion. The cognitive subject is supposed to eliminate itself? Tell that to an enthusiast, a collector, a connoisseur. No, a field of study interests us so much more when knowledge and emotion are intimately and inextricably linked.

Herodotus

THE GELDING AS CRITIC

Since the Queen had little time to spare, the painter and his model agreed on a limited number of sittings. Although the project in question was a small-format portrait, these sittings stretched over a period of eighteen months, from May 2000 to December 2001. The portrait was not a commission by the royal family and, when it was finished, Lucian Freud presented it to the Queen as a gift. He didn't want there to be the slightest doubt about his personal independence. Freud and Elizabeth spent the sessions engaged in lively conversation. There was no lack of topics, as both loved horses and dogs. Queen Elizabeth II has been a true horsewoman all her life, like her Renaissance namesake.[1] Some of Freud's most impressive images show naked people surrounded by their sleeping or dozing dogs, but he also had a strong connection with horses. He began riding early in life and later became a notorious frequenter of the racetrack and the betting shop, gambling away vast sums. Besides painting and his countless affairs, this was the third passion of his life. Several of the fleshy men in his paintings are bookmakers and shady figures from the turf. As a painter, Freud was a perfectionist; sittings for a portrait could easily eat up hundreds of hours. The animals he painted also had to be extraordinarily patient, spending days in his studio, unless he chose to work in their stables, where he did indeed paint a handful of his great horse portraits in the last decade of his life.[2] These include *Grey Gelding*, a portrait he painted in 2003.

A photo from the same year (Plate 31) shows Freud leading his model to the well-advanced portrait on the canvas. Both protagonists, the painter and the sitter, are clothed in similar tones, somewhere between a dirty white and grey. The colour of Freud's hands is reflected in that of the horse's nostrils, while its brown leather bridle corresponds to the patterned silk scarf loosely looped around the artist's neck. But the 'partner look' shared by the two is limited to garment and flesh tones. When it comes to art and its appraisal, the two go their separate ways. While the painter's focus is directed to the image, the horse turns its head away, its eyes closed – a look of disinterest or reluctance. There's no trace of the lively and jolly-looking animal of the portrait; in contrast with its painted image, the living gelding is playing dead.

It is not the first time that Lucian Freud, grandson of the founder of psychoanalysis, has posed before the camera, creating a *tableau vivant* of a narrative, myth or legend. We have a whole cluster of stories here, where the *pictor doctus* appears both as stage director composing the scene and in a cameo role as the subject. Two young scholars from his grandfather's Viennese circle, Ernst Kris and Otto Kurz, once collected and analysed such narratives,[3] and of course the grandchild of Sigmund Freud must have been keenly aware of the interrelationships at play between them. Kris and Kurz's focus was mainly on the short stories and anecdotes which emerged in the earliest literature on art, given literary form by authors such as Plato, Xenophon and Pliny, and later retold by Vasari. These placed the artist himself, his origins, his inspirations and his talent, at the centre of the narrative. Especially popular were accounts where art was conceived of as *mimesis*, an imitation or mimicry of nature, and which conjured up fabulous tales of the animal subjects themselves, deceived by their own portrait, barking at their artificial companion, running away from it or trying to copulate with it. 'It is almost impossible', write Kris and Kurz, 'to estimate the frequency with which this anecdote and similar ones occur. We already meet it in antiquity in a number of variations: a stallion attempts to mount a mare painted by Appeles; quails fly at a picture on which Protogenes has painted a quail in the background; the painted picture of a snake silences the twittering of birds . . .'[4]

It is almost as if Bernhard Grzimek, zoologist and behavioural scientist, in his experiments with animals and horses in particular, was inspired by the ancient literature on art. In the early 1940s, as an army veterinary surgeon in Berlin and in occupied Poland, Grzimek undertook experiments showing living animals first a stuffed horse, then painted portraits, to see how they reacted to these dummies.[5] The results would have delighted Pliny: the horses showed animated curiosity towards not only the stuffed animal, but also their painted counterparts. They looked at, sniffed and touched the artworks and kept coming back to them. There was just one elderly mare who showed complete indifference, and initially Grzimek thought that made her intelligent enough to see through the deception, until he realized she did not show any interest in her living companions either.

The grey gelding led by Lucian Freud to its portrait is also either indifferent or hostile. Now, one might argue that this is not the first time he's been introduced to his portrait, after all. As the model, he will have seen it several times throughout the process of its creation. In short, the horse is bored. Or is he responding as a critic, like the monkeys painted by Gabriel von Max? Is he expressing his displeasure at the portrait, intimating to the artist that he is not a second Apelles? Has the horse even recognized who is represented in this likeness? Has he recognized *himself* in the painting? It's a difficult question that should probably be answered in the negative. Not many animal species undergo the moment of realization experienced by a human child aged between twelve and eighteen months, famously described by Jacques Lacan as the 'mirror stage',[6] when, with a cry of joy, the child recognizes the other person as an image *of itself.* Freud's gelding might have been expected not only to show an interest in his depicted colleague, like Grzimek's horses, but even to experience his mirror stage in the presence of Freud's canvas and give a jubilatory neigh as if to exclaim, 'Gosh, that's me!' But apparently the intelligence of the beautiful animal does not extend quite that far.

The study of animal intelligence has long moved beyond the stage of the experiments that a hundred years ago accompanied the rise and fall of Clever Hans. Today, horses are no longer required to learn to read or calculate square roots to prove their mental agility. Indeed, this dated concept of intelligence has been replaced by that of *cognition.* The field of equine cognition studies combines research into the physiology of horses, the functioning of the senses, the nerve cells and the brain, with questions of ethology, or behavioural science.

From this deeper ethological understanding are derived recommendations for dealing with animals – advice which is often directly compatible with the teachings of writers of generations past, from Xenophon through to the English and French riding instructors of the seventeenth century (Cavendish, de la Guérinière), and which relies on gentleness and understanding of the animal rather than on compulsion and severity (as with the sixteenth-century Italian school of Grisone).[7]

The invention of the Turing machine by Alan Turing in 1936 – the same year that Lacan coined the term 'mirror stage', which also involves a kind of feedback concept – and the ensuing 'cognitive revolution' triggered by cybernetics have, since the 1950s, led to an impressive acceleration and differentiation in the way we explore how horses perceive their environment, how they interpret their sensory perceptions, how they interact with their peers, their environment and other species, including humans.[8] Research into the cognition of different species of mammals has overcome the divide that Descartes tore through living nature. For some years now, this field of study has even been undoing the double bond which is so fiercely defended by philosophy: the association of consciousness with thinking and thinking with language. Research into the evolution of human intelligence[9] owes as much, if not more, to studies into the behavioural ecology and cognitive ethology of monkeys, dogs and horses, as to human psychology and ethnology. The horse – for 6,000 years our primary mode of transport – is still a great conveyor of knowledge: our friend, our companion and teacher.

Besides behavioural ecology and cognition studies, the search for fields which offer the most potential for equine studies now and for the future also brings us back to archaeology.[10] Many regions and cultures of the world have a history only because of archaeology. This includes the regions to which all horse cultures of history, from the Arabian to the American, can trace their roots: the vast areas to the north and east of the Black Sea and Caspian Sea and the huge land mass of Central Asia. For the historical events and evolutions in these parts of the world, researchers have very few written sources at their disposal, among them Herodotus' *Histories*. Finding evidence of the ancient history that stretches much further back than the use of writing, the history of the colonization of these territories, the establishment of sovereign states, the birth of countless languages and the invention of hunting and war techniques, all relies on patient prospecting by archaeologists.[11] This includes breakthroughs in palae-ontology and historical zoology over the last fifty years regarding the early history of the coexistence of humans and horses.

Historians who have studied the history of people in the period over which equine history extends, such as the medievalist Hermann Heimpel and the historical theorist Reinhart Koselleck, have regis-tered the tone and the unusual tension that history acquires as soon as they broaden their field of observation to include an awareness of the horse. As Koselleck recognized,[12] the horse was an outstanding agent of modernization. Without the horse's role in the dynamics of production, circulation and warfare, it would have been much harder to usher in the wave of modernization in the late eighteenth century – the notorious 'saddle period' – and it certainly would have developed differently than under the circumstances in which horses met the demand for kinetic energy.

On the other hand, as Hermann Heimpel strongly reiterates,[13] horses represent bridges to the past, offering a connection to the time of Charlemagne and beyond to the earliest periods of humanity's his-tory. Horses link the man of 'late culture', as formulated by Heimpel's contemporary, the philosopher Arnold Gehlen, with the 'primitive man' who had first domesticated the animals. Horses were not only agents of modernization in the most recent period, beginning roughly with Napoleon, they were also *agents de liaison* connecting us with the earliest stages of that realm we call history. During this entire period, horses have been our companions, our fellow travellers and fellow sufferers. Indeed, in retrospect it almost seems as though they have enabled something like solidarity between modern man and his Neolithic ancestors: do the nodding, snorting creatures pawing at the ground not place us side by side with the inhabitants of Botai and Dereivka? Together with man, horses opened up the realm of history, and at the point when it looked like it was all coming to an end (from the point of view of conservative thinkers), Equidae and human parted ways. Meanwhile, we've put the theories of the 'end of history' behind us, and history, instead of ending silently or disappearing into the archives, has certainly marched onwards, albeit more generally without horses than with them. However, our perception of history has changed: it seems at once both to have expanded spatially and to have shrunk chronologically over time.

On the threshold of modernity, as the many histories of the ancient world found their way into the collective singular of *one* history, the geographical expanse of history was still largely focused on Europe and Asia Minor and limited culturally to the realm of the written word. The pre-literate peoples and regions of the world were by definition *ahistorical*. Since then, the scope of history has continually expanded to encompass the globe as an entirety. The modern techniques of historical epistemology, which owe much to archaeology, ethnology, palaeo-biology and other precise scientific fields, have blown open the closed doors of philology and textual criticism to such an extent that possession or non-possession of a written script is no longer a deciding factor for having a voice in history. The scope of history, which until relatively recently could still be thought of as a closed solar system, where everything orbited around the deeds and woes of those peoples who possessed a system of written chronicling, found itself suddenly expanding to encompass the larger evolutionary contexts of pre-literate humanity, of animals, plants, landscapes and continents. The image of history as it had been taught until very recently at school suddenly looked crumpled and shrivelled, rather like Max Ernst's *Europe After the Rain*.

Although history has responded to these challenges, much remains to be done. When looking for new ways to think about history and describe it, we ought not to overlook the oldest approaches. Perhaps, after all, it is time to read Herodotus again. Hardly any other author of ancient literature has become as topical as the incomparable chronicler from Halicarnassus. No matter how far and wide the narrator of 'countless legends' travelled or how much he saw with his own eyes, whether he truly fact-checked his stories or simply made most of it up, he did at least – like very few who followed in his footsteps – raise his head above the parapet of all-too-*human* history. Herodotus, who felt the sting of exile four centuries before Ovid, also shared with him a love of spinning a yarn and a firm belief in the gods and the fates. He collected trusted tips for gold mining – relying on giant ants or young girls with feathers – and meticulously noted the wedding rites, mating customs and death cults of the peoples he encountered. He tells of the horse oracle that brought Darius to the throne,[14] and of the Scythians' custom of burying their rulers together with their horses.[15] Stallions and mares, as he knew, had lead roles in the cast of history; they lent sovereignty to kings and were interred alongside them.

Posterity has been both kind and cruel to Herodotus. He has been praised as much as chastised. His detractors would expose him as a writer of fiction or criticize him for his hellenocentricism. It cannot be denied that he sometimes described the life and customs of the peoples on the fringes of the known world rather as an entomologist would describe the impulses and appetites of a rare beetle. But perhaps his anthropological myopia is less significant than his hyperopia with regard to the natural and preternatural. Perhaps, rather than protecting Herodotus against his critics, we need to defend him against his admirers. His devotees included, in particular, humanists such as Wolfgang Schadewaldt, who in his Tübingen lecture praised the 'father of history' (Cicero). Herodotus, he argued, was the first to understand that he was dealing 'with all these things as they have occurred at the hands of people, and thus with history as one great people-occurrence'.[16] So, did he see Herodotus as the inventor of history as the cosmos of humanity, an early precursor of Giambattista Vico? But what if a modern-day reader were to find contemporary relevance in this ancient author in the very fact that his field of view was not restricted to mankind alone? In fact, one should read Herodotus for other reasons, as endorsed by late humanism: from him we learn the art of a compelling historic narrative with not only human protagonists as its subject, but also stones, clouds and gods. And, indeed, horses.

History is acquainted with many different actors: some are huge composite bodies, composed like an army of dozens of divisions and thousands of men with tanks and typewriters, while others are minuscule and inconspicuous, like a pill or a cloud of microbes. Some live a thousand years, others a mere couple of hours. Ultimately, historians must decide for themselves whether to allow horses more space in the scenes they conjure up of the past; horses are, after all, just one species of historical actor among many. When we consider

But why is the horse here? *Iphigenia*, Joseph Beuys, 1973.
Photo: Abisag Tüllmann.

The idea of the horse: *La querelle des universaux*, René Magritte, 1928.

the significance they took on over time and what they achieved in their alliance with mankind, we have to admit that they were a very special kind of actor: particularly fast, particularly steeped in history and particularly beautiful. Herodotus was astute in seeing this.

A HORSE PASSES ON

Westphalia after the Second World War was anything but an island of the blessed. The impression of peace, the memory of the nineteenth century – these were but mirages. The forests, where the last remaining units of the Wehrmacht had been surrounded by the Americans, were full of discarded or superficially buried weapons and crates of ammunition. Despite being strictly forbidden, we country boys sought out and found in the woods the toxic moraine heaped up by the war. We compiled our own secret arsenals, and occasionally someone would blow himself up with his stockpile. My grandfather knew what we were up to and kept mum. In a drawer in his workshop, he had two battered bullets from an aircraft machine gun. An English fighter plane had shot at him and his horse when they were out ploughing in March 1945. He was hurled into a furrow and the animals bolted, but by some miracle were all unharmed. As fascinated as I usually was by tales of the war, this was one story I did not like hearing. The smashed-up bullets, encrusted with soil from the field, sent a chill down my spine. One of the two horses from then was still in my grandfather's stable. I could picture the look of terror on his face, and imagined what it would have been like if he had been hit – the sudden burning and the blood on his dun coat. I pictured how he would have lain in the field, helplessly trying to rear up in his harness while still hitched up to the wooden plough and the other horse. The actor in the network, dying.

I did once see a horse writhing in its own blood. It was a slender brown mare named Cora, one of the most beautiful animals I ever rode as a child. My mother would take her out hacking in the week while her real owner, a building contractor from the nearby city who had come into some money, was off managing his diggers and building sites. Gentle-natured, with something of a sense of humour, Cora used to get up to mischief from time to time: she had a pronounced tendency to leap over the fence of her pasture when the whim took her, to go and have a little explore. On one of these impromptu outings, she got caught up in some barbed wire which a farmer was about to use to replace the fence around his sheep's field and had left lying on the ground. The mare lay on the ground – the tendons of both front legs lacerated, her dark brown legs covered in blood – looking around wildly, her eyes full of a desperate plea for help. The forester who was passing by, a former sergeant in the Wehrmacht, offered to shoot her, and the village policeman, alerted by the neighbours, proposed the same solution. It was the intervention of her owner that saved the injured mare's life. By the evening, he had arranged for her to be transported to what was then the most sophisticated veterinary clinic in the area, where Cora was carefully nursed back to health after weeks suspended in straps. When fully healed and back on her feet, she returned to the farm and resumed her old way of life in her field, with the fences slightly increased in height. But the look of that desperate animal, the blood on the grass and the voices of men all talking about shooting her continued to haunt my dreams for a long time to come.

Who can bear to see a horse in agony? The horse, that tragic animal – the sight of its death is unbearable. Its long legs buckling as it sinks down to its knees. The slow collapse of its great body, the broken look in its eyes – nobody can bear to look upon it. Horses are killed like soldiers; if too severely wounded, they are given the *coup de grâce*. But they are not gassed, and when this did happen, in Flanders in the First World War, it was unintentional, collateral damage, as we say today. Man reserves gassing for his own kind and for insects.

The sight of suffering animals chisels through the armour of the toughest soldier: 'I felt sorry for the horses, not the people. But I felt sorry for the horses till the very last day.'[17] There's hardly any reportage from the two world wars, barely a diary or a letter without an expression of lamentation for the horses. Did Goethe not feel the same? 'The badly injured animals could not die in peace,' he wrote of the campaign in France,[18] with a vivid description of the sufferings of the mortally wounded and cruelly mistreated animals. 'It seems', remarks Marlene Baum in her analysis of Goethe's poetics, 'as though the suffering inflicted by this war is exemplified and dramatically portrayed through the horses, as we find remarkably few corresponding examples of human suffering.'[19] For one and a half centuries, it seems – from Goethe to the Second World War – the suffering and death of horses was actually something of a formula for pathos, a means to convey the suffering of war per se. It provided a symbol for anyone who wished to enunciate the widespread suffering, but felt unable to voice that of their fellow man. But even those who wanted to shout their indictment loud and clear, like Picasso when he painted *Guernica*, could not do so without the image of the horse.

In a concise, almost taciturn, scene, barely longer than a page, Thomas Hardy describes the death of a horse. One night in May, in the early hours of the morning, the young Tess Durbeyfield is driving home on the narrow country roads of southern England, her sleeping brother beside her in the waggon. The old gelding Prince up-front pretty much knows the way by himself, so Tess closes her eyes, not noticing as she dozes off. Woken by a sudden jolt, she hears a hollow groan, sees a black mass on the road ahead and knows that something terrible has happened. The groans are coming from Prince, speared by the pointed shaft of the silently oncoming morning mail-cart, piercing his breast 'like a sword, and from the wound his life's blood was spouting in a stream, and falling with a hiss into the road'. Tess, in her despair, tries to close the wound with her hand, which only results in her being spattered all over with blood. 'Then she stood helplessly looking on. Prince also stood firm and motionless as long as he could; till he suddenly sank down in a heap.'[20] Tess's father refuses to sell his old horse to the knacker for a few shillings, and so the body of the dead Prince is buried in the garden the next day. The shadow of the dead horse looms over the young Tess for the rest of her life's journey.

I've never seen a horse die. But I did know one that for a long time was closer to death than to life. It was a large, strong draught horse, a Belgian stallion, a young animal of impetuous temperament and tremendous strength. That is, until the day in June 1954 when, while out mowing a meadow surrounded by a stone wall that had warmed up in the sun, he stepped on the tail of a sleeping adder. It was the last reported sighting of a venomous snake in these valleys of southern Westphalia; since then, it's thought that there are only harmless grass snakes and slow-worms in these parts. The last adder of Westphalia flared up like the devil and bit the stallion in the chest. The horse managed to get back to his stable unaided, then stood in his box, more dead than alive, swaying, but unable to lie down, too weak to eat a handful of oats, too feeble even to drink some water. For four weeks this heavy animal stood, sickly, miserable, poisoned to the very tips of his golden mane; even the vet, with all his experience of large animals, doubted he would survive. The owner would wake in the night and go to check whether his horse was still alive. The stallion, this mountain of a horse that seemed even bigger at night than by day, stood silently in his stall, swaying and staring into space with dull, clouded eyes. After four weeks, the animal gave a deep groan one morning and, at the site of the snakebite, the skin of his breast burst open and from the putrid wound out poured a gush of dark pus, several bucketsful of wound exudate. The stallion moved, and slowly, still dazed, he allowed himself to be led out of the box, into the open, where he stopped again, dazzled by the light and too weak to take another step. He had survived.

Notes

THE LONG FAREWELL

1. Cf. D. Edgerton, *The Shock of the Old. Technology and Global History since 1900*, London, 2006, pp. 32 ff.
2. M. Serres, *Erfindet Euch neu! Eine Liebeserklärung an die vernetzte Welt*, Berlin, 2013, p. 9.
3. Cf. E. R. Curtius, *Die französische Kultur. Eine Einführung*, Berne and Munich, 1975, pp. 6, 28 ff.
4. J. Clair, *Les derniers jours*, Paris, 2013, p. 135.
5. Ibid., p. 136.
6. Hegel gave this lecture for the first time in winter 1822–3, then on another four occasions, every two years (winters of 1824–5, 1826–7, 1828–9 and 1830–31).
7. Alexandre Kojève, Gottfried Benn, Arnold Gehlen.
8. Cf. A. Gehlen, 'Post-Histoire' (the transcript of an unpublished lecture from 1962), in H. Klages and H. Quaritsch (eds), *Zur geisteswissenschaftlichen Bedeutung Arnold Gehlens*, Berlin, 1994, pp. 885–98, here p. 891.
9. R. Koselleck, 'Der Aufbruch in die Moderne oder das Ende des Pferdezeitalters', in 'Historikerpreis der Stadt Münster 2003', Münster City Historian Prize booklet, 18 July 2003, pp. 23–37.
10. Ibid., p. 25.
11. Cf. I. Babel, *The Complete Works of Isaac Babel*, ed. N. Babel, translated by P. Constantine, New York and London, 2002.
12. H. Heimpel, 'Geschichte und Geschichtswissenschaft', *Vierteljahrshefte für Zeitgeschichte*, vol. 5, 1/1957, pp. 1–17, here p. 17.

I THE CENTAURIAN PACT—*ENERGY*
Hell for Horses

1. Cf. the elegant sculpture by Reinhold Begas, 1888, displayed in the garden of the Alte Nationalgalerie on Berlin's Museum Island; see pp. 269–71.

2. M. de Guérin, *Der Kentaur*, translated by Rainer Maria Rilke, Wiesbaden, 1950, pp. 14 f.

3. H.-E. Lessing, *Karl Drais: Zwei Räder statt vier Hufe*, Karlsruhe, 2010, p. 49. Cf. H.-E. Lessing, *Automobilität: Karl Drais und die unglaublichen Anfänge*, Leipzig, 2003; H.-E. Lessing, 'Die apokalyptischen Draisinenreiter', *Frankfurter Allgemeine Zeitung (FAZ)*, 29 April 2010, p. 9; H.-E. Lessing, 'Fahrräder sind die Überlebenden der Pferde', *FAZ* 30 October 2013, p. N4.

4. A. Mitscherlich, *Reiterbuch. Bilder, Gedanken und Gesänge*, Berlin, 1935, pp. 9 f.

5. Ibid., p. 84.

6. Ibid., p. 88.

7. Ibid. Unlike Timo Hoyer (*Im Getümmel der Welt: Alexander Mitscherlich – Ein Porträt*, Göttingen, 2008, p. 84), I would not emphasize a desire for freedom as one of the conceptual motifs that recur in Mitscherlich's later work. What links his *Reiterbuch* with the later, well-known texts by a more mature Mitscherlich is a deep scepticism of modern technology (cf. *Die Idee des Friedens und die menschliche Aggressivität*, Frankfurt am Main, 1970, pp. 131 f.) and an increasing tendency towards psycho-historical mourning (*Auf dem Weg zur vaterlosen Gesellschaft, Die Unfähigkeit zu trauern*).

8. Cf. the outstanding study by Silke Tenberg, 'Vom Arbeitstier zum Sportgerät: Zur Soziologie der Mensch-Pferd-Beziehung in der Moderne', University of Osnabrück, 2011.

9. Friedrich Schiller, *Schillers Werke, Nationalausgabe*, vol. XII, Weimar, 1982, pp. 89–107 and 427–61 (commentary), here p. 97.

10. L. S. Mercier, *Tableau de Paris*, Hamburg and Neuchâtel, 1781, p. 42. This first edition is available in its entirety as a Google book. Schiller read and excerpted the second edition (nouvelle edition), which was published as an eight-volume work in 1782–3 in Amsterdam. On examination of the quotations, he doesn't appear to have made use of the complete translation of this edition by Georg Walch, *Paris, ein Gemälde von Mercier*, Leipzig, 1783–4; cf. *Schillers Werke*, vol. XII, p. 427.

11. Ibid., p. 97.

12. 'Paris . . . c'est le paradis des femmes, l'enfer des mules, et le purgatoire des solliciteurs', *Nouvelles récréations et joyeux devis*, Lyons, 1561, p. 114.

13. J. Florio, *Second Fruits*, London, 1591, p. 205.

14. R. Burton, *The Anatomy of Melancholy*: 'England is a paradise for women, and hell for horses; Italy a paradise for horses, hell for women, as the diverbe goes.' Section 3, member 1, subsection 2; Reprint of the 1932 New York edition, 1977, Part 3, p. 265.

15. F. J. L. Meyer, *Briefe aus der Hauptstadt und dem Innern Frankreichs*, Tübingen, 1802.

16. *Morgenblatt für gebildete Leser*, no. 50, dates 27 February 1838 to 12 March 1838, p. 197.

17. The report by al-'Amraoui, first published in Fez, 1909, was recently reprinted in France: Idriss al-'Amraoui, *Le paradis des femmes et l'enfer des chevaux. La France de 1860 vue par l'émissaire du sultan*, La Tour d'Aigues, 2012. The preface by Yadh Ben Achour tells of the circumstances surrounding the origins of the text and al-Tahtawi's influence, pp. 5–12.

18. Ibid., p. 81.

19. Ibid., p. 107.

20. A. Schopenhauer, *Werke in fünf Bänden*, vol. V: *Parerga und Paralipomena*, Zürich, 1991, p. 552.

21. Cf. Mercier, *Tableau de Paris*, 'Les heures du jour', quoted by D. Roche, *La culture équestre de l'Occideur XVIe–XIXe siècle. L'ombre du cheval*, Paris, 2008, pp. 85 f.

22. Cf. Roche, *La culture*, p. 86. Complaints about the noise in cities can be found in countless personal testimonies by craftsmen and migrant workers who moved to the city from the country in the nineteenth century. For an example from Vienna, cf. F. Lenger, *Metropolen der Moderne. Eine europäische Stadtgeschichte seit 1850*, Munich, 2013, p. 236.

23. Cf. A. Farge, *Der Geschmack des Archivs*, Göttingen, 2011, p. 55.

24. Cf. G. Bouchet, *Le cheval à Paris de 1850 à 1914*, Geneva, 1993, p. 45.

25. Roche, *La culture*, pp. 35 ff. According to J.-P. Digard, *Une histoire du cheval*, Paris, 2004, p. 149, there were already 3 million horses in France in 1840 and this figure was consistent until 1935.

26. Roche, *La culture*, p. 36.

27. W. J. Gordon, *The Horse World of London*, London, 1893, p. 164.

28. C. McShane and J. A. Tarr, *The Horse in the City. Living Machines in the Nineteenth Century*, Baltimore, 2007, p. 16.

29. Ibid.

30. As in 1866, quoted by M. G. Lay, *A History of the World's Roads and of the Vehicles that Used Them*, New Brunswick, 1992.

31. Ibid. Also Lenger, *Metropolen der Moderne*, p. 168, speaks of the 'unimaginable quantities of horse manure' covering the streets when omnibuses and trams were still pulled by horses.

32. Gordon, *Horse World*, p. 187.

33. Ibid., pp. 187 ff.

34. McShane and Tarr, *The Horse*, p. 28.

35. Ibid.; Bouchet, *Le cheval à Paris*, pp. 228 ff. on transportation and slaughter methods used by Parisian knackers; also cf. Roche, *La culture*, p. 116.

36. McShane and Tarr, *The Horse*, p. 31.

37. Ibid., p. 33. For France, cf. Roche, *La culture*, pp. 70 ff.

38. Lay, *A History of the World's Roads*, pp. 91 ff.

39. This is equivalent to 'Watch out!' and was the customary exclamation used in the streets to warn of approaching carriages, riders, beasts of burden and similar potential hazards.

40. Mercier, *Tableau de Paris*, p. 55.

41. Ibid., p. 56.

42. Lay, *History*, p. 150.

43. Roche, *La culture*, p. 113.

44. Lay, *A History of the World's Roads*, p. 151.

45. McShane and Tarr, *The Horse*, p. 54.

46. Roche, *La culture*, p. 96.

47. Bruno Latour examined various objects, including door handles, seat belts and the famous 'Berlin key', where an entire social situation (or network) is associated with a technical object; cf. B. Latour, *Der Berliner Schlüssel: Erkundungen eines Liebhabers der Wissenschaften*, Berlin, 1996, pp. 37 ff. A number of items within the 'Centaurian Pact' could be described as 'Latourian objects', e.g. kerbstones and stirrups.

48. Roche, *La culture*, p. 97; Lay, *A History of the World's Roads*, p. 93.

49. McShane and Tarr, *The Horse*, pp. 103 ff.

50. Ibid., pp. 105 ff.

51. Gordon, *Horse World*, p. 19.

52. C. Gray, 'Where Horses Wet Their Whistles', *New York Times*, 31 October 2013, with reference to a study by Michele Bogart, Stony Brook University, New York.

53. Ibid.

54. Up until the first half of the twentieth century, oats were the next most important cereal in Germany after rye. Worldwide, oats were in third

place, after wheat and maize. Today, they account for less than 1 per cent of worldwide cereal production.

55. Roche, *La culture*, p. 70.

56. T. Veblen, *Theorie der feinen Leute*, Munich, 1981, p. 111.

57. E. Kollof, 'Das Pariser Fuhrwesen', p. 202.

58. Ibid., p. 206. An overview of the abundance of luxury vehicles in the nineteenth century is provided by A. Fürger in *Fahrkunst: Driving, Mensch, Pferd und Wagen von 1800 bis heute*, Hildesheim, 2009, especially pp. 250 and 250A.

59. M. Praz, *Der Garten der Erinnerung. Essays 1922–1980.* Frankfurt, 1994, pp. 268 f.

60. S. Longstreet, *A Century on Wheels: The Story of Studebaker. A History, 1852–1952*, New York, 1952, pp. 66 ff.

61. J. P. Digard, *Une histoire du cheval. Art, techniques, société*, Paris, 2004, pp. 157 f.

62. S. Giedion, *Die Herrschaft der Mechanisierung. Ein Beitrag zur anonymen Geschichte*, Frankfurt, 1982, p. 191.

63. McShane and Tarr, *The Horse*, p. 59.

64. Ibid., p. 62.

65. Ibid., pp. 64 f.

66. The London tram network had some 135 miles of track in 1893; Gordon, *Horse World*, p. 26.

67. Arne Hengsbach, 'Das Berliner Pferdeomnibuswesen', *Jahrbuch für brandenburgische Landesgeschichte*, 14 (1963), pp. 87–108.

68. Digard, *Une Histoire du cheval*, p. 166.

69. Ibid., p. 167.

70. McShane and Tarr, *The Horse*, p. 1: 'The nineteenth-century city represented the climax of human exploitation of horse power. Humans could not have built nor lived in the giant, wealth-creating metropoles that emerged in that century without horses.'

71. Bouchet, *Le cheval à Paris*, p. 200. For a 'brief' history of the replacement of horses by cars, see D. L. Lewis and L. Goldstein (eds), *The Automobile and American Culture*, Ann Arbor, 1983; for the 'long' history, see C. M. Merki, *Der holprige Siegeszug des Automobils 1895–1930. Zur Motorisierung des Straßenverkehrs in der Schweiz*, Vienna, 2002.

72. Giedion's long book was first published in English under the title *Mechanisation Takes Command* (Oxford, 1948). It was due to the efforts of Henning Ritter and his former comrades-in-arms that more than thirty years later a German version of the classic was published, with an

afterword by Stanislaus von Moos: *Die Herrschaft der Mechanisierung: Ein Beitrag zur anonymen Geschichte*, Frankfurt, 1982.

73. Roche, *La culture*, p. 27.

74. W. Ehrenfried, 'Pferde im Postdienst', *Archiv für deutsche Postgeschichte* 1 (1987), pp. 5–29, here p. 5.

75. Contrary to the legend, Henry Ford, who stocked replacement parts from 1917, was not actually the inventor of the *spare part*. Individual agricultural machinery manufacturers such as W. A. Woods had been experimenting with spare parts even before the turn of the century; see Giedion, *Die Herrschaft der Mechanisierung*, p. 187.

76. P. Richter, *Süddeutsche Zeitung*, 29 March 2014.

A Pastoral Incident

1. Silke Tenberg, 'Vom Arbeitstier zum Sportgerät: Zur Soziologie der Mensch-Pferd-Beziehung in der Moderne', University of Osnabrück, 2011, p. 15.

2. H. Küster, *Am Anfang war das Korn. Eine andere Geschichte der Menschheit*, München, 2013, p. 235. It was the increase in the horse population and the expansion of their fields of activity that was responsible for the increase in oat cultivation, rather than stabling and feeding.

3. J. Ritter, *Vorlesungen zur philosophischen Ästhetik*, Göttingen, 2010, p. 137.

4. G. Simmel, 'Philosophie der Landschaft', in *Die Güldenkammer*, 3, 1912–13, pp. 635–44, here p. 640.

5. Ritter, *Vorlesungen*, p. 136; also H. Küster, *Die Entdeckung der Landschaft: Einführung in eine neue Wissenschaft*, Munich, 2012, pp. 30 f.

6. W. Sombart, *Die deutsche Volkswirtschaft im neunzehnten Jahrhundert und im Anfang des 20. Jahrhunderts*, 1st edn, Berlin, 1912; quotation from 5th edn, Berlin, 1921.

7. Ibid., p. 4.

8. Ibid.

9. L. Börne, 'Monographie der deutschen Postschnecke', in L. Börne, *Sämtliche Schriften*, vol. I, Düsseldorf, 1964, pp. 639–67, here p. 640.

10. J. W. von Goethe, *Tagebücher* (Hist.-krit. Ausgabe), vol. II, part 1, Stuttgart and Weimar, 1790–1800, p. 179.

11. L. Sterne, *A Sentimental Journey Through France and Italy*, London, 1768, chapter 25.

12. Wolfgang Schivelbusch, *Geschichte der Eisenbahnreise*, Munich, 1977, p. 35–45.

13. See also M. Scharfe, 'Straße und Chaussee. Zur Geschichte der Wegsamkeit', in *Zeit der Postkutschen*, Frankfurt, 1992, pp. 137–49.

14. C. von Clausewitz, *On War*, edited and translated by M. Howard and P. Paret, Princeton, NJ, 1976.

15. Ibid.

16. Ibid.

17. Ibid.

18. P. Marivaux, *La voiture embourbée*, here quoted from the German translation, *Die Kutsche im Schlamm*, Zurich, 1985, pp. 19 f.

19. L. Sterne, *The Life and Opinions of Tristram Shandy, Gentleman*, 2nd edn, London, 1760.

20. Sombart, *Die deutsche Volkswirtschaft*, p. 4.

21. F. Kafka, 'A Country Doctor', translated by M. Pasley, in *The Transformation ('Metamorphosis') and Other Stories*, London, 1992.

22. On the image of the horse in Kafka's 'A Country Doctor', see the observations of Ernst Osterkamp in his pioneering work, *Die Pferde des Expressionismus: Triumph und Tod einer Metapher*, Munich, 2010, pp. 60–64.

23. Gustave Flaubert, *Madame Bovary*, translated by G. Wall, London, 1992, p. 56.

24. Ibid., p. 31.

25. Ibid., p. 51.

26. In the commentary to her German translation of *Madame Bovary*, E. Edl refers to the 'meaningful name' of the doctor. G. Flaubert, *Madame Bovary*, translated by E. Edl, Munich, 2012, p. 712.

27. Flaubert, *Madame Bovary*, translated by G. Wall, p. 51.

28. Ibid., p. 146.

29. Ibid., p. 147.

30. Ibid., p. 150.

31. Hippolytus – meaning 'the freer of horses' – was the son of Theseus and the Amazon Hippolyta, and famously died in a driving accident; see below p. 59.

32. Flaubert, *Madame Bovary*, p. 163.

33. M. Scharfe, 'Die alte Straße', in *Reisekultur. Von der Pilgerfahrt zum modernen Tourismus*, edited by H. Bausinger, K. Beyrer and G. Korff, Munich, 1991, pp. 11–22.

34. T. De Quincey, *The English Mail-Coach and Other Essays*, London, Toronto and New York 1912, pp. 30–39.

35. F. M. F. Bouwinghausen von Wallmerode, *Taschenbuch für Pferdeliebhaber, Reuter, Pferdezüchter, Pferdeärzte und Vorgesezte großer Marställe*, Tübingen, 1799, p. 56.

36. In the Monatsschlössl at Hellbrunn Palace, south of Salzburg.

37. F. A. de Garsault, *Traité des voitures, pour servir de supplément au nouveau parfait maréchal, avec la construction d'une berline nouvelle nommée inversable*, Paris, 1756.

38. J. H. M. Poppe, *Geschichte der Erfindungen in den Künsten und Wissenschaften, seit der ältesten bis auf die neueste Zeit*, vol. 3, Dresden, 1829, pp. 59 f.

39. J. G. Herklotz, *Beschreibung einer Maschine die das Durchgehen der Reit- und Wagenpferde verhindert*, Dresden, 1802.

40. J. Riem, *Zwei untrügliche bereits erprobte Mittel, sich beim Durchgehen der Pferde gegen alle Gefahr zu schützen*, Leipzig, 1805.

41. Poppe, *Geschichte der Erfindungen*, vol. 3, p. 63.

42. Comte G. de Contades, 'Bibliographie sportive' in *Le driving en France 1547–1896*, Paris, 1898.

43. The life of the coach as a dramatic capsule has been described in works from *Boule de suif* (1880), Guy de Maupassant's story of the Franco-Prussian War, to *Stagecoach*, John Ford's 1939 Western. Cf. J.-L. Rieupeyrout, *Der Western: Geschichte aus dem Wilden Westen*, edited by Joe Hembus, Bremen, 1963, pp. 80 f., for more on the close links with Maupassant's tale.

44. S. Kracauer, *Jacques Offenbach und das Paris seiner Zeit*, Frankfurt, 1976, p. 38.

45. Flaubert, *Madame Bovary*, p. 227.

46. Ibid., p. 228.

47. M. Praz, *Der Garten der Erinnerung, Essays*, vol. 1, Frankfurt, 1994, p. 270.

48. G. W. F. Hegel, *Philosophy of Nature*, volume II, edited by M. J. Petry, London, 2014.

49. K. Bücher, *Arbeit und Rhythmus*, 2nd edn, Leipzig, 1899.

50. Ibid., p. 28.

51. Flaubert, *Madame Bovary*, pp. 227–8.

52. L. Börne, 'Monographie der deutschen Postschnecke', in Börne, *Sämtliche Schriften*, vol. I.

53. A. Corbin, *Village Bells: Sound and Meaning in the Nineteenth-century French Countryside*, Frankfurt, 1995, p. 4.

54. Ibid., p. 6.

55. W. H. Riehl, *Culturstudien aus drei Jahrhunderten*, 2nd edn, Stuttgart, 1859, p. 336.

56. W. Burkert, *Lore and Science in Ancient Pythagoreanism*, translated by E. L. Minar, Jr., Nürnberg, 1962, p. 375 (includes information on Nicomachus and other sources).

57. Burkert, *Lore*, p. 376.
58. In a special issue on the history of technologies, the journal *Annales*, edited by Marc Bloch and Lucien Febvre, also published the results of a survey on the work and fate of the village blacksmith, which covered a diverse range of issues from tools, fuel, the function of the blacksmith as a vet, recruitment and professional training, to the social function of the forge as a village meeting point and the chances of them disappearing or staying; L. Febvre, 'Une enquête: La forge de village', *Annales*, 7, 1935 edition, pp. 603–14.
59. W. Burkert, 'Einbruch des Kentauren', *Zeitschrift für interkulturelle Germanistik (ZiG)*, VIII/3, 2014, pp. 83–4. The Swiss Böcklin was unabashed when answering the unresolved question of what centaurs eat: muesli, of course, because of the oats.
60. P. Kipphoff, 'Im Wasserbad der Gefühle', *Die Zeit*, 23 May 2001.

Riding West

1. Comanche was, of course, the only survivor of the US cavalry unit that was wiped out in the battle with the Sioux. On the Sioux side there were no lack of survivors, and whenever a Sioux reached the age of 100, he would claim to have been the last survivor of Little Bighorn. Comanche, the horse belonging to Captain Myles Keogh, outlived his master by fifteen years. After his death in 1891, the stallion was stuffed and exhibited at the World Exposition in Chicago in 1893. Comanche then continued his posthumous wanderings, resting at various stops, losing multiple replacements of body parts to souvenir hunters (mane and tail) before coming to his final rest in his current location at the Natural History Museum of the University of Kansas. Cf. D. Stillman, *Mustang: The Saga of the Wild Horse in the American West*, Boston and New York, 2008, pp. 113, 121 ff.; J. Hembus, *Western-Geschichte 1540–1894*, Munich, 1979, pp. 468 ff.
2. Stillman, *Mustang*, p. 108; for more on Custer, Keogh and Comanche, cf. ibid., p. 317.
3. 'The year after the Civil War, 100,000 settlers passed through the city of St. Louis immigrating west. Between 1860 and 1870, a million Americans poured into the western territories of the United States. Many of the Indians west of the Mississippi were determined to resist this migration.' L. A. DiMarco, *War Horse: A History of the Military Horse and Rider*, Yardley, PA, 2008, p. 271.
4. See p. 72.
5. The cavalry in the Middle Ages must of course have had a similar experience with the appearance on the field of the English longbow

archers, whose arrows were actually able to stop an enemy attack; cf. John Keegan who, in his classic *The Face of Battle: A Study of Agincourt, Waterloo and the Somme* (London, 2014), investigated the military and technical prowess that lay behind the victory of Henry V's troops over the superior French cavalry. Cf. also the more recent P. Edwards, *Horse and Man in Early Modern England*, London, 2007, pp. 145 ff.

6. DiMarco, *War Horse*, pp. 234 ff.

7. Ibid., p. 238.

8. Cf. also Stillman, *Mustang*, pp. 93 ff.

9. 'The army understood that Indian military power was more a function of the horse than any other factor. The army killed many of these horses to deny them to the Indians, and dispersed the remaining horses as war booty.' DiMarco, *War Horse*, p. 278; see also pp. 285 f.

10. In the 1970 film *Little Big Man* directed by Arthur Penn, Dustin Hoffman played Jack Crabb, the son of a white settler, who grew up near a Washita tribe and witnessed the Washita massacre.

11. Stillman, *Mustang*, pp. 111 f.

12. A view promoted in particular by Maximilian zu Wied, *Reise in das innere Nord-America*, Coblenz, 1839–41.

13. The 'Plains way of life', writes the American anthropologist Ruth M. Underhill, is actually the most recent of all the ways of life of the Native North Americans, associated as it is with the possession of horses, possible for the first time from around 1600: 'But, once this magnificent new find came into use, it was like the discovery of gold in modern days, drawing people from every language and every background. ... The Plains Indian, far from being the typical red man, was a modern product, a *nouveau riche*.' R. M. Underhill, *Red Man's America: A History of Indians in the United States*, revised edition, Chicago, 1971, p. 144.

14. 'Apparently the function of the horse in Indian warfare was seldom more than that of conveying the warrior to the area (not the *scene*) of operations, where he dismounted, dragoon-wise, to fight, or preferably to surprise the enemy. Such Indian forces were really, or normally, mounted infantry.' F. G. Roe, *The Indian and the Horse*, Norman, OK, 1955, p. 230.

15. P. S. Martin and H. E. Wright (eds), *Pleistocene Extinctions: The Search for a Cause*, New Haven, CT, 1967; P. S. Martin and R. G. Klein, (eds), *Quaternary Extinctions: A Prehistoric Revolution*, Tucson, AZ, 1984.

16. R. M. Denhardt, *The Horse of the Americas*, Norman, OK, 1948, pp. 14 ff.; R. B. Cunninghame Graham, *The Horses of the Conquest*, Norman,

OK, 1949, p. 19; C. Bernand and S. Gruzinski, *Histoire du Nouveau Monde*, Paris, 1991, pp. 67, 473. For the *'à la gineta'* riding style, see p. 82.

17. A. W. Crosby Jr, *The Columbian Exchange. Biological and Cultural Consequences of 1492*, Westport, CT, 1972, p. 80.

18. Ibid., p. 81.

19. Ibid., p. 82.

20. According to contemporary reports, the Apaches appear to have begun riding between 1620 and 1630. In the middle of the seventeenth century they were already 'a typical horse people', according to F. G. Roe, *The Indian and the Horse*, Norman, OK, 1955, p. 74.

21. S. C. Gwynne, *Empire of the Summer Moon: Quanah Parker and the Rise and Fall of the Comanches, the Most Powerful Indian Tribe in American History*, New York, 2010, pp. 29 f.

22. On the 'wars' amongst Native Americans themselves and the role horses played in these, cf. Roe, *The Indian*, pp. 222 f. and especially p. 227: The horse was 'not only the means of war; it was also the end. In plain English, what we persist in terming "wars" were more basically and much more commonly horse raids.'

23. Gwynne, *Empire*, pp. 30 f.

24. Ibid., p. 31.

25. Ibid., p. 34.

26. J. C. Ewers, *The Horse in Blackfoot Indian Culture*, Washington, 1955, p. 1.

27. Ibid., p. 3 (Haines, Wyman, Denhardt amongst others). Roe, *The Indian*, criticizes the 'stray legend' which traced the explosive spread of horses over the prairies of North America and the Pampas in South America back to individual horses which had escaped from the earlier conquistadors, thus indirectly contributing to the connection between Native Americans and horses. He maintains that this is too early; see Roe, *The Indian*, pp. 38 ff.

28. The first serious essay on the impact of horses on the life and culture of the Great Plains was published by Clark Wissler under the title 'The Influence of the Horse in the Development of Plains Culture', *American Anthropologist*, 16, 1 (1914), pp. 1–25. The bibliography of further discussions can be found in E. West, *The Contested Plains: Indians, Goldseekers and the Rush to Colorado*, Lawrence, KS, 1998, pp. 345 f. John C. Ewers, a student of Wissler's, published the unrivalled classic of the genre in 1955 (*The Horse in Blackfoot Indian Culture*). In 1941 Ewers founded the Museum of the Plains Indian in Browning, Montana, and as curator supervised an exhibition which brought him into

close contact with his most important informants, older Blackfoot members. He was appointed first director of the newly founded National Museum of American History in 1964.

29. F. R. Secoy, *Changing Military Patterns on the Great Plains (17th Century Through Early 19th Century)*, Seattle, WA, 1953, pp. 3 ff.

30. Cf. the maps in Secoy, *Changing Patterns*, pp. 104–6.

31. Ewers, *The Horse*, p. 13.

32. Ibid., pp. 20 ff.

33. Ibid., pp. 71 ff., 81 ff.

34. Cf. the differentiated depiction by Roe, *Indian*, pp. 188–206; West, *Contested Plains*, pp. 64 ff.

35. West, *Contested Plains*, p. 72.

36. Ewers, *The Horse*, pp. 9 f.

37. West, *Contested Plains*, pp. 64 f.

38. Gwynne, *Empire*, pp. 138 ff.

39. W. P. Webb, *The Great Plains*, New York, 1931, p. 183.

40. W. P. Webb, *The Great Frontier*, Boston, MA, 1952, p. 244.

41. DiMarco, *War Horse*, pp. 234 f.

42. For the sake of simplicity here, I am ignoring any other parts of the armament such as lances, swords, cutlasses and guns. Other parts of the respective systems, such as saddles, bridles and stirrups are also omitted. For stirrups, see pp. 219–21.

43. L. S. Mercier, *Les écoles espagnoles dites de la Brida et de la Gineta (ou Jineta), Revue de cavalerie*, Paris, 1927, pp. 301–15; J.-P. Digard, 'Le creuset moyen-oriental des techniques d'équitation', in B. Koechlin, F. Sigaut, J. M. C. Thomas and G. Toffin (eds), *De la voûte céleste au terroir, du jardin au foyer. Mosaïque sociographique. Textes offerts à Lucien Bernot*, Paris, 1987, pp. 613–18; L. Clare, 'Les deux façons de monter à cheval en Espagne et au Portugal pendant le siècle d'or', in J.-P. Digard, *Des chevaux et des hommes. Équitation et société*, Lausanne, 1988, pp. 73–82, provides many references to French Baroque literature on handling horses and on both Spanish riding schools.

44. Cf. above, p. 75, note 16.

45. Cf. the classic work by Steven Runciman, *A History of the Crusades*, 3 vols, Cambridge, 1951–4; see also W. Montgomery Watt, *The Influence of Islam on Medieval Europe*, Edinburgh, 1972.

46. D. P. Sponenberg, Virginia Tech, Blacksburg, VA, 2011: 'North American Colonial Spanish Horse'; see http://centerforamaricasfirsthorse.org.

47. In an inspired study, R. Düker recalls that the enthusiastic veneration of the Arab horse and the admiration of the Arab riding style, widespread

in Europe since the eighteenth century, was brought to America in the nineteenth century, and he shows this in the essays on different riding schools penned by cavalry colonel T. A. Dodge for *Harper's Magazine* in the 1880s. Dodge wanted to recognize the modernity and forward-looking approach of the American cavalry, which moved away from the stiff and heavy European schools towards the sleek elegance of the Arab riders; R. Düker, 'Als ob sich die Welt in Amerika gerundet hätte. Zur historischen Genese des US-Imperialismus aus dem Geist der Frontier', Ph.D. thesis, Berlin, 2005; see edoc.hu-berlin.de, pp. 191 ff. The empirical historical hippologist evaluates the question of the originally Moorish equine knowledge brought over to the Americas by the Spaniards in a more cautious and differentiated manner than the older diffusionist school of anthropology. See also J.-P. Digard, 'El caballo y la equitación entre Oriente y America. Difusíon y síntesis', in *Al-Andalus allende el Atlántico*, Granada, 1997, pp. 234–52; here, in particular, p. 247.

48. Watt, *The Influence of Islam*, pp. 34, 37–48.

49. S. Steiner, 'Jewish Conquistadors, America's first cowboys?' *The American West*, Sept/Oct 1983, pp. 31–7; S. Steiner, *Dark and Dashing Horsemen*, New York, 1981.

50. S. B. Liebman, Hernando Alonso, 'The First Jew on the North-American Continent', *Journal of Inter-American Studies*, 5/2 (1963), pp. 291–6.

51. Denhardt, *The Horse*, Chapter 6: 'El Otro Mexico', pp. 87–100.

52. Steiner, 'Jewish Conquistadors', p. 37.

53. I. Raboy, *Jewish Cowboy: Der Yiddischer Cowboy*, [no location], 1942.

54. The 'rough rider' was originally a bronco-buster who accustomed wild or semi-wild horses to a saddle and reins.

55. Preliminary List of Jewish Soldiers and Sailors who served in the Spanish-American War, *American Jewish Year Book 1890/91*, pp. 539 f.

56. His work hangs in the Mission Inn in Riverside, California; K. Holm, 'Schlacht im Steakhaus', *Frankfurter Allgemeine Zeitung*, 19 July 2010, p. 28.

57. The strongest impact left by Remington's iconography has been on film, i.e. the Western. 'Western directors', writes Joe Hembus, 'have always admitted that Remington was the main source of their optical inspiration' (*Western-Geschichte*, p. 563).

58. T. Roosevelt, *Ranch Life in the Far West*, Flagstaff, AZ, 1985.

59. E. Jussim, *Frederic Remington, the Camera and the Old West*, Fort Worth, TX, 1983, p. 50.

60. Ibid., p. 81.

61. T. Roosevelt, *The Rough Riders: A History of the First United States Volunteer Cavalry* (1899), 3rd edn, New York, 1906.

62. Ibid., p. 36; my italics.

63. Owen Wister, *The Virginian*, first published in New York in 1902, was the first real Wild West novel and was dedicated to Theodore Roosevelt.

64. See p. 89.

65. H. Böhringer, *Auf dem Rücken Amerika:. Eine Mythologie der neuen Welt im Western und Gangsterfilm*, Berlin, 1998, p. 38: 'The Western film marked the end of the Wild West and continued the legendary memory of it . . . It fashioned the consciousness of America.'

66. Cf. Düker, 'Als ob sich die Welt', 'Teddy's Rough Riders', pp. 198 ff. Incidentally, in his book *Rough Riders,* Roosevelt himself established the relationship between the closure of the frontier and recruitment of his men for what should be called America's first imperial war. According to Roosevelt, the majority of the regiment actually came from the south-west: 'They came from the Four Territories which yet remained within the boundaries of the United States; that is, from the lands that have been most recently won over to white civilization, and in which the conditions of life are nearest those that obtained on the *frontier* when there still was a *frontier*.' (Roosevelt, *Rough Riders*, p. 18; my italics.)

67. 'As it turned out, we were not used mounted at all, so that our preparations on this point came to nothing. In a way, I have always regretted this. We thought we should at least be employed as cavalry in the great campaign against Havana in the fall; and from the beginning I began to train my men in shock tactics for use against hostile cavalry. My belief was that the horse was really the weapon with which to strike the first blow.' (Ibid., p. 39).

68. E. Morris, *The Rise of Theodore Roosevelt*, New York, 1979, p. 275. The meaning the West held for Roosevelt is given even more emphasis in M. L. Collins, *That Damned Cowboy: Theodore Roosevelt and the American West 1883–1898*, New York, 1989.

69. Düker, 'Als ob sich die Welt', pp. 35 ff.

70. D. Rünzler, *Im Westen ist Amerika*, Vienna, 1995, put it in this incontestable formulation: 'The "Wild West" became a myth almost as soon as the frontier, the border between wilderness and civilization, ceased to exist.' (p. 10). Düker, 'Als ob sich die Welt', goes a step further and refers to Roosevelt's *Rough Riders* as an 'attempt to write a dramatized version of a mythical history' (p. 47).

71. Rünzler, *Im Westen*, p. 13. Incidentally, Cody himself stood with one foot on the stage and the other in current events, as the French film historian J.-L. Rieupeyrout put it (*Der Western*, ed. Joe Hembus, Bremen, 1963, p. 95).

72. Hembus, *Western-Geschichte*, p. 601.
73. Düker, 'Als ob sich die Welt', p. 51.
74. Rieupeyrout, *Der Western*, p. 43.
75. Hembus, *Western-Geschichte*, p. 196.
76. H. Melville, *Moby-Dick*, New York, 1851.
77. Hembus, *Western-Geschichte*, p. 563.

The Shock

1. On 1 April 1926, Stauffenberg joined the 17th Bavarian Cavalry Regiment in Bamberg and attended the army cavalry school in Hanover from 1928 to 1929, where he finished sixth best in his year; P. Hoffmann, *Claus Schenk Graf von Stauffenberg und seine Brüder*, Stuttgart, 1992, pp. 84, 95. In December 1942, as a major in the administration of the army's general staff, he obtained approval to set up an Eastern voluntary association that would 'pave the way for a Cossack cavalry division in the German forces'; H. Meyer, *Geschichte der Reiterkrieger*, Stuttgart, 1982, p. 188.
2. Stauffenberg to his wife Nina, letter of 17 September 1939, Stefan George Archiv, Stuttgart.
3. R. Kapuscinski, *Die Erde ist ein gewalttätiges Paradies. Reportagen, Essays, Interviews aus vierzig Jahren*, Munich and Zurich, 2002, pp. 14 f. In his *Buch des Flüsterns*, published in 2009 in Romanian and translated into German in 2013, Varujan Vosganian described the same image of a battlefield left after the recovery of human bodies with only the corpses of horses, so that one had the impression that, 'on the fields there hadn't been a war between men, but between horses' (p. 479). The fact that the Romanian author was familiar with the passage by Kapuscinski cannot be ruled out.
4. The concept of a riding nation is so true that alongside the Soviet Union, Poland had at its command 'the last cavalry . . . that independently operated in a traditional form' (Meyer, *Reiterkrieger*, p. 187).
5. Cf. the Wikipedia entry for 'Charge at Krojanty'.
6. Historian Janusz Piekalkiewicz writes that the Polish Uhlans 'were not suicide soldiers, and this was by no means a conscious mounted assault against tanks by the Polish cavalry. There were of course multiple attacks against the German cavalry when armoured vehicles came to help or situations where the Polish cavalry were attacked by tanks. The only chance of survival for them was to attempt, in a breakneck manoeuvre, to ride past the tanks as quickly as possible.' J. Piekalkiewicz, *Pferd und Reiter im II. Weltkrieg*, Munich, 1992, p. 14.

7. Of course it didn't really happen like that, Wajda admitted in a later interview, asserting that he intended it as an allegory. This differentiation seems to have gone unnoticed by most of the film's audience.

8. Catalogue published by the National Museum in Warsaw for the exhibition *Ross und Reiter*, Polenmuseum Rapperswil, 1999, pp. 17 ff., 22 ff.

9. H. Guderian, *Erinnerungen eines Soldaten*, Heidelberg, 1951, p. 63.

10. Piekalkiewicz, *Pferd und Reiter*, pp. 65 ff.

11. Clausewitz, *On War*: '. . . cavalry is suited to movement and major decisions. Therefore, its preponderance is important in operations over great distances, and in cases where one expects to carry out major and decisive blows. Bonaparte will serve as an example.' (p. 289).

12. J. Ellis, *Cavalry: The history of mounted warfare*, Newton Abbot and Vancouver, 1978, p. 157. The significant rise in the infantry's firepower, which was to lead to a gradual change in the relative strengths of the infantry and cavalry branches, was already noticeable under Frederick the Great, as Clausewitz notes in *On War*.

13. In his book on animals in the First World War, Éric Baratay made a very impressive effort to describe the phenomenon of a cavalry attack, from the perspective of the animals as well as the riders; É. Baratay, *Bêtes des tranchées: Des vécues oubliés*, Paris, 2013, pp. 63 f.

14. Meyer, *Reiterkrieger*, pp. 196 ff.

15. G. A. Craig, *The Battle of Koniggratz: Prussia's Victory Over Austria, 1886*, Philadelphia, 1964.

16. M. Howard, *The Franco-Prussian War: The German Invasion of France 1870–71*, London, 1961, p. 216.

17. The figures from the Franco-Prussian War in DiMarco, *War Horse*, pp. 259 ff., show without a shadow of a doubt that the unfettered violence in wars was sometimes aimed at animals, as history writers have known since Herodotus, even when, unlike him, they have preferred to keep quiet about it. Cf. the gruesome scene in Herodotus (V 111 f.), in which the King of Salamis's page severs the foreleg of the charger belonging to the Persian army commander. M. Kretschmar provides examples of the elimination of horses through targeted use of long-range weapons (arrow shots) in *Pferd und Reiter im Orient: Untersuchungen zur Reiterkultur Vorderasiens in der Seldschukenzeit*, Hildesheim, 1980, pp. 428 f. Ludwig Uhland also calls the severance of the forelegs of enemy horses 'folly' in his *Schwäbischen Kunde* (1814).

18. Howard, *Franco-Prussian War*, p. 157.

19. DiMarco, *War Horse*, p. 261.

20. Ibid., pp. 289–308.

21. M. E. Derry, *Horses in Society: A Story of Animal Breeding and Marketing, 1800–1920*, Toronto and London, 2006, p. 102.
22. W. Churchill, *The River War: A Historical Account of the Reconquest of the Sudan*, London and New York, 1899.
23. Derry, *Horses in Society*, p. 115.
24. P. Liman, *Der Kaiser: Ein Charakterbild Kaiser Wilhelms II, 1888–1911*, Leipzig, 1913, p. 110.
25. Meyer, *Reiterkrieger*, p. 196.
26. F. von Bernhardi, *Gedanken zur Neugestaltung des Kavallerie-Reglements*, Berlin, 1908, p. 28. The cavalry general and sometime colleague of Schlieffen published three further texts on the function and future of the military cavalry before the First World War alongside his 1908 exposé on cavalry regulations: *Unsere Kavallerie im nächsten Kriege*, Berlin, 1899; *Reiterdienst*, Berlin, 1910; and *Die Heranbildung zum Kavallerieführer*, Berlin, 1914. He was soon translated into English: *Cavalry in Future Wars*, London and New York, 1906, and *Cavalry*, New York, 1914.
27. Bernhardi, *Die Heranbildung*, p. 7.
28. Bernhardi, *Unsere Kavallerie*, p. 6.
29. Bernhardi, *Das Heerwesen*, in S. Körte, F. W. von Loebell, G. von Rheinbaben, H. von Schwerin-Löwitz, A. Wagner (eds), *Deutschland unter Kaiser Wilhelm II*, vol. 1, Berlin, 1914, p. 378.
30. Bernhardi, *Unsere Kavallerie*, p. 6.
31. DiMarco, *War Horse*, p. 307.
32. T. Travers, *The Killing Ground. The British Army, the Western Front, and the Emergence of Modern Warfare 1900–1918*, London, 1987, pp. 89 ff.
33. In his study, *The Social History of the Machine Gun*, London, 1975, pp. 128 ff., John Ellis provides a range of examples for Haig's obstinate adherence to traditional doctrines on the deployment of cavalry in the First World War. Even the polite hints by his king in a speech of June 1916 regarding the high cost of the upkeep of so many largely useless cavalry horses did not persuade Haig; Ellis, *Social History of the Machine Gun*, p. 130.
34. E. Köppen, *Heeresbericht*, Munich, 2004, pp. 182 f.
35. A. Hochschild, *Der große Krieg: Der Untergang des alten Europa im Ersten Weltkrieg 1914–1918*, Stuttgart, 2013, pp. 172, 224.
36. S. Butler, *The War Horses: The Tragic Fate of a Million Horses Sacrificed in the First World War*, Wellington, 2011, p. 79.
37. There is a summary of this school in D. Kenyon, *Horsemen in No Man's Land: British Cavalry & Trench Warfare*, Huddersfield, 2011.

38. G. Phillips, 'The Obsolescence of the Arme Blanche and Technological Determinism in British Military History', *War in History*, IX, 1/2002, pp. 39–59.

39. R. Netz, *Barbed Wire: An Ecology of Modernity*, Middletown, CT, 2004, p. 90.

40. Ibid., pp. 87 ff.; also Hochschild, *Der große Krieg*, p. 174.

41. Cf. R. Bruneau, 'La mission militaire française de remonte aux États-Unis pendant la Grande Guerre', in D. Roche, *Le cheval et la guerre du XVe au XXe siècle*, Paris, 2002.

42. G. M. Tempest, 'All the Muddy Horses: Giving a Voice to the "Dumb Creatures" of the Western Front' (1914–18), in R. Pöppinghege (ed.), *Tiere im Krieg. Von der Antike bis zur Gegenwart*, Paderborn, 2009, pp. 217–34, here p. 218. In her dissertation, *The Long Face of War: Horses and the Nature of Warfare in the French and British Armies on the Western Front*, New Haven, CT, 2013, Gene Tempest gives a detailed and knowledgeable outline of the fate of around 2.7 million horses deployed on the Western Front on both British and French sides. See also Butler, *War Horses*, p. 118. The number of horses killed on the British side is given here as being 256,000 (compared to 558,000 British soldiers).

43. Butler, *War Horses*, p. 101.

44. Ibid.

45. Meyer, *Reiterkrieger*, p. 192.

46. The connection with centenary commemorations and memorials is clear in studies such as Baratay, *Bêtes de tranchées*, Paris, 2013; R. Pöppinghege, *Tiere im Ersten Weltkrieg. Eine Kulturgeschichte*, Berlin, 2014.

47. E. H. Baynes, *Animal Heroes of the Great War*, London, 1926.

48. John Moore, *Our Servant the Horse: An Appreciation of the Part Played by Animals During the War (1914–1918)*, London, 1931.

49. F. Schauwecker, *So war der Krieg. 200 Kampfaufnahmen aus der Front*, Berlin, 1928, here pp. 101–6.

50. E. Johannsen, *Fronterinnerungen eines Pferdes*, Hamburg-Bergedorf, 1929.

51. E. M. Remarque, *All Quiet on the Western Front* (*Im Westen nichts Neues*, Berlin, 1929), first translated into English by A. W. Wheen, London, 1929.

52. German cavalry officers and Uhlans were often depicted, particularly in British caricatures from the time of the First World War, as the personification of a narrow-minded, reactionary and bloodthirsty Junker caste, representatives of their supreme commander.

53. Jünger did not invent this name, yet it is difficult not to think of the name of the protagonist, Karl Rossmann, in Kafka's novel *Amerika*.

54. Ernst Jünger, *Kriegstagebuch*, ed. Helmuth Kiesel, Stuttgart, 2010, p. 430.

55. Ibid., p. 593.

56. R. Koselleck, 'Der Aufbruch in die Moderne oder das Ende des Pferdezeitalters', in 'Historikerpreis der Stadt Münster 2003', Münster City Historian Prize booklet, 18 July 2003, p. 37. Meyer, *Reiterkrieger*, p. 192, quotes similar figures (2,750,000 equids in the German Wehrmacht, of which an estimated 1,600,000 died) and gives 1943 as the year with the highest deployment of horses (1,380,000). These figures match those in W. Zieger, *Das deutsche Heeresveterinärwesen im Zweiten Weltkrieg*, Freiburg, 1973, p. 415. Zieger also calculates a 5 to 8 per cent lower casualty rate than the 68 per cent of the First World War. Meyer, *Reiterkrieger*, p. 186, estimates the horse deployment by the Red Army to be 3.5 million.

57. Meyer, *Reiterkrieger*, p. 192. Further details on the number of horses in partially motorized and non-motorized units is given in P. L. Johnson, *Horses of the German Army in World War II*, Atglen, PA, 2006, pp. 9 ff.

58. Zieger, *Heeresveterinärwesen*, p. 421.

59. For example in K. C. Richter, *Die Geschichte der deutschen Kavallerie 1919–1945*, Stuttgart, 1978.

60. Koselleck, 'Der Aufbruch', p. 37.

61. As in N. Davies, *White Eagle, Red Star. The Polish-Soviet War, 1919–1920*, London 1983, p. 229.

62. Budyonny's astonishing political ascent from 1920 and his narrow survival of the cleansing of the officer corps from 1937 to 1938 is, however, linked more to his proximity to Stalin than to his fame as cavalry leader.

63. Davies, *White Eagle, Red Star*, p. 268.

64. There is an abundance of information on the alliance between the nobility and riding going back to ancient times. On the ancient Greeks and Romans, for example, see R. L. Fox, *The Classical World: An Epic History From Homer to Hadrian*, London, 2005. M. de Montaigne derides the 'hippolatry' of the European nobility in his essay 'Of War Horses, or Destriers', The *Essays of Michel de Montaigne*, translated by Charles Cotton, 1877, vol. 8.

65. Meyer, *Reiterkrieger*, pp. 195 f.

66. C. Simon deals with this theme first in 1947 in *La Corde raide*, then in 1960 in *La Route des Flandres*, in 1989 in *L'Acacia* and again in 1997 in *Le Jardin des Plantes*.

67. C. Simon, *The Acacia*, translated by R. Howard, New York, 1991.

68. R. Barthes, *Mythen des Alltags. Vollständige Ausgabe*, Berlin, 2010, p. 136.
69. Cf. DiMarco, *War Horse*, p. 349.

The Jewish Horsewoman

1. Cf. S. Koldehoff, 'Vom unbekannten Meister zum echten Rembrandt', *Die Welt*, 7 November 2010.
2. Julius S. Held, 'Rembrandt's "Polish" Rider', *Art Bulletin*, 26:4 (December 1944), pp. 246–65.
3. Handwritten notes from the R. B. Kitaj Estate, quoted from the literature accompanying the exhibition 'R. B. Kitaj 1932–2007: Obsession' at the Jewish Museum, Berlin, 2012–13.
4. Not only do interpreters of Kitaj's work occasionally confuse Michael Podro with Richard Wollheim (for example R. I. Cohen, 'The "Wandering Jew" from Medieval Legend to Modern Metaphore', in B. Kirshenblatt-Gimblett and J. Karp (eds), *The Art of Being Jewish in Modern Times*, Philadelphia, PA, 2008, pp. 147–75), they also only comment on one book in the picture, that in the window. They overlook the fact that the traveller holds another in his left hand (which in Rembrandt is the hand holding the reins) and that there is a third balancing precariously on the headrest of his seat. Podro, as is also mentioned in this context, had a strong affinity for rail travel. He particularly enjoyed the evening commute from Essex, where he taught at the university from 1969 until his retirement in 1997, back to London, during which he and the colleagues travelling with him would hold an impromptu seminar about the latest exhibitions and publications in the field of art history; C. Saumarez Smith, 'Professor Michael Podro' (obituary), *The Independent*, 1 April 2008.
5. Held, 'Rembrandt's "Polish" Rider', p. 259.
6. Ibid., pp. 260 ff.
7. M. Podro, *The Critical Historians of Art*, New Haven, CT, and London, 1982, p. 215.
8. See the post by stlukesguild on the thread 'RIP: R. B. Kitaj' on the discussion forum wetcanvas.com, 27 October 2007.
9. F. Nietzsche, 'Nachgelassene Fragmente, Herbst 1884 bis Herbst 1885', in *Werke: Kritische Gesamtausgabe*, Part 7, Vol. 3, Berlin and New York, 1974, p. 292.
10. C. Battegay, 'Fest im Sattel. Von Herzl bis Mel Brooks: Wie die Juden aufs Pferd kamen', *Jüdische Allgemeine*, 20 November 2012.

11. J. Hoberman, 'How Fiercely That Gentile Rides!: Jews, Horses, and Equestrian Style', in J. Kugelmass (ed.), *Jews, Sports, and the Rites of Citizenship*, Urbana, IL, 2007, pp. 31–49, here p. 33.

12. Hoberman, 'How Fiercely', p. 39; on this subject see also M. Samuel, *The Gentleman and the Jew*, Westport, CT, 1950. The roots of this cultural malaise could lie deep: 'In early Israel,' writes S. P. Toperoff, 'the horse was never included among the domesticated animals, such as the ass or the ox. Indeed, the ass was a symbol of peace, but the horse was a symbol of war, and in the Bible the horse is always represented, with few exceptions (e.g. Isaiah 28:28) as a fighting animal.' S. P. Toperoff, *The Animal Kingdom in Jewish Thought*, Northvale, NJ, and London, 1995, p. 123.

13. C. Magris, *Inferences from a Sabre*, translated by M. Thompson, New York, 1991, p. 68. Krasnov's portrait is in fact distorted, as it is well known that Trotsky could ride and in moments of crisis would mount his horse to bring the situation under control, to rally together dispersing or fleeing soldiers and to lead them back into battle; O. Figes, *A People's Tragedy: The Russian Revolution, 1891–1924*, London, 1996, pp. 708, 712.

14. F. P. Ingold, *Dostojewski und das Judentum*, Frankfurt, 1981, p. 40.

15. Ibid., pp. 35 ff.

16. Ibid., pp. 43, 45.

17. Ibid., pp. 47 f.

18. M. Landmann, *Das Tier in der jüdischen Weisung*, Heidelberg, 1959, pp. 106 f.

19. P. Longworth, *The Cossacks*, New York, 1970. More recent accounts are more critical on this point; cf. A. Kappeler, *Die Kosaken: Geschichte und Legenden*, Plunich, 2013. An exception is the relevant Wikipedia article (as at 1 August 2015), which makes no reference to the traditional anti-Semitism of the Cossacks. On the history of the pogroms in the nineteenth and twentieth centuries, J. Dekel-Chen, D. Gaunt, N. M. Meir and I. Bartal (eds), *Anti-Jewish Violence: Rethinking the Pogrom in East European History*, Bloomington and Indianapolis, 2011, as well as S. Hoffman and E. Mendelsohn (eds), *The Revolution of 1905 and Russia's Jews*, Philadelphia, PA, 2008.

20. U. Herbeck, *Das Feindbild vom 'jüdischen Bolschewiken': Zur Geschichte des russischen Antisemitismus vor und während der Russischen Revolution*, Berlin, 2009, p. 294.

21. Ibid., pp. 300 ff.

22. Ibid., p. 294; also chapter 4.4: 'Die Pogrome von Budennyjs Reiterarmee im Herbst 1920', pp. 384 ff.

23. I. Babel, *1920 Diary*, translated by H. T. Willetts, New Haven, CT, and London, 1995, p. 28.
24. Ibid., p. 64.
25. Ibid., p. 77.
26. Ibid., p. 19.
27. Ibid., p. 36.
28. The often noted ambivalence of the narrator in *Red Cavalry* and his open admiration of the Cossacks, their ferocity and their naïve or revolutionary savagery (C. Luplow, *Isaac Babel's Red Cavalry*, Ann Arbor, 1982, pp. 38 ff.) are literary devices characteristic of these expressionistic stories. There are also allusions to the older, 'Byronic' tradition of admiration for the freedom-loving Cossacks, for example in Tolstoy. In his *1920 Diary*, which dispenses with such artifices, Babel's proximity to his people and his empathy for their suffering is unwaveringly tangible. There are indeed passages of undisguised sympathy for the Cossacks in the *1920 Diary*, however the brotherly tone with which they are expressed has nothing to do with the Nietzschean 'sympathy for the devil' that the *Red Cavalry* narrator allows himself.
29. Babel, *1920 Diary*, p. 24.
30. Ibid., pp. 75, 78.
31. Ibid., p. 44.
32. Ibid., p. 23.
33. Longworth, *Cossacks*.
34. T. Segev, *Es war einmal ein Palästina: Juden und Araber vor der Staatsgründung Israels*, Berlin, 2005, p. 9.

II A PHANTOM OF THE LIBRARY–*KNOWLEDGE*

Blood and Speed

1. Besides his numerous historical, political and philosophical works, Xenophon, known because of his industrious nature and elegant writing style as the 'Attic bee', was the author of two important works on horse handling, *On Horsemanship* (*Peri Hippikes*) and *Hipparchicus* (*Hipparchikos*). To this day, both texts impress readers with their affection and understanding of the animals derived from experience.
2. Georg Graf Lehndorff, *Handbuch für Pferdezüchter*, Potsdam, 1881, was reprinted four times in the author's lifetime, twice revised by his son Siegfried. A reprint of the seventh edition from Berlin, 1925, was published in 2008.

3. R. H. Dunlop and D. J. Williams, *Veterinary Medicine*, St Louis, MO, 1996, chapter 18: 'The Launching of European Veterinary Education', and chapter 19: 'An Increasing Demand for Veterinary Schools', pp. 319–50; A. v. d. Driesch and J. Peters, *Geschichte der Tiermedizin*, chapter 4: 'Die tierärztlichen Ausbildungsstätten', pp. 133 ff.

4. A. Mayer on the development of the physiology of movement, in A. Mayer, *Wissenschaft vom Gehen: Die Erforschung der Bewegung im 19. Jahrhundert*, Frankfurt, 2013, particularly chapter 4, pp. 143 ff.

5. S. Saracino, 'Der Pferdediskurs im England des 17. Jahrhunderts', *Historische Zeitschrift*, vol. 300, issue 2 (2015), pp. 341–73, here pp. 344 ff. and 371.

6. E. Graham, 'The Duke of Newcastle's "Love ... For Good Horses": An Exploration of Meanings', in P. Edwards et al. (eds), *The Horse as Cultural Icon: The Real and the Symbolic Horse in the Early Modern World*, Leiden and Boston, MA, 2012, pp. 31–70.

7. Now in the Mr and Mrs Paul Mellon Collection, Upperville, Virginia.

8. D. Roche, *La gloire et la puissance: Histoire de la culture équestre, XVIe–XIXe siècle*, Paris, 2011, p. 217; W. Behringer, *Kulturgeschichte des Sports: Vom antiken Olympia bis ins 21. Jahrhundert*, Munich, 2012, pp. 204 ff.

9. G. Schreiber, *Glück im Sattel oder Reiter-Brevier*, Vienna, 1971, p. 146.

10. The Vienna Riding School was the 'survivor' of the former unity.

11. This story is also told in the older literature; M. von Hutten-Czapski, *Die Geschichte des Pferdes*, Berlin, 1876, pp. 546 ff.; P. Goldbeck, *Entstehung und Geschichte des englischen Vollblut-Pferdes*, Saarburg, 1899.

12. M. Stoffregen-Büller, *Pferdewelt Europa: Die berühmtesten Gestüte, Reitschulen und Rennbahnen*, Münster, 2003, pp. 132 ff.; W. Vamplew and J. Kay, *Encyclopedia of British Horseracing*, London, 2005, passim.

13. Stoffregen-Büller, *Pferdewelt*, p. 133.

14. Behringer, *Kulturgeschichte des Sports*, pp. 196 f.

15. The lines which they founded, Herod, Eclipse and Matchem, are named after their only male offspring, who ensured the survival of the respective line (Herod = great-grandson of Byerley Turk; Eclipse = great-grandson of Darley Arabian; and Matchem = grandson of Godolphin Arabian).

16. D. Defoe, *A Tour through the Whole Island of Great Britain*, P. N. Furbank and W. R. Owens (eds), New Haven, CT, and London, 1991, p. 32. On the hippophilia and racing enthusiasm of the English kings, cf. also Saracino, 'Der Pferdediskurs im England', pp. 348 ff.

17. C. Eisenberg, *'English Sports' und deutsche Bürger: Eine Gesellschaftsgeschichte 1800–1939*, Paderborn, 1999, p. 26.

18. C. R. Hill, *Horse Power: The Politics of the Turf*, Manchester, 1988.

19. O. Brunner, *Adeliges Landleben und europäischer Geist*, Salzburg, 1949, pp. 331 f.

20. Vamplew and Kay, *Encyclopedia*, pp. 106 f.

21. Eisenberg, 'English Sports', p. 29.

22. T. Veblen, *Theorie der feinen Leute*, Köln, 1958, pp. 62 ff.; on the cult of the fast horse, cf. pp. 111 ff.

23. R. Black, *The Jockey Club and its Founders*, London, 1893, p. 349.

24. Eisenberg, 'English Sports', p. 30.

25. Ibid., p. 31.

26. S. Deuchar, *Sporting Art in Eighteenth-Century England: A Social and Political History*, New Haven, CT, and London, 1988, pp. 25 ff., p. 66.

27. N. Elias, 'An essay on sport and violence', in N. Elias and E. Dunning, *Quest for Excitement: Sport and Leisure in the Civilising Process*, Dublin, 2008.

28. Stoffregen-Büller, *Pferdewelt*, p. 141.

29. W. Seitter, *Menschenfassungen: Studien zur Erkenntnispolitikwissenschaft*, Weilerswist, 2012, chapter AI, 'Heraldik als Erkennungssystem', pp. 13–33.

30. Goldbeck, *Entstehung*, p. 16.

31. H. Delbrück, *Geschichte der Kriegskunst*, vol. 4: *Die Neuzeit*, Berlin, 1962, pp. 151–246; H. Meyer, *Geschichte der Reiterkrieger*, Stuttgart, 1982, pp. 176–227 (mostly agrees, sometimes word for word, with Delbrück); L. A. DiMarco, *War Horse: A History of the Military Horse and Rider*, Yardley, PA, 2008, pp. 150–92.

32. C. Simon, *The Flanders Road*, translated by R. Howard, London, 1961, p. 116. This is part of the racing scene in which erotic fantasies merge with images of French cavalry squadrons being destroyed by German fighter bombers in summer 1940.

33. L. Machtan, *Der Kaisersohn bei Hitler*, Hamburg, 2006.

34. N. M. Fahnenbruck, '. . . reitet für Deutschland': Pferdesport und Politik im Nationalsozialismus*, Göttingen, 2013, pp. 152 ff., 236 ff.

35. Ibid., pp. 170 ff.

36. 'The first English sport successfully exported to Germany was horse racing,' says Eisenberg in 'English Sports', p. 162.

37. Fahnenbruck, '. . . reitet für Deutschland', p. 40; also Eisenberg, 'English Sports', p. 163.

38. F. Chales de Beaulieu, *Der klassische Sport*, Berlin, 1942, p. 37.

39. Ibid., p. 50.

40. A. Jäger, *Das Orientalische Pferd und das Privatgestüte Seiner Majestät des Königs von Württemberg*, Stuttgart, 1846 (reprinted Hildesheim, 1983).

41. K. W. Ammon, *Nachrichten von der Pferdezucht der Araber und den arabischen Pferden*, Nuremberg, 1834 (reprinted Hildesheim, 1972), p. 37.

42. 'Friedrich Wilhelm Hackländer 1816–1877', J. Bendt and H. Fischer (eds), *Marbacher Magazin* 81/1998, pp. 21 ff. The royal private stud was transferred to Marbach in 1932 and was combined with the court and state studs located there.

43. R. von Veltheim, *Abhandlungen über die Pferdezucht Englands, noch einiger Europäischen Länder, des Orients u.s.w., in Beziehung auf Deutschland*, Braunschweig, 1833, p. 16: 'Were it not for the enjoyment of racing, which requires a consistently pure bloodline of Oriental descent, there would never have been the possibility of maintaining a sufficient number of pedigree stallions to contribute to the required level of noble blood, which, as with all mixed lineages, is gradually lost and needs to be refreshed from time to time.'

44. S. Széchenyi, *Über Pferde, Pferdezucht und Pferderennen*, Leipzig, 1830 (reprinted, Hildesheim, 1979), p. 27; also p. 26: 'I know of no better or more appropriate way to pick out the best horse among many than through racing.'

45. Eisenberg, *'English Sports'*, p. 166.

46. According to Brehm, the court of Louis XV swarmed with so many 'large pintos and other Baroque horses' that this under-appreciated horse, 'a maltreated, cantankerous animal was bought a year later by an English Quaker in Paris, as a godly deed, from the cart of a timber merchant'. *Brehms Tierleben*, vol. 12, 4th edn, Leipzig and Vienna, 1915, p. 689.

47. A. von Arnim, 'Pferdewettrennen bei Berlin (1830)', in *Werke in sechs Bänden*, vol. 6: *Schriften*, Frankfurt, 1992, pp. 988–92, here p. 990.

48. Goldbeck, *Entstehung*, pp. 8 ff.

49. One hundred and sixty Arab and Berber stallions were introduced to England from 1660 to 1770. F. Chales de Beaulieu, *Vollblut: Eine Pferderasse erobert die Welt*, Verden, 1960, p. 55.

50. According to Goldbeck, *Entstehung*, p. 17, citing H. Goos, *Die Stamm-Mütter des englischen Vollblutpferdes*, Hamburg, 1885; also the chapter on 'sport princes' in Behringer, *Kulturgeschichte des Sports*, pp. 184–97.

51. See above, pp. 75, 82.

52. M. Jähns, *Ross und Reiter in Leben und Sprache, Glauben und Geschichte der Deutschen*, vol. 2, Leipzig, 1872, pp. 100 f., 152 f.

53. J. Burckhardt, *The Civilization of the Renaissance in Italy*, translated by S. Middlemore, London, 1990.

54. J. J. Sullivan, *Blood Horses: Notes of a Sportswriter's Son*, New York, 2004, pp. 52 f., 89; also K. Conley, *Stud: Adventures in Breeding*, New York, 2003.

55. An equestrian portrait by George Stubbs of the family includes his mother Susannah and uncle Josiah Wedgwood II on horses, along with other family members; cf. J. Browne, *Charles Darwin*, v. 1, London, 1995, pp. 7 and p. 2 and the first plates (after p. 110).

56. C. Darwin, *On the Origin of Species*, London, 1859; R. J. Wood, 'Robert Bakewell (1725–1795), Pioneer Animal Breeder and his influence on Charles Darwin', in *Folia Mendeliana*, Brno, 1973, pp. 231–42. Darwin's enthusiastic reception among agricultural economists and animal breeders is evident in the work written five years after the publication of *Origin* by R. Weidenhammer, *Die landwirthschaftliche Thierzucht als Argument der Darwin'schen Theorie*, Stuttgart, 1864. According to the *Augsburger Allgemeinen Zeitung*'s critic in 1868, Darwin showed us 'that Moses had prescribed maintaining the purity of breeds, that Homer had described the lineage of Aeneas's horse . . . and Virgil had recommended keeping genealogical charts when breeding cattle. The golden experience of ancient times was not lost when Charlemagne carefully nurtured his noble stallions and even the Irish in the dark ages of the ninth century made sure there was good blood when breeding horses.' *Augsburger Allgemeinen Zeitung*, no. 15, 1868, p. 234. Also M. E. Derry, *Horses in Society: A Story of Animal Breeding and Marketing, 1800–1920*, Toronto and London, 2006, chapter 1: 'Modern Purebred Breeding: A Scientific or Cultural Method?' pp. 3–10.

57. F. Galton, *Inquiries into Human Faculty and Its Development*, London, 1883, p. 55.

58. B. Lowe, *Breeding Racehorses by the Figure System*, was published posthumously by William Allison, London, 1895, and included an impressive series of photos of famous horses taken by the photographer Clarence Hailey at Newmarket.

59. The *General Stud Book*, published by J. Weatherby, was first published in 1793 and had been revised five times by the time Lowe's work was published in 1895.

60. H. Goos, *Die Stamm-Mütter des englischen Vollblutpferdes*, Hamburg, 1885; J. P. Frentzel, *Familientafeln des englischen Vollbluts*, Berlin, 1889.

61. Cf. for example, R. Henning, *Zur Entstehung des Englischen Vollblutpferdes*, Stuttgart, 1901 (reprinted Hildesheim, 2007).

The Anatomy Lesson

1. D. Roche, *La culture équestre de l'Occideur XVIe–XIXe siècle. L'ombre du cheval*, Paris, 2008, vol. 1, chapter 7, pp. 231 ff., here pp. 258 f.

2. D. Ashton and D. B. Hare, *Rosa Bonheur: A Life and a Legend*, New York, 1981, p. 88.

3. After a period in the collections of A. T. Stewart and Cornelius Vanderbilt, it is now in the Metropolitan Museum in New York.

4. L. Eitner, *Géricault: His Life and Work*, London, 1982, p. 125; K. Kügler, 'Die Pferdedarstellungen Théodore Géricaults. Zur Entwicklung und Symbolik des Pferdemotivs in der Malerei der Neuzeit', MA thesis, Kiel, 1998, p. 76.

5. According to his first biographer, C. Clément, *Géricault: Étude biographique et critique*, Paris, 1867, p. 104.

6. Eitner, *Géricault*, pp. 133 f., describes some of the speculation surrounding his sudden departure. It also remains unclear whether Géricault worked on *Berberpferden* to the end or had given up the project months beforehand.

7. W. Whitney, *Géricault in Italy*, New Haven and London, 1997, p. 93, speaks of 'some eighty-five paintings and drawings related to the *Race of the Barberi Horses*', which are well known today.

8. W. Behringer, *Kulturgeschichte des Sports: Vom antiken Olympia bis ins 21. Jahrhundert*, Munich, 2012, p. 219.

9. J. W. von Goethe, *Italian Journey [1786–1788]*, translated by W. H. Auden and Elizabeth Mayer, London, 1962.

10. Whitney, *Géricault in Italy*, p. 113.

11. Ibid., p. 99.

12. Eitner, *Géricault*, pp. 128 f.

13. It is thanks to the precise chronology of the painter's individual working stages, reconstructed by Whitney, in *Géricault in Italy*, pp. 93 ff., that we can see this phase-change so clearly.

14. Eitner, *Géricault*, p. 126.

15. R. Simon, 'L'Angleterre', in *Géricault. Dessins & estampes des collections de l'École des Beaux-Arts*, edited by E. Brugerolles, Paris, 1997, pp. 77–81, here p. 80.

16. Ashton and Hare, *Rosa Bonheur*, pp. 83, 87; Brugerolles (ed.), *Géricault*, p. 244.

17. Ashton and Hare, *Rosa Bonheur*, p. 87.

18. To cite just one author of the many who could be mentioned here: I. Lavin, *Passato e presente nella storia dell'arte*, Turin, 1994.

19. Ashton and Hare, *Rosa Bonheur*, p. 82, cites M. Richard, *Étude dú cheval de service et de guerre*, Paris, 1859, as her most important source.

20. J. F. Debord, 'À propos de quelques dessins anatomiques de Géricault', in Brugerolles (ed.), *Géricault*, pp. 43–66, here in particular pp. 51 ff.

21. This is what Ozias Humphry claimed in his *Memoir* of George Stubbs of 1876, which dated back to discussions with Stubbs in his latter years; M. Warner, 'Stubbs and the Origins of the Thoroughbred', in M. Warner and R. Blake, *Stubbs and the Horse*, New Haven, CT, and London, 2004, pp. 101–21, here p. 103.

22. R. Musil, *The Man Without Qualities*, vol. 1, translated by S. Wilkins, London, 1996, chapter 13, p. 41: 'A racehorse of genius crystallizes the recognition of being a man without qualities.'

23. One example is the famous stallion Gimcrack, which between 1764 and 1769 changed hands five times and was painted multiple times, amongst others by Stubbs; F. Russell, 'Stubbs und seine Auftraggeber' in H. W. Rott (ed.), *George Stubbs 1724–1806. Die Schönheit der Tiere*, Munich, 2012, pp. 78–87, here p. 85.

24. Carlo Ruini, an illustrator of horse anatomies preceding Stubbs by one and a half centuries, carelessly sprinkled numbers and letters all over his illustrations; C. Ruini, *Anatomia del cavallo, infermità, et suoi rimedii*, Venice, 1618.

25. B. S. Albinus, *Tabulae sceleti et musculorum corporis humani*, Leiden, 1747. O. Kase, ' "Make the knife go with the pencil" – Wissenschaft und Kunst in George Stubbs's "Anatomy of the Horse" ', in Rott (ed.), *George Stubbs 1724–1806*, pp. 43–59, here pp. 52 ff.

26. Stubbs was in his early thirties when he produced the sketches in 1757–8. As he was unable to find a suitable engraver and had to complete it himself, the folio collection was not published until 1766. It brought him instant fame, although he was already in high demand as a horse and animal painter by this time; Warner, 'Stubbs and the Origins of the Thoroughbred', and M. Myrone, 'G. Stubbs – Zwischen Markt, Natur und Kunst', in Rott (ed.), *George Stubbs 1724–1806*, pp. 8–21.

27. Stubbs chose an ochre tone as the background, which in the case of *Whistlejacket* had a hint of green – a non-colour, of absolute neutrality.

28. According to Werner Busch in 'Stubbs Ästhetik', in Rott (ed.), *George Stubbs 1724–1806*, pp. 23–41, here p. 32.

29. Cf. for example M. Warner, 'Ecce Equus: Stubbs and the Horse of Feeling', in Warner and Blake, *Stubbs and the Horse*, pp. 1–17, here p. 11.

30. Busch, 'Stubbs Ästhetik', p. 39.

31. Kase, '"Make the knife go with the pencil"', pp. 48 ff.; on Lafosse, see also pp. 191–2.

32. Ibid., p. 50.

33. U. Krenzlin, *Johann Gottfried Schadow: Die Quadriga. Vom preußischen Symbol zum Denkmal der Nation*, Frankfurt, 1991, p. 28.

34. J.-O. Kempf, *Die Königliche Tierarzneischule in Berlin von Carl Gotthard Langhans. Eine baugeschichtliche Gebäudemonographie*, Berlin, 2008, pp. 120 ff.

35. 'The royal veterinary school was therefore tailored to the needs of the cavalry and was subordinate to the *Obermarstallsamt* in administrative terms.' Kempf, *Tierarzneischule*, p. 28.

36. M. Foucault, *Die Geburt der Klinik: Eine Archäologie des ärztlichen Blicks*, Munich, 1973.

37. 'The motif of a circular garland with *bucrania* dates back to Hellenistic and Roman sacrificial rites. The head of the sacrificial animal was decorated with ribbons and pendants at the sacrificial altar as a visible symbol. This decoration was an integral part of the artistic decoration of the temple.' Kempf, *Tierarzneischule*, p. 179.

38. Eitner, *Géricault*, p. 231.

39. Géricault had previously copied Stubbs's *Anatomy*; Eitner, *Géricault*, pp. 227, 351.

40. By the time of Géricault's death in January 1824, the horses were not yet fully paid off and were immediately sold for 7000 francs; Eitner, *Géricault*, p. 280.

41. Ibid., p. 235; then Kügler, 'Pferdedarstellungen', p. 81.

42. H. Alken, *The National Sports of Great Britain, with Descriptions in English and French*, London, 1821, plate 6, 'Doing their best'; also S. Deuchar, *Sporting Art in Eighteenth-Century England: A Social and Political History*, New Haven, CT, 1988, and Kügler, 'Pferdedarstellungen', pp. 84 f.

43. Anyone who thinks the opposite, such as L. de Nanteuil, 'L'homme et l'oeuvre', in *Géricault. No. special de Connaissance des Arts*, Paris, 1992, pp. 14–55, here p. 51, has their eyes closed to the unity of the work and the integrality of the artist's intentions. Blinder still is the admiration of L. Mannoni, *Etienne-Jules Marey. La mémoire de l'oeil*, Paris, 1999, p. 150. The best argument in defence of Géricault as a sports painter is given by K. Kügler, who points to the blurred background and the painter's 'transitory parallel movement'; in other words, the dynamism of the viewer's position showing new and original aspects of the picture; Kügler, 'Pferdedarstellungen', p. 83.

44. Cf. the study by A. Mayer, *Wissenschaft vom Gehen: Die Erforschung der Bewegung im 19. Jahrhundert*, Frankfurt, 2013, chapter 4, pp. 143 ff.; also A. Rabinbach, *The Human Motor: Energy, Fatigue and the Origins of Modernity*, Princeton, NJ, 1992, chapter 4, pp. 84 ff.

45. É. Duhousset, *Le cheval. Études sur les allures, l'extérieur et les proportions du cheval. Analyse de tableaux représentant des animaux. Dédié aux artistes*, Paris, 1874; an expanded edition was published in 1881 as *Le cheval. Allures, extérieur, proportions*. Also É. Duhousset, 'Le cheval dans l'art', *Gazette des beaux-arts*, XXVIII (1884), pp. 407–23; and XXIX (1884), pp. 46–54.

46. Mannoni, *Etienne-Jules Marey*, pp. 205 f.; F. Dagognet, *Etienne-Jules Marey : A Passion for the Trace*, New York, 1992, pp. 138 ff.

47. Mayer, *Wissenschaft vom Gehen*, pp. 155 f.

48. C. C. Hungerford, *Ernest Meissonier: Master in His Genre*, Cambridge and New York, 1999, p. 168.

49. H. Loyrette, *Degas*, Paris, 1991, p. 392.

50. Mayer, *Wissenschaft vom Gehen*, pp. 156 f.; Hungerford, *Meissonier*, p. 168.

51. His second major work, *La Méthode graphique dans les sciences expérimentales*, first published in 1878, was lengthened and reprinted in 1885 with a 'Supplément sur le développement de la méthode graphique par la photographie'.

52. The flood of studies on the origins of visual modernism, the origins of films and observational modernism in the last few decades has led to one aspect in particular – the debate about whether, when galloping, there is a moment when all four of the horse's hooves are in the air – receiving unprecedented attention, while the other 99 per cent of equine history, along with mountains of pertinent literature, have remained *terra incognita*, other than to the relatively small circle of experts, researchers, aficionados and enthusiasts, who know *everything*.

53. On Marey, cf. above all Mannoni, *Etienne-Jules Marey*; on Muybridge, cf. R. Solnit, *River of Shadows: Eadweard Muybridge and the Technological Wild West*, New York and London, 2003.

54. Mannoni, *Etienne-Jules Marey*, pp. 158 f.

55. Loyrette, *Degas*, p. 385.

56. Ibid, p. 464.

57. Elsewhere, Loyrette notes that the 'the anatomical inaccuracy of the horse's movement' is 'a throwback to a time when there were no photographs by Muybridge and Marey to consult'; H. Loyrette, *Degas: The Man and His Art*, translated by I. Mark Paris, New York, 1993, p. 123.

58. D. Sutton, *Edgar Degas. Life and Work*, New York, 1986, p. 160.

59. These were the details Degas focused on when copying the classics; *Degas. Klassik und Experiment*, edited by Alexander Eiling for Staatliche Kunsthalle, Karlsruhe, 2013, pp. 202 ff.

Connoisseurs and Conmen

1. M. Stoffregen-Büller, *Pferdewelt Europa. Die berühmtesten Gestüte, Reitschulen und Rennbahnen*, Münster, 2003, pp. 153 f.

2. P. Mellon and J. Baskett, *Reflections in a Silver Spoon: A Memoir*, New York, 1992, p. 265.

3. Even for Virginia, Paul Mellon's new passion was not without its consequences, as James Salter observes; 'in the 1920s and 30s Paul Mellon, a passionate hunter, bought up large areas of land and friends followed suit. From then on, the land was dedicated to horses and hunting. One could hear the excited, muffled barking of dogs on the hunt, while galloping horses appeared between the trees, with riders jumping over stone walls and trenches, going up and down slopes, slowing down a little and then accelerating again into a full gallop.' J. Salter, *Alles was ist*, Berlin, 2013, p. 49.

4. Mellon, *Reflections*, pp. 162 ff.

5. The catalogue from the Mellon collection (see note 6) contained numerous works dedicated to foxes and fox hunting, such as nos. 172: T. Smith, *The Life of a Fox* (1843), 181: W. C. Hobson, *Hobson's Fox-Hunting Atlas* (1848), 183: C. Tongue, *The Fox-Hunter's Guide* (1849), 330: E. Somerville and M. Ross, *Dan Russel the Fox* (1911), 324: J. Masefield, *Reynard the Fox* (1919) and 372: S. Sassoon, *Memoirs of a Fox-Hunting Man* (1929).

6. J. B. Podeschi, *Books on the Horse and Horsemanship: Riding, Hunting, Breeding and Racing, 1400–1941* (catalogue of the Paul Mellon Collection), New Haven, CT, 1981, p. ix.

7. F. H. Huth, *Works on Horses and Equitation. A Bibliographical Record of Hippology*, London, 1887; reprint by Georg Olms in the series *Documenta Hippologica*, Hildesheim and New York, 1981.

8. Gérard de Contades, *Le Driving en France 1547–1896*, Paris, 1898.

9. *Leçons de Science hippique générale ou Traité complet de l'art de connaître, de gouverner et d'élever le Cheval*, vol. 3, Paris, 1855.

10. Mennessier de la Lance, *Essai*, vol. 1, Paris, 1915, p. 659.

11. It was his 'love of equine science and his eighteen years of research and observation,' says Bouwinghausen, that 'put him a good position to publish useful entries on the development of the science, year after year, in this pocket book'. Bouwinghausen, 'Letter to the public', in *Taschenbuch für Pferdeliebhaber*, 3rd edn, Tübingen, 1795.

12. The second contract with Cotta of 29 March 1800, DLA Marbach, Cotta-Archiv, Agreement 2, Bouwinghausen.

13. See above, p. 154.

14. J. G. Prizelius, *Handbuch der Pferdewissenschaft zu Vorlesungen*, Lemgo, 1775, seems to be the first to include the term as part of a book title.

15. W. Gibson, *A new Treatise on the diseases of Horses*, London, 1750; W. Osmer, *A Treatise on the Diseases and Lameness of Horses*, London, 1759; J. Gaab, *Praktische Pferdearzneikunde*, Erlangen, 1770; D. Robertson, *Pferdearzneikunst*, Frankfurt, 1771; L. Vitet, *Médecine vétérinaire*, vol. 3, Lyons, 1771; C. W. Ammon, *Handbuch für angehende Pferdeärzte*, Frankfurt, 1776.

16. D. Roche, *La gloire et la puissance. Histoire de la culture équestre, XVIe–XIXe siècle*, Paris, 2011, p. 217.

17. Henry, Earl of Pembroke, *Military Equitation, or a method of breaking Horses and teaching soldiers to ride, designed for the use of the Army*, London, 1778.

18. La Guérinière, *École de Cavalerie*, German translation, p. 46 (my italics).

19. J.-O. Kempf, *Die Königliche Tierarzneischule in Berlin von Carl Gotthard Langhans. Eine baugeschichtliche Gebäudemonographie*, Berlin, 2008, p. 22.

20. A. von den Driesch and J. Peters, *Geschichte der Tiermedizin: 5000 Jahre Tierheilkunde*, Stuttgart, 2003, p. 126.

21. R. Froehner, *Kulturgeschichte der Tierheilkunde*, 3rd edn, Konstanz, 1968, p. 78.

22. Some works on equine art or equine science contain sections on 'horse examination' and 'assessment methods'. For example, W. Baumeister, *Anleitung zur Kenntniß des Aeußern des Pferdes*, 5th edn, Stuttgart, 1863, pp. 312 ff.

23. C. Bourgelat, *Traité de la conformation extérieure du cheval*, Paris, 1768–9, German translation: *Anweisung zur Kenntniß und Behandlung der Pferde*, translated from the French by J. Knobloch, Prague and Leipzig, 1789.

24. Claudia Schmölders pays Bourgelat too great a compliment when she claims that he baptizes horse enthusiasts (C. Schmölders, 'Der Charakter des Pferdes. Zur Physiognomik der Veterinäre um 1800', in

E. Agazzi and M. Beller (eds), *Evidenze e ambiguità della fisionomia umana*, Viareggio, 1998, pp. 403–22, here p. 410). Bourgelat may have been an ambitious teacher of equestrian art and a founder of a school, but he was neither the first, nor was he without rival. His greatest role model, de Solleysel, to name just one, preceded him by over a century.

25. Ibid., p. 6.
26. E. Panofsky, *The Codex Huygens and Leonardo da Vinci's Art Theory*, London, 1940, pp. 51–8 and plates 39–48.
27. Bourgelat, *Anweisung*, vol. II, p. 14.
28. 'The study of the signs of beauty and health in a horse is a science, by virtue of which we learn to judge the beauty of a horse in both its outer appearance, as well as in respect to its quality and utility.' J. G. Naumann, *Ueber die vorzüglichsten Theile der Pferdewissenschaft: Ein Handbuch für Officiere, Bereiter und Oeconomen*, Berlin, 1800, p. 24.
29. F. Schiller, *On the Aesthetic Education of Man*, translated by E. M. Wilkinson and L. A. Willoughby, Oxford, 1967, letter no. 6, p. 43.
30. Some examples include J. A. Kersting, *Zeichenlehre oder Anweisung zur Kenntniß und Beurtheilung der vorzüglichsten Beschaffenheit eines Pferdes: Ein Buch zur Uebersicht für Roßärzte und Pferdeliebhaber nach den bewährtesten Grundsätzen und Erfahrungen*, Herborn, 1804; E. Schwabe, *Zeichenlehre, oder Anweisung zur Kenntniss und Beurtheilung der vorzüglichsten Beschaffenheit eines Pferdes*, Marburg, 1803.
31. J. G. Naumann, *Ueber die vorzüglichsten Theile*, p. xi.
32. S. Széchenyi, *Über Pferde, Pferdezucht und Pferderennen*, Leipzig and Pesth, 1830, p. 128.
33. Xenophon, 'On Horsemanship', *Hiero the Tyrant and Other Treatises*, translated by R. Waterfield, London, 1997, p. 95.
34. With comments, explanations and annotations by J. F. Rosenzweig, Leipzig, 1780.
35. A. Mortgen, *Enthüllte Geheimnisse aller Handelsvortheile der Pferdehändler* ('Secrets of the Horse Trade Revealed'), Weimar, 1824; quote from the 3rd edition, Weimar, 1840. The work also contains an 'Appendix on the easiest and simplest means of nicking the tail and the advantages of such for the trader'.
36. Ibid., p. 5.
37. Ibid., p. 8.
38. Ibid., p. 28.
39. Ibid., p. 29. A. Mortgen's confessions seem to have been a great success with the public, as fifteen years later, in 1839, a sequel to his book of advice was published within Tennecker's equine almanac, *Jahrbuch der*

Pferdezucht ('Almanac of Horse Husbandry'), a successor to Bouwing-hausen's *Taschenbuch für Pferdeliebhaber* ('Handbook for Horse Lovers'). Once again it was not the Jewish horse trader himself who tells his story, but another with whom he shared it and who writes it down for posterity. This time it is Tennecker himself, the editor of the 'Almanac of Horse Husbandry', who puts his name to the main story and relates the accounts supposedly entrusted to him by a certain Moses Aron, a Berlin horse trader. Tennecker is no less sparing with the anti-Semitic clichés than Dr Lentin, the narrator of the story of the late Abraham Mortgen; S. von Tennecker, *Redensarten und Manieren der Pferdehändler, von Moses Aron, Pferdehändler in Berlin: Ein Anhang zu Enthüllte Geheimnisse aller Handelsvortheile der Pferdehändler* ('The Ways and Words of Horse Traders by Moses Aron, Berlin Horse Trader: An Addendum to "Secrets of the Horse Trade Revealed"'), in *Jahrbuch der Pferdezucht, Pferdekenntniß, Pferdehandel, die militärische Campagne-, Schul- und Kunstreiberei und Roßalzneikunst in Deutschland und den angrenzenden Ländern auf des Jahr 1839* ('Almanac of Horse Husbandry, Horse Knowledge, Horse Trading, Military Equestrianism and Horse Doctoring in Germany and the Neighbouring Countries, for the Year 1839') 15th edn, Weimar, 1839, pp. 231–472.

40. W. G. Ploucquet, *Über die Hauptmängel der Pferde*, Tübingen, 1790, p. 4.
41. Ibid., p. 22.
42. Ibid., p. 32.
43. Ibid., p. 33.
44. Ibid., p. 35.
45. Ibid., p. 72.
46. Ibid., p. 77.

Researchers

1. D. Rayfield, *The Dream of Lhasa: The Life of Nikolay Przhevalsky*, London, 1976.
2. The animal later named by Nikolay Mikhailovich Przhevalsky, *Equus przewalskii*, is not a direct ancestor of the domestic horse, but a subspecies of *Equus ferus*, the wild horse. Its distribution is limited to the area of the Dzungarian Basin and parts of south-western Mongolia. For further differences, see L. Boyd and D. A. Houpt (eds), *Przewalski's horse: The History and Biology of an endangered Species*, Albany, New York, 1994, as well as the relevant site from Cologne Zoo: http://www.koelner-zoo.de/takhi/Seiten/biologie-takhi_dt.html.

3. Przewalski has been described as taxonomically prolific, lending his name to a gazelle, a gecko, a type of poplar, a rhododendron, an ephedra and a horse. He brought back 20,000 zoological and 16,000 botanical specimens from his journeys. C. Tyler, *Wild West China: The Taming of Xinjiang*, London, 2003, p. 13.

4. The best synopsis of the story of the Przewalski horse since its discovery, along with a summary of the associated literature and research, is found in the edited reissue by W. Meid of S. Bökönyi, *Das Przewalski-Pferd oder das mongolische Wildpferd: Die Wiederbelebung einer fast ausgestorbenen Tierart*, Innsbruck, 2008. Przewalski's official report of his first three research journeys was also translated into German (Bökönyi, p. 154); a summary of the fourth journey, edited by Sven Hedin, was published in 1922 in Leipzig.

5. D. Schimmelpenninck van der Oye, *Toward the Rising Sun: Russian Ideologies of Empire and the Path to War with Japan*, DeKalb, IL, 2001, chapter 2, pp. 24–41.

6. K. E. Meyer and S. B. Brysac, *Tournament of Shadows: The Great Game and the Race for Empire in Central Asia*, Washington DC, 1999, chapter 9, pp. 223–40, in particular pp. 224 f. On personality and character, the researcher as a scientific conqueror and Przewalski's role models, see also R. Habermas, 'Born to go wild? Missionare, Forscherinnen und andere Reisende im 19. Jahrhundert', unpublished manuscript of a lecture in Erfurt in 2014, gratefully received from Mrs Habermas; here, particularly, p. 16 on the 'heroic outdoor research all-rounder', who already back then must have seemed to 'come from another time'.

7. Ibid., pp. 33 ff.

8. N. T. Rothfels, 'Bring 'em back alive: Carl Hagenbeck and exotic animal and people trades in Germany, 1848–1914', Ph.D. thesis, Harvard University, 1994; L. Dittrich and A. Rieke-Müller, *Carl Hagenbeck (1844–1913): Tierhandel und Schaustellungen im Deutschen Kaiserreich*, Frankfurt, 1998, pp. 53–64.

9. Rayfield, *The Dream of Lhasa*, p. 261.

10. S. Bökönyi, *Das Przewalski-Pferd oder Das mongolische Wildpferd: Die Wiederbelebung einer fast ausgestorbenen Tierart*, Budapest and Innsbruck, 2008.

11. German Reichstag session reports from 4 March 1899; http://reichstagsprotokolle.de

12. F. Boas, *The Mind of Primitive Man*, New York, 1911; resumed by B. L. Whorf, *Language, Mind and Reality*, Madras, 1942.

13. E. Strittmatter, *Poetik des Phantasmas: Eine imaginationstheoretische Lektüre der Werke Hartmanns von Aue*, Heidelberg, 2013, p. 232.

14. Ibid., p. 233.

15. M. Jähns, *Ross und Reiter in Leben und Sprache, Glauben und Geschichte der Deutschen: Eine kulturhistorische Monografie*, 2 vols, Leipzig, 1872, vol. 1, p. 7.

16. Ibid., p. 12. Jähns, the political philologist, uses a 'purified spelling' approach which, as can be seen here, suppresses long vowels and consonants (although he himself complains of some 'inconsistencies'). However, unlike the Grimm brothers, he maintains the conventional approach to upper and lower case.

17. Ibid., p. 13.

18. Ibid., p. 36.

19. Ibid., p. 38.

20. Ibid., p. 39.

21. For a selection from Grimm, see S. Martus, *Die Brüder Grimm: Eine Biografie*, Berlin, 2009, pp. 488 ff.

22. Ibid., pp. 419–62.

23. Ibid., p. 162.

24. This is admittedly only true of the German language and Western horse culture. For the East, the work by the Freiherrn von Hammer is stronger than that of Jähn from a philological point of view; J. v. Hammer-Purgstall, *Das Pferd bei den Arabern*, Vienna, 1855–6, reprint of the *Documenta Hippologica* series, Hildesheim, 1981.

25. Jähns, *Ross und Reiter*, vol. 2, p. 329.

26. Ibid., p. 330.

27. Ibid. p. 410.

28. Ibid., pp. 406 f.

29. Ibid., p. 418.

30. Ibid., pp. 434–45.

31. Cf. in particular, *Das französische Heer von der Großen Revolution bis zur Gegenwart*, Leipzig, 1873; *Handbuch einer Geschichte des Kriegswesens von der Urzeit bis zur Renaissance*, Leipzig, 1880; *Heeresverfassungen und Völkerleben*, Berlin, 1885.

32. 'We know who helped Germany into the saddle! Yes, now she will be able to ride . . .' Jähns, *Ross und Reiter*, vol. 1, p. vi.

33. See above, p. 175.

34. See A. Mayer, *Wissenschaft vom Gehen: Die Erforschung der Bewegung im 19. Jahrhundert*, Frankfurt, 2013, pp. 146 ff. for more on the dispute between the schools of the riding instructors François Baucher and the

Vicomte d'Aure. On these two, see also Mennessier de la Lance, *Essai*, vol. 1, Paris, 1915, vol. 1, pp. 44–50 (d'Aure) and pp. 85–91 (Baucher).

35. A. Rabinbach, *The Human Motor: Energy, Fatigue and the Origins of Modernity*, Princeton, NJ, 1992, pp. 133 ff.

36. G. Bonnal, *Équitation, par le Commandant Bonnal*, Paris, 1890.

37. Ibid., p. 224.

38. L. Mannoni, *Etienne-Jules Marey. La mémoire de l'oeil*, Paris, 1999, p. 256.

39. U. Raulff, *Der unsichtbare Augenblick*, Göttingen, 1999, pp. 65 ff.

40. If the Codex Huygens drawings are indeed to be attributed to him.

41. E. Panofsky, *Le Codex Huygens et la théorie de l'art de Léonard de Vinci*, Paris, 1996, p. 23 (Panofsky's commentary focuses on Folio 22 of the Codex).

42. According to Marc Bloch in his review of R. Lefebvre des Noëttes, '*La force motrice animale à travers les âges*', *Revue de synthèse historique*, XLI, 1926, pp. 91–9, here p. 92.

43. R. Lefebvre des Noëttes, *La force motrice animale à travers les âges*, Paris 1924, p. 30.

44. R. Lefebvre des Noëttes, *Le cheval de selle à travers les âges: Contribution à l'histoire de l'esclavage*, 2 vols, Paris, 1931.

45. Ibid., pp. 174–90.

46. Ibid., pp. 185 f.

47. Ibid., p. 188. See also R. Lefebvre des Noëttes, 'La "Nuit" du Moyen Age et son Inventaire', *Mercure de France*, 235 (1932), No. 813, pp. 572–99.

48. M. Bloch speaks of antiquity being in 'une sorte de sommeil de l'invention technique', a technological slumber; for example in note 13, p. 94.

49. Bloch, for example, in note 13, pp. 94–8. In 1935 Bloch returned to the point ('Les "inventions" médiévales', *Annales d'histoire économique et sociale*, 7 (1935), pp. 634–43, and contested the causal link between improved harnesses and the introduction of the watermill which Lefebvre des Noëttes claimed, but he agreed that his main thesis of the connection between cheaper manpower and technical inventions was worth further consideration. According to Bloch, the watermill was an ancient invention, but had only been used since the Middle Ages; Bloch, 'Avènement et conquête du moulin à eau', *Annales*, 7 (1935), pp. 538–63.

50. On the story of the critical reception of Lefebvre des Noëttes, see M.-C. Amouretti, 'L'attelage dans l'Antiquité. Le prestige d'une erreur scientifique', *Annales E. S. C.* 1991, book 1, pp. 219–32. The most relevant studies on the way his theory was received were the long dissertation by P. Vigneron, *Le cheval dans l'antiquité gréco-romaine*, 2 vols, Nancy, 1968; J. Spruytte, *Études expérimentales sur l'attelage. Contribution à*

l'histoire du cheval, Paris, 1977; and G. Raepsaet, *Attelages et techniques de transport dans le monde gréco-romain*, Brussels, 2002.

51. L. White, Jr, 'The Contemplation of Technology', in *Machina ex deo. Essays in the Dynamism of Western Culture*, Cambridge, MA, 1968, pp. 151–68, here p. 157; below, p. 242.

52. J. A. Weller, Roman traction systems; http://www.humanist.de/rome/rts, p. 2.

53. According to Schillings in a letter to the 6th International Congress of Zoology in Bern, quoted by H. Gundlach, 'Carl Stumpf, Oskar Pfungst, der Kluge Hans und eine geglückte Vernebelungsaktion', *Psychologische Rundschau*, 57 (2), pp. 96–105, here p. 99. This excellent review provides the exact chronology of the events of the summer of 1904 and sheds light on the background of the scholarly dispute regarding 'Clever Hans'.

54. Ibid., p. 102.

55. K. Krall, *Denkende Tiere. Beiträge zur Tierseelenkunde auf Grund eigener Versuche. Der kluge Hans und meine Pferde Muhamed und Zarif*, Leipzig, 1912. Also see the document on the case of 'Clever Hans' and the 'Elberfeld horse', compiled by the first qualified female agronomist in Germany, Henny Jutzler-Kindermann, *Können Tiere denken?* St Goar, 1996.

56. Ibid., p. 69.

57. P. Kurzeck, *Ein Sommer, der bleibt*, audio book, Berlin, 2007, 4 CDs, here CD 1.

58. The tough practitioners from the manège were convinced that they were 'tricks' the horses had been taught.

59. O. Pfungst, *Das Pferd des Herrn von Osten (Der kluge Hans). Ein Beitrag zur experimentellen Tier- und Menschen-Psychologie. Mit einer Einleitung von Prof. Dr. C. Stumpf*, Leipzig, 1907. The English translation, *Clever Hans (The Horse of Mr. von Osten)*, was published in 1911 in New York and can now be found online in its entirety as the Project Gutenberg eBook of *Clever Hans*. Gundlach, 'Carl Stumpf' (see note 53) portrays with convincing arguments the unusual genesis of the book and deals with the question of authorship.

60. 'Hans can neither read, count nor make calculations. He knows nothing of coins or cards, calendars or clocks, nor can he respond, by tapping or otherwise, to a number spoken to him but a moment before. Finally, he has not a trace of musical ability.' Pfungst, *Clever Hans*, p. 23.

61. Prof. Dr Carl Stumpf, Head of the Psychological Institute of Berlin University, was the student Pfungst's scientific supervisor and Head of the Examination Board which visited Hans on 11 and 12 September 1904. More on this in Gundlach, 'Carl Stumpf', p. 101.

62. Krall, *Denkende Tiere*, p. 7.

63. Ibid., pp. 48–53.

64. Ibid., p. 59.

65. Ibid., p. 8.

66. This is the often quoted work by Krall, *Denkende Tiere* (see note 55).

67. M. Maeterlinck, 'Die Pferde von Elberfeld. Ein Beitrag zur Tierpsychologie', *Die neue Rundschau*, XXV, 1 (1914), pp. 782–820, here p. 788.

68. Ibid.

69. Ibid., p. 801.

70. Ibid., p. 818.

71. Ibid., pp. 810 f.

72. Ibid., p. 818.

73. As late as 1977 in *Thinking with Horses* (London), Henry Blake claimed that horses could communicate in more subtle ways than men, in particular through 'extrasensory perception and telepathy'.

74. Ibid., p. 816.

75. Cf. the so-called 'Elberfeld Fragment', in F. Kafka, *Nachgelassene Schriften und Fragmente I. Apparatband*, edited by M. Pasley, Frankfurt, 2002, p. 71. See also I. Schiffermüller, 'Elberfelder Protokolle. Franz Kafka und die klugen Pferde', in R. Calzoni (ed.), *'Ein in der Phantasie durchgeführtes Experiment'. Literatur und Wissenschaft nach 1900*, Göttingen, 2010, pp. 77–90.

76. Kafka, 'Elberfeld', pp. 226 f. For the English translation of this extract, see Franz Kafka, *The Burrow: Posthumously Published Short Fiction*, trans. M. Hofmann, London, 2017.

77. As Schiffermüller argues in 'Elberfelder Protokolle', p. 79.

78. G. Deleuze and F. Guattari, *Kafka: Toward a Minor Literature*, translated by D. Polan, Minneapolis and London, 1986.

79. D. Grünbein, 'Der kluge Hans', *Sinn und Form*, LXVI, 1(2014), pp. 28–35.

80. R. Koselleck, 'Der Aufbruch in die Moderne oder das Ende des Pferdezeitalters', in 'Historikerpreis der Stadt Münster 2003', Münster City Historian Prize booklet, 18 July 2003, pp. 23–37.

81. Ibid., p. 37.

82. See p. 109.

83. A. Alföldi, *Der frührömische Reiteradel und seine Ehrenabzeichen*, Baden-Baden, 1952, especially pp. 53 and 120 f.; A. Alföldi, *Die Struktur des voretruskischen Römerstaates*, Heidelberg, 1974.

84. J. F. Gilliam, text for an Alföldi retrospective, manuscript in the Institute of Advanced Study archive, Faculty, Alföldi Box I.

85. L. White, Jr, *Medieval Religion and Technology. Collected Essays*, Berkeley, CA, 1978, p. xv.

86. M. McLuhan, *Understanding Media. The Extensions of Man*, London, 1964, pp. 192 f.

87. See Xenophon's instructions for how soldiers should jump onto the horse from the side or behind in Xenophon, *Hipparchichus*, 7, 1–2, and *Vegetius*, I, 18.

88. For an early historical overview of this significant piece of technical riding equipment (the stirrup), see R. Zschille and R. Forrer, *Die Steigbügel in ihrer Formen-Entwicklung. Characterisirung und Datirung der Steigbügel unserer Culturvölker*, Berlin, 1896, pp. 2 f.

89. L.White, Jr, *Medieval Technology and Social Change*, London, Oxford and New York, 1962, chapter II: 'The Origin and Diffusion of the Stirrup', pp. 14 ff.

90. Ibid.

91. L.White, Jr, 'The Medieval Roots of Modern Technology and Science', in *Medieval Religion and Technology. Collected Essays*, pp. 75–92, here p. 78.

92. W. Schivelbusch, *Geschichte der Eisenbahnreise, Exkurs: Geschichte des Schocks*, Munich, 1977, pp. 134–41, here p. 135.

93. White, *Medieval Technology*.

94. Ibid.

95. In the 1970s, it was the epigones of Walter Benjamin, and in the 1980s and 1990s the followers of *microstoria* and *close reading*, who cultivated this kind of synthetic history. The idea that through pious and patient immersion in historic details ('devotion to the insignificant'), one can reach comprehensive panoramas of interpretation, has long been part of the medicine cabinet of the historical apothecary. I confess that I myself still like to take the occasional sniff from this vial.

96. Their scathing response to White's book is in contrast to the positive reaction by historian of ideas Ernst Kantorowicz: 'It (*Medieval Technology and Social Change*, 1962) is, in my opinion, the best book on medieval problems (mine included) that I have read in twenty years. . . . It is so good because he comes close to fulfilling a dream of mine, which I can never hope to materialize: an oecology of history. He only grabs a few points: the stirrup, the horse-shoe, the harnesss, the beans, and a few other things; but the cosmica he combines with the introduction of these gadgets are amazing, and they would please English historians far more, because they are "material", than all the

"metaphysical" things that I would do.' Kantorowicz to Maurice Bowra, 22 March 1962, Bowra papers, Wadham College, Oxford.

97. White, *Medieval Technology*, p. xiv.

III THE LIVING METAPHOR—*PATHOS*
Napoleon

1. On the nature, history and symbolism of the donkey, see J. Person, *Esel: Ein Portrait*, Berlin, 2013.

2. A. Rüstow, *Freedom and Domination: A Historical Critique of Civilization*, Princeton, NJ, 1980, p. 110. (German title: *Ortsbestimmung der Gegenwart. Eine universalgeschichtliche Kultukritik*, Zurich, 1950, p. 74.)

3. D. Roche, *La gloire et la puissance: Histoire de la culture équestre, XVIe–XIXe siècle*, Paris, 2011, chapter 'Art équestre, art de gouverner', pp. 220 ff.

4. S. Freud (1923), 'The Ego and the Id', translated by J. Riviere, *The Standard Edition of the Complete Psychological Works of Sigmund Freud*, vol. 19, ed. J. Strachey, London, 1961.

5. H. Blumenberg, *Theorie der Unbegrifflichkeit*, Frankfurt, 2007, p. 61.

6. K. Pomian, *Vom Sammeln: Die Geburt des Museums*, Berlin, 1988, pp. 50 ff.

7. 'The king is not king without his horse.' Yves Grange, 'Signification du rôle politique du cheval (XVIIIe et XIXe siècles)', in J. P. Digard (ed.), *Des chevaux et des hommes*, Avignon, 1988, pp. 63–82, here p. 65.

8. S. Lewitscharoff, *Blumenberg*, Berlin, 2011, p. 10.

9. On the concept of composition, cf. B. Latour, 'Ein Versuch, das "Kompositionistische Manifest" zu schreiben', a lecture given to the Munich University Society on 8 February 2010; http://www.heise.de/tp/artikel/32/32069/1.html

10. H. von Kleist, *The Marquise of O— and Other Stories*, translated by D. Luke and N. Reeves, London, 1978, p. 116.

11. Kafka's country doctor unexpectedly stumbles upon two horses in precisely such a pigsty and it is with them that the protagonist starts out on his hellish nocturnal journey.

12. Kleist, *The Marquise of O— and Other Stories*, p. 211.

13. J. Traeger, *Der reitende Papst. Ein Beitrag zur Ikonographie des Papsttums*, Munich, 1970, p. 97.

14. I will leave Kleist at this point, although there is still much more to say about the (also apocalyptic) importance of the horse as a symbol of justice (Traeger, *Der reitende Papst*, pp. 102 ff.). The doubling of horses – to make a pair of black horses – could allude to the horses of the Dioscuri, Castor and Pollux, on Rome's Capitoline Hill. Kleist himself hints at this when he describes the black horses peering out of the pig-sty, after the servant Herse had lifted off the roof boards: 'there they stood, poking their heads through the roof *like geese* . . .' (Kleist, *The Marquise of O— and Other Stories*, p. 124).

15. Exceptions were Dijon and Rennes, where 'one initially sufficed with toppling over the Sun King's riders and temporarily leaving their horses be . . .' V. Hunecke, *Europäische Reitermonumente: Ein Ritt durch die Geschichte Europas von Dante bis Napoleon*, Paderborn, 2008, p. 284.

16. Ibid., p. 288.

17. Ibid., p. 13. 'At the time of Cassiodorus (*c*.490–580 CE), the Roman equestrian monuments still formed "vast herds" ("*greges abundantissimi equorum*").'

18. We know a thing or two about Caesar's cavalry and also about his Gallic opponents (the curious work by M.-W. Schulz, *Caesar zu Pferde*, Hildesheim, 2009), but we have no graphical representations of how he himself rode a horse.

19. Hunecke, *Reitermonumente*; U. Keller, *Reitermonumente absolutistischer Fürsten*, München, 1971; J. Poeschke et al. (eds), *Praemium Virtutis III. Reiterstandbilder von der Antike bis zum Klassizismus*, Munich, 2008.

20. Other significant exceptions to this rule are the equestrian statues of Prince Eugene (by sculptors Fernkorn and Pönninger, 1865) in Vienna's Heldenplatz and Peter the Great (by Falconet, 1782) in St Petersburg's Senate Square.

21. See p. 404, note 29.

22. J. A. S. Oertel painted the scene of the toppling of the New York monuments in 1852.

23. Hunecke, *Reitermonumente*, p. 289.

24. Cf. the outstanding study by D. O'Brien, *After the Revolution: Antoine-Jean Gros, Painting and Propaganda under Napoleon*, Philadelphia, PA, 2006; and M. H. Brunner, *Antoine-Jean Gros: Die Napoleonischen Historienbilder*, Ph.D. thesis, Bonn, 1979.

25. C. Henry, 'Bonaparte franchissant les Alpes au Grand-Saint-Bernard. Matériaux et principes d'une icône politique', in D. Roche (ed.), *Le cheval et la guerre du XVe au XXe siècle*, Paris, 2002, pp. 347–65.

26. Hunecke, *Reitermonumente*, p. 291.

27. Nicolas Villaumé, *Histoire de la révolution française*, 1864, p. 312, cited by J. Burckhardt, *Kritische Gesamtausgabe*, vol. 28: *Geschichte des Revolutionszeitalters*, Munich and Basle, 2009, p. 521.

28. L. S. Mercier in *Le nouveau Paris*, vol. 2, p. 374, is of the same opinion as Couthon: 'Had Robespierre mounted a horse, he might have rallied the crowd around him.' Cf. also the account by J. Burckhardt, *Geschichte des Revolutionszeitalter*, p. 521.

29. Burckhardt, *Geschichte des Revolutionszeitalters*, pp. 795 f. It is reasonable to doubt Johannes Willms's speculation that Sieyès only took riding lessons to 'cut a *bella figura* next to Bonaparte'. J. Willms, *Napoleon: Eine Biographie*, Munich, 2005, p. 203.

30. The idea of the historical loser who would not have lost the game had he mounted a horse at the right time linked Napoleon not with Robespierre, but with Louis XVI who failed to respond on horseback, when revolutionaries stormed the Tuileries on 20 June 1792. As an eyewitness wrote to his brother Joseph: 'Si Louis XVI s'était montré à cheval, la victoire lui fût restée.' ('Had Louis XVI mounted his horse, victory would have been his.') Also see Roche, *La gloire*, p. 270.

31. According to the English historian and conservationist Jill Hamilton, on this day Napoleon opted for a bigger and taller mount than usual; J. Hamilton, *Marengo: The Myth of Napoleon's Horse*, London, 2000, p. 58.

32. Quoted in Traeger, *Der reitende Papst*, p. 12.

33. Louis Antoine Fauvelet de Bourrienne, *Memoirs of Napoleon Bonaparte*, London, 1836.

34. See Hegel's famous letter to Niethammer of 13 October 1806, in G. W. F. Hegel, *Hegel: The Letters*, translated by C. Butler and C. Seiler, Bloomington, IN, 1985, p. 114.

35. G. W. F. Hegel, *Vorlesungen über die Philosophie der Weltgeschichte*, vol. 4, Leipzig, 1944, p. 930.

36. 'His way in love was only a *despotisme de plus*.' J. Burckhardt, 'Napoleon I. nach den neuesten Quellen', in *Kritische Gesamtausgabe*, vol. 13, *Vorträge 1870–1892*, Munich and Basle, 2003, pp. 292–340, here p. 300.

37. Hamilton, *Marengo*, p. 151. Regarding Napoleon's horse, see also L. Merllié, *Le cavalier Napoléon et ses chevaux*, Paris, 1980; P. Osché, *Les chevaux de Napoléon*, Aosta, 2002, as well as various articles on the website of *Napoleonica: Revue internationale d'histoire des deux Empires Napoléoniens*, edited by the Fondation Napoléon.

38. Hamilton, *Marengo* (with reference to Madame de Rémusat), p. 6.

39. 'Napoleon rode *sans grâce*, exclusively Arabians, *parce qu'ils s'arrêtent à l'instant*. He loved to gallop down steep paths and often fell, which

was not talked about. He was also unlucky at carriage driving: he once completely overturned a four-horse carriage in St Cloud.' Burckhardt, vol. 13, *Vorträge 1870–1892*, p. 298. Napoleon behaved in just as dissolute a manner when hunting, which according to Burckhardt he primarily loved because of the vigorous riding; ibid., p. 304; also Roche, *La gloire*, pp. 274 f.; on Napoleon's accidents, cf. also Hamilton, *Marengo*, p. 95.

40. Hamilton, *Marengo*, pp. 31 f.

41. 'Like his general staff and his dragoons, in Egypt he adopted the bit and saddle of the Mamelukes. He also brought a whole squadron of Mamelukes with him back to France – the first cavalry unit to ride in Arab style – and he included them in the order of battle of the French army.' D. Bogros, 'Essai d'analyse du discours français sur l'équitation arabe', in *Des chevaux et des hommes: equitation et société*, Avignon, 1988.

42. Ibid., pp. 65, 70. On the Napoleonic cavalry and their deployment, cf. Roche, *La gloire*, pp. 299 ff.

43. Hamilton, *Marengo*, pp. 91 f.; Osché, *Les chevaux*, p. 270.

44. Cf. the beautiful catalogue from the exhibition *Chevaux et cavaliers arabes dans les arts d'Orient et d'Occident*, L'Institut du monde arabe, Paris, 2002 (with extensive bibliography).

45. This painting, which was once a key exhibit at the Princeton University Art Museum, New Jersey, disappeared into storage several years ago during a gallery renovation.

46. Gaethgens, references in T. W. Gaethgens, 'Das nazarenische Napoleonbildnis der Brüder Olivier', in M. Kern (ed.), *Geschichte und Ästhetik. Festschrift für Werner Busch zum 60. Geburtstag*, Munich, 2004, pp. 296–312, here p. 303.

47. B. Baczko, 'Un Washington manqué: Napoléon Bonaparte', in B. Baczko, *Politiques de la révolution française*, Paris, 2008, pp. 594–693, here pp. 596 ff.

48. Ibid., p. 603.

49. Ibid., pp. 604 f.

50. F. Furet, 'La Révolution, de Turgot à Jules Ferry', in *La révolution française*, Paris, 2007, p. 478.

51. See Emmanuel, comte de Las Cases, *Mémorial de Sainte-Hélène*, London, 1823, here quoting Baczko, *Politiques*, pp. 681 f.

52. O. Figes, *A People's Tragedy: The Russian Revolution, 1891–1924*, London, 1996, p. 673.

53. Ibid.

54. W. Hegemann, *Napoleon oder 'Kniefall vor dem Heros'*, Hellerau, 1927, p. 579.

55. Ridden to death? In the light of films such as *The Man Who Shot Liberty Valance* (1962), we can hardly say the cliché is long gone. James Stewart plays a lawyer who seemingly beats the gunslinger Lee Marvin with his Colt alone, but in truth he is armed with the book of law.

56. F. Kafka, *The Transformation ('Metamorphosis') and Other Stories*, translated by M. Pasley, London, 1992, pp. 154 f. All the subsequent quotes from the short story come from this edition.

57. R. Musil, *The Man Without Qualities*, vol. 1, translated by S. Wilkins, London, 1996, p. 42.

The Fourth Rider

1. Cf. the official site of the US Army Joined Force Headquarters (http://www.usstatefuneral.mdw.army.mil/military-honors/caparisoned-horse) or see references to specific horses such as Black Jack or Sergeant York.

2. Wikipedia article on the 'Riderless horse', last visited on 24 June 2015.

3. W. Brückner, 'Roß und Reiter im Leichenzeremoniell. Deutungsversuch eines historischen Rechtsbrauches', in *Rheinisches Jahrbuch für Volkskunde*, vol. 15/16 (1964–5), pp. 144–209, here pp. 156, 159. Curiously the author, although he begins and ends with the funeral of J. F. Kennedy (pp. 144 f., 209), and indeed mentions the boots in the stirrups, does not mention their reversal. On the custom of reversing the saddle of the deceased, see J. von Negelein, 'Das Pferd im Seelenglauben und Totenkult, Part II', in *Zeitschrift des Vereins für Volkskunde in Berlin* 12, Berlin, 1902, pp. 13–25, here p. 16.

4. Cf. also *Handwörterbuch des deutschen Aberglaubens*, H. Bächtold-Stäubli (ed.), vol. VI, Berlin and Leipzig, 1935, Sp. 1673.

5. H. Heimpel, *Die halbe Violine: Eine Jugend in der Haupt- und Residenzstadt München*, Frankfurt, 1978, pp. 196 f.

6. Negelein, 'Das Pferd im Seelenglauben und Totenkult, Part I', in *Zeitschrift des Vereins für Volkskunde in Berlin* 11, Berlin, 1901, pp. 406–20, here p. 410.

7. R. Koselleck, *Zeitschichten. Studien zur Historik*, Frankfurt, 2000, p. 101.

8. Ibid., p. 102.

9. R. Koselleck, 'Der Aufbruch in die Moderne oder das Ende des Pferdezeitalters', in 'Historikerpreis der Stadt Münster 2003', Münster City Historian Prize booklet, 18 July 2003, p. 29. 'Anyone who could be trampled under hoof could also be subjugated.'

10. N. Luhmann, *Macht*, Stuttgart, 1975, pp. 23 ff.

11. C. Darwin, *The Expression of the Emotions in Man and Animals*, New York, 1872.

12. J. Burkhardt, *Recollections of Rubens*, translated by M. Hottinger, London, 1950, p. 146.

13. It did not escape the painter's notice that horses genuinely have unusually large and agile eyes. They are larger than those of any other land mammal and give them a particularly broad field of vision. M.-A. Leblanc, *The Mind of the Horse. An Introduction to Equine Cognition*, Cambridge, MA, 2013, pp. 126 ff.

14. A. Schaeffer, *Ross und Reiter. Ihre Darstellung in der plastischen Kunst. In Gemeinschaft mit Robert Diehl herausgegeben von Albrecht Schaeffer*, Leipzig, 1931, p. 11.

15. S. Freud, 'Analysis of a Phobia in a Five-Year-Old Boy' (1909), translated by A. and J. Strachey, in *The Standard Edition of the Complete Psychological Works of Sigmund Freud*, vol. 10: *Two Case Histories ("Little Hans" and "The Rat Man")*, London, 1955.

16. Ibid.

17. Ibid.

18. Ibid.

19. Ibid.

20. On the phenotype and history of the desperado, cf. H. von Hentig, *Der Desperado: Ein Beitrag zur Psychologie des regressiven Menschen*, Berlin, 1956.

21. E. Pagels, *Apokalypse: Das letzte Buch der Bibel wird entschlüsselt*, Munich, 2013, pp. 12 f.

22. E. Jones, *On the Nightmare*, London, 1949.

23. Ibid., Part III, 'The Mare and the Mara: A Psycho-Analytical Contribution to Etymology', pp. 241–339.

24. Ibid., p. 246.

25. M. Jähns, *Ross und Reiter in Leben und Sprache, Glauben und Geschichte der Deutschen*, Leipzig, 1872.

26. Ibid., vol. 1, p. 77, quoted in Jones, *Nightmare*, p. 248.

27. Jones, *Nightmare*, pp. 260 f.

28. For a cautious critique of Jones and a comparison with Jung, who also connects the nightmare with incestuous desire, albeit a different, less sexual or carnal concept than Freud and Jones, cf. J. White-Lewis, 'In Defense of Nightmares: Clinical and Literary Cases', in C. Schreier Rupprecht (ed.), *The Dream and the Text: Essays on Literature and Language*, Albany, New York, 1993, pp. 48–72.

29. J. Starobinski, *Trois fureurs*, Paris, 1974 (German translation: *Besessenheit und Exorzismus. Drei Figuren der Umnachtung*, Berlin, 1978); here Chapter 3, 'Die Vision der Schläferin', pp. 141–83.
30. Ibid., pp. 179 f.
31. Ibid., p. 159.
32. Ibid., p. 160.
33. N. Powell, *Fuseli: The Nightmare*, New York, 1973.
34. Starobinski, *Besessenheit*, p. 164.
35. Ibid., p. 162.
36. Ibid., p. 150.
37. Ibid., p. 162.
38. Ibid., p. 167.
39. Ibid., p. 172.
40. The place name is difficult to make out in the manuscript, so this may be wrong.
41. Koselleck dates his note '23 XII. 02'; the sheet can be found in the Reinhart Koselleck estate, Deutsches Dokumentationszentrum für Kunstgeschichte, Bildarchiv Foto, Marburg. I am grateful to Felicitas and Katharina Koselleck for their help deciphering his handwriting.
42. On the absurd in Koselleck, cf. J. E. Dunkhase, *Absurde Geschichte: Reinhart Kosellecks historischer Existentialismus*, Marbach, 2015.

The Whip

1. Bloodhound Gang, 'The Bad Touch', song lyrics, refrain.
2. This distinctive branch of curiosity about sex is no contemporary invention. In his art history study, *Kunst-Geburten. Kreativität, Erotik, Körper*, Berlin, 2014, p. 138, Ulrich Pfisterer describes a festival in Florence in 1514 when a mare was locked in the Piazza della Signoria with some stallions and their mating was staged as a spectacle for an audience of some 40,000 women and girls.
3. P. F. Cuneo, 'Horses as Love Objects: Shaping Social and Moral Identities in Hans Baldung Grien's *Bewitched Groom* (circa 1544) and in Sixteenth-Century Hippology', in P. F. Cuneo (ed.), *Animals and Early Modern Identity*, Burlington, VT, and Farnham, Surrey, 2014, pp. 151–68, here pp. 159 f.; also K. Raber, 'Erotic Bodies: Loving Horses', in P. F. Cuneo, *Animal Bodies, Renaissance Culture*, Philadelphia, PA, 2013, pp. 75–101.
4. J. J. Sroka, *Das Pferd als Ausdrucks- und Bedeutungsträger bei Hans Baldung Grien*, Zurich, 2003, does not explicitly interpret the

engraving as a treatment of the theme of sodomy, but hints at such with a general allusion to the erotic electricity of the scene and the mare 'as a symbol for sexuality and the power of female seduction' (p. 112); cf. also J. J. Sroka, 'Das Pferd als Metapher für menschliche Triebe bei Dürer, Baldung und Füssli', in K. Corsepius, D. Mondini, D. Senekovic, L. Sibillano and S. Vitali (eds), *Opus Tesselatum. Modi und Grenzgänge der Kunstwissenschaft. Festschrift für Peter Cornelius Claussen*, Hildesheim, 2004, pp. 151–61.

5. For England in the early modern period, cf. E. Fudge, 'Monstrous Acts: Bestiality in Early Modern England', *History Today*, 50 (2000), pp. 20–25. Another classic treatment of the subject is R. v. Krafft-Ebing, *Psychopathia sexualis*, 12th edn, Stuttgart, 1903, p. 399: 'Evidence suggests that bestiality in cattle and horse stables was not at all rare . . . the reaction of Frederick the Great to a cavalryman who had desecrated a mare – "the man is a beast and should be sent to the infantry".'

6. M. Treut, homepage for the film, *Of Girls and Horses*; http://www.maedchen-und-pferde.de/start-english.html, last viewed 24 June 2015.

7. H. A. Euler, 'Jungen und Mädchen, Pferde und Reiten', paper presented at the meeting 'Jugend im Wandel', Warendorf, 28 November 1998.

8. L. Rose, quoted by K. Greiner, 'Was hat die denn geritten?', *Süddeutsche Zeitung Magazin*, 20 March 2015, p. 19.

9. G. Deleuze and F. Guattari, *A Thousand Plateaus: Capitalism & Schizophrenia*, translated by B. Massumi, Minneapolis, MN, 1987.

10. Herodotus, *Histories*, Book Four, translated by T. Holland, London, 2013, p 303.

11. Ibid.

12. Ibid.

13. A. Mayor, *The Amazons: Lives and Legends of Warrior Women across the Ancient World*, Princeton, NJ, 2014, p. 20. See also R. Rolle, 'Amazonen in der archäologischen Realität', in *Kleist Jahrbuch 1986*, Berlin, pp. 38–62 and, also by Renate Rolle, the companion book to the exhibition *Amazonen. Geheimnisvolle Kriegerinnen* in Speyer, Germany, from September 2010 to February 2011.

14. Mayor, *Amazons*, p. 132.

15. Ibid., p. 172.

16. Ibid., p. 173.

17. W. Koestenbaum, *Humiliation*, New York, 2011, p. 10.

18. Ibid., p. 7.

19. M. de Montaigne, *The Complete Essays*, translated by M. A. Screech, London, 1991. Even such a clear symbol of despotism could be inverted

and used in the sense of voluntary servitude as a gesture of humility or reverence. Hegel, in a letter to the publisher Cotta, described the Prussian king's embarrassment at his subjects volunteering to harness themselves to his carriage. The background was political unrest in the German states. 'Things are quiet here. A few days ago the King could scarcely prevent those who happened to be about him as he rode away from a spectacle of show riders – i.e., the *people*, to use the official term for them – from disharnessing the horses and pulling him home themselves. His admonition to them not to sink to the level of animals, coupled with his assurance that he would otherwise be obliged to go home on foot, allowed him to ride away to loud applause.' G. W. F. Hegel, *Hegel: The Letters*, translated by C. Butler and C. Seiler, Bloomington, IN, 1985, p. 675.

20. E. Pfeiffer (ed.), *Lou Andreas-Salomé: Lebensrückblick* (1951); 5th edn, Frankfurt, 1968, p. 81.

21. *Looking Back: The Memoirs of Lou Andreas-Salomé* (German title: *Lebensrückblick*), translated by B. Mitchell, New York, 1991.

22. F. Nietzsche, *Kritische Studienausgabe*, vol. 4, Munich, 1980, p. 85.

23. *Kritische Studienausgabe*, vol. 10, no. 210, p. 77.

24. L. Lütkehaus, *Nietzsche, die Peitsche und das Weib*, Rangsdorf, 2012: Lütkehaus dedicates this illuminating study to the infamous line, its context and possible literary relationship to Turgenev's novella *First Love*.

25. *Kritische Studienausgabe*, vol. 10, no. 367, p. 97.

26. *Kritische Studienausgabe*, vol. 4, p. 86.

27. E. Künzl, *Der römische Triumph. Siegesfeiern im antiken Rom*, Munich, 1988, pp. 42 f.

28. W. Matz, *Die Kunst des Ehebruchs. Emma, Anna, Effi und ihre Männer*, Göttingen, 2014.

29. K. Robert, *Degas*, London, 1982, p. 40.

30. Gustave Flaubert, *Madame Bovary*, translated by G. Wall, London, 1992.

31. Ibid.

32. T. Hardy, *Far from the Madding Crowd*, London, 1874.

33. Ibid.

34. L. Tolstoy, *Anna Karenina*, translated by R. Edmonds, London, 1954, p. 200.

35. Ibid., p. 210.

36. There is much to say about the poetics of characters' names, from the weary, cold-sounding three-syllable names for the husbands, to the more interesting two-syllable names for their wives' lovers and horses such as Frou-Frou.

37. See above, 'A Pastoral Incident', p. 57.
38. Tolstoy, *Anna Karenina*, p. 641.
39. V. Shklovsky, *Leo Tolstoi*, Frankfurt, 1984, p. 313; also the following pages (on the genesis of *Kholstomer*).
40. This is the title of the classic study by Leo Marx on the advance of technology (locomotives, steamboats) into the perceived paradise of the American wilderness: L. Marx, *The Machine in the Garden: Technology and the Pastoral Ideal in America*, Oxford, 1964.
41. T. Hardy, *Tess of the d'Urbervilles*, London, 1892.
42. Ibid.
43. Tolstoy, *Anna Karenina*, p. 217.
44. Ibid.
45. Ibid., p. 218.
46. Ibid., p. 229.
47. Ibid., p. 802.
48. Ibid.
49. Ibid., p. 79.
50. J. Starobinski, 'Die Skala der Temperaturen – Körperlesung in *Madame Bovary*', in *Kleine Geschichte des Körpergefühls*, Frankfurt, 1991, pp. 34–72.
51. Starobinski, 'Die Skala', p. 65.
52. J. W. von Goethe, *The Sorrows of Young Werther*, translated by M. Hulse, London, 1989.

Turin: a Winter's Tale

1. *Der gefährliche Augenblick* ('The Dangerous Moment') is the title of Jünger's next illustrated book, published in 1931 in Berlin.
2. Julia Encke clearly encapsulates the focus of Jünger's illustrated books of the Great War in J. Encke, *Augenblicke der Gefahr: Der Krieg und die Sinne. 1914–1934*, Munich, 2006, p. 39.
3. On the emotional impact of images of animal combatants, see also H. Kean, *Animal Rights: Political and Social Change in Britain since 1800*, London, 1998, pp. 171 f.
4. S. Neitzel and H. Welzer, *Soldaten: Protokolle vom Kämpfen, Töten und Sterben*, Frankfurt, 2011, p. 85.
5. First published in the *Illustrierten Kriegszeitung* ('Illustrated War Bulletin') of the Austro-Hungarian 32nd Infantry Division, 10 January 1917; reprinted in J. Roth, 'Der sterbende Gaul', in *Werke in 6 Bänden*, Vol. 1, Appendix, Cologne, 1989, p. 1103.

6. E.g. C. Simon, *The Flanders Road*, translated by R. Howard, London, 1961, p. 81: 'And after a moment or so he recognized it: what was not a rough mass of dried mud but . . . a horse, or rather what had been a horse . . .'

7. The exceptions – see p. 122, the mounted police officer in Jerusalem – prove the rule.

8. Cf. his readings of the poignant letter from Rosa Luxemburg to Sophie Liebknecht (24 December 1917), in which the inmate, Luxemburg, describes the torture of a buffalo that she addresses as 'my poor, beloved brother'; also the famous passage about Count Dohna's drowned horse in Karl Kraus's play, *The Last Days of Mankind*.

9. E. Lasker-Schüler, 'Am Kurfürstendamm. Was mich im vorigen Winter traurig machte . . .', in *Gedichte*, 2nd edn, Berlin, 1920, pp. 48–50.

10. C. Rowe, *Die Mathematik der idealen Villa*, Basle, 1998, p. 7.

11. L. S. Mercier, *Le Tableau de Paris*, Hamburg and Neuchâtel, 1781; in particular the chapter entitled 'Fiacres', pp. 67 ff.

12. On this topic, cf. K. Hamburger, *Das Mitleid*, Stuttgart, 1985; H. Ritter, *Die Schreie der Verwundeten: Versuch über die Grausamkeit*, Munich, 2013; U. Frevert, *Vergängliche Gefühle*, Göttingen, 2013, chapter III, 'Mitleid und Empathie ', pp. 44–74.

13. In an early draft of the following passage, I only described three figures: the beaten horse, the wounded soldier and the working child (U. Raulff, 'Ansichten des Unerträglichen. Drei Figuren des Mitleids', *Neue Zürcher Zeitung*, 11 January 2014.) I am grateful to Ernst Halter for drawing my attention to the fourth of these figures, the orphan.

14. One of the most gruesome vignettes in Dunant's account is the passage where the wounded masses are shattered and crushed a second time by the wheels and hooves of the artillery driving over them. He also describes the horses as being 'more human than their riders', who, 'with every hoof step spare the victims of this fierce and furious battle'.

15. J. Kuczynski and R. Hoppe (eds), *Geschichte der Kinderarbeit in Deutschland 1750–1939*, vol. 1: *Geschichte*, by J. Kuczynski; vol. 2: *Dokumente*, by R. Hoppe, Berlin, 1958.

16. E. P. Thompson, *The Making of the English Working Class*, London, 1963.

17. E. Halter, *Heidi: Karrieren einer Figur*, Zurich, 2001, p. 10.

18. Ibid., p. 12.

19. Ibid., p. 15.

20. Queen Victoria to her Home Secretary, quoted by H. Ritvo, *The Animal Estate: The English and Other Creatures in the Victorian Age*, Cambridge, MA, and London, 1987, p. 126.

21. The actual title, 'Bill to Prevent the Cruel and Improper Treatment of Cattle', was worded in broad terms to include all draught animals such as horses, donkeys and mules.

22. Cf. the classic study by K. Thomas, *Man and the Natural World: A History of the Modern Sensibility*, New York, 1983, chapter IV, 'Compassion for the brute creation', pp. 143–91; cf. also the excellent Ph.D. thesis by Mieke Roscher, *Ein Königreich für Tiere: Die Geschichte der britischen Tierrechtsbewegung*, Marburg, 2009, pp. 47 ff., and Ritvo, *Animal Estate*, pp. 125 ff., and H. Kean, *Animal Rights*, pp. 13 ff.

23. S. Johnson, *The Works of Samuel Johnson*, edited by A. Murphy, 12 vols, London, 1792.

24. Kean, *Animal Rights*, p. 20.

25. J. Bentham (1789), *An Introduction to the Principles of Morals and Legislation*, London, 1970, p. 283.

26. K. Miele, 'Horse-Sense: Understanding the Working Horse in Victorian London', *Victorian Literature and Culture*, 37 (2009), pp. 129–40.

27. D. Donald, *Picturing Animals in Britain: 1750–1850*, New Haven, CT, and London, 2007, pp. 215–32, 347 (with further citations).

28. L. Gompertz, *Moral Inquiries on the Situation of Man and of Brutes*, New York, 1824, published in the year of the foundation of the SPCA, is rightly considered to be the founding manifesto of English animal protection and the main text for all nature protection movements.

29. Roscher, *Königreich*, pp. 111 f.; M. Zerbel, 'Tierschutzbewegung', in *Handbuch zur 'Völkischen Bewegung' 1871–1918*, edited by U. Puschner, Munich, 1996, pp. 546–57.

30. S. and F. W. von Preußen, *Friedrich der Große: Vom anständigen Umgang mit Tieren*, Göttingen, 2012, pp. 77–83.

31. I am grateful to Barbara Picht for this information and Werner Busch for his interpretation.

32. C. A. Dann, *Bitte der armen Thiere, der unvernünftigen Geschöpfe, an ihre vernünftigen Mitgeschöpfe und Herrn die Menschen* (1822) and C. A. Dann, *Nothgedrungener durch viele Beispiele beleuchteter Aufruf an alle Menschen von Nachdenken und Gefühl zu gemeinschaftlicher Beherzigung und Linderung der unsäglichen Leiden der in unserer Umgebung lebenden Thiere* (1832). Both texts can be found in *Wider die Tierquälerei: Frühe Aufrufe zum Tierschutz aus dem württembergischen Pietismus*, edited by M. H. Jung, Leipzig, 2002.

33. Jung, 'Nachwort', in *Wider die Tierquälerei*, pp. 113–20, here p. 113.

34. Dann, *Bitte der armen Thiere*, p. 29.

35. M. H. Jung, 'Die Anfänge der deutschen Tierschutzbewegung im 19. Jahrhundert', in *Zeitschrift für württembergische Landesgeschichte*, Stuttgart, 1997, pp. 205–39, here p. 226.

36. Ibid., p. 239.

37. F. T. Vischer, 'Noch ein vergebliches Wort gegen den himmelschreienden Thierschund im Lande Württemberg', *Der Beobachter*, no. 327, 28 November 1847. The following two pieces appear in no. 328, 30 November 1847 and no. 329 of 1 December 1847.

38. F. T. Vischer, *Briefe aus Italien*, Munich, 1908, p. 94, letter of 25 January 1840.

39. Ibid., pp. 133 f., letter of 7 March 1840. The dispute with the coachman comes up again in Vischer's 1869 satirical novel *Auch Einer*, now presented as a personal experience of the book's protagonist. Earlier outpourings of rage by Vischer about dog and horse knackers also recur here. Cf. *Auch Einer*, Frankfurt, 1987, pp. 35, 296.

40. F. T. Vischer, *Kritische Gänge*, 6 vols, Stuttgart, 1860–73, vol. 1, pp. 155 f.

41. F. T. Vischer, 'Noch ein Wort über Tiermißhandlung in Italien', in *Kritische Gänge*, 2nd edn, vol. 6, Munich, 1922, pp. 326–36, here p. 326.

42. Ibid., p. 328.

43. Ibid., p. 331.

44. Roscher, *Königreich*, p. 113. Like the Catholics, the Jews were also reproached for their alleged indifference towards the suffering of animals, as seen in the practice of ritual slaughter. All of these partly secular, partly religious assumptions are firmly rejected by the philosopher Michael Landmann; M. Landmann, *Das Tier in der jüdischen Weisung*, Heidelberg, 1959.

45. F. Nietzsche, *Werke III*, Munich, 1984, p. 835.

46. Nietzsche biographer Curt Paul Janz remarks: 'Nietzsche never showed any particular affinity to animals, he only used "the animal" as an abstract creature snug in its instinctive security as a counter position to contrast with the man who is made insecure by his moralistic prejudices and alienated from his natural foundation . . .' C. P. Janz, *Friedrich Nietzsche: Biographie*, vol. 3, *Die Jahre des Siechtums*, Munich, 1979, p. 34. This finding is reaffirmed in a study by Vanessa Lemm, *Nietzsche's Animal Philosophy: Culture, Politics, and the Animality of the Human Being*, New York, 2009.

47. In fact, Nietzsche did once have dealings with real animals, during his military service with the horse-drawn artillery in the winter of 1867–8, which after a short, proud period of happiness riding the 'fieriest and most

restless animal in the battery' ended with a serious accident in March 1868 and a lengthy convalescence; *Friedrich Nietzsche: Chronik in Bildern und Texten*, edited by R. J. Benders and S. Oettermann, Munich, 2000, pp. 172–9.

48. As related by E. F. Podach, *Nietzsches Zusammenbruch*, Heidelberg, 1930.

49. Cf. Gottfried Benn's poem 'Turin' in the *Statische Gedichte* of 1938, whose last verse is: 'Indes Europas Edelfäule/an Pau, Bayreuth und Epsom sog,/umarmte er zwei Droschkengäule,/bis ihn sein Wirt nach Hause zog.' ('While Europe's noble rot/Supped at Pau, Bayreuth, and Epsom,/He put his arm around two cart-/Horses, until his landlord dragged him home.' Gottfried Benn, *Impromptus: Selected Poems and Some Prose*, translated by M. Hofmann, Farrar, Straus and Giroux, 2013) The originally single horse-drawn carriage is doubled for rhyming effect.

50. Davide Fino was a kiosk owner and Nietzsche's landlord in Turin.

51. Podach, *Nietzsches Zusammenbruch*, p. 82.

52. His book *La catastrofe di Nietzsche a Torino*, Turin, 1978, is published in German: A. Verrecchia, *Zarathustras Ende: Die Katastrophe Nietzsches in Turin*, Vienna, 1986.

53. Verrecchia, *Zarathustras Ende*, p. 261.

54. Ibid, p. 260.

55. Ibid., pp. 262–72; the additions of the kiss and the 'brother', p. 267. Since then every narrator of Nietzsche's last days in Turin has found abundant anecdotal material to guide their narratives. Recent examples are R. Safranski, *Nietzsche: Biografie seines Denkens*, Munich, 2000; P. D. Volz, *Nietzsche im Labyrinth seiner Krankheit*, Würzburg, 1990, p. 204; L. Chamberlain, *Nietzsche in Turin: An Intimate Biography*, New York, 1999.

56. Cf. among others Janz, *Friedrich Nietzsche*, vol. 3, pp. 34 f.

57. Letter from F. Nietzsche to Reinhart von Seydlitz, 13 May 1888, in F. Nietzsche, *Briefwechsel. Kritische Gesamtausgabe*, vol. 5, 3rd section, 'Letters January 1887–January 1889', Berlin and New York, 1984, pp. 314.

58. See above, pp. 231–2.

59. F. Dostoevsky, *Crime and Punishment* (1866), translated by D. McDuff, London, 1991, pp. 72–3.

60. G. Pochhammer, 'Tierquälerei, Doping, Betrug', *Süddeutsche Zeitung*, 4 March 2015, p. 24.

IV THE FORGOTTEN PLAYER—*HISTORIES*
Teeth and Time

1. T. Hardy, *Far from the Madding Crowd*, London, 1874.
2. Koselleck never warmed to Jaspers and his 1949 book; at the time it was published he responded with ridicule and mockery, he recalls fifty-five years later in an interview; R. Koselleck and Carsten Dutt, *Erfahrene Geschichte: Zwei Gespräche*, Heidelberg, 2013, p. 37.
3. In a recently published collection of essays, Glen Bowersock discusses Jaspers's 'Axial Age' (*The Axial Age and its Consequences*, R. N. Bellah and H. Joas (eds), Cambridge, MA, 2012), pointing out that Hegel, cited by Jaspers, labels the turning point of history as the incarnation of Christ, described as an 'angel', while Jaspers talks of an 'axis'; G. W. Bowersock, 'A Different Turning Point for Mankind?', *New York Review of Books*, 9 May 2013, pp. 56–8, here p. 56. On the discussion of the 'Axial Age', see also the excellent summary by H. Joas, *Was ist die Achsenzeit? Eine wissenschaftliche Debatte als Diskurs über Transzendenz*, Basle, 2014.
4. K. Jaspers, *The Origin and Goal of History*, translated by M. Bullock, Abingdon, 2011, p. 16.
5. A. Weber, *Das Tragische und die Geschichte*, Hamburg, 1943, p. 60.
6. Ibid., pp. 58 f.
7. O. Spengler, 'Der Streitwagen und seine Bedeutung für den Gang der Weltgeschichte', in *Reden und Aufsätze*, Munich, 1937, pp. 148–52, here p. 149.
8. Ibid., p. 150.
9. H. Freyer, *Weltgeschichte Europas*, 2 vols, Wiesbaden, 1948, vol. 1, p. 25.
10. Ibid., pp. 26, 28 f.
11. Ibid., pp. 33, 35.
12. Jaspers, *Origin and Goal*, p. 46.
13. Ibid. (my italics).
14. Joseph Wiesner, *Fahren und Reiten in Alteuropa und im Alten Orient*, Leipzig, 1939. This slim volume is based on a lecture given the previous year to the Vorderasiatisch-Ägyptischen Gesellschaft (Near East and Egyptian Society) in Berlin. It simultaneously served as the author's postdoctoral thesis in the Faculty of Classical Archaeology at the University of Königsberg. It was reprinted in the original version in 1971 in Hildesheim. My thanks go to Karl-Heinz Bohrer, taught by Joseph Wiesner after the war at Landschulheim Birklehof, for making me aware of the volume.

15. Ibid., pp. 24, 29.

16. Ibid., p. 37.

17. Ibid, p. 34.

18. Ibid., p. 39.

19. As General Bamme puts it: 'Considering what my *métier* is, I might even aspire to the proposition that world-history in the grand style, such as that represented by the progress of the Huns and Mongols, has never been made anywhere but from the saddle, that is to say, in plain terms by a kind of primeval hussar'; T. Fontane, *Before the Storm*, translated by R. J. Hollingdale, Oxford and New York, 1985, p. 163.

20. A. Rüstow, *Ortsbestimmung der Gegenwart: Eine universalgeschichtliche Kultukritik*, vol. 1: *Ursprung der Herrschaft*, Erlenbach-Zurich, 1950, p. 68. Rüstow concluded his reflections on the early historical relationship to bovids and equids with the noteworthy sentence, 'The chief representative of the equids which has been decisive in world history is nevertheless the horse.' Ibid., p. 66.

21. E. Canetti, *Crowds and Power*, translated by C. Stewart, New York, 1962.

22. G. Deleuze and F. Guattari, *Anti-Oedipus: Capitalism and Schizophrenia*, translated by R. Hurley, M. Seem and H. R. Lane, Minneapolis, MN, 1983.

23. P. Raulwing, *Horses, Chariots and Indo-Europeans*, Archaeolingua Series Minor 13, Budapest, 2000, p. 61.

24. 'Jaspers', writes Bowersock, 'was totally innocent of archaeology.' The fact that earlier archaeology worked from a 'fond commun de l'humanité' to produce the image of the hero and its tradition, is evidenced in the work by F. Benoit, *L'héroisation équestre*, Aix-en-Provence, 1954, here p. 9.

25. N. Di Cosmo, 'Inner Asian Ways of Warfare in Historical Perspective', in N. Di Cosmo (ed.), *Warfare in Inner Asian History (500–1800)*, Leiden, 2002, pp. 1–20, here pp. 2–4 (with references for further reading).

26. J. K. Fairbank, *Chinese Ways in Warfare*, Cambridge, MA, 1974, p. 13.

27. D. W. Anthony, *The Horse, the Wheel, and Language*, Princeton, NJ, 2007, p. 222.

28. Ibid., p. 223.

29. Ibid., p. 224.

30. According to the archaeologist Marsha Levine, quoted by A. Hyland, *The Horse in the Ancient World*, Stroud, 2003, p. 3.

31. V. Horn, *Das Pferd im Alten Orient*, Hildesheim, 1995, pp. 20 f. On the discussion about the finds at Dereivka, cf. H. Parzinger, *Die Kinder*

des Prometheus: Eine Geschichte der Menschheit vor der Erfindung der Schrift, Munich, 2014, p. 390.

32. Anthony, *The Horse*, pp. 205 f.: 'Riding leaves few traces on horse bones. But a bit leaves marks on the teeth, and teeth usually survive very well. Bits are used only to guide horses from behind, to drive or ride. They are not used if the horse is pulled from the front, as a pack-horse is . . . The absence of bit wear means nothing, since other forms of control (nosebands, hackamores) might leave no evidence. But its presence is an unmistakable sign of riding or driving.'

33. Ibid., p. 220.

34. Ibid., p. 221.

35. Hyland, *Ancient World*, p. 5. Cf. also C. Baumer, *The History of Central Asia*, vol. 1: *The Age of the Steppe Warriors*, London, 2012, pp. 84 f.

36. J. Clutton-Brock, *Horse Power: A History of the Horse and the Donkey in Human Societies*, Cambridge, MA, 1992, pp. 20 ff.; E. West, 'The Impact of Horse Culture', *History Now*, New York; online at www.gilderlehrman.org/history-by-era/early-settlements/essays/impact-horse-cultures.

37. J. Osterhammel, *The Transformation of the World: A Global History of the Nineteenth Century*, translated by P. Camiller, Princeton, NJ, 2014.

38. R. H. Thurston, *The Animal as a Machine and a Prime Motor – And the Laws of Energetics*, New York, 1894. The essay, 'The Animal as a Prime Mover', summarized the main themes of the book by Thurston, and was published in the journal *Science*, Vol. 1, No. 14, 5 April (1895).

39. F. Cottrell, *Energy and Society: The Relation Between Energy, Social Change, and Economic Development*, Westport, CT, 1955.

40. Ibid., p. 6.

41. Ibid., p. 20.

Conquest

1. E. Canetti, *Crowds and Power*, translated by C. Stewart, New York, 1962.

2. F. Kafka, *The Transformation ('Metamorphosis') and Other Stories*, translated by M. Pasley, London, 1992.

3. J. H. Zedler, *Das Grosse vollständige Universal-Lexicon Aller Wissenschafften und Künste*, Leipzig, 1732–54.

4. Pausanias, *Description of Greece*, translated by W. H. S. Jones and H. A. Ormerod, Cambridge, MA, and London, 1918.

5. Herodotus, *Histories*, Book Six, translated by T. Holland, London, 2013.

6. J. Dünne and S. Günzel (eds), *Raumtheorie*, Frankfurt, 2006; W. Köster, *Die Rede über den 'Raum': Zur semantischen Karriere eines deutschen Konzepts*, Heidelberg, 2002; R. Maresch and N. Werber, *Raum, Wissen, Macht*, Frankfurt, 2002. In his study, *Die Geopolitik der Literatur: Eine Vermessung der medialen Weltraumordnung*, Munich, 2007, Niels Werber criticizes the 'banalization of space' in favour of the atopic communications universe of media theory. A non-banal theory of space would, in contrast, if it were historically informative, take into account the vector function of the horse.

7. As argued by, for example, the sociologist Markus Schroer, a theoretician who has turned away from the current theories on the destruction of space and its replacement by time in the last two decades (mostly the media theories from McLuhan to Baudrillard). In his postdoctoral thesis, *Räume, Orte, Grenzen: Auf dem Weg zu einer Soziologie des Raums*, Frankfurt, 2006, Schroer stressed, that it is 'exactly the opposite . . . space only comes into being through the mutual accessibility of formerly isolated places'. In this respect, a medium does not lead to a 'successive loss of space', but rather 'a constant increase in space . . . as each medium opens up and creates additional spaces'. (p. 164).

8. M. de Certeau, *The Practice of Everyday Life*, translated by S. Rendall, Oakland, CA, 1984. As far as I am aware, Karl Schlögel is the only contemporary German historian to have undertaken a precise and systematic study of the history of space and the spatial dimensions of military, ideological, scientific, artistic and everyday movements. He sets out his history and poetics of space in K. Schlögel, *Im Raume lesen wir die Zeit. Über Zivilisationsgeschichte und Geopolitik*, Munich, 2003, and in 'Narrative der Gleichzeitigkeit oder die Grenzen der Erzählbarkeit von Geschichte', in *Grenzland Europa. Unterwegs auf einem neuen Kontinent*, Munich, 2013. His 'cartographic' view of history (we read time in space) would appear to be entirely compatible with my proposed 'vectorial' vision. His recent work, *Archäologie des Kommunismus*, Munich, 2013, describes the railway as the producer of Russian space and informal communication space (p. 69).

9. Henri Bergson, *Creative Evolution*, translated by A. Mitchell, London, 1911, p. 216.

10. Henri Bergson, *Time and Free Will*, translated by F. L. Pogson, London, 1913.

11. Bergson, *Creative Evolution*, p. 326.

12. Unfortunately the otherwise excellent essay by Jan van Brevern on the 'marathon' as a space of memory is written entirely without *horse*

sense. The equestrian element of movement only emerges as a topic of criticism of F. T. Vischer; J. von Brevern, 'Bild und Erinnerungsort. Carl Rottmanns Schlachtfeld von Marathon', *Zeitschrift für Kunstgeschichte*, 71, Vol. 4 (2008), pp. 527–42.

13. De Certeau, *The Practice of Everyday Life*, p. 117.

14. C. Schmitt, *The Nomos of the Earth in the International Law of the Jus Publicum Europaeum* (1950), translated by G. L. Ulmen, New York, 2006.

15. A. W. Crosby, Jr, *The Columbian Exchange: Biological and Cultural Consequences of 1492*, Westport, CT, 1972, p. 79.

16. Ibid., p. 81.

17. F. Schürmann, 'Herrschaftsstrategien und der Einsatz von Pferden im südwestlichen Afrika, ca. 1790–1890', in R. Pöppinghege (ed.), *Tiere im Krieg. Von der Antike bis zur Gegenwart*, Paderborn, 2009, pp. 65–84, here p. 83.

18. W. W. Howard, *Horrors of Armenia: The Story of an Eye-witness*, New York, 1896.

19. W. W. Howard, 'The Rush to Oklahoma', *Harper's Weekly*, 18 May 1889, pp. 391–4, here p. 392.

20. Anon., 'The Oklahoma Land Rush, EyeWitness to History'; online at www.eyewitnesstohistory.com (2006). See also the impressive final scene of the 1992 film *Far and Away*, whose director, Ron Howard, ends with a panorama of the Land Run of 1893 (available on YouTube).

21. I. Hobson, 'Oklahoma, USA, and Kafka's Nature Theater', in A. Flores (ed.), *The Kafka Debate: New Perspectives For Our Time*, New York, 1977, pp. 273–8, here pp. 274 f.

22. R. Stach, *Kafka: Die frühen Jahre*, Frankfurt, 2014, pp. 451, 566; H. Binder, *Kafka in Paris*, Munich, 1999, pp. 108 ff.

23. A. von Chamisso, 'Das Riesenspielzeug', in *Sämtliche Werke*, vol. 1, Munich, 1975, p. 336.

24. On Lynn White, Jr, see pp. 220–23.

25. P. Edwards, *Horse and Man in Early Modern England*, London, 2007.

26. On McShane and Tarr, see p. 31.

27. On G. M. Tempest, see above, note 42 on p. 393.

28. We should not let the few brief remarks by Fernand Braudel on the 'fight against distance' go unmentioned: F. Braudel, *Geschichte als Schlüssel zur Welt: Vorlesungen in deutscher Kriegsgefangenschaft 1941*, Stuttgart, 2013, pp. 126 f.

29. W. Kaschuba, *Die Überwindung der Distanz. Zeit und Raum in der europäischen Moderne*, Frankfurt, 2004, particularly the chapter 'Fahrplan und Prinzip Post', pp. 43–7; P. Borscheid, *Das Tempo-Virus. Eine Kulturgeschichte der Beschleunigung*, Frankfurt, 2004.

30. B. Latour, *We Have Never Been Modern*, translated by C. Porter, Cambridge, MA, 1993.

31. Ibid., p. 104.

32. Ibid., pp. 106 f.

33. A.-G. Haudricourt, *La technologie science humaine: Recherches d'histoire et d'ethnologie des techniques*, Paris, 1987, p. 141. The essay which the quote comes from, 'Contribution à la géographie et à l'ethnologie de la voiture', was first published in 1948.

34. B. Latour, *Der Berliner Schlüssel. Erkundungen eines Liebhabers der Wissenschaften*, Berlin, 1996, p. 76.

35. Haudricourt, *La technologie*, p. 141.

36. Ibid., p. 142.

37. A. de Gaudemar, 'Haudricourt, retour à la terre', *Libération*, 22 August 1996, p. 28.

38. A.-G. Haudricourt, *Des gestes aux techniques: Essai sur les techniques dans les sociétés pré-machinistes. Texte inédit présenté et commenté par J.-F. Bert*, Paris, 2010, p. 129.

39. M. Heidegger, *Sein und Zeit*, 12th edn, Tübingen, 1972, pp. 68ff.

Out of the Picture

1. I am grateful to Jakob Hessing for making me aware of this joke.

2. R. Netz, *Barbed Wire: An Ecology of Modernity*, Middletown, CT, 2004, p. 74.

3. M. Baum, *Es schlug mein Herz, geschwind zu Pferde!: Zur Poesie des Pferdemotivs in Goethes Alltag und in seinem Werk*, Jena, 2005, p. 75. Paul Virilio, who reverses the perspective, sees the similarity of the saddled horse to 'a seat that moves, a piece of furniture, a hippomobile that is not satisfied merely in assisting the body in the requirements of parking, of rest, like a chair, but also in moving from one place to another'. P. Virilio (1984), *Negative Horizon: An Essay in Dromoscopy*, translated by M. Degener, London and New York, 2005, p. 43.

4. E.-G. Güse, U. Müller-Harang, M. Oppel, D. Ahrendt and C. Terzy, *Dichterhäuser in Weimar: Goethehaus, Goethes Gartenhaus & Schillerhaus*, Weimar, 2005, p. 59.

5. W. Benjamin, *Kritiken und Rezensionen, Gesammelte Schriften,* R. Tiedemann and H. Schweppenhäuser (eds), vol. 3, Frankfurt, 1972, p. 59.
6. Virilio, *Negative Horizon,* p. 45.
7. A. Schaeffer, *Ross und Reiter. Ihre Darstellung in der plastischen Kunst. In Gemeinschaft mit Robert Diehl herausgegeben von Albrecht Schaeffer,* Leipzig, 1931, p. 10.
8. Ibid.
9. Ibid., p. 11.
10. H. Blumenberg, *Löwen,* Frankfurt,, 2001.
11. Henri Michaux tried to correct this mistake. 'Le pigeon est un obsédé-sexuel,' as he puts it at the beginning of the chapter 'Histoire naturelle' in *Un barbare en Asie, Oeuvres completes,* vol. I, Paris, 1998, pp. 277–409, here p. 353.
12. O. Weiniger, *Über die letzten Dinge,* Vienna and Leipzig, 1904, p. 125.
13. S. Lewitscharoff, *Blumenberg,* Berlin, 2011.
14. A. Warburg, *Werke in einem Band,* edited by M. Treml et al., Berlin, 2010, in particular the lecture 'Der Eintritt des antikisierenden Ideal-stils in die Malerei der Frührenaissance' (1914), pp. 281–310; see also E. H. Gombrich, *Aby Warburg: Eine intellektuelle Biographie,* Frankfurt, 1981, pp. 228–45.
15. Warburg, *Werke,* 'Eintritt des antikisierenden Idealstils', p. 295.
16. Gombrich, *Aby Warburg,* p. 56.
17. W. Hogrebe, *Ahnung und Erkenntnis: Brouillon zu einer Theorie des natürlichen Erkennens,* Frankfurt, 1996.

Herodotus

1. W. Behringer, *Kulturgeschichte des Sports: Vom antiken Olympia bis ins 21. Jahrhundert,* Munich, 2012, p. 194.
2. On this topic, see the catalogue from the beautiful exhibition in Siegen: *Lucian Freud und das Tier,* 2015.
3. E. Kris, O. Kurz, *Legend, Myth, and Magic in the Image of the Artist: A Historical Experiment,* translated by A. Laing and L. M. Newman, New Haven, CT, 1979.
4. Ibid., p. 62.
5. B. Grzimek, *Und immer wieder Pferde,* Munich, 1977, pp. 105 ff.
6. Lacan first presented his thoughts on the 'mirror stage' in 1936 at the 14th International Congress for Psychoanalysis in Marienbad and pub-lished them in 1949 in an extended form.

7. S. Saracino, 'Der Pferdediskurs im England des 17. Jahrhunderts', *Historische Zeitschrift*, vol. 300, issue 2 (2015), pp. 342, 358 f.

8. M.-A. Leblanc, *The Mind of the Horse: An Introduction to Equine Cognition*, Cambridge, MA, 2013; here, in particular, chapters 2 and 3, pp. 22–70.

9. M. Tomasello, *Eine Naturgeschichte des menschlichen Denkens*, Berlin, 2014.

10. See above. p. 325.

11. C. Baumer, *The History of Central Asia*, London, 2012.

12. R. Koselleck, 'Der Aufbruch in die Moderne oder das Ende des Pferdezeitalters', in 'Historikerpreis der Stadt Münster 2003', Münster City Historian Prize booklet, 18 July 2003, p. 37.

13. H. Heimpel, 'Geschichte und Geschichtswissenschaft', *Vierteljahrshefte für Zeitgeschichte*, vol. 5, 1/1957, pp. 1–17, here p. 17.

14. Herodotus, *Histories*, Book Three, translated by T. Holland, London, 2013.

15. Ibid., Book Four. Cf. F. Hartog, *Le miroir d'Hérodote: Essai sur la représentation de l'autre* (1980), new edn, Paris, 2001, p. 248, on the Scythian horse burials.

16. W. Schadewaldt, *Die Anfänge der Geschichtsschreibung bei den Griechen. Tübinger Vorlesungen*, vol. 2, Frankfurt, 1982, p. 128.

17. See p. 294; S. Neitzel and H. Welzer, *Soldaten: Protokolle vom Kämpfen, Töten und Sterben*, Frankfurt, 2011, p. 85.

18. J. W. von Goethe, *Werke. 'Hamburger Ausgabe': Autobiographische Schriften II*, vol. 10, edited by Erich Trunz, Nördlingen, 1989, p. 238.

19. M. Baum, *Es schlug mein Herz, geschwind zu Pferde!: Zur Poesie des Pferdemotivs in Goethes Alltag und in seinem Werk*, Jena, 2005, p. 15.

20. T. Hardy, *Tess of the d'Urbervilles*, London, 1892, p. 42.

Acknowledgements

For all their information, criticism and inspiration, I would like to thank:
Sonja Asal, Stephan Askani, Veronika Askani, Achim Aurnhammer, Lina Baruch, Martin Bauer, Gerda Baumbach, Jutta Bendt, Andreas Beyer, Gottfried Boehm, Knut Borchardt, Glen Bowersock, Ulrich von Bülow, Jan Bürger, Werner Busch, Daniele Dell'Agli, Antonia Egel, Detlef Felken, Anne Rose Fischer, Jens Malte Fischer, Heike Gfrereis, Gerd Giesler, Lionel Gossman, Anna Grauvogel, Valentin Groebner, Eckart Heftrich, Klaus Heinrich, Ole Heinzelmann, Alexa Hennemann, Jakob Hessing, Walter Hinderer, Regina Hufendiek, Lorenz Jäger, Dietmar Jaegle, Robert Jütte, Joachim Kalka, Joachim Kersten, Jost Philipp Klenner, Hans Gerd Koch, Reinhart Koselleck, Jochen Langeheinecke, Verena Lenzen, Marcel Lepper, Wulf D. von Lucius, Jürgen Manthey, Peter Miller, Helmuth Mojem, Lothar Müller, Pia Müller-Tamm, Lutz Näfelt, Joachim Nettelbeck, Caroline Neubaur, Ute Oelmann, Stephan Opitz, Ernst Osterkamp, Norbert Ott, Reinhard Pabst, Peter Paret, Barbara Picht, Marie Louise von Plessen, Anson Rabinbach, Birgit Recki, Myriam Richter, Sandra Richter, Henning Ritter, Karol Sauerland, Benedicte Savoy, Stephan Schlak, Karl Schlögel, Thomas Schmidt, Danielle Schönwitz, Heinz Schott, Ellen Strittmatter, Dirko Thomsen, Michael Tomasello, Adelheid Voskuhl, Jannis Wagner, Ulrike Wegner, Yfaat Weiss, Meike Werner, Johannes Willms and Heinrich August Winkler.

For their tireless support I thank Lucie Holzwarth, Chris Korner, Magdalena Schanz, Jens Tremml and Christa Volmer.

Even with all this intellectual and practical support, this book would not have been possible without the encouragement and understanding of Helga and Max Raulff. To them I extend my special thanks.

Index

Page references in *italic* indicate illustrations and their captions.